ONE

UNFOLDING GOD'S ETERNAL PURPOSE
FROM HOUSE TO HOUSE

HENRY HON

Imagine all the people
Living life in peace

You may say I'm a dreamer
But I'm not the only one
I hope someday you'll join us
And the world will be as one

Imagine, John Lennon, 1971

DEDICATION

I am dedicating this book to One Body Life, which has a mission to support and build up assemblies in homes everywhere. This includes the preaching of Jesus Christ as the good news, the encouragement for believers to focus on and enjoy the Lord Jesus, and the gathering of diverse believers in one body. One Body Life has no intention to federate or organize home assemblies, but simply to connect believers together in the one fellowship of Jesus Christ. All proceeds from the sales of this book will be used for the sole purpose of this mission. For tax purposes, One Body Life is a 501(c)(3) non-profit organization approved by the IRS. For more information about One Body life, go to: www.onebody.life.

I will continue to commit myself to my family, whom I love: my wife, my four children and their spouses, and my grandchildren (four at present). I sincerely pray and hope that they will continue to love and serve the Lord for the rest of their lives even when I am away in body. I want them to remember how they were raised to enjoy and serve the Lord in our home through the years and continue this pattern in their homes and in the homes of their friends.

TABLE OF CONTENTS

FOREWORD

ONE! The simplicity of this title provides strategic insight into Henry Hon's thinking and the contents of this book. It is a clear call for every believer, through God's empowering grace and our inspired obedience, to become the answer to the prayer that Jesus prayed to our Father.

" . . . that they may be made perfect in one, and that the world may know that You have sent Me, and have loved them as You have loved Me." John 17:23

Hon has a clear vision of how we can become one without dismantling church structure as it exists in many parts of our world today. Simultaneously, he is committed to seeing the same experience of life and vibrancy of early Christians expressed today. They carried the life of Jesus into the very centers of their living in homes – from house to house – compelling the world around them.

When it comes to meeting from house to house, Hon is not a novice. His journey has had him assembling in this way since 1986. His experience has taught him that this form of worship is not in itself the answer. Rather, it is obedience to Jesus' Command to "love one another," just as He has loved us.

He clearly demonstrates that God has given us all we need to become one – the Eternal life, Truth and Jesus' Glory. However, Hon is not content to leave us with profound theological truth alone; this book is filled with practical examples of how we can both embrace the truth and live the life God calls us to live.

This life work is given to us by one who has lived its reality. I urge you to take the time to digest the truth contained in *ONE!*

Gaylord Enns

Author of *Love Revolution: Rediscovering the Lost Command of Jesus*

PREFACE

It was 1971 when John Lennon wrote what is widely regarded as his signature song: "Imagine." His composition captured the imagination of that generation and subsequent ones. Lennon dreamed of a world where all people were together as one with nothing separating them. Two thousand years ago, Jesus prayed that His people be one. He prayed this epic prayer the night that He was going to die on the cross. This prayer was recorded in John 17 in the Bible.

Lennon dreamed of world peace, of one, and asked that we imagine that no one has their own possessions. Later, it was "…derided by many who point out the contradiction of a multimillionaire asking the rest of the world to imagine no possessions."[1] Many people have fantasized and imagined a utopia, but very few have led by example; and, furthermore, who has actually sacrificed their life for it? Jesus did much more than speak of diverse people being One; He lived an exemplary life warmly receiving and loving all people; and, as proof of His commitment, He died for this oneness. His death and resurrection made this oneness a reality, and it is being manifested increasingly in these days.

Lennon's beautiful song became an anthem of sorts in many countries due to the world's hunger for equality and oneness; however, seemingly, people the world over are more divided than ever. Because of humanity's selfish nature, this dream of being one cannot happen. That is why Jesus Christ gave people three gifts through His death and resurrection: eternal life, the truth, and His glory. After each gift, He said that "you may be one." This is a crucial point: All three gifts are needed for oneness among people.

When "Imagine" was written in 1971, it was on the heels of the Civil Rights Movement, in the midst of the time of hippies, peace rallies against the Vietnam War, and what can be described as a counterculture revolution. Coinciding with this period, in the late 1960s, God did something wonderful. Christian historians call it a revival. Hundreds of thousands of mostly young people came to Jesus all across the United States and Europe. This happened outside of mainstream Christianity. It took place in communes, coffee houses, on street corners and on college campuses, and came to be known as the "Jesus Movement." Those who participated were called "Jesus People" and "Jesus Freaks."

It was during this period in 1969 that I came to know and enjoy Jesus Christ, and started pursuing and serving Him. I was one of the "Jesus Freaks." Although I was only sixteen at the time, I began to see the vision as presented in the New Testament that Jesus Christ is building His one body and that all His followers are one and should practice this oneness together. I had a longing to be one: one body, one Spirit, one Lord, one faith, one hope, and one fellowship in Jesus Christ. Enjoying Jesus Christ for His one body became more than just my motto — it became and still is my purpose of living.

This book represents the realization of my imagining. I long to see God's people becoming and functioning as one according to the vision of Lord's Prayer and through the three gifts Jesus gave to all of His believers. We are not just dreamers, but explorers and

1   http://www.beatlesbible.com/people/john-lennon/songs/imagine/

pioneers — as many before us — endeavoring to bring the reality of this oneness, step-by-step, into practice and manifestation. Will you come join us?

About Me

I was born in Hong Kong, the youngest of five boys. My parents were divorced, so my mom raised me. Our family immigrated to the US when I was eight years old. Since we were poor, I started working when I was nine years old to contribute to our family, and have never stopped working. I grew up in Berkeley, California, and graduated from UC Berkeley with an engineering degree. I have been a serial entrepreneur since then.

Through the introduction by one of my brothers, I was fortunate enough to earn a good income from computer programming and an insurance business. So I decided to invest and started a folding bicycle company with my oldest brother. It is now the largest folding bicycle company in the world. Since then I have started a few technology companies, and today I am still involved in some capacity in both the bicycle company and a technology startup.

I have been married to a wonderful woman, with the same vision, for forty years, and she has borne and raised two sons and two daughters with me. All four of our children have also graduated from UC Berkeley, and are now married as well. We currently have three grandsons and one granddaughter. Our family is a "melting pot" reflecting American society: My wife is European American, and my kids have married Americans with ancestry from Africa, Europe and Southeast Asia. So as you can imagine, we are looking forward to more beautifully blended grandchildren.

I consider myself just a regular worldly guy, working in businesses my whole life with their seductive frills, enjoying the human life of raising a family, and going through typical struggles and failures. Yet, the life of Christ and God's purpose is intertwined with mine, and I can directly contribute to the building up of His body, the assembly.

My Life in Christ

I began my spiritual journey as a believer in Jesus Christ when I was sixteen. At the time I was not seeking God or desiring to be a Christian. In fact, though raised by a Christian mom, I had abandoned Christianity and was enjoying my teenage years as an accomplished athlete in high school. But one weekend, after succumbing to my mom's nagging, I finally agreed to attend a particular Christian conference. It was not in a church, but outside with a group of young people singing impromptu that attracted me. Ten to fifteen minutes or so after joining in their singing, I was filled up with the joy of Jesus Christ and of the Holy Spirit. That weekend I decided to serve the Lord Jesus and gave my life to Him. I didn't know it, but I became part of His "revival."

With a desire to live and serve the Lord, I have pursued the principles and experiences of various Christian persuasions over the decades: Evangelical–a strong desire to preach the gospel, with a focus on mission and bringing people to a new birth in Christ; Fundamental–a focus on the inerrancy of the Bible and therefore a strong emphases on Bible study and adherence to its teachings; Charismatic–a focus on being Spirit-filled and experiences in the power of the Spirit and the releasing of the spirit; and Mysticism–a focus on seeking to know and experience the constant union with God, knowing the cross by self-denial, and following the Spirit's leading through intuition. In pursuing each of these, I have received help. However, eventually and invariably, I grew frustrated and found deficiencies with each. Today, I would not be classified by any of these affiliations; however, I still possess elements of each and therefore am comfortable accepting and fellowshipping with all kinds of believers, no matter their proclivity or denomination.

Since my youth, I have been a diligent student of the Bible. My scriptural understanding is influenced by the traditions of the Plymouth Brethren (Darby, Mueller, Mackintosh, Vine), Watchman Nee, and Witness Lee. I have never been to Bible school, but through learning a great spectrum of Bible teachings and having them as a foundation and influence, I have received fresh insight and understanding of the Word (not heard from others). This has affected my walk and open fellowship with other believers. Whatever I have understood and have written in this book is curated and condensed from what has practically guided every aspect of my life. I am not just passing on biblical doctrines and theories, but a revelation of God's eternal purpose that is practical and positively effective in everyday living.

In the first fifteen years after being gained by Christ, my understanding was that in order to serve the Lord, I needed to be a good preacher — a dynamic speaker; therefore, I did my best to learn to speak publically — from open-air preaching to teaching weekly at a church, and eventually speaking in conferences. I was growing increasingly dissatisfied with my own performance and the long-term results of people that were inspired by this type of speaking.

Additionally, though I had received the vision of the oneness of believers, I was frustrated in its actual practice: it wasn't happening. While church groups that grew out of the Jesus Movement were typically against the traditions and divisiveness of mainline denominations, they competed amongst themselves to possess the mantle of being in the forefront of what God was doing. Being in such a group, we expected Christians to leave their churches and join our group if they, too, saw the vision of one body. Needless to say, that didn't work well; rather, it produced even more divisions in the body.

During this time of dissatisfaction and reflection concerning the way for me to serve the Lord and how to practice oneness, I received help from Witness Lee, who opened my eyes to see from the New Testament that the way to build up the assembly, His body — from bringing people to know the Lord Jesus to mutual edification — was in the homes. I began to understand that the life of fellowship in the one body of Christ should take place from house to house. Therefore, since mid-1980, my focus of service and fellowship has been in the homes, house by house.

Over these last thirty years, it has been a joy to participate in the Lord's move in building up His body in the homes. The first positive outcome is that my entire family — our four children with their spouses — actively believe in the Lord, and most of them also host gatherings for fellowship in their homes. They all contributed and participated in the assembly in our home as they were growing up and brought their network of friends with them into fellowship.

Simultaneously, as I progressed in learning to assemble and fellowship in the homes from house to house, I found that it is in this environment that oneness is manifested. People from diverse backgrounds have been received and accepted, and hundreds of people over the years have come to Christ and have grown spiritually. Additionally, any differences that would normally divide Christians have become a non-factor in the one fellowship of Jesus Christ. As I am seeing this oneness among believers spreading to more and more homes, house by house, I am no longer imagining, but witnessing the manifestation of what Jesus prayed for in John 17. Undeniably, His prayer is answered and it will continue to be expressed more and more.

One line in the song "Imagine" that resonated with me is "…no religion." Religion is a big divider among people and that includes the Christian religion. Even Christians are divided within their own religion with various sets of laws, traditions, and formalities. Jesus Christ is not a religion. He is life! This is precisely why the assembly in homes is what God needs for the maturation of His one body. There are no prerequisites: we simply need to focus on Jesus Christ and have a love for one another which is seen by receiving and being open to fellowship with all kinds of believers.

The Lord's intention is for a joyful and purposeful life for each of His believers. No one was meant to be a passive spectator. On the contrary, each person is needed to function as a member of His body in the course of their normal living. In various capacities, all believers need to become teachers, shepherds, ministers, and good-news-bearers, right in the comfort of their own home. When an environment exists where the three gifts that Jesus gave (eternal life, truth, and glory) are the focus, and are enjoyed, the manifestation of the oneness of people is evident and contagious. This has been my discovery and experience; it has been an adventure and a joy to advocate as well as to help fellow believers do the same from house to house.

My intention for writing this book is to explore and expound on the three gifts that Jesus gave in John 17 that, when taken together, result in divine oneness. My hope is that people of all ages, backgrounds and spiritual conditions will be inspired by the unveiling of the truth and begin to enjoy the Lord as the eternal life in their daily living. Simultaneously, this enjoyment will cause a rising up to serve others and the entering into the delight of the one fellowship with all other believers for the building up of the one body of Christ.

"…that they may be ONE." –Jesus Christ.

ACKNOWLEDGEMENT

I would not be able to write this book if it not for Sylvia, my wife, who has always supported me both as a life-companion and as a spiritual partner over these 40 years of marriage. She has stayed true and faithful through all my various struggles. Also, without my children and their spouses, I would not have the rich and wide-ranging experiences that I have had. They have endured all of my "crazy" ideas and through their growth in the faith of Jesus Christ, I continue to be encouraged in my own ministry.

I also want to acknowledge a close friend, Jeremy Tibbets, who was the one encouraging me over the last few years to get my message out to a wider audience. Jeremy came to enjoy the Lord Jesus in our home when he was a single 20-year-old. After he was married a year later and over the next ten years, my wife and I had a weekly home fellowship in his home with his wife, Paula, and their friends. As a believer that stayed up-to-date with many contemporary Bible teachers, Jeremy saw a need for a message that presented God's entire revelation that is, at once, logical and easy to understand, spiritual and practical, and backed by a living testimony. His encouragement was a major motivation for me to write this book and I am grateful. Even though he is the founder and CEO of the fastest-growing and nationally-acclaimed tree service company, I hope and pray that he will take time out to join me in unfolding God's eternal purpose to others.

As I have increased meeting, fellowshipping and networking with many believers from diverse backgrounds and churches, they have opened my eyes to recognize that the Lord is working and moving everywhere among all of His people. It is because of them that my heart is enlarged, which has led to fresh discoveries of seeing the Lord and His purpose in the Bible. Through them, I have gained more confidence to love and receive *all* believers, and to actively find and greet more and more seekers of the Lord Jesus.

INTRODUCTION

Overall church membership in western society has been declining over the last few decades — and is currently declining at a faster rate than previous years.[2] For all the good works and evangelizing that Christian churches have done over the centuries, there is a growing awareness and criticism toward churches for elements of hypocrisy, self-righteousness, intolerance and divisiveness. Additionally, there is a perception that many leaders are driven by power and material gain. While Jesus Christ is viewed positively by 91 percent of people surveyed in the USA,[3] only 41 percent of non-Christians are favorable to Evangelical churches.[4]

This should not be the case: The body of believers should reflect and express Jesus, since it is His body. If that is the reality then His body should receive the same favorability as Jesus. The fact that there is such a wide mismatch in favorability means that churches are not expressing Jesus. This was not the case in the beginning, when Jesus Christ died for the sins of the world, resurrected on the third day, ascended forty days later, and poured out His Spirit on the 50th day (Pentecost) — something marvelous, mysterious, supernatural, and yet normal was lived out in the human lives of His believers, His corporate body: They were in favor with all the people around them.

> And they, continuing daily with one accord in the temple, and breaking bread from house to house, did eat their meat with gladness and simplicity of heart, praising God and having favor with all the people and the Lord added to the church [assembly] daily those being saved.
>
> – Acts 2:46-47

The first significant factor mentioned in the above verses was that the believers continued in one. This "one accord" and the fact that all the believers were active and functioning joyfully in their homes, from house to house, brought forth an environment where the people around them approved of them. Because of this favorability, people who witnessed the believers assembling in homes were drawn to Jesus Christ and were saved. Salvation was a daily occurrence. What a revival!

This was an answer to the Lord's Prayer in John 17. He prayed:

> ...that they all may be one, as You, Father, [are] in Me, and I in You; that they also may be one in Us, that the world may believe that You sent Me.
>
> – John 17:21 NKJV

Just as the believers being one attracted people, resulting in daily salvations in Acts, the recovery of this oneness of believers assembling from house to house in this day will usher in another revival. Today's dream is that it will be the last revival before the Lord's second

---

2   http://www.churchleadership.org/apps/articles/default.asp?articleid=42346&columnid=4545
3   http://www.publicpolicypolling.com/pdf/2011/PPP_Release_US_1117424.pdf
4   http://www.pewforum.org/2014/07/16/how-americans-feel-about-religious-groups/

coming. Believers should *not* embrace the belief that being one will only happen in eternity. If this were the case, then the gifts that Jesus gave His believers in John 17 are not effective. If John Lennon can be a dreamer, then Christians today need to be visionaries and join into the Lord's Prayer and allow the Lord's three gifts of eternal life, truth and His glory to manifest this oneness of believers together within the Trinity.

This book will be, hopefully, like a big "reset" button for readers and an encouragement to return to Jesus Christ and God's purpose as revealed in the Bible. Let's not be chained down by traditions of Christianity — what has been done and taught for centuries so it "must continue as is." Rather let's consider the Bible with fresh eyes without the distorted lens of historical Christianity. Let's pray that the readers of this book will hit "reset" and return to the beginning and become one.

Defining Church and Assembly

Since the matter of "church" is probably the biggest item of Christianity after faith in Jesus Christ, it is impossible to be reset back to the beginning without receiving fresh eyes on this matter of church. To begin with, the word "church" in the Bible is a mistranslation from the Greek word *ekklesia*. The accurate translation is "assembly" or "congregation." Literally, *ekklesia* means the "called out ones." The common usage of this word during the apostles' time was for a called out assembly of people, such as a town square meeting, whose citizens were "called out" to attend. Therefore, the correct translation of *ekklesia* is assembly, or congregation (Thayer's Greek Lexicon).

The word "church" actually comes from a very different Greek word. The etymology (etymology.com) of the word "church" is said to be from *kyriake (oikia)*, or *kyriakon doma* meaning, "the lord's house." It refers to an actual place of worship, which included a place to worship idols. This word started being used to identify a Christian place of worship around the fourth century AD, when Constantine established Christianity as the Roman state religion. It was during this time that Christians began meeting in dedicated worship buildings, rather than in homes or in public places.

In 1525, William Tyndale translated the first printed Bible into English. He translated the word *ekklesia* as "congregation" or assembly. This was in direct contradiction to the Roman Church.[5] At that time, the Roman Church feared that removing the word "church" from the Bible would threaten their authority and hierarchy. This was one of the major reasons Tyndale was killed and burned at the stake by the Roman Church in 1536.[6] When King James authorized his translation of the Bible in 1611, eighty-four percent of the New Testament was translated directly from Tyndale's Bible. But King James made one translation rule clear: *ekklesia* was to be translated "church" and not "congregation" or "assembly." [7]

King James was the head of the Church of England (the Anglican church) and all forty-seven translators were members. Once again, for political and control reasons, the King James Version of the Bible mistranslated the Greek word *ekklesia* to "church." Since then, just about every English version of the Bible has kept to this translation of "church."

---

5   http://www.bl.uk/onlinegallery/sacredtexts/tyndale.html
6   https://en.wikipedia.org/wiki/Tyndale_Bible
7   http://www.kjvonly.org/other/kj_instructs.htm

It is much simpler and honest when words are used exactly for what they mean. Even today the primary dictionary meaning of church is "a building that is used for Christian religious services" (Merriam-Webster). Christians who are more advanced in seeing the body of Christ (Eph. 1:22–23) have to constantly clarify and redefine "church" as the believers, not the building.

Considering this, for the sake of accuracy and in support of Tyndale who gave his life for the translation of the Bible, for this book, the word for *ekklesia* will be translated "assembly." When the word "church" is used, it will refer to either a physical place for Christian worship or an organized group of Christians associated with one or more dedicated physical buildings for worship.

Many Churches (Ministries), but Only One Assembly (Body)

Additionally, churches belong to a specific work of ministers, pastors, or priests (the clergy), and because of this churches are defined by the teachings and practices of their respective clergy. But the assembly as defined in the New Testament is very different from how churches operate today in their very nature. This is not to denigrate what God may be doing in the various churches and the faithfulness of many of the clergy serving in the churches. However, in order to come back to the beginning to understand God's eternal purpose, it is imperative that a distinction be made between the assembly as defined by the New Testament and churches as they are known today. In fact, churches as ministries can be many, but the assembly of believers can only be one. The lack of this understanding among Christians is a source of confusion and division.

Many Christian churches in general, as ministries, have been used by God to spread the gospel and to gather believers for teaching the Bible. They have served society with various good deeds, but when compared with the pattern of the assembly of believers *(ekklesia)* as described in the New Testament, institutional churches fall far short. Some Bible teachers have pointed out the various unscriptural practices of institutional churches and have become ultra-critical — to the point that those under their influence would completely alienate themselves from *all* churches and even the Christians active in them. This is divisive and damaging to the Lord's body.

On the other hand, many Christians that have left organized churches and are meeting in homes desiring deeper relational fellowship begin with high expectations and inspiring experiences. Eventually, many of these home groups become ingrown and stagnate, with no outreach and without a higher purpose other than "good fellowship" within their own group. They can become even more divisive, controlling, and directionless when compared to Christians in institutional churches. Therefore, one of the most well-known proponents of house churches (also known as "organic churches") Frank Viola in his blog dated April 2016 has given a negative assessment to the general state of house churches.[8] Broadly speaking the "organic church" or "simple church" movement fell short of building up the assembly, also.

---

8   http://frankviola.org/2016/04/21/organicchurch/

The assembly, as unveiled in the Scriptures, is dynamic, living, fluid, expanding, and proactive. Though in homes from house to house, it is the living body of Christ with a mission to reach the unsaved, shepherd weaker believers, expand and blend fellowship with more and more homes, and build up the practical and manifested oneness of all believers. Believers will have complete freedom to be who they are in Christ and function according to their God-given capacity. There is no separation among God's people, but rather fellowship among all believers no matter how diverse they are. The principal location of the assembly will take place in each other's homes from house to house. This is the vision of the assembly that God is after and He will build up such a testimony on earth in this age.

Organized churches and the assembly in homes do not have to conflict with each other, and Christians do not have to pick one over the other; they serve different purposes. Institutional churches are often set up to further a particular ministry led by specific ministers with diverse purposes, whereas the assembly existing in homes is for the building up of the oneness and fellowship among dissimilar believers that may span various ministries. The assembly is for each believer to function according to the gift that the Spirit has given them.

Believers may attend a certain church in support of that ministry and simultaneously gather during the week from house to house with and among diverse believers for the assembly. In fact, this book is calling upon pastors — the clergy of churches — to encourage those under their ministry to do just that. Their job as gifted ministers is to equip and encourage those under their leadership to be able to blend and fellowship with disparate believers in one, and to reach out to all.

The author is not advocating an ecumenical movement where all Christian churches work out their differences to come under one umbrella organization. Rather, the oneness among believers does not need to be organized. Loving one another in the one body is innate within each believer based on the organic life of Jesus Christ in each one.

The Bible Presented from the Viewpoint of ONE

Since the entire revelation of God's eternal purpose is contained in the Scriptures, this book is intended to be more like a Bible study, to help people read and understand the Bible directly for themselves. For this reason, Scripture is prominently quoted as part of this book. The goal is to present the Bible in a way that provides the encompassing story of God's eternal purpose in Jesus Christ in a linear fashion, so that readers can follow and study it logically. It is critical that readers are impacted by the Spirit, who enlightens them directly with the understanding of Scriptures, rather than solely relying on man's interpretation. The commentaries on the Scriptures in this book serve as an opening and a challenge for readers to consider (or reconsider), so that they have confidence in their understanding of the Bible as a whole. This is in contrast to understanding a Scripture here and a portion there, which might not be interpreted in context.

Many of the crucial points of Christian truth, life, and service are still quite hidden to most believers. If there is familiarity to the topics presented, it may be a hodgepodge of unrelated and conflicting subjects that, if not fitted together as a puzzle, won't unveil the entire view of God's eternal purpose accomplished by His economy.

This book is an attempt to synthesize the main points of Christian theology and experiences, categorized into the three gifts given by the Lord Jesus to make believers one. Although each chapter as separate points can be (and has been) explored by a multitude of writers over the centuries within Christian literature, this book has curated and condensed the many points through the vision of God's eternal purpose: ONE.

To support his thesis of ONE through three gifts, the author has discovered a number of fresh and helpful understandings of portions of the Bible that he didn't learn from others. They have been very helpful to him in his pursuit of the Lord for His purpose. However, just because he discovered them does not necessarily mean others have not had the same insight throughout church history. So, he is asking for help from readers to verify their scriptural correctness and corroborate these findings with other Bible teachers. He believes that taken as a whole, the information presented in this book is theologically and experientially balanced and accurate, even if a number of points may be different from traditional understanding. Therefore, he hopes that readers will consider the entire book before rendering a final judgment.

While the system of institutional churches of various stripes has been well established for more than a thousand years, the recovery of the independent assembly in homes, house by house, according to the New Testament, is still in its infancy. Ironically, it is the assembly (God's desire) located in homes that all the apostles labored to build up. Yet two thousand years later, it is still obscure.

However, the Lord Jesus, according to His desire, has not given up and is recovering the assembly back to its rightful prominence. Since it is a fresh discovery by many believers in recent decades, trial and error is still taking place as believers learn and negotiate their way back to assembling as prescribed by the early apostles. The author hopes that through this book many more believers will be inspired and find real joy in the building up of the assembly from house to house, according to God's eternal purpose. For those already practicing the assembly in a home, this book will serve as a way of trading notes so that believers can learn and network together in the one fellowship of Jesus Christ. Let's pray and live expecting the next and last revival. Reset to ONE; revival next!

> ...fulfill my joy by being like-minded, having the same love, [being] of one accord, of one mind.
>
> – Philippians 2:2

1.

THE LORD'S PETITION: ONE

I do not pray for these alone, but also for those who will believe in Me through their word; that they all may be one, as You, Father, are in Me, and I in You; that they also may be one in Us, that the world may believe that You sent Me.

— John 17:20–21

The entire revelation of God concerning the mystery of His eternal will has been recorded in the Bible. Outside of what is already written in the Bible, no one can add to its revelation or claim to have additional truth that is not already written in the Bible. Neither can anyone remove what is already revealed in God's Word. The Bible is full of mysteries concerning God, Jesus Christ, and God's purpose in relation to His people; yet it also contains history, stories, laws, parables, and ethical and moral standards. Because of this, readers of the Bible often come away with an assortment of impressions of what this book is conveying. Casual readers, and even many serious students of the Bible, can be confused or distracted by what may seem to be a thick forest of topics.

However, the Scriptures have only one major topic: Jesus Christ (John 5:39). Jesus Himself affirmed this. The mystery the Bible unveils is Jesus — *who He is,* both individually and corporately (in His body), what He has accomplished, and what He is doing today. Therefore, though there are tens of thousands of books written concerning the Bible, those that are of the most spiritual value are those that explore and expound on Jesus Christ or the relationship between Jesus and His believers.

Embodied in Jesus Christ is God's eternal purpose, His pleasure and His will (Eph. 1:9, 3:11). Therefore, to truly know Jesus Christ, one must know more than Jesus' activity in the Gospels; one must also know His purpose, His pleasure, and what He is doing today. Only then will followers of Jesus be able to participate in accomplishing His eternal will. This is crucial.

But the sad fact is that many Christians are self-centered and only care about what God is doing for them. They seek after God's will in order to meet their own personal goals.

What about God's Purpose and Will?

If we dive into the heart of Jesus Christ and understand His purpose, we will realize that, as believers, if we don't take His purpose to be our purpose and His pleasure to be our pleasure, then our lives on earth will be driven by selfish motives and the result is vanity.

In Matthew 16:13 Jesus asked His disciples, "Who do men say that I, the Son of Man, am?" The answer to this simple question determined everything for His disciples, and it determines everything for us: Faith in Jesus Christ makes the difference in whether someone receives eternal life...or not. Some have answered that Jesus was a great teacher, a prophet, or a revolutionary. However, it takes revelation from the Father for a person to recognize that Jesus is the Christ — the Son of the living God, the promised Messiah.

A few verses later Jesus looked at the disciples and asked them the question, "But who do *you* say that I am?" (Matt. 16:15, emphasis added). Peter's answer, "You are the Christ, the Son of the living God" (16:16), would change his life.

Like Peter, people are truly blessed when they see and believe who Jesus is. As soon as Peter answered with this wonderful revelation, Jesus immediately responded that He would build His assembly, and this assembly would crush the gates of Hades. Peter received eternal life by believing that Jesus was the Son of God (John 20:31; 1 John 3:24), but notice what else happened: The Lord immediately explained His mission *as the Christ*, commissioned by God, to His disciples.

Half of the revelation Peter received was from the Father, and the other half was from the Son, the Christ. The first part of the revelation was to know Jesus as the Christ, the Son of the living God; the second part was to know that Jesus' mission is to build an assembly that will crush the gates of Hades. Together, the two parts of this revelation make up the whole of Jesus' entire purpose for coming to earth.

Furthermore, this assembly is to be built on the rock. Some have misinterpreted this rock to be Peter. The problem is that "Peter" in the Greek means a stone that can be moved and thrown, and "rock" in the Greek means a solid rock mass on which a structure can be built. So in 1 Peter 2:5, Peter declares that all other believers are similar to him, a living stone. In context, the rock on which the assembly is built can only be Jesus Christ and more specifically, on the revelation of Jesus Christ. It is the revelation directly from the Father of who Jesus Christ is, and the singular focus on Him alone that is the foundation for the building up of the Lord's assembly — God's eternal purpose. All other ground is sinking or shifting sand.

Becoming ONE Is the Building Up of the Assembly

When Jesus said that He will build His assembly (ekklesia), it was the first time this word was used in the Scriptures. This word was used again two chapters later in Matthew 18. After that, the word was not mentioned again until Acts and the epistles. For something so important that Jesus was commissioned to build up and for which He died, it is unusual that Jesus only used this word "ekklesia" (assembly) in a couple of instances. By definition, ekklesia is just a group of people that are called out to assemble, but is that it? What is so special about this group of people? How does this group of people interact with each other? What is this group of people projecting to the world around them?

The night prior to Jesus going to die on the cross, which is commonly known as the last supper, He unveiled His heart and spoke of extraordinary and mysterious things to His disciples. He was describing and defining the assembly (ekklesia) that He will build up. Though the word "assembly" was not used, clearly Jesus was describing His called out people and their relationship within the Trinity. The last supper was recorded from John chapter 13 to 17. Jesus started the evening in chapter 13 by washing His disciples' feet, a job that was commonly performed by the lowliest of slaves in those days. Jesus then gave a new commandment: That you love one another as I have loved you (13:34). This one commandment encapsulates the relationship between every believer in the assembly and was exemplified by Jesus serving His disciples as a slave. He said that it is by the manifestation of loving one another as Jesus loved that the followers of Jesus are made known to all (John 13:35). The banner designating the assembly is their love for one another.

In Chapter 14, Jesus spoke of His imminent death by saying that He is going away. Though the disciples were saddened by Jesus' disclosure that He is leaving them, Jesus encouraged them by telling them that it is profitable that He goes away to die, because He will come back as the indwelling comforter or helper. If He does not go away, He can only be with them. But if He dies, then He will come back as the Spirit to dwell in them and they will dwell in both Him and the Father. This is another unveiling of the assembly: It is a group of people with Jesus living in them to constantly help them from within, and they are living in the very being of the Father and the Son.

In Chapter 15, Jesus said that He is the vine and all the believers are the branches of this vine. A vine is the sum total of all the branches. A vine is not a vine without branches. At best it would just be a stump, but not a vine. By this one description, Jesus opened up the heavenly and mysterious reality that through His death and resurrection, all believers are a part of Him, His body. He has expanded and increased Himself from one person in Jesus to millions as this universal vine. The assembly is this vine: full of life, growth and multiplication. The vine is constantly bearing fruit: multiplying in an increasing number of people and displaying all the attributes of God. When the universe looks at this vine, what is seen is the vibrant eternal divine life coursing through all the branches, extending, life transforming; and love, joy, peace with other attributes of the Spirit are expressed in humanity (Gal. 5:22).

Jesus continues in Chapter 16 to describe the Spirit of truth that will guide the assembly of believers into everything real concerning the Trinity. Everything that the Father is and all that Jesus Christ has accomplished will be declared and made real to all believers through the Spirit. The assembly becomes the recipient and the expression of the unsearchable riches of the entire Trinity. How awesome!

Finally in chapter 17, Jesus ended the supper with a monumental and wonderful prayer to the Father. This prayer is the conclusion of that evening as described above. This is Jesus' outpouring from the deepest part of His heart for His followers according to the eternal purpose of God. This prayer unveils what He was sent to accomplish as the Christ. The focus of His prayer was that His people become ONE. He declared this three times: "that they may be ONE." In His prayer, He revealed that through His death and resurrection He gave His people three gifts. The result of each gift is that "they may be ONE" and even as one as the Father and the Son are ONE. What a mysterious and extraordinary oneness! God is literally one, though He is distinctly three: the Father, Son, and Spirit. The building up of the assembly occurs when millions of distinctively individual believers become one just as the Father and the Son are one.

After the gospels, in the epistles, the assembly was described in more ways: household (sons) of God, bride of Christ, body of Christ, new man, warrior, temple, God's kingdom, and eventually the New Jerusalem. All these various descriptions point to God's desire to be one with human beings. His eternal life and divine nature joined and mingled together with humankind; additionally, man will have their being in God--The two become ONE. Just as the Father, the Son and the Holy Spirit are perfectly one, God's people will become part of this perfect oneness. As the three of the Trinity are in perfect love, fellowship, and purpose, God extends Himself and envelopes humankind into this same oneness. His people living in ONEness are the manifestation of their perfect union with God. This is the heart of Jesus, His desire and purpose.

It can then be said that this ONEness or becoming ONE as prayed for by Jesus is the consummate definition and description of what He is building, the assembly. The ultimate expression of God's eternal purpose is simply ONE.

ONEness Experienced and Expressed

Below are just a few of the verses showing the expression and manifestation of oneness through the Lord's new commandment with its ancillary instructions:

> "A new commandment I give to you, that you love one another; as I have loved you, that you also love one another.
>
> – John 13:34

> Therefore let us not judge one another anymore, but rather resolve this, not to put a stumbling block or a cause to fall in [our] brother's way.
>
> – Rom 4:13

> And be kind to one another, tenderhearted, forgiving one another, even as God in Christ forgave you.
>
> – Eph. 4:32

> That there may be no division in the body, but that the members may have the same care for one another.
>
> – 1 Cor. 12:25, ESV

> But whoever has this world's goods, and sees his brother in need, and shuts up his heart from him, how does the love of God abide in him?
>
> – 1 John 3:17

Generally, when the matter of oneness or unity is discussed among Christians, it is related to unity in their own church, denomination or group. It is centered on the need for unity within their own defined group. On the other hand, there are the ecumenical discussions where various Christian institutions are negotiating a kind of unification among themselves. Neither of these are the oneness that Jesus prayed for in John 17. Being ONE in the Trinity is outside of any human organizations. It crosses organizational barriers. It cannot be arranged systematically. It stems from the eternal life within each believer. Being one is not a result of negotiation or human coordination, but it is an organic outcome from each individual's own relationship within the Father, the Son, Jesus Christ, and Holy Spirit.

Unity in the secular world and sadly among most Christian churches is based on uniformity of interest or viewpoints. The oneness in Jesus Christ crosses all boundaries and separations. Anyone with the faith of Jesus Christ can immediately enjoy the innate oneness with another who also has the faith of Jesus regardless of differing political or doctrinal views. There can be immediate fellowship in the Holy Spirit and prayer to the same Father. Fellowship can include testifying of our salvation experiences, enlightening from the word concerning Jesus Christ or sharing the challenges of daily life. This fellowship leads to praying for one another and rejoicing in God's love and mercy. A bond is immediately realized and the love for one another is instant and genuine.

For too long, the followers of Jesus have allowed divergent doctrinal understandings, Christian practices and personalities, worldly politics, and many other variations to divide them. No wonder the world has not believed and instead has mocked the name of Christ. Christians have spent much time and energy in evangelism, but how many have entered into the prayer of Jesus to announce John 17 to help bring His people to ONEness. The Lord promised that when His people are ONE then the world will believe. Wouldn't that be the most powerful gospel? The verses above are a sampling of experiences of being one. Just consider what the world will see when there is a manifestation of this oneness through the various expressions of His love through believers.

This oneness can be expressed in work places, buses, schools, neighborhoods, and any place where believers can have a chance to meet one another. Right there in regular daily life, connections can be made and oneness manifested. Over time, fellowship can continue over the phone, and even welcoming one another into each other's homes.

The ONEness prayed for by the Lord Jesus is real, practical, and genuine. There is unpretentious joy and rejoicing. Each person can be who they are, just as they are, yet living in the transforming life of Christ and fellowshipping in the love of God with all kinds of different followers of Jesus.

Zion Is the Place of ONEness

Behold, how good and how pleasant [it is] for brethren to dwell together in unity! [It is] like the precious oil upon the head, running down on the beard, the beard of Aaron, running down on the edge of his garments. [It is] like the dew of Hermon, descending upon the mountains of Zion. For there the LORD commanded the blessing--Life forevermore.

– Psa. 133

For the LORD has chosen Zion; He has desired [it] for His dwelling place:

– Psa. 132:13

The Lord's prayer in John 17 corresponds to God's desire in the Old Testament. Back in those days there was a mountain in Jerusalem called Zion, which is the site where the Jewish temple was built. The temple is a pre-figure of the assembly which is the dwelling place of God for eternity (Eph. 2:21-22). The assembly that the Lord Jesus is building is literally called Zion (Heb. 12:22-23). Zion signifies the place of oneness or unity. It is oneness that is God's dwelling place. God desires the oneness of His people. He commands the blessing of eternal life on Zion, on oneness. Therefore, God's people in oneness, in unity, are joyful and pleasant. On the people in oneness, there is the anointing of the Spirit signified by the anointing oil on Aaron. There is the dew signifying the freshness of the experiences of Christ every morning. Zion, the place of oneness, is God's desire and even is the joy of the entire earth (Psa. 48:2). The entire earth is waiting for the manifestation of the oneness of God's people. This oneness will usher in peace and joy for the whole earth. No wonder that this is the unique calling of every believer: keep the oneness of the Spirit (Eph. 4:1-3).

God's Amazing Three Gifts

In order to have this transcendent ONEness among believers, which is the manifestation of the building up of His assembly, Jesus in His prayer gave the believers three gifts: eternal life (the Father's name), the truth (the Word), and His glory. Each is given to every believer, and makes it possible for them to be one, just as Jesus is one with the Father. It is through the believers being one in such a way that the world will believe that Jesus is truly the Son of God (John 17:21b).

Knowing, understanding, and experiencing these three gifts is how believers are made one; they are essential to accomplishing His purpose of creating "oneness." This book explores these three gifts for the purpose of the Lord's continuing work of building up His assembly by bringing believers into this mysterious yet practical oneness.

This same testimony of oneness among the believers from all nations, ethnicities, and socioeconomic diversity (Col. 3:11) will cause the world to believe that He is the Son of God, and be convinced of God's eternal love for humankind (17:23). This is the most powerful testimony for the gospel to cause people to believe — believers brought into one through the eternal life, the truth and the glory of Jesus Christ!

The First Gift – Eternal life, The Father's Name

> . . . as You have given Him authority over all flesh, that He should give eternal life to as many as You have given Him. And this is eternal life, that they may know You, the only true God, and Jesus Christ whom You have sent. . . . Now I am no longer in the world, but these are in the world, and I come to You. Holy Father, keep through Your name those whom You have given Me, that they may be one as We [are].
>
> – John 17: 2–3, 11

The eternal life (the Father's name) is the first element, which is related to being born of God in order to become God's child. It is this process that results in God becoming the believers' Father, and, in turn, they receive His name. John 17:3 clearly states that knowing the Father results in eternal life for those who are in the faith of Jesus Christ. When one believes into Christ, this person receives a new birth. He or she is born anew. This is known as "regeneration," and can only be produced through God's divine, eternal life. This is what it means to be "born...of God" (John 1:13). Being born of God is not just a metaphor; it is a reality. God is now the believers' Father, not just their Creator. In addition to receiving God's eternal life, they partake of His divine nature (2 Pet. 1:4). The reality of God as the believers' Father is even more real than their earthly (biological) fathers from their "first" birth, because God is the Father constantly and eternally. Believers have actually received the Spirit of the Son by which they can call out to God in the most intimate way, "Abba, Father" or "Daddy, Father" (Gal. 4:6).

It is by being kept in this life of the Father, enjoying the Father's name, that believers are made one. The believers are one because they have the same eternal life and divine nature. All believers have the same Father. They all originate from the same source; they become genuine brothers and sisters within the same family. In many cultures, those that are born from the same earthly father have the same name — their family (last) name. Similarly, believers bear the same "name" as their heavenly Father because they are born of Him. So being kept in the Father's name is to remain in the enjoyment of the reality that all believers are in one family with the same Father and in the same name. If believers are not kept in the enjoyment of this divine life, then they will gravitate back to their divisive old nature.

The Father and the Son, though distinct, are one in life and nature; therefore, they are both eternally one. Thus, all believers that abide in this life and nature of God are automatically one in Christ. This is the most basic factor of the believers' oneness. 1 John 3:14 states, "We know that we have passed from death to life, because we love the brethren." This new life causes believers to love one another; this divinely natural love is the proof that they are no longer in death, but in the Father's life.

Every believer, upon receiving Jesus Christ as their Savior, being born anew, immediately feels a connection with other believers. They don't know much, if at all, concerning various Christian doctrines, practices, or denominational affinities, but are just happy to meet any other believers. Their first thought is not to what denomination a person belongs, but simply that, "You believe in Jesus Christ. Praise the Lord! Let me tell you, I just found Jesus!" This is real, spontaneous, unadulterated love for other believers. There is oneness immediately in the eternal life.

But instead of being kept in that life, in the Father's name, many believers over the centuries picked up assorted doctrines and practices and made them their own. Sitting under the tutelage of various Bible teachers, they began to align themselves with certain schools of theology — a *way* of practicing baptism, a *method* for holy living, or steps to receiving miraculous gifts. It may have seemed that they were learning a lot of Christian and scriptural things, but the more they learned, the more they began to separate themselves from other believers. They began to identify themselves with a certain type of Christian. They may have even taken on an identifying name such as Baptist, Catholic, or Methodist. Soon, believers were labeled: he is a Pentecostal; she is a reformed Christian; he is a dispensationalist.

This is not being kept in the Father's name. This is the leaving of the Father's name to take on other names.

Oh, how believers need to be kept uniquely in the Father's name! This is the first and most basic element of believers being brought into one. Those that are in the Father's name will not bring about problems with other believers by promoting anything that would cause other believers to be distracted from the eternal life, the Father's name.

Those that are kept in the Father's name will receive all their fellow believers as true brothers and sisters into the one fellowship of the divine life. They will seek to grow in the eternal life and desire to help other believers to grow in this life too. They will not want to remain as a babe, but will strive to reach maturity.

A babe in this life is a person that is easily carried away from the Father's name. These believers are easily distracted by the world — by political causes, law keeping, doctrinal debates, various Christian practices, or personalities. In Ephesians 4:14, Paul said believers should no longer be like babies, tossed and carried about by every wind of teaching. Men use both secular and biblical teachings with craftiness, carrying off the "babes" into their schemes or systematized error — that is, a system in error. The enemy's schemes cause divisions and eventually sects in the body of Christ, resulting in separation among believers.

Conversely, mature believers in the divine life are immovable because of the Father's name. They are no longer diverted or confused by various doctrines or practices. They are guarded and kept to remain in the Father's life. Such followers of Christ are able to fellowship easily with all believers, even with distracted babes. Mature believers can bring those confused by diverse doctrines and Christian practices back to the enjoyment of the Father's name.

Part 1 in this book will explore how the followers of Jesus can grow in God's life. It is through their spiritual eating, drinking, breathing, exercise, and rest that God's eternal life grows and matures in them.

The Second Gift – Truth

The second gift the Lord gave believers to bring them into oneness is *truth.* The Lord prayed in John 17:14 and 17, "I have given them Your word…Sanctify them by Your truth. Your word is truth." It is in this truth that believers are made one. Jesus continued to pray, "That they all may be one, as You, Father, *are* in Me, and I in You; that they also may be one in Us, that the world may believe that You sent Me" (17:21). How deep and mysterious is the oneness of all believers in the triune God, in the Father and the Son! How powerful is this manifestation that will cause the world to believe.

John 17:17 states, "Your word is truth." The "word" in this verse does not refer to the actual words in Scripture (the Bible). The Bible contains and conveys the Word; however, people can read and study the Scriptures, yet *miss* the Word. John 1:1 says, "In the beginning was the Word and the Word was with God and the Word was God." This verse alone shows that "word" in John 17:17 is not referring to the Bible since the Bible was not written in the beginning of eternity! Then, in 1:14 John writes, "The Word became flesh…" This "Word" is God Himself, incarnate. God became man, in the form of Jesus Christ. *The* Word is Jesus. Jesus confirmed this in John 5:39–40 when He said, "You search the Scriptures, for in them you think you have eternal life. But you are not willing to come to Me that you may have life." Here Jesus clearly separated Himself from the Scriptures. One can read and study the Scriptures without coming to Jesus. Life is in Jesus, not in mere Scripture absent of Jesus.

The Greek word for "word" is *logos*. It means "a speech, something said, and reasoning." It is the root word for "logical" (Gr. *logikos*). Jesus being the "Word" is the expression of God as speech, and that Word comes in a way that is reasonable and can be understood logically. John 1:18 reveals God is hidden and no one can see or perceive Him but the Son, who is the Word and who declares (or manifests) God. It is through the Word — Jesus Christ — man can see and know God. Words can be written down, passed on and reproduced in an accurate manner; this is how the Word has been recorded in the Scriptures. God will be manifested to those who seek Jesus as the Word in the Scriptures, through understanding and reasoning. Believers need to do more than simply read and study the Bible because it contains the Word; they should simultaneously come to Jesus, seek Him, see Him, speak to Him, know Him, handle Him, and have fellowship with Him; otherwise, they will miss the words of eternal life (1 John 1:1–2).

John 1:14 says, "The Word became flesh and dwelt among us…full of grace and truth." A few verses later in verse 18 John writes, "For the law was given through Moses, *but* grace and truth came through Jesus Christ." These two verses reveal that grace and truth were introduced through the Word, Jesus Christ, when God became flesh.

According to Vine's Expository Dictionary, truth, as used in the New Testament, is "the reality lying at the basis of appearance and manifestation." According to this definition, truth is much more than not telling a lie or saying something factual; it is the reality of the universe. When a person realizes what is hidden behind what appears and what is manifested, *that is truth*. No wonder "truth" has such prominence! It is one of the two items that came through Jesus Christ. It is important to elevate the understanding of the word "truth" to a high and spiritual level, and not relegate it to a simple secular concept such as, "Tell me the truth! Did you take a cookie?"

John says that Jesus Christ is full of grace and truth. He continued to say that grace and truth came through Jesus Christ. Based on the above definition, when a person receives Jesus Christ, they possess *the* truth, *the* reality. They will know and discern what is real, what is behind the entire "shadow" of the universe (Col. 2:16–17). Without Jesus Christ, men are stuck knowing only what they can see and what is physically manifested. Men's lives and all that they strive for — money, fame and material gain — are all vanity. Even the physical universe is not reality! Receiving and believing into Jesus Christ brings people out of the pit of vanity, emptiness, and false reality, and into truth, veracity, and something solid that is eternal.

The more a believer stands in truth alone, the more open and receptive in fellowship that believer will be with all other believers. When a believer is established in the truth, that person is not blown about by various doctrines and practices. Neither will there be objections to or insistence on any non-essential doctrines, nor the wide array of Christian practices. This is because that person will be peaceful, comfortable, confident and grounded in the truth of Jesus Christ.

Part 2 in this book is dedicated to exploring the major points of the truth. Jesus said: The truth shall make you free (John 8:32). The understanding of truth is the fuel and the freedom to fellowship in oneness among God's people.

The Third Gift – Jesus' Glory

In John 17:22, Jesus said, "And the glory which You gave Me I have given them, that they may be one just as We are one." The Lord Jesus prayed that the glory that was given to Him by the Father would be given to the believers that they may be one. Glory in the Greek means "good opinion, praise, honor, an appearance commanding respect, magnificence, excellence, manifestation of glory" (Vine's Expository Dictionary). Therefore, the highest glory is the result whenever God is expressed and manifested.

The glory given to Jesus was through His death and resurrection. Luke 24:26 made it clear that it was through death that Jesus entered into glory. In John 12:23–24, Jesus said that the hour had come for Him to be glorified; then He spoke of going to His death and resurrection in order to bear much fruit. He likened Himself to a seed of wheat that needs to experience death in order to bring forth many more grains in resurrection. That was the glory given to Him in resurrection. In Jesus' opening prayer, He anguished over the fact that the hour had arrived for Him to be glorified; again, He was referring to His imminent crucifixion. In the rest of the prayer, He prayed as if He had already been resurrected and all three gifts were already given to His disciples.

As the Son of God, the second of the Trinity, Jesus as God *already* has glory (John 1:14). In fact, it is the same glory as the Father (John 17:5). Since the glory of the Son in His divinity is the same glory as of the Father, there was no need for the Father to give Him glory. The glory that was given to Jesus in the above-referenced verses was given to Him *after* His death and resurrection, affirming the glory of the Father was given to Him *as a man.* Jesus in His humanity didn't possess the glory of God before His crucifixion, but after His death and resurrection, *still completely human,* He was glorified with the same divine glory as the Father and the Son. Not only was Jesus' humanity brought into glory, but He brought all of His people who were born human beings into the same divine glory. This is the "much fruit" that He bore as the "grain of wheat." It was through this process that God was fully expressed in humanity or glorified.

Just as Jesus served God and man for His glorification, His followers who have received His glory are on the same path. They are to serve God and man in humility, as a slave, in ministering Christ to people on earth. As Jesus is interceding on the throne in heaven, His followers would continue His service to preach the gospel, to teach the truth, to make disciples and to build up His assembly, His body, on earth. This is the unique purpose for all believers. They are one in this glory to fulfill God's purpose.

Philippians 2 – A Description of How Jesus Obtained This Glory

Philippians 2 clearly describes the process from which Jesus received glory from the Father, which is the same glory that He has given to the believers in order to bring believers into one. In Philippians 2, Paul was expressing the same aspiration as the Lord's Prayer in John 17. He desired that believers be one — that they be one in mind, be of one accord, and have the same love for one another. However, Paul addressed a problem: "Vain glory" disrupted this oneness among the believers. Vain (or empty) glory is human glory that lifts oneself up and thinks of oneself as higher or better than other people. This self-glory (or ego) caused discord and created fractions (Phil 2:14) among the believers in Philippi.

The remedy for this discord, according to Paul, was that the believers are to have the mind of Christ. What is the mind of Christ and its result? Let's read:

> Let this mind be in you, which was also in Christ Jesus: who, being in the form of God, thought it not robbery to be equal with God, but made Himself of no reputation, taking the form of a bondservant, and coming in the likeness of men. And being found in appearance as a man, He humbled Himself and became obedient to the point of death, even the death of the cross.
>
> – Philippians 2:5–8

Jesus left His glory and His reputation as God to become a man, but not just *any* man; He became a humble bondservant who died performing His service. And it was not until after His death that Paul said Jesus was glorified:

> Therefore God also highly exalted him, and gave to him the name which is above every name; that at the name of Jesus every knee should bow, of those in heaven, those on earth, and those under the earth, and that every tongue should confess that Jesus Christ is Lord, to the glory of God the Father.
>
> – Philippians 2:9–11, WBT

As a man in resurrection, Jesus was glorified. He received glory from the Father as the exalted One with the highest name. This humble Jesus, as a servant of God and man, received the highest glory, and in turn it glorified the Father. This is what Jesus meant when He prayed in John 17:1: "Glorify your Son, that your Son may glorify You."

This glory that was given to Jesus is the same glory given to the believers. To have the same glory as Jesus, believers need to have the same mind as Jesus — a mind to become nothing but a servant to others. To the secular and religious world, this does not sound like glory! Glory in the secular or religious world typically means a person is served and that their directives are followed. The higher one is exalted, the more people will serve them and attend to their needs and wishes. This is the glory of man, the glory of this world today. But the glory of the Lord Jesus is not so. Jesus said:

> Yet it shall not be so among you; but whoever desires to become great among you, let him be your servant. And whoever desires to be first among you, let him be your slave — just as the Son of Man did not come to be served, but to serve, and to give His life a ransom for many.
>
> – Matthew 20:26–28

Just as the glory given to Jesus was not of this world, the glory that He gave to His believers is not of this world; it is exactly like the glory given to Him by the Father. It is a glory through death and resurrection.

As in Philippi, where there was discord among believers, much of the discord today that leads to sectarianism is due to personalities. Individuals who have allowed ego and pride to take over (which is the world's glory) have caused disunity in the body and sectarianism. Even among small groups of believers, pride and ego among various personalities is a sure way to cause friction and split up a group. This kind of dividing is generally not between young or weak believers, but between those that are prominent; those who want to serve God. It is ironic that many who desire to serve God end up not being able to be one with other believers because of ego and self-glory. The solution is to understand, receive, and live according to the glory of Jesus Christ.

This glory is absolutely contrary to the typical hierarchy of leadership among believers. Those in leadership expect others to follow them, and those under such leadership will identify themselves with their leaders to the detriment of fellowshipping with believers outside their group. The problem is not with mature believers serving diligently who may have garnered a title such as "Pastor," "Minister," "Elder," or "Priest," who have stayed in the position of a servant. Trouble occurs when leaders expect others to follow their directions and are offended when those directions are not followed; when this happens, it is certain they are no longer participating in the glory of Jesus Christ.

It is only in the glory of Jesus that the services of each believer lead to ONEness, and the more each serves, the more oneness is produced and manifested. This is the Lord's glory given to each and every believer that they may be ONE.

ONE in Life, Truth, and Glory

The three precious gifts that the Lord gave His believers certainly will bring the believers into one: the Father's name (eternal life), the truth (His Word), and the Lord's glory (service). Since these three gifts given by the Lord are the elements to build up His assembly — *His body* — by bringing believers into one, they are key and crucial to the Christian life. This book will explore and expound on these three gifts, by bringing focus to the Lord Jesus' prayer for this matter of the building up of His body into one. When believers consider and focus on these three gifts as factors or elements to becoming one, they will be brought into the heart of God's purpose and pleasure, and in turn they will be full of the joy of the Lord and have purpose and eternal value in their lives.

The following is a general sketch of the rest of this book, covering these three gifts:

1. The Eternal life, the Father's Name

There are two innate functions of life that define life: metabolism and reproduction. In fact, without these two items, life cannot be classified as life. In addition, life needs four elements to survive and thrive: nutrients, air (environment), exercise, and sleep. If these four elements are present, life will spontaneously grow, reproduce, and mature. When believers are born anew and experience the divine eternal life, these four spiritual essentials will cause growth of this wonderful life in the believers. If these four elements are present, the Christian's spiritual life will be healthy and strong; they will be able to go through the challenges of everyday life with joy and in victory.

2. The Truth (His Word)

The truth is the "nutrient" for the spiritual life and the "knowledge" to inspire believers to live and serve God. The goal of this part of the book is not to exhaustively touch on all the points of the truth, but to give a solid framework for understanding and appreciating the major points. Studying and understanding these points of truth will open up the rest of the Scriptures, both the Old and New Testament, for discovering all the riches of the truth. This part will focus on the person and work of Jesus Christ, the New Covenant of grace, God's eternal purpose, and the way of His economy to accomplish this purpose. This knowledge will expand the receiving of and fellowshipping with all believers with confidence and inspire believers with purpose in their life.

3. His Glory

Even though this glory that the Lord gave the believers leads through suffering and humble service, there is true joy and rejoicing through this process as the believer ministers the eternal life to those around them. They will be able to fulfill their calling for the ministry of the Spirit in the midst of their regular daily living with the people that are right around them. Every believer has the privilege and responsibility to build up the body of Christ through their ministry. This part will help believers learn what it means to bring those they love and care for to eternal life, what it means to cherish and nourish them to maturity, and what it means to build up assemblies in homes, from house after house. This is the work of faith, the labor of love, the endurance of hope, and the fruit that will be the believer's joy and crown.

2.
GOD IS STILL MOVING TO FULFILL HIS PURPOSE

In order to appreciate the significance of the Lord's Prayer in John 17, a comparison needs to be made against the backdrop of today's Christianity.

A Short History of the "Church"

After the death and resurrection of Jesus Christ, His subsequent ascension, and out-pouring of the Spirit, something completely outside of and apart from religion was initiated: the unique oneness that the Lord Jesus prayed for was immediately manifested. Believers lived and assembled in the joy and freedom of the Spirit. They were freed from religious laws and regulations, from a dedicated place of worship, and from the hierarchy of religious offices. They gathered in homes from house to house without any rituals or regulations. They were full of the joy of the Spirit, experienced oneness of fellowship with all believers, and peace with all. The supernatural beginning of this assembly at the beginning of Acts was something new within the realm of existing "religion" at that time.

All religions have two things in common: they have a designated place of worship such as a temple, and a mediatory class of "holy men" such as priests or clergymen. When the body of Christ was formed after Jesus' resurrection and ascension, something profound happened: The assembly of His believers began meeting in homes. Thousands of believers in the assembly in Jerusalem gathered together in homes, in house after house. Additionally, every believer actively functioned as a member of the body with a direct connection to the Head (Jesus Christ), without a mediatory class (1 Tim. 2:5). This was the initiation of the body of Christ, and this normal and healthy condition should have continued for all believers of Jesus Christ from generation to generation.

Alas, this blissful condition only lasted a short time. Within about thirty years, early believers became distracted by various teachings that advocated law keeping, ritualistic observances, and Greek philosophies (Col. 2:6–23). Believers, because they were babes in Christ, started to divide among themselves over preferences of various apostles (1 Cor. 1:12). Others positioned themselves as leaders, drawing people to themselves rather than Christ, forming sectarian groups and separating themselves from the general body of believers (Acts 20:30). Most of the Epistles Paul wrote addressed these distractions with the intent of directing believers back to Jesus Christ and His mysterious purpose: building up His one body. Paul's two letters to the Corinthians are good examples of this.

Persecution ensued, beginning in the 1st century AD and continuing through the 3rd century. This only caused the resurrection life of Christ to grow and multiply through "death," a testimony of the victorious life of Jesus Christ in believers. During this time of persecution, believers were not able to organize which actually helped them to greatly multiply through small communities gathering in homes. But the seeds of distraction were already sown — a mixture of Jewish laws and rituals and Greek philosophies — which sidetracked believers from their focus solely on Jesus Christ; therefore, Christian communities, by and large, were susceptible and eventually succumbed to the allure of Emperor Constantine who made Christianity the official state religion during the 4th century. Being accepted and honored by the state seemed like a victory for persecuted Christians in the Roman Empire. However, the church Constantine established was completely foreign to the concept of the original 1st century gathering of believers, and it contradicted the revelation of the New Testament. Buildings dedicated to Christian worship were selected and constructed, a clergy class of Christians was uplifted to rule over the common believers, and various Jewish and heathen liturgies were brought into Christian gatherings. Constantine, who referred to himself as the "chief priest" of all cults in his empire, also tried to act in concordance with church tradition[9] and some say purposely converted to Christianity. The result of his merging of Christianity and cults marred the assembly Jesus established. This resulted in the disappearance of the simplicity of a common brotherhood meeting in homes and from house to house with the sole focus on Jesus Christ as the Head.

By the 4th century, the Christian community had accepted the current collections of writings in the Bible to be inspired by God. The same twenty-seven writings and letters in today's New Testament were canonized by the beginning of the 5th century. In the meantime, the Roman state (Catholic) church grew in prominence, while church and politics became completely intertwined. Because of this, the Roman church became more powerful than kings. Although the Bible had been canonized as being divinely inspired, the actual reading of the Bible became more obscure. One of the biggest reasons for this was because the Roman church discouraged reading (and thus understanding) the Bible. It was restricted to the clergy class of priests and monks. The Roman church's reasoning was that the Scriptures were too hard and complicated for common believers to understand; therefore, believers needed the interpretation and teaching from the clergy. The hidden motive, however, was to keep the common people in the dark concerning divine revelations in the Scriptures; by doing so, the clergy had complete control over the laity. The clergy, alone, could decide the meaning of the Scriptures and what the common people could and could not believe and do.

From the 5th century to the 15th century, for a period of about 1000 years (also known as the Dark or Middle ages), the Roman church was repressive and people were persecuted for the unauthorized owning or reading of the Bible. Without the freedom to read the Bible, the populace was completely subjected to the leadership of the Roman church. The revelation concerning Christ and His purpose was kept in the dark — so much so that even the concept of salvation was completely distorted. The fact that salvation is *by faith* in Jesus Christ alone was lost and was replaced with the buying of indulgences for an uncertain salvation. In essence, if people wanted salvation, they were required to pay the Roman church.

---

9   Odahl, Charles M. *Constantine and the Christian Empire*. London: Routledge, 2004. Print.

A significant invention in the 15th century prompted a change in this situation: a printing machine called the Gutenberg Press, which led to a mass production of books in Europe.[10] The first complete book printed was the Bible. With the development of the printing press, the Bible became more and more accessible outside the control of the Roman church. Common people could have access to the revelation God intended for His people, without the medium of the clergy's interpretation that controlled people's knowledge and understanding. Interestingly, the availability of the Bible for common people coincided with the decline of the Roman church's power and dominance. As more and more people questioned the doctrines and practices of the Roman church, viewing them as contrary to the revelation in the New Testament, individuals (mostly in central Europe) began to rise up and challenge the Roman church in an attempt to reform it. The most famous of these reformers was Martin Luther, who was actually a monk in the Roman church. He is credited as the catalyst of the Reformation movement. The Reformation, which was intended to reform the Roman church, became a widespread advancement of various groups of believers who actually departed and separated from the Roman church in the 16th century.

Martin Luther's famous act in challenging the Roman church was a document called the Ninety-five Theses, which he announced in 1517. Luther's strong belief that acceptance by God was only through faith and not through any other means is what propelled him to create the document, which mainly challenged the pope's authority and the sale of indulgences. Martin Luther is credited with championing and recovering from obscurity the basic tenet that justification before God is only by the faith in Jesus Christ. History testifies that this period of time was the beginning of God's recovery — or bringing back to light — of the truth of the Scriptures that was lost (or covered over) by the Roman church. This new freedom to explore the Scriptures directly, without the shackle of the Roman church, unchained the human mind and intellect. During that period other men rose as leaders of the reformation such as John Calvin. This, in turn, opened the door for the secular world to rebel against the authority and influence of the Roman church. Significantly, by the 17th century, the secular world entered into what is known as the "Age of Enlightenment" where individualism, science, skepticism and toleration became a driving force in transforming society; no longer would it be dominated by institutional religious churches.

Though Martin Luther's intention was to reform the Roman church, the church viewed him a threat to its theocratic rule and, ultimately, made a decision to eliminate him. Luther took refuge and came under the protection of a German prince. For almost a century, Europe had been under the universal rule of the Roman church, and the kings of Northern Europe had longed to be unshackled from Roman authority. Taking advantage of the Reformation, many regional kings aligned themselves politically with the reformers, and ultimately formed state churches independent from Rome. Those that adhered to Luther's teachings, called Lutherans, became the state church of Germany. Many other state churches followed such as the Church of England, the Church of Denmark, and the Dutch Reformed Church. These churches joined themselves politically with the state, and the monarch became the authority (or head) of the church. Though some critical truth was uncovered from the

---

10   McLuhan, Marshall. *The Gutenberg Galaxy: The Making of Typographic Man.* Toronto: U of Toronto, 1962. Print.

Reformation, which was indeed full of spiritual activity and enlightenment, by and large the common people eventually just switched from the regulations of one Roman institution to one under the state. Though the Reformation originated with the Lord's fresh move through various reformers, in a rather short time the resulting churches became institutionalized with a mixture of politics, human organization, and hierarchy.

Since the work of the Spirit to fully bring back and recover the truth in the Bible and God's eternal purpose was not yet fulfilled, men continued to seek the Lord through the study of Scripture and for a fresh move of the Holy Spirit. As these men discovered something new from the Scriptures, or when the Spirit used men to continue His move without the restraints of rituals and regulations, they would speak out and preach their discoveries with the inspiration of the Spirit. However, just as the Roman church rejected the first reformers, state churches also rejected any preaching that might disrupt their set ways and system. These preachers found that established churches did not embrace the idea of the Spirit of the Lord moving forward; most preachers were rejected or persecuted or they left their church voluntarily.

This has been a common recurring pattern in church history. Seeking believers would rediscover a new doctrine or practice, which would help and inspire many Christians. This became their ministry. At the same time, institutional churches would reject the movement. Often, as the movement formed to spread new discoveries to help more believers, the followers formed themselves into a group. After a few decades, the group would become organized and institutionalized, ready to reject anything new the Spirit was revealing if it fell outside their new system of doctrine and practices. This cycle can be identified with Luther, Calvin, Wesley (Methodist), and Parham (Assemblies of God), all the way to the present day, albeit in a much smaller scale, among independent churches. In a way, this is understandable.

God's purpose from the beginning was for the assembly of believers to work as in the beginning of Acts. In Acts, every believer was living in a direct relationship with Him, and each one functioned normally as a member in His body in oneness with all believers. This is not yet realized, (the systemization and rigidity of control by a growing number of institutional churches hampering the move of the Spirit has prevented this), but fortunately men continue to seek the Lord and to search out the Scriptures. This allows the Lord to persist in His work of building up His body through a fresh enlightenment of the Word and the continuing move of His Spirit. Therefore, even the writing of this book is a result of the conviction that something fresh is being discovered and needs to be presented to help energize fellow believers in understanding the Scriptures. May this be for the believers' enjoyment of the grace of the Lord and encouragement to follow the leading of the Spirit as He builds up the body of Christ!

Where We Are Today

There are both positive and negative aspects — and results — of this recovery-degradation cycle. After 500 years, the truth and mystery concerning the person and work of Jesus Christ hidden in the New Testament is readily available. The way of salvation by faith in Jesus Christ alone is well accepted and established. Major doctrines such as Calvinism versus Arminianism have been thoroughly discussed and debated, and just about all the practices in the New Testament have been uncovered and discussed. Now, all these items are available and easily accessible for believers to consider before the Lord. Believers can search the Scriptures on their own, and allow the Word of God, coinciding with the Holy Spirit, to enlighten their understanding and open their spiritual eyes. They can discern for themselves what is healthy to keep and practice and what non-essentials are not worth fighting over. This of course is a far cry from pre-Reformation times, when the truth of the Bible was completely hidden and the Bible itself was not even available to common people.

However, the negative results of this cycle are just as profound. Many denominations and independent Christian groups have separated and divided believers in direct opposition to the building up of the one body of Christ and continue to do so in this day. Since anyone can pick up something new from the Bible or from spiritual experiences, it is rather easy to start a group, which often becomes a "church," whether big or small. There are now tens of thousands of church institutions, each with its own identifier (Baptist or Lutheran, for example). Believers that have identified themselves with one of these groups, and have become loyal to its system of doctrine and practices, may then, with a bias, overlook teachings and practices within their church system that may be unscriptural and even contrary to God's desires. For example, some Catholic believers do not agree with the infallibility of the pope or praying to a saint's image. However, since they are loyal to the Catholic Church, they often overlook or do not object to unscriptural beliefs that may be contrary to God's commandment. As a result, the body of Christ is more splintered than ever, and the one fellowship of the body of Christ, with believers loving one another according to the Lord's new commandment, seems just as foreign as ever.

What can be learned from history that would prevent further division among believers? How can believers receive the benefits of the continuous, but new and fresh move of the Spirit? The author believes there is a general lack of understanding and delineation between various ministries and churches and the assembly.

In short (since this will be developed later in this book), ministries are based on individual believers whom the Lord has raised up to do a certain work. For example, they may teach the Bible, preach the gospel, or offer help for specific sub-groups such as the elderly, youth, or various ethnic groups. There are tens of thousands of such ministries, and there should be many more (1 Cor. 12:4–11). The more gifted ministers will continue to discover new things of the Lord, broadcast their discoveries to help many believers, and draw a following. Leadership and organization is necessary for such ministries and operations. For example, a ministry existing to distribute food to the poor would need some sort of organization, if done on a wide scale.

Though the Spirit continues to move, the assembly that is described in the New Testament with all the believers in the one fellowship of Jesus Christ and meeting in homes, house by house, is almost completely neglected. The true assembly has no hierarchy, nor man's organization. Hierarchy is defined as levels of authorities to direct and control believers. All the various ministries should be for the building up of the assembly, but instead the opposite occurs. Whole churches are formed around various ministries. Not only are major denominational churches formed around powerful ministers such as Luther, Calvin and Wesley but also every church today is centered on the ministry of a particular teacher or preacher.

The assembly, on the other hand, consists of all believers having equal opportunities to speak no matter what their preferred doctrine or Christian practices and no matter from which minister they have received help (1 Cor. 1:9–13). Even with the best intentions, churches built around ministries cannot help but to enable divisions among the believers if the church becomes centered on emphasizing its ministry alone. Since there is often a clear direction for a particular ministry, it is understandable that believers that disturb this direction will not be welcomed. As a result, believers look for churches that suit them the best. The assembly, on the other hand, is one; by definition it receives all believers, no matter their preferences or distinctiveness (Rom. 14).

The Three Gifts Mirrored in Ephesians 4 Needed Today

I, the prisoner in [the] Lord, exhort you therefore to walk worthy of the calling wherewith you have been called, with all lowliness and meekness, with long-suffering, bearing with one another in love; using diligence to keep the unity of the Spirit in the uniting bond of peace. [There is] one body and one Spirit, as ye have been also called in one hope of your calling; ... and he has given some apostles, and some prophets, and some evangelists, and some shepherds and teachers, for the perfecting of the saints; with a view to [the] work of [the] ministry, with a view to the edifying of the body of Christ; until we all arrive at the unity of the faith and of the knowledge of the Son of God, at [the] full-grown man, at [the] measure of the stature of the fulness of the Christ; in order that we may be no longer babes, tossed and carried about by every wind of that teaching [which is] in the sleight of men, in unprincipled cunning with a view to systematized error; but, holding [or speaking] the truth in love, we may grow up to him in all things, who is the head, the Christ: from whom the whole body, fitted together, and connected by every joint of supply, according to [the] working in [its] measure of each one part, works for itself the increase of the body to its self-building up in love.

– Ephesians 4:1-4, 11-16, DBY

John 17 was the Lord's Prayer before He went to be crucified and resurrected. In Ephesians 4:1–16, Paul applies the three gifts that Jesus gave to all believers in a divisive environment similar to situations Christians faced throughout church history up until today. Ephesians 4 is the remedy to bring believers from being carried away into various religious systems and bring them back to the oneness and building up of the body of Christ.

When a person first receives faith and believes into the Lord Jesus Christ, they are immediately born of God and receive the Father's name and the Spirit. Spontaneously and innately, they are one with all other believers in Jesus Christ. Every believer already has the oneness of the Spirit; that is why in Ephesians 4:2–3 believers are charged to "keep the unity of the Spirit" with all lowliness and long-suffering. "Keep" means that it is already there. There is no waiting to receive this, and no one needs to be taught this. The reason that oneness or unity is inborn is because there is only one body, one Spirit, one Lord, one faith, one God and Father. This is the initial oneness that all believers need to remain in — or come back to, if they have been distracted.

Then Ephesians 4:14 speaks of little children being tossed about by winds of doctrines used by men to deceive young believers into a system of error. Many believers become distracted by various winds of doctrines and practices that ultimately blow them into a sectarian system. If they are caught up in a system, their loyalty belongs to that system and those that are adherent to the same system. They no longer identify themselves as just a member in the one body and the one fellowship; rather, they identify themselves as a sub-group. This separates them from other believers that are not in that particular system of doctrines and practices.

The remedy that Paul gave matches the gift of truth in Jesus' prayer in John 17. Believers need to grow and arrive at the oneness of the faith and of the knowledge of the Son of God (Eph. 4:13), which is the truth that needs to be spoken to one another (4:15). This is the mature oneness. While babes are being tossed around, tricked and caught up in various systems, those that are growing in the eternal life and are anchored in truth will arrive into oneness with all believers in the same faith. They are not defined by any systems set up by men, and yet they are one with all those that are in the faith, even babes caught in a system of men. They can receive and fellowship with all believers because to them every believer is an equal member in the one body and belongs in the one fellowship, even those who ignorantly identify themselves by another name (1 Cor. 1:12).

It is wonderful and amazing how the simple faith gives men eternal life: Jesus is God who came as a man to die for man's sins, was resurrected on the third day, and is now Lord of all and indwells every believer. This is it. Even some of the most important doctrines for Christians such as the Trinity or the inerrancy of Scriptures are not essential; nowhere in Scripture does it say that a person needs to believe in the Trinity, or believe every word of the Bible as the Word of God, in order to have eternal life. The oneness of the faith that believers should arrive at is simple. Once arriving at this simplicity of the faith, it is easy to receive all believers with the same faith in the one fellowship.

On the other hand, the knowledge of the Son of God is infinitely vast. It will take eternity to know the Son of God in full. And in the present, the constant focus and seeking of this knowledge is the maturing oneness among believers. For example, this knowledge would include knowing and appreciating the triune God, appreciating and discovering more types of Christ in the Old Testament, or considering the mystery of Christ and His assembly more in depth. It is also through exploring and digging into the Scriptures that believers can know and experience the Son of God which keeps them growing in this oneness of the body. A person who has arrived at the knowledge of the Son of God means that the person's focus is not on peripheral doctrines or Christian practices (though they may be helpful), but rather solely on knowing and experiencing the Son of God. Such knowledge will not divide since it is the destination of all believers — the Son of God.

Finally, a person who has arrived at the truth (the faith and the knowledge of the Son of God) will receive and minister to all other believers. Instead of separating and being complacent in a religious position, they will be inviting, accepting, and caring to all in the body. They will serve and minister Christ in meekness, long-suffering and love, as a servant, "with all lowliness and gentleness, with longsuffering, bearing with one another in love" (Eph. 4:2). This verse in Ephesians describes the glory of the Lord and the pathway He took to glory. In order to keep the oneness of the Spirit, believers need to lay aside their own glory to be lowly, gentle, suffer long, and bear others in love. This is a servant in the Lord, living with servant characteristics. Without such an attitude, it is impossible to stay in oneness with believers. Just a few verses later in Ephesians 4:12 and 16, believers are told that every member is a minister and every member in the body should share to contribute toward the building up of the body of Christ.

Yes, there may be more gifted members such as those called to be apostles, prophets, evangelists, and shepherd/teachers (4:11), but their function is not to usurp and replace the function of each believer. They are to equip them so that every believer can do the work of the ministry (4:12) according to the grace given to each member (4:7). Each believer has the privilege and responsibility to minister Christ for the building up of the body of Christ, so that others will also arrive at the mature oneness of the truth. The participation in this ministry is the glory that the Lord Jesus has given all the believers.

A Renewed Vision to Build the Assembly

The purpose of this book is not to cast a blanket criticism on institutional churches as divisive or spiritually stuck, but to emphasize the need to see and build up the assembly from house to house. There are certainly ministers that believers should be wary of if they teach against the truth or purposely try to form a sect with prideful motives (Rom. 16:17), but the Lord uses and has used many ministers and pastors for His purpose in their work among organized churches. However, ministers and pastors could be even more useful if they encouraged their followers and church members to assemble according to the Scriptures, in the homes, with complete freedom. They would then seek to experience fellowship with *all* believers, even when some of those believers are under the teaching of a ministry that is contrary to their own. This would exemplify that their ministry is properly building up the assembly according to the revelation in the New Testament, rather than simply building a church around their ministry.

Another major reason various ministries become divisive (and to no fault of the ministers) is because of the laziness of believers in seeking the Lord through the Scriptures or due to a church culture of merely being a spectator. That is why Paul didn't blame the *ministers* for causing divisions; he blamed the *believers* for being spiritual babes (1 Cor. 3:1–4). It is so easy and effortless for Christians to just join a church and follow its leadership and practices without seeking the Lord for personal discernment. The end result is a group of believers that have passively gravitated toward a divisive mindset.

To accomplish His purpose, the Lord will continue to attempt to initiate something fresh within all individual believers. In Revelation 2 and 3, John portrays the Spirit continually speaking to believers in many different kinds of churches, in order that individuals would rise up and heed the Spirit's call. God is calling His children to rise up and overcome the current condition of the church, even when it seems good. Without the persistent rising up of individuals that seek the Lord and place themselves under His direct headship, churches will inevitably become corrupt and slip into human hierarchy, institutionalizing a system of doctrines and practices. Let's pray that the many individual believers in the body of Christ that are unsatisfied with the status quo would heed the Spirit's call to overcome further degradation and apathy!

Learning from the Past

Just as in secular learning where each subsequent generation builds upon previous discoveries, mistakes and knowledge, so does biblical understanding and spiritual experiences. For example, today's researchers do not need to start from scratch to discover electricity before inventing the next generation of electronic products. If that were the case, every generation would be stuck in the 17th century. Instead, they can quickly learn from the collection of knowledge before them — including failed experiments — so that new discoveries can continue leading to better electronic products.

It is similar with spiritual knowledge. Today, believers don't need to fight the battle of the doctrine of the Trinity, debate whether Christ is both God and man, argue whether people are justified by faith alone, or figure out what it means to experience the new birth (regeneration). Rather, they can build on previous battles won and learn from mistakes made, in order to progress as a body of believers toward the consummation of what God is after in His eternal purpose.

It is profoundly important that believers learn from past mistakes. This will enable them to present something new, fresh and inspiring that can render spiritual help without creating more harm in the body of Christ. Can the Lord continue His recovery and building work without adding another organizational system that excludes other believers and ministries? Absolutely. In the spirit of the Lord's continuing work of building up His body, major points of truth will be discussed in subsequent chapters — truth that was already uncovered in the past from the Scriptures. These points will be combined with what the author believes to be fresh insight and discovery, and uniquely delivered through the lens of the Lord's final prayer in John 17 — for the genuine and mysterious oneness of His believers.

Ultimately, the author hopes believers will be encouraged to become one. This will happen according to the Lord's Prayer in John 17 and by embracing the three gifts given to each of God's children. Understanding, knowing and enjoying these three gifts, which will be explored in upcoming chapters, would fulfill God's purpose of building up the Lord's one mystical body, with three divinely natural results:

1. Believers would be released to enjoy the divine eternal life that they have received. By focusing on Jesus being the resurrection life in them, they would trust this life, grow,

and be spontaneously shaped according to the nature of this divine life. As a result, they would express the image of the Lord Jesus in oneness with all believers.

2.	Believers would methodically connect spiritual truth recovered from past centuries with fresh discoveries that can be simply understood by Christians, including new believers. The result of this fuller knowledge would be an enjoyment of the "unsearchable riches of Christ" (Eph. 3:8). Believers would possess the ability to walk according to God's eternal will, and be open to receive, fellowship with, and love all kinds of believers.

3.	Each and every believer would be inspired and equipped for their mission to serve God and humanity. This is to minister Christ to humankind for their salvation, growth and maturity in the divine life. Thus, Christ's body will be built up practically in homes (from house to house), while seeking to blend in fellowship with all believers to become one for God's satisfaction and glory.

Part 1

ONE IN THE ETERNAL LIFE, THE FATHER'S NAME

(Chapters 3–6)

> ...that He should give eternal life to as many as You have given Him. And this is eternal life, that they may know You, the only true God, and Jesus Christ whom You have sent.
>
> Now I am no longer in the world, but these are in the world, and I come to You. Holy Father, keep through Your name those whom You have given Me, that they may be one as We [are].
>
> —John 17:2-3, 11

To most Christians, the concept of eternal life means everlasting life; they will live forever. Before they die and before eternity, however, they believe they should do their best to follow the example of Jesus and the laws in the Bible to live properly before God and man. After they die they believe they will go on to heaven and live forever in a wonderful environment of celestial's mansions with God and loved ones for eternity. Most unbelievers think of the Christian faith in this way, too. It is atypical for believers to consider that eternal life actually begins the very moment a person believes in the Lord Jesus Christ.

This is the meaning of being "born again," "born anew," or "born from above." Another word for what happens when a person believes in Jesus is "regeneration." Being born anew means being born with a new life...*another* life. This new, regenerated life is the eternal divine life. At the time of faith, believers literally receive God's divine eternal life into them. This new life may be likened to a newborn baby that needs to grow. A believer's spiritual growth should take place while they are still living in this world, raising families and going to work to make a living. The divine eternal life needs to progress, develop, bear fruit and mature, and this should take place while a believer is still on earth. However, this thinking is foreign to most Christians.

The first gift that the Lord Jesus gave His believers is eternal life, the Father's name. As previously shown, having the Father's name means that believers have His eternal and divine life. Since believers are born of God, God is their Father; thus, they have His name — the Father's name. Since believers have received this gift, they are one with the Father. Just as the Father, Son and the Holy Spirit have one life — the eternal life — those with the faith of Jesus Christ have the exact same life. This is why believers can be one to the same extent as the Father and the Son (Jesus Christ). The more the divine life grows in a believer, the more this "oneness" toward other diverse believers will naturally grow, widen, and deepen. The eternal life is one in all other believers. The ability to be one with other followers of Christ in receiving, accepting, honoring, fellowshipping, and caring for them is the sign of spiritual maturity, the maturity of the eternal divine life in the believers.

Four Essentials for Growth

Each living being, whether animal or human, needs four items to live and thrive. These four essential items include: nutrients (eating and drinking), breath (environment), exercise, and sleep. Life will not continue if even one of these items is missing. Additionally, the very basic definition of life is that it reproduces itself. If something cannot or does not reproduce, then it is either not life or life is deadened. Similarly, the eternal life in man also needs these four essential items in order to grow, bear fruit, and mature. Since the eternal divine life exists in the spiritual realm, nutrients, breath, exercise, and sleep are also spiritual; yet, these things need full cooperation with the believer's physical and psychological being.

When believers are born anew (again) with the new life of Jesus Christ, they become like a spiritual babe that needs to grow. According to 1 Peter 2:2, no matter how long someone has been a believer, they need to respond like a new born babe coming to the Word of God for "milk" to thrive. Just as nourishment (food and drink), breath, exercise and sleep are required for human beings to develop and mature, Christians need those same things *spiritually* in order to develop and mature. When these things are present, life grows spontaneously and innately. There is no need to be anxious about whether one will grow spiritually, because a person's spiritual life will automatically grow and function well under these conditions.

The next four chapters will cover these four items:
1. Nutrient (eating and drinking)
2. Environment for breathing
3. Exercise
4. Sleep (rest)

Fruit of the Spirit

> But the fruit of the Spirit is love, joy, peace, longsuffering, kindness, goodness, faithfulness, gentleness, self-control…
>
> – Galatians 5:22–23

Most Christians, after accepting Jesus Christ, spend a lot of effort trying to behave according to what is portrayed in the Bible. They focus on overcoming their sins and failures, and they do their best to be holy in order to have a "good" testimony. Though these efforts seem admirable, they can all become a distraction from doing the things that will actually help them grow spiritually (Gal. 3:1–5). And if they are not growing, then trying to live the Christian life becomes a very frustrating endeavor. Consider the fruit of the Spirit: that is what the Christian life should be. Fruit is just the product of life and growth, not self-effort and work. If believers will focus on the four essentials for life and growth then the outcome, fruit, includes all the things that make a believer become a duplicate of Jesus Christ (Rom. 8:29). A believer with the fruit of the Spirit, as listed, is certainly one with all believers in the body, and a joy for all people to be around. This is the result of the eternal divine life lived and expressed in people growing in life.

Therefore, it is critical to understand these four essentials for life and stay in them regularly day by day. Anyone who does this will spontaneously grow over time in the speed of life, however long it takes for life to grow.

3.

EATING THE WORD; DRINKING THE SPIRIT

This chapter on *life* will focus on the believer's need for spiritual nourishment from eating and drinking. Spiritual breath, exercise and sleep will be considered in later chapters.

The Real Food and Drink!

Who or what is the spiritual nutrient for eternal life in the believers? It is Jesus Christ. Jesus said in John 6:54, "Whoever eats My flesh and drinks My blood has eternal life…" It is amazing that Jesus Christ came to be food and drink, asking men to eat and drink Him. Eating and drinking are not only essential for life but they are also two of the most enjoyable activities for man. Additionally, what human beings eat and drink actually becomes their body's composition. Food and drink provide the energy to live, but they also become part of the person's physical constitution. There is truly oneness between the physical body and any food or drink consumed.

The *real* food and drink, however, is Jesus Christ. He came to have such an amazing relationship with man! Eating and drinking Him is the beginning of the new life. It is also how believers continue their Christian journey, and it is what they will continue to enjoy for eternity.

"Eating" Jesus Christ occurs when a person hears and understands the Scriptures concerning Him. When a believer is inspired by the knowledge of Jesus — when that knowledge makes sense to him or her, and they appreciate it — they have received spiritual nourishment. The believer then responds with faith in His Word and believes. Based on the Word of God that is heard, the follower of Jesus speaks back to Jesus with thanksgiving, praise or a request, applying it to life situations. Upon believing, the Spirit transmits into the person and operates within them, giving them joy, peace and love, and making the words spoken and promised 2000 years ago real and tangible. This continual interaction of believing Jesus while "hearing" the Word is the drinking of the Spirit.

This is the simplicity of eating and drinking Jesus.

Generation, Continuation, and Destination

Jesus Christ came that man may eat and drink Him, to generate life in man:

> This is the bread which comes down from heaven, that one may eat of it and not die. I am the living bread which came down from heaven. If anyone eats of this bread, he will live forever; and the bread that I shall give is My flesh, which I shall give for the life of the world. The Jews therefore quarreled among themselves, saying, 'How can this Man give us His flesh to eat?' Then Jesus said to them,

> 'Most assuredly, I say to you, unless you eat the flesh of the Son of Man and drink His blood, you have no life in you. Whoever eats My flesh and drinks My blood has eternal life, and I will raise him up at the last day. For My flesh is food indeed, and My blood is drink indeed. He who eats My flesh and drinks My blood abides in Me, and I in him. As the living Father sent Me, and I live because of the Father, so he who feeds on Me will live because of Me.
>
> – John 6:50–57

These verses are both repugnant and wonderful; they clearly declare believers are to eat and drink Jesus Christ in order to have life and live. This is the purpose for which Jesus came down from heaven. He entered the material world as "bread" for man to consume in order to have life. In God's eyes only the *eternal life* is life. John 6:53 states that unless a person eats and drinks Jesus, no life is in them. However, the very first time a person eats and drinks Him, they receive the eternal divine life, which is the new birth.

To continue to live after the new birth, Christians need to eat regularly. Just like people need to eat physically, believers need to spiritually eat, in order to live and grow. These verses in John 6:50–57 show that the generation of a believer's life in Christ begins with the eating and drinking of Jesus Christ, followed by a continual "eating" throughout life. He is the true food and drink. By eating and drinking Him, a believer's relationship with Jesus Christ is as intimate and as one as the relationship between Jesus and the Father. Jesus is the unique nourishment for believers.

God is not looking for worshipers in the way of bowing before Him to sing His praise. He is looking for people to eat and drink Him, to consume Him. How absurd would it be if people bowed before a plate of food, worshipping it, while they were starving? God does not want to be outside of man for man to worship. He wants to be food and drink for man to enjoy, ingesting Him so that the two may become one.

Consider this example further. What if a person was really weak due to hunger, but he needed to get out of bed to help his daughter move. A plate of food is available for him to eat every day, but instead of eating the food, he prays: "Oh food, please help my daughter to move, you know I can't do it. I am so weak, please strengthen me. Oh food, I beg you to send someone to help her move." This sounds so bizarre, but this is exactly what most religions think when praying to God for help. Now, what if this dad simply gives thanks, eat and enjoy the food in front of him? The food would become energy in him to strengthen him, so he could get up and help his daughter move.

Was it the man who helped his daughter to move, or was it the food that he ate, the food in him? The fact is, it was *both:* The food in him, together with his physical self, helped his daughter move. The food could not get up from the plate to help the daughter move, nor could the father get up from bed to help his daughter move. But together by eating the food and getting up, the job was done. God does not want to be outside of man to do things externally for man; rather, He wants to be *in* man to live and work together with man. He wants a relationship with man such that it will be hard to know whether it is God working or man working, that it would not be possible to know whether it is human or divine love, patience, or joy, because God and man became one through eating and drinking.

This is the meaning of John 6:57, where Jesus said, "I live because of the Father. He who eats Me shall live because of Me." The only way a believer can live Jesus similar to the way Jesus lived the Father is through eating Jesus. This is the wonder and mystery of God in Jesus Christ, being food to man. It is utterly different from religious concepts concerning worshipping and praying for help from an external God.

How can believers love others as Jesus loves? Eat Jesus. How can believers forgive others the way Jesus forgives? Eat Jesus. How can believers be one with all other believers? Eat Jesus. How can believers live like Jesus? The only way is…to eat Jesus.

Christ Knocking at the Door: Continue to Dine with Him

The apostle John wrote in his revelation that Christ is knocking at the door, desiring believers to continue to dine with Him:

> Because you say, 'I am rich, have become wealthy, and have need of nothing' — and do not know that you are wretched, miserable, poor, blind, and naked — Behold, I stand at the door and knock. If anyone hears My voice and opens the door, I will come in to him and dine with him, and he with Me.
>
> – Revelation 3:17, 20

The assembly in ancient Laodicea was made up of believers, but as a whole, the assembly began to decay, becoming degraded, wretched, miserable, poor and blind. The worst part is that they thought they were rich and wealthy. While these believers imagined everything was fine, the Lord Jesus was actually knocking outside their door. These believers had gained a wealth of Bible knowledge and spiritual experiences in the past, but were blinded by those experiences, so much so that they were not aware of their true condition. They replaced the living Christ who can be experienced *now* with old knowledge and good memories. They thought they knew everything, but Christ was not in their midst; He was outside knocking.

The people in this type of assembly believe their experiences and knowledge make them rich, but they miss the Christ who should be rich to them in the present; sadly, Jesus says these people are actually poor and miserable. They stopped enjoying the Christ who is always new and available. They live life in a religious shell, going through the motions, while the Lord is outside their door knocking, shut out. He desires to be brought back inside the assembly. Although the knocking is on the door of the assembly, it is the responsibility of each believer to open the door and let the Lord in for eating and drinking with Him.

These believers are missing something profound: dining with the Lord. They are not enjoying Him. They hold on to the past, but miss His present nourishment. Believers in this kind of degraded situation miss the reality of the Lord. However, Jesus is not seeking to condemn and judge His children. He wants to dine with them and to feast with them, because this is the way to be recovered from spiritual degradation. He deeply desires Christians to eat Him and drink Him.

To continue as a believer, no matter how much a person may already know about the Bible or how much they have experienced Christ, they can never "graduate" from eating and drinking. This is the only way to progress as a believer or as an assembly: through the daily nourishment of Christ Himself. Once a believer stops receiving daily nourishment, degradation (or deterioration) kicks in and will only worsen over time. Sadly, believers are often not even aware or able to process that this is happening. It is critical that believers hear the Lord knocking and open the door to Him when they depart from being nourished.

The Reward Is to Eat and Drink More of Christ

Eating and drinking Christ is a reward for those who overcome, and the believers' portion for eternity:

> He that has an ear, let him hear what the Spirit says to the assemblies. To him that overcomes, I will give to him to eat of the tree of life which is in the paradise of God…He that has an ear, let him hear what the Spirit says to the assemblies. To him that overcomes, to him will I give of the hidden manna…
>
> – Revelation 2:7, 17, DBY

Most of the seven churches described in Revelation 2 and 3 were not in a good spiritual condition. They had become religious, which brought deadness, worldliness, hierarchy, heresies and many other negative things into the assemblies. To be religious means to stray from focusing on the Lord Himself, and instead establish rules for what is "right and wrong," or what is okay or not okay to do — making formalities and regulations the center of the assembly.

Degradation started with the very first assembly: Ephesus. Jesus said the Ephesians had "left [their] first love" (Rev. 2:4). They had not kept Him preeminent, and they had stopped feeding on Him as the unique source of spiritual nourishment. Remember Laodicea? The Lord was outside knocking, and His desire was to come back inside to feast with the believers. To each assembly in Revelation 2 and 3, even to Philadelphia (the only one Jesus spoke of positively), the Lord called for overcomers. Believers are to triumph over all religious distractions and come back to Jesus alone — to enjoy Him as their food and drink. The reward for those who overcome is more enjoyment of Jesus. Therefore, believers eat to overcome and overcome to eat. Eating Jesus is the beginning, the way, and the destination.

The Tree of Life first makes its appearance at creation. In Genesis 2:9 and 16, God told the first humans "you may freely eat" of the Tree of Life positioned in the center of the garden. Solomon also mentioned this life-giving tree in the book of Proverbs saying, "The fruit of the righteous is a tree of life" (Prov. 11:30).

The real Tree of Life is Jesus. Revelation 2:7 and 17 reveal the reward for overcoming degradation is the blessing of eating from the Tree of Life, and the hidden manna. When the believer's life begins to deteriorate, the way to recovery is to eat and drink Jesus. When Jesus declared He is the vine tree in John 15, He also declared He is the life (John 11:25); therefore, *He is the Tree of Life.*

In John 6:22–40, Jesus referred to Himself as the manna from heaven, the living bread. Today, Jesus as the "bread of life" (John 6:35) is "hidden" in heaven, but believers can be sustained and nourished by this invisible Bread if they overcome to eat Him every day.

Eating and Drinking Christ Is the Eternal Destiny

> Then the angel showed me the river of the water of life, bright as crystal, flowing from the throne of God and of the Lamb through the middle of the street of the city; also, on either side of the river, the tree of life with its twelve kinds of fruit, yielding its fruit each month. The leaves of the tree were for the healing of the nations.
>
> – Revelation 22:1–2, ESV

These verses describe a couple of the major features of the New Jerusalem in eternity. This city is actually a sign showing the composition of all of God's people throughout time and space in perfect union with God. God and His people are one for eternity. At the center of the city, which is likened to the peak of a mountain, is the throne of the God-man, Jesus, from which flows the river of the water of life; this is the Spirit flowing throughout the city. In the middle of the river, easily accessible from the street, is the Tree of Life producing new fruit every month. This imagery reveals that for eternity God's people will continue to eat Him and drink Him. He will be fresh and new forevermore. Believers will never grow tired or bored of participating in Him, being nourished by Him, and enjoying Him as their source. This is the believer's destiny.

Eat and Drink to Remember Jesus

The most important symbol for believers that the Lord Himself established is to eat and drink to remember Him.

> And when He had given thanks, He broke *it* and said, 'Take, eat; this is My body which is broken for you; do this in remembrance of Me.' In the same manner *He* also *took* the cup after supper, saying, 'This cup is the new covenant in My blood. This do, as often as you drink *it*, in remembrance of Me.'
>
> – 1 Corinthians 11:24–25

What is commonly known as communion (or the Lord's table), initiated by Jesus the night that He went to be crucified, is a continual reminder that Jesus is the real food and drink. This was practiced every day among the early believers. Perhaps this was because every time they ate physical food they were reminded that *Jesus is the real food.* Eating and drinking is truly the most amazing example of the intimate relationship and oneness with the Lord Jesus.

Physically, what people eat and drink actually becomes part of their being. The Lord Jesus was outside His believers, but through "eating" and "drinking" Him, He became inextricably a part of them. Eating and drinking Jesus is the way to remember Him. Just as the source of a person's physical energy comes from eating and drinking, in the new covenant, the believer's source of vigor comes from enjoying Jesus by partaking of Him. Jesus' part is to do everything necessary to supply, energize, and fulfill His eternal purpose in those that ingest Him.

The Word Is Tangible Food to Assimilate Christ

The Word of God is the Bread — the nourishment believers need to live:

> But He answered and said, "It is written, 'Man shall not live by bread alone, but by every word that proceeds from the mouth of God.'"
>
> – Matthew 4:4
>
> Your words were found, and I ate them, And Your word was to me the joy and rejoicing of my heart; For I am called by Your name, O LORD God of hosts.
>
> – Jeremiah 15:16

The Word of God conveyed in the Bible is tangible for His people to receive food. His Word is the provision that sustains and nourishes the believer's inner man. When children of God eat the Word, the result is joy and rejoicing, and a satisfaction available to them continually regardless of their environment.

The Lord's Word Is Spirit and Life

> It is the Spirit who gives life; the flesh profits nothing. The words that I speak to you are spirit, and they are life.
>
> – John 6:63

Earlier in John 6, Jesus spoke of eating His flesh and drinking His blood in order to have life. Many who heard this speech were offended. It sounded like cannibalism! The Lord explained He was not speaking of His physical body, since "the flesh profits nothing" (John 6:63). He was speaking of the Spirit. Eating His flesh and drinking His blood means partaking of and ingesting His Spirit. His Spirit is living and real, yet mysterious, intangible, and difficult for people to apprehend. Therefore, Jesus made eating of Him much more practical by referring to His words as Spirit and life. His words are substantial and understandable. When a person receives His words by faith, they are filled with the Spirit, who is life. Therefore, it is paramount that believers ingest His Spirit through His words, in order to have life.

> And receive the helmet of salvation and the sword of the Spirit, which *[Spirit]* is the word of God.
>
> – Ephesians 6:17

Paul shows clearly in Ephesians 6:17 that the Word of God is His Spirit. The Spirit and His Word are like "two sides of the same coin." To possess the Spirit the believer needs His Word; but to take in His Word, the believer needs to utilize their spirit to contact the Spirit in His Word. Ephesians 6:18 continues on to say that the way to take in the Spirit in the Word is by praying in the Spirit; therefore, whenever believers come to the Word, they need to utilize their praying spirit.

The Spirit of God Is the Living Water for Drinking Christ

> In the last, the great day of the feast, Jesus stood and cried saying: If any one thirst, let him come to me and drink. He that believes into me, as the scripture has said, out of his belly [innermost being] shall flow rivers of living water. But this he said concerning the Spirit, which they that believed into him were about to receive; for the Spirit was not yet, because Jesus had not yet been glorified.
>
> – John 7:37–39, DBY

For some Jewish feasts, God required people to physically eat and drink for seven days as a religious service. Knowing that man (male and female) was still thirsty in their inner being after practicing their religion (they were filled up physically), Jesus called people on the last day of the feast to *come to Him* (John 7:37) spiritually to drink. The unique way of drinking Jesus was to believe into Him. Upon belief in Christ, spiritual thirst is quenched and satisfied, and Jesus becomes the source of the water of life in the believer's innermost being. A "river" flows out from their spirit and soul. Not only are they filled, but they can also quench others' thirst. This drinkable and out-flowing water is the coming Spirit. God's Spirit is eternal, but the drinkable Spirit "was not yet" (7:39) and could not enter into men and women until after Jesus Christ died for their redemption and was resurrected in victory; only then did He become the life-giving Spirit (1 Cor. 15:45).

> For in one Spirit we were all baptized into one body — Jews or Greeks, slaves or free — and all were made to drink of one Spirit.
>
> – 1 Corinthians 12:13, ESV

Drinking of the Spirit by believing into Jesus Christ immerses the believer into the one body of Christ. Before drinking of the Spirit, people can be from various nationalities and social statuses that can have conflict with each other. Paul stated, for example, that there was enmity between Jews and Gentiles (Eph. 2:14–15) and that slaves and the free were a world apart (Col. 3:10–11). But when people drink of the one Spirit, they are baptized into one body where all the differences between people are eliminated. Therefore, it is important to keep drinking the Spirit for a person's inner being to be satisfied, but also to become one with all His believers. This powerful verse supports the Lord's Prayer in John 17 and connects how drinking Jesus is an essential item for life, making diverse believers one.

Drinking the Spirit by Believing

> This only I want to learn from you: Did you receive the Spirit by the works of the law, or by the hearing of faith? Are you so foolish? Having begun in the Spirit, are you now being made perfect by the flesh? Therefore He who supplies the Spirit to you and works miracles among you, does He do it by the works of the law, or by the hearing of faith?
>
> – Galatians 3:2–3, 5

The Galatian believers were being deceived. Some Christian teachers were telling them they needed to go back to law keeping in order to please God, to try and perfect themselves by the flesh – the fallen man – who is without Christ. Because of this, the apostle Paul reminded them of what they already had: they had previously received salvation, beginning with faith. They should continue their spiritual journey in the same way – through faith. The supplying of the Spirit is by faith as well. Believers recognize that their life in Christ began with simply believing into Jesus Christ; unfortunately many also foolishly labor to keep God's laws by the efforts of their flesh *after* being a Christian. Paul encourages Christians to turn back to their simple faith, no matter how far along they have progressed as believers.

> That the blessing of Abraham might come upon the Gentiles in Christ Jesus, that we might receive the promise of the Spirit through faith.
> – Galatians 3:14

The blessing of Abraham in the Old Testament was the good land, but in the New Testament, the reality of the promise of Abraham is the Spirit of God. God wants people to receive the Spirit, through believing into the Lord Jesus Christ. This is faith. It is only through faith that anyone can receive the Spirit as the "good land" of God into their inner being.

> In Him you also trusted, after you heard the word of truth, the gospel of your salvation; in whom also, having believed, you were sealed with the Holy Spirit of promise.
> – Ephesians 1:13

In Ephesians 1:13, Paul reveals that it is from believing in the good news of Jesus Christ that the Holy Spirit is received. The Holy Spirit even becomes a seal in the believers. A seal is a permanent mark placed on an object to verify ownership and authenticity; this permanent mark is the Holy Spirit. Upon belief, the Spirit was permanently sealed into the believer's inner being.

Blending the Spoken Word with Faith

> For indeed the gospel was preached to us as well as to them; but the word which they heard did not profit them, not being mixed with faith in those who heard it.
> – Hebrews 4:2

In the Old Testament, the Israelites heard the good news concerning God bestowing upon them the good land, but when they saw obstacles in the way, they didn't believe God's Word. Because of their unbelief, they didn't enter the good land, but wandered in the wilderness for forty years. Today, the good news of the real good land – Jesus Christ and the Spirit – is announced to all those wanting to hear. If this good news is going to profit the hearer, faith must be actively mixed, blended, or united with the gospel heard. There are things to learn concerning who Jesus Christ is and what He has accomplished for man, but they are only profitable and made real through believing this full and wonderful gospel.

> Jesus said to him, 'If you can believe, all things are possible to him who believes.' Immediately the father of the child cried out and said with tears, 'Lord, I believe; help my unbelief!'
>
> – Mark 9:23–24

Since faith is essential in receiving all that God has done for man and wants to provide for man, every man (male and female) needs to *ask* for faith. The question is whether or not a person believes enough to ask for help. What a simple and honest prayer from this man in Mark 9:23! A believer should pray the same upon hearing difficult things concerning whom the Lord is and what He has accomplished: "Lord, I believe; help my unbelief!" This is the way to receive more faith…*simply ask.*

Tasting through Understanding

The way to eat the Word and drink the Spirit is through the understanding and tasting of Christ.

> As newborn babes desire earnestly the pure mental milk of the word, that by it ye may grow up to salvation, if indeed ye have tasted that the Lord is good.
>
> – 1 Peter 2:2–3, DBY

The Greek word for "word" here is *logikos,* which is where the English word for "logic" or "logical" is derived from. Therefore, the "milk of the word" is nourishment from something of reason, or logic. God's Word is full of logic, and for His children's understanding. Read the Scriptures concerning Jesus Christ, who He is, what He has done, His purpose, and His relationship to man; consider it, and follow its logic. When the Scriptures unveiling Jesus Christ makes sense to someone and they understand, it becomes milk for the mind, soul, and the inner being. The milk of the Word causes growth specifically relating to the knowledge of Jesus Christ the Lord. Peter writes in 1 Peter 2:3 that the ingesting of this nourishing milk is what it means to "taste the Lord." The way to receive nourishment from the milk is to focus on Jesus Christ when reading to understand the Scriptures. The Lord is sweet, and He is so good when He is tasted. People simply do not know how good the Lord is until they taste Him. When they do, they will desire more of this milk of the Word.

This can only happen through the proper studying, consideration and retention of the knowledge of God and Jesus the Lord.

> Grace and peace be multiplied to you in [the] knowledge of God and of Jesus our Lord.
>
> – 2 Peter 1:2, DBY

The knowledge of God and of Jesus Christ as Lord will cause grace and peace to multiply. Many believers who study the Bible focus on countless other topics such as end times, miraculous gifts, or abortions. They strive to answer the "how to's" — how to pray, how to tithe, how to live or how to become holy, to name a few. The number of other topics one can pick from the Bible is endless, but the knowledge that can multiply grace and peace is only of God and Jesus Christ. The entire Bible unveils who God is, His Son Jesus Christ, and His eternal plan. Read, study, and understand the Bible by focusing on the proper knowledge to gain what is profitable!

> That the God of our Lord Jesus Christ, the Father of glory, would give you [the] spirit of wisdom and revelation in the full knowledge of him.
>
> – Ephesians 1:17, DBY

> Until we all arrive at the unity [or oneness] of the faith and of the knowledge of the Son of God, at the full-grown man, at the measure of the stature of the fullness of the Christ.
>
> – Ephesians 4:13, DBY

In order to have the knowledge of Jesus Christ, it is necessary to be of a sober mind; only then will Christians be able to consider and understand His words. They also need a spirit of wisdom and revelation, which is received through prayer. Believers who possess an excellent knowledge of the Son of God will grow and mature so that they can love and receive all believers in oneness without disputes and judgment. Possessing mere scriptural knowledge which does not focus on Jesus Christ's person and work, and pursuing it, can lead to friction and disputes among believers. Therefore, it is critical to pay full attention to the knowledge of Jesus Christ and let *that* be what saturates the Christian's mind.

Take the Spirit–Word through Prayer, Praise and Thanksgiving

> And take the helmet of salvation, and the sword of the Spirit, which [Spirit] is the word of God. With all prayer and petition pray at all times in the Spirit, and with this in view, be on the alert with all perseverance and petition for all the saints.
>
> – Ephesians 6:17–18, NASB

Paul tells his readers in Ephesians 6:17–18 that the Spirit is the Word of God, and the way to receive this Word is with all kinds of prayers. On one hand, when reading the Bible, Christians need to use logic to understand what they are reading; simultaneously, they also need to use their praying spirit in order to enter into fellowship with God's Spirit, which is His Word. It is important to turn what is read and understood into prayer — a conversation with the Lord.

Conversing with the Lord concerning the wonders in His Word will lead to petition. "Petition" means asking specifically for something in relation to anyone the Lord brings up in the believer's heart while praying. The things that are read and prayed can then be applied to those people.

> In God will I praise [his] word; in Jehovah will I praise his word. In God have I put my confidence: I will not fear; what can man do unto me? Thy vows are upon me, O God: I will render thanks unto thee.
>
> – Psalm 56:10–12, DBY

Here the psalmist makes the need to praise the Word (or turn God's Word to praise) evident. And for God's vows (His promises), which are now fulfilled in the New Testament, Christians need to offer thanks. Believers should thank Him for His Word and His vows; they are real because they are all fulfilled in Christ (2 Cor. 1:20).

Use and Apply the Word to Teach and Admonish One Another

For the Word to dwell in the believers richly, they must use and apply the Word to teach and admonish one another.

> Let the word of Christ dwell in you richly in all wisdom, teaching and admonishing one another in psalms and hymns and spiritual songs, singing with grace in your hearts to the Lord.
>
> – Colossians 3:16

Teaching, admonishing and singing are all words that modify the verb "dwell." This indicates that the way for the Lord's Word to "dwell in you richly" (Col. 3:16a) is by teaching, admonishing and singing. The more someone teaches the Word of Christ to others, the richer His Word will dwell in them. Before the New Testament was penned and canonized, much of the Word of Christ and the apostles' teachings were formulated into various lengths of songs from long ones to short ones. As believers "sing" these songs, they also teach and admonish. By singing and teaching the content of these songs, the Word of Christ dwells in believers richly, in all wisdom.

> And how from childhood you have been acquainted with the sacred writings, which are able to make you wise for salvation through faith in Christ Jesus. All Scripture is breathed out by God and profitable for teaching, for reproof, for correction, and for training in righteousness, that the man of God may be complete, equipped for every good work.
>
> – 2 Timothy 3:15–17, ESV

It is crucial for believers to know Scripture specifically in the knowledge of Jesus Christ, the Son of God. Not only does it contain the way to salvation, but it is also "breathed out" by God (2 Tim. 3:16). Therefore, when Christians pray the Word that they read, they are actually breathing in the breath of God, the Spirit. Believers who come to know the Scripture in such a living way in both knowledge and Spirit can, in turn, use this Word to minister to people around them. Being filled with Scripture, both in understanding and in breath, equips people to be men and women of God in order to minister Christ in every work that they do. Without such knowledge and Spirit of the Scripture, they will not be adequately equipped to serve the Lord according to His purpose.

Practice: Prayer and Praise with the Word

Now it is time to practice! There is no "right" way to do this; any way is fine! Begin by reading a verse or two. Then, turn those verses into prayer, praise and thanksgiving. Speak to the Lord using these verses as the basis. Personalize the verses by changing the pronouns from "*the* Lord" or "*your* people," to "*my* Lord" or "to *me.*" Apply the verses to others the Lord brings to mind while praying, praising God for or giving thanks for them.

Here is an example using one of the verses above for prayer, praise, and thanksgiving:

> Grace and peace be multiplied to you in [the] knowledge of God and of Jesus our Lord.
>
> – 2 Peter 1:2, DBY

"Lord Jesus, thank you for grace and peace. Lord, multiply grace and peace to me. Praise You for making grace and peace so available. I love you Lord. I pray for more knowledge of You. Grant me more knowledge of God and Yourself that grace and peace will multiply more to me. Lord Jesus, I also pray for _____ (insert a name). I pray that he/she will know you and receive grace and peace. Thank you for unveiling yourself to him. I praise and pray in your name, Amen."

Now try a verse and practice yourself.

4.

BREATHING – LIVING IN CHRIST, THE GOOD LAND

Breathing is another requirement for life. However, in order to breathe, there must be an environment of air. Breathing is a nonstop function that continues throughout a person's walk each day; wherever anyone goes, whatever they do — they need to breathe!

This chapter will explore the environment believers live in, and the function of "spiritual breathing" as they go about daily life. For the believer, the environment they live in is Christ; it is full of "living air" for them to breathe as they walk through each day.

Every believer should ask themselves two questions relevant to this topic of spiritual breathing: How "big" is Christ in their life, and where can they "breathe" Him? God has given a blessing to every believer: the vast and unsearchably rich Christ, or the "good land." Believers who lift up their eyes to see Christ as the good land will enjoy Him wherever they journey day to day. Continuously, Christ is the Spirit that dwells in believers and surrounds them in such a way that it is impossible to be separate from Him. The Spirit supplies believers abundantly as they continue in fellowship through the practice of unceasing prayer.

An Overview of This Chapter

The believers' experience of Christ should progress from the Passover Lamb to daily manna, finally arriving at God's chosen destination: the good land. This land is so rich and vast that whatever the believer sees and wherever he or she walks, 24/7, is Christ Himself. The key for believers to possess and enjoy such a rich and vast land is to lift their eyes to see Christ as the reality in everything.

The promised blessing to Abraham was the good land, a physical piece of land. The reality of the good land for the believers of Jesus, however, is the Spirit. After the crucifixion, Jesus Christ, in resurrection, took the form of the Spirit. Therefore, through faith, the believer's spirit and the Lord as *the* Spirit are one — impossible to separate. Because of this, followers of Jesus are not only surrounded by the *real* good land, but the good land is in them.

The Spirit that believers have received in their spirit is the praying Spirit. Just like a person's lungs breath continually, the believer's spirit *prays* unceasingly. Having constant fellowship with the Lord in prayer is innate and normal for every believer. Seeing Christ in everything reminds Christians to pray, to give thanks and to make requests on others' behalf.

Believers should practice praying unceasingly by turning everything around — every activity, every situation — to prayers of fellowship. Seeing Jesus Christ as the reality of everything positive actually reminds believers to pray and to give thanks. They can do this at work, at home, at play, in everything — as they walk through daily life.

Typology – the Shadow of Things Depicting Jesus Christ

The "good land" in the Old Testament is a type of Christ for believers to live and walk in. He's the good and spacious land.

> So let no one judge you in food or in drink, or regarding a festival or a new moon or sabbaths, which are a shadow of things to come, but the substance is of Christ.
>
> – Colossians 2:16–17

The writers of the Old Testament describe key figures that parted seas, healed illnesses, and heard the voice of God. They foretold things to come and painted a picture of the seemingly odd system of sacrifices and offerings. Many of these things, such as the Israelites' diet, certain festivals and Sabbaths, were commandments of God; people were judged by whether they practiced such instruction or not. Paul alluded to these things in Colossians 2:16–17, calling them "shadows" (or "types") of Christ.

Typology is a kind of symbolism seen throughout the Old Testament — something that represents something else. When a person in the Old Testament is identified as a "type of Christ," it means that person behaved in a way that corresponds to Jesus' character or actions in the New Testament. An object or even an event in the Old Testament can also represent some quality or characteristic of Jesus.

In these verses above, a number of rituals and Old Testament practices are mentioned: eating, drinking, festivals, new moon celebrations, and Sabbaths. These items were given meticulous detail in the Old Testament. They instructed Israel in how to live: what rules the nation was to abide by concerning what to eat and drink (and what not to), how to conduct their annual festivals, and what each Israelite could and could not do during the Sabbath day. There were condemnations and judgments attached to breaking laws relating to these items. In Colossians 2:16–17, Paul told the believers they were no longer judged by rules governing these practices, because these rituals were merely a shadow of things to come. The substance or the reality that cast that shadow is Jesus Christ. Believers are freed from performing these religious rituals since all these Old Testament practices are just shadows. These religious rituals, people or objects were never the reality; they were the *type*.

The reality of eating and drinking is Jesus Christ, the true substance of food and drink. He is "clean" food for all to eat and drink. He satisfies man's inner hunger and thirst. The reality of each festival of enjoyment and feasting is Jesus Christ. He brings God's people together for enjoyment in the building up of the body and to render worship to God. Jesus is the reality of the beginning of a new moon. In Christ everything is new; old things have passed away. Failures of the past should be forgotten. Every time a believer turns to Jesus Christ, they receive a new start.

Finally, He is the true Sabbath rest. Jesus finished all His work and He is resting. Believers now come to Him to rest, and should abide in Him and rest in Him for eternity. Resting means believers are filled, satisfied, and peacefully joyful in Him.

The Passover Lamb in Egypt—the Feast of Redemption

Just before the Israelites escaped Egypt and crossed the Red Sea, God gave specific instructions for what they were to do:

> Speak to all the congregation of Israel, saying: 'On the tenth of this month every man shall take for himself a lamb, according to the house of his father, a lamb for a household.
>
> Now you shall keep it until the fourteenth day of the same month. Then the whole assembly of the congregation of Israel shall kill it at twilight. And they shall take some of the blood and put it on the two doorposts and on the lintel of the houses where they eat it.
>
> And thus you shall eat it: with a belt on your waist, your sandals on your feet, and your staff in your hand. So you shall eat it in haste. It is the LORD's Passover. For I will pass through the land of Egypt on that night, and will strike all the firstborn in the land of Egypt, both man and beast; and against all the gods of Egypt I will execute judgment: I *am* the LORD. Now the blood shall be a sign for you on the houses where you are. And when I see the blood, I will pass over you; and the plague shall not be on you to destroy you when I strike the land of Egypt.'
>
> – Exodus 12:3, 6–7, 11–13

Passover was the last of the ten plagues that afflicted Egypt before Moses was to lead the children of Israel out from under Egyptian slavery. God was about to judge Egypt by allowing the firstborn son of each family to die. For the Israelites' firstborn son to be saved from death, each family was to kill a lamb, put the blood on the outside doorposts of the house, and eat the lamb inside. God passed over the houses where He saw the lamb's blood, delivering those inside the house from the judgment of the death plague. While inside the house, God's people enjoyed eating the lamb, which would provide them with the energy needed to leave Egypt later that night. From that point on, Passover became an annual feast that God's people were to enjoy as a memorial.

> The next day John saw Jesus coming toward him, and said, 'Behold! The Lamb of God who takes away the sin of the world!'
>
> – John 1:29
>
> Therefore purge out the old leaven, that you may be a new lump, since you truly are unleavened. For indeed Christ, our Passover, was sacrificed for us. Therefore let us keep the feast, not with old leaven, nor with the leaven of malice and wickedness, but with the unleavened bread of sincerity and truth.
>
> – 1 Corinthians 5:7

The first introduction of Jesus Christ to the world came from John the Baptist, who said, "Behold, the Lamb of God!" (John 1:29) Jesus is the true Lamb that was to shed His blood so that the world would be free from sin and God's judgment. Jesus, the reality of the shadow of thousands of years of Passover lamb sacrifices, perfectly fulfilled this "type" at His crucifixion. Paul makes it clear in 1 Corinthians 5 that Jesus is the real Passover Lamb sacrificed for the world. Because of faith in Jesus Christ, believers are freed from God's judgment of death.

Once freed from spiritual death, it is important to keep feasting on Him as the Passover Lamb who provides life and the means to escape corruption and sin. Jesus is both the Lamb and the Bread that believers should continue to eat for the rest of their journey on earth.

Manna—the Living Heavenly Bread for Daily Eating

God provided the Israelites with bread (or "manna") while they were in the wilderness for sustenance; manna is another beautiful picture, or type of Christ.

> And when the layer of dew lifted, there, on the surface of the wilderness, was a small round substance, as fine as frost on the ground. So when the children of Israel saw it, they said to one another, "What is it?" For they did not know what it was. And Moses said to them, "This is the bread which the LORD has given you to eat.
>
> – Exodus 16:14–15

> And the house of Israel called its name Manna. . . . that they may see the bread with which I fed you in the wilderness, when I brought you out of the land of Egypt.'"
>
> – Exodus 16:31–32

> And the children of Israel ate manna forty years, until they came to an inhabited land; they ate manna until they came to the border of the land of Canaan.
>
> – Exodus 16:35

After the Israelites left Egypt, they wandered in the wilderness for forty years because of unbelief that God could actually bring them into the good land. During their wandering, their food was bread from heaven called manna, which means, "What is it?" God provided this bread six days a week, and it sustained the Israelites for forty years.

> Our fathers ate the manna in the desert; as it is written, 'He gave them bread from heaven to eat.' Then Jesus said to them, 'Most assuredly, I say to you, Moses did not give you the bread from heaven, but My Father gives you the true bread from heaven. For the bread of God is He who comes down from heaven and gives life to the world.' Then they said to Him, 'Lord, give us this bread always.' And Jesus said to them, 'I am the bread of life. He who comes to Me shall never hunger, and he who believes in Me shall never thirst.'
>
> – John 6:31–35

Jesus referenced the Israelites eating manna in the wilderness when responding to the people's questions in Capernaum, but proclaimed that what their forefathers ate in the wilderness was not the *true* bread from heaven. It was only a type. Jesus told them He is the real living Bread from heaven. Though God miraculously gave manna to Israel, it was still only physical bread; those that ate manna nonetheless died. But Jesus Christ — the real Bread of Life — is for all men to eat. Whoever eats of Jesus, the living Bread from heaven, shall have eternal life. The real ingesting of Jesus is to believe into Him.

The Good Land—the Unsearchable Riches of Christ

The "good land" with all of its produce is the most beautiful picture of the all-inclusive and expansive Christ.

> And they ate of the produce of the land on the day after the Passover, unleavened bread and parched grain, on the very same day. Then the manna ceased on the day after they had eaten the produce of the land; and the children of Israel no longer had manna, but they ate the food of the land of Canaan that year.
>
> – Joshua 5:11–12

The Israelites were called to fulfill God's purpose in the Old Testament. Doing so occurred in three stages: during the Israelites' time in Egypt, in the wilderness, and finally when they reached the good land. Notice that in each stage, eating was prominently mentioned. In Egypt, the Israelites ate the Passover lamb, and that lamb was their salvation. In the wilderness, they ate manna that sustained them for forty years. In the good land, which God promised to give them, they began eating the produce of the land. Manna actually continued for about four days after entering the good land before it stopped. Clearly, eating the produce of the land replaced manna.

Scripture reveals that the manna stopped the day after the Israelites began eating the produce of the land. The food from the Promised Land not only replaced but also advanced their diet. While the manna never changed — it was the same bread for forty years — the food in Canaan was varied and abundant. This will become evident later in this chapter.

Just as the lamb and the manna are types of Jesus Christ, the following verses reveal He is also the land and the produce of the land for His people to enjoy.

> For the LORD your God is bringing you into a good land, a land of brooks of water, of fountains and springs, that flow out of valleys and hills; a land of wheat and barley, of vines and fig trees and pomegranates, a land of olive oil and honey; a land in which you will eat bread without scarcity, in which you will lack nothing; a land whose stones are iron and out of whose hills you can dig copper. When you have eaten and are full, then you shall bless the LORD your God for the good land which He has given you.
>
> – Deuteronomy 8:7–10

From these verses, one can appreciate the beauty and riches in the good land. Canaan was vast for exploration and abounding in resources, food, and even minerals. There was no scarcity; in this land, God promised the Israelites "you will lack nothing" (8:9).

Jesus Christ is truly the reality of this good land. It is an expansive description of who He is. The Passover lamb was enjoyed just once a year. Manna was eaten daily. It was tiny compared to a piece of land, and never varied in flavor or amount for forty years. However, the good land of Christ is immense and believers are surrounded with all kinds of enjoyment in Him. As a believer progresses spiritually, his or her enjoyment of Christ increases more and more.

Interestingly, Deuteronomy 8:10 was the first time in the entire Old Testament the Israelites were told they would "bless the Lord." Man had never blessed God until this point in history; this blessing would be connected to man's satisfaction from partaking of the food the good land produced.

God's purpose was fulfilled *in this land*.

> As you therefore have received Christ Jesus the Lord, so walk in Him, rooted and built up in Him and established in the faith, as you have been taught, abounding in it with thanksgiving.
>
> – Colossians 2:6–7
>
> To me, who am less than the least of all the saints, this grace was given, that I should preach among the Gentiles the unsearchable riches of Christ.
>
> – Ephesians 3:8

Paul declared the believer needs to walk in Christ Jesus and be rooted in Him, in Colossians 2:6–7. Both of these descriptions provide beautiful images of the land. First, believers are to take root in Jesus and second, He is the vast land to walk in, the "unsearchable riches" Paul spoke of in Ephesians 3:8.

The root system of a plant draws all of its nourishment from the land, and the root firmly establishes the plant. Any plant that takes root downward will grow upward. Likewise, believers are to dig down and take root in Jesus Christ, in order to grow.

Like a firmly established plant, believers need to be drawing nourishment from Christ (the land) continuously. The growing up of the plant is the building up of the body of Christ. The building up of the believers into one, functioning as the body of Christ, results from drawing nourishment from Jesus. Believers are not built up through negotiation, compromise, strategies, planning, or some sort of human coordination. These things can never produce genuine oneness among all types of believers. The only way for a true building up of the body to occur is for each individual believer to be rooted in Christ — the land — and to grow from the nourishment He provides.

Then in Ephesians 3:8, Paul said Gentiles should come to know and enjoy the "unsearchable riches of Christ." This clearly speaks of the vastness of Jesus, and the diversity of His riches. He is not limited to being the Lamb and manna, but His unsearchable riches far exceed what can be described of the good land. Throughout the Scriptures, Jesus Christ can be surveyed as the good land: real water for His children to drink, the real sun to provide growth and warmth, the true Sabbath rest, and the real house to dwell in. He is the real husband, door, light, shepherd, rock, lion, and road. Hundreds of physical items in the Scriptures describe the reality of Jesus. But that reality runs deeper than the human mind can comprehend; He is actually the reality of every positive tangible thing in this universe. By implication, applying Him to this modern age, Jesus is the real electricity that provides energy for His people, the real car that transports people, the real rocket that brings people to the heavens, and the real mobile phone that keeps people connected to Him anywhere. The unsearchable riches of Christ can be infinitely explored and enjoyed!

Possessing the Good Land

Possessing the good land depends on seeing and walking in the good land. Believers need to appreciate the immensity of Jesus Christ.

> And the LORD said to Abram, after Lot had separated from him: "Lift your eyes now and look from the place where you are — northward, southward, eastward, and westward; for all the land which you see I give to you and your descendants forever. Arise, walk in the land through its length and its width, for I give it to you."
>
> – Genesis 13:14–17

In order to see the spaciousness of the good land, believers need to lift up their eyes. Focusing downward on personal situations results in missing Christ; believers who do so forget how big He is. Two important questions believers should ask themselves include:

- Do you only know Him as the Lamb that takes away your sins?
- Though your sins are washed, are you still trying hard to perfect yourself by keeping God's laws?

If the answer to one or both of these questions is "yes," the result may be a joyless Christian life. Some believers progress forward to the point of spending time in the Bible daily, in pursuit of knowing Christ as the manna in their "quiet time." However, when they face challenges at work or frustrations at home, they become anxious and angry. Christ disappears from their realization and experience.

This is a sign that the believer is not yet enjoying the "good land" in Christ; rather, he or she is stuck looking down at themselves and their situations. When this happens, it is critical for the believer to lift up his or her eyes to see that in all four directions, as far as they can see, Jesus Christ is available to experience and enjoy. The writer of Hebrews exhorts believers to "[look] unto Jesus, the author and finisher of our faith" (Heb. 12:2). When believers see Jesus, they will be released from bondage and supplied with the unsearchable riches of Christ (Heb. 2:9).

When God's children see Jesus Christ as this vast and rich land, they will rise up and walk through its length and width. He is for the taking! Yes, Christ is big enough to include everything — at work, at home, with friends, even in recreation. He is so vast that one can never step outside of Him, no matter where they walk. He is the rich supply, regardless of needs. Jesus Christ is truly the good land!

> In order that you may be fully able to apprehend with all the saints what is the breadth and length and depth and height; and to know the love of the Christ which surpasses knowledge; that you may be filled even to all the fullness of God.
> – Ephesians 3:18–19, DBY

In an attempt to describe the vastness of Christ, Paul points out Jesus' four dimensions without being able give an actual measurement…because Jesus is unlimitedly spacious. Though His vastness and depth surpass knowledge, believers can still know and apprehend Him experientially. As they explore the good land — Christ — they are filled and become a more complete expression of God. Enjoying the Passover lamb in Egypt or the manna in the wilderness has limitations; neither can fulfill God's purpose.

In the Old Testament, God's instruction commanded the temple only be built in the good land; it could not be built anywhere else. The building up of the temple was a type of the building up of the assembly in the New Testament. It is not until believers enjoy the unlimited Christ as the reality of everything around them, together with one another and indiscriminately with all kinds of believers, that they can be filled and God's purpose be fulfilled: the building up of His body.

To apprehend the dimension of this immense Christ, Paul instructs that "all the saints" are needed (3:18). The word "all" in the original Greek does not emphasize quantity (meaning every single person), but "types" or "kinds." Thus, this phrase means a variety of saints are needed to capture the depths of the love of Christ. Therefore, the sheer number of believers gathered is not what enables them to grasp the vast dimensions of Christ. Fellowship that occurs with believers from all kinds of diverse backgrounds and environments is what empowers them to apprehend the immeasurable scope of Christ.

As individuals, believers can only enjoy Christ based on the environment they are in. For example, a stay-at-home mom's environment includes the children she takes care of, her house, and her interactions with other moms. Christ exists in that environment for her to enjoy, but she will not know Christ in an environment she never enters — such as a global business operation. However, a believer who engages often in this kind of business environment will find Christ there to enjoy and experience. If these two believers are isolated from each other and never fellowship, each will not know Christ in the other person's environment; their apprehension of Christ is limited and one-dimensional.

This same concept can be applied in a spiritual sense to an entire category of people. Let's say that a person only fellowships with believers in their own church consisting of a particular ethnic group, a particular political leaning, or a particular doctrinal understanding. This, then, remains the only environment they experience of Christ, which is limited to one particular track. Then, one day they begin to fellowship with believers of other ethnicities and perhaps with opposing political views. They will find those believers are experiencing Christ as well. As they enter into the fellowship of Jesus Christ with them, what they receive is not their political views, but their Christ. They are able to enjoy Him in a way that they may have never considered, since that is not their normal environment. They will begin to realize Christ is just as enjoyable in the new environment, as in their own. Their "apprehension" of Christ expands! Therefore, the more kinds or types of believers a Christian is in fellowship with, the more he or she will lay hold of this vast all-inclusive Christ. It is the enjoyment of Christ as the vast, good land that brings believers into oneness for God's building.

Thus, the building up of the temple — the body of Christ, which is the one fellowship of Jesus Christ — can only take place when believers explore the vast and diverse Christ as the good land in fellowshipping with all kinds and type of believers. This is the corporate aspect of enjoying Christ as the good land.

Believers Cannot Get Out of Christ; Learn to Walk in Him

Moses My servant is dead. Now therefore, arise, go over this Jordan, you and all this people, to the land which I am giving to them — the children of Israel. Every place that the sole of your foot will tread upon I have given you, as I said to Moses.

– Joshua 1:2–3

Where can I go from Your Spirit? Or where can I flee from Your presence? If I ascend into heaven, You *are* there; if I make my bed in hell, behold, You are *there*. *If* I take the wings of the morning, *and* dwell in the uttermost parts of the sea, even there Your hand shall lead me, and Your right hand shall hold me. If I say, "Surely the darkness shall fall on me," even the night shall be light about me.

– Psalm 139:7–11

As you therefore have received Christ Jesus the Lord, so walk in Him,

– Colossians 2:6

Is it hard to believe that once a person receives the faith of Jesus Christ and is joined to Him, that they cannot be removed or detached from Him, no matter what happens? Many believers have such a small Christ they think that if they do certain things, socialize at certain places, or behave in a certain way they will find themselves outside of Christ and miss Him. Psalm 139 contradicts this idea, however; no matter where believers go or what they do, they cannot get away from Christ. The believer must stand firm in this assurance, and boldly declare that even when failures bring the weight of hell and darkness, they can never get out of Him! A believer can go anywhere in this universe and never be outside of Christ. It is not behavior that keeps believers in Him; it is the realization that they are already in Him that *keeps* them in Him experientially. They simply need to walk in Him according to what they are seeing.

Wherever the believer goes, wherever they tread, Christ is the land for them to possess. It is simply not possible to be outside of Christ! This is what it means to learn how to explore the vast Christ — to consider and enjoy His riches, no matter what situations and challenges impact daily life.

Most Christians may consider whether they are in Christ and able to enjoy Him based on a set of criteria or behaviors. If they behave in a certain way, then they are in Christ; if they misbehave, they are excluded from the pleasure of being in Christ. In actuality, whether a believer can enjoy Him — whether they are in the right condition to delight in Him or not — depends on faith in God's Word. In 2 Corinthians 5:7, Paul says that, "We walk by faith and not by sight." The word "sight" in this verse refers to an individual's own perception, which can be very deceptive. Faith, however, is the ability to spiritually see the real situation in God's realm. And the reality is, believers are in Christ as a vast land that they cannot get out of. It is by this faith that believers need to walk in Christ. This faith of always being in Christ allows believers to turn their focus from their behavior and criteria to behold Jesus Christ in their daily living. This is the individual aspect of enjoying Christ as the good land.

The Good Land in the Believer's Spirit

Now Christ is the Spirit; thus, the all-inclusive Christ as the Spirit is the good land in the believer's spirit.

> Now the Lord [Jesus] is the Spirit; and where the Spirit of the Lord *is*, there *is* liberty.
>
> – 2 Corinthians 3:17

> And so it is written, "The first man Adam became a living being." The last Adam [Jesus Christ] became a life-giving spirit.
>
> – 1 Corinthians 15:45 3

In both of these verses, Paul declared Jesus Christ, *today,* is the Spirit. The God who became man, died on the cross and resurrected, is now in a spiritual form. Because He is the Spirit, believers can be in Him and He in them.

The Greek word for "spirit" is *pneuma* meaning, "breath" or "wind." It is the origin of the word "pneumatic." Air is in people, but air also surrounds them. The air in a person is their life. The air surrounding a person, regardless of what they are doing, is the environment of their daily living. This is the Spirit to believers: The Spirit is in them and they are in the Spirit. They are completely joined and mingled together with the Spirit, within and without. Therefore, a believer does not have to fulfill certain laws in order to enjoy Jesus as the Spirit; rather, they are liberated and free to live in Him just as they are.

The Good Land for the Believer's Enjoyment

The all-inclusive Christ is the good land for the believer's enjoyment.

> That the blessing of Abraham might come upon the Gentiles in Christ Jesus, that we might receive the promise of the Spirit through faith.
>
> – Galatians 3:14

According to the Old Testament (Gen. 12:7; 13:15; 17:8), what was promised to Abraham was a piece of land called the "good land." That was the physical blessing that Abraham's seed was to receive, the shadow (type). Today the blessing of Abraham that is available to all believers, even the Gentiles, is the Spirit. This is the reality (or the antitype) of the good land for believers today. The Spirit is the real, vast and abundantly rich land for believers to enjoy and live in. No matter where the believer walks, what he or she does, or what time of day it is, the Spirit is available for enjoyment as the all-inclusive blessing.

> For I know that this shall turn out for me to salvation, through your supplication and the [bountiful] supply of the Spirit of Jesus Christ.
> – Philippians 1:19, DBY

The root word for "supply" in the Greek is the word *epichorēgia,* which means "to supply bountifully, abundantly; to supply all things necessary." While Paul (the writer of Philippians) was a prisoner chained to a guard, the Spirit of Jesus Christ was supplying abundantly all that he needed. The Spirit was ministering to him. Surely Paul experienced the "good land," even while in chains. Regardless of the challenging situations facing believers, they can find themselves in the Spirit — the vast and rich land that supplies, saves and delivers them.

> So then, those who are in the flesh cannot please God. But you are not in the flesh but in the Spirit, if indeed the Spirit of God dwells in you. Now if anyone does not have the Spirit of Christ, he is not His.
> – Romans 8:8

The word "flesh" in Romans 8:8 refers to the fallen old self, without Christ. A person devoid of Christ cannot please God. However, believers are no longer in the flesh but in the Spirit. The Spirit is now their land, realm, even their universe. The Spirit of God and Christ dwells in the believers and the believers are dwelling in the Spirit. There is nothing more a believer needs to do to be "in." They are to simply rest and enjoy the reality that they are *already* in the Spirit.

One Spirit
Through faith in Jesus Christ, believers are joined to Him in perfect union. Thus, the Spirit with the believer's spirit is one Spirit.

> But he who is joined to the Lord is one spirit.
> – 1 Corinthians 6:17

> You received the Spirit of [sonship] adoption by whom we cry out, "Abba, Father." The Spirit Himself bears witness with our spirit that we are children of God.
> – Romans 8:15b–16

Once the believer is joined to the Lord they become one spirit. His Spirit and their spirit together become one. There is no more separation or even the possibility of becoming two again.

The physical act of eating food is a good illustration. When a person ingests food, the food and the person's body become one. It is no longer possible to separate digested food from the body (see Chapter 9 concerning the human spirit). This is how believers become children of God: by *their* spirit and *God's* Spirit becoming one. That is the meaning of being "born again," "born anew," or "regeneration." How is it possible for a believer to "come out of" the good land, if the good land is now part of their very being?

> The Lord Jesus Christ be with your spirit. Grace be with you. Amen.
> — 2 Timothy 4:22

The Lord Jesus became the life-giving Spirit after resurrection, and that Spirit is now indwelling the spirit of His believers; therefore, the Lord Jesus Christ is with their spirits. Today, believers are in the good land and the good land is in them; their response should be to lift up their eyes and see Christ in everything around them, and in all they are doing!

The Mind-Set of the Spirit and Breathing Prayer

First, to live according to the Spirit is to have the mind-set of the Spirit:

> …in order that the law's requirement would be accomplished in us who do not walk according to the flesh but according to the Spirit. For those who live according to the flesh think about the things of the flesh, but those who live according to the Spirit, about the things of the Spirit. For the mind-set of the flesh is death, but the mind-set of the Spirit is life and peace.
> — Romans 8:4–6, HCSB

The requirements of the law set a high standard. In fact, it is so high that only God can fulfill His own law. How can believers fulfill this law, with such extreme requirements? It is by walking according to the Spirit. For example, the way to fulfill the requirement to love and forgive one another as Christ is not by self-effort; it can only be done by walking according to the Spirit. Paul says in Romans 8:5 the unique characteristic of one living according to the Spirit is when they constantly think about the things of the Spirit. To live according to the Spirit is to consider the things of the Spirit. So then, *what are the things of the Spirit?*

Those in the good land experience the Spirit in everything around them. Everywhere they look, and whatever they do are things of the Spirit for their contemplation, consideration, and appreciation. This is the mind-set of the Spirit that gives life and peace, and what leads to fellowship with the Lord. The believer can switch from the mind-set of the flesh to the mind-set of the Spirit in a split second. It is that quick to embrace life and peace and to fulfill the requirement of the law.

For example, think of commuting to work. The believer can experience Christ as the car that provides transportation, the gas that provides power, the air conditioning that cools, and even as he or she passes by a call box, the person to call when in need. This kind of thinking concerning the things of the Spirit will spontaneously lead the believer to fellowship with the Lord, and result in an outpouring of thanksgiving — for the Lord is so many things! In such enjoyment of the good land, believers will also experience Christ as their patience and love. When someone driving a car cuts a person off who is in such fellowship with Christ, their spontaneous reaction will be one of understanding and forgiveness because they are enjoying and resting in the good land.

Or, let's say that upon arriving home from work after a long day, someone finds their spouse has forgotten to do something important that they promised to do. Before reacting, the believer prays inwardly and thinks on how Christ is the real husband and how He came to give His life in love for them — He is the faithful servant. Instead of reacting in anger and death, when the believer's mind-set is full of appreciation for all the blessings of Christ around them, they will not only remain in life and peace, but also, in turn, minister the same life and peace to their spouse.

Breathing in the Believer's Spirit

Next, to live according to the Spirit means breathing — this is unceasing prayer in the believer's spirit.

> And I will pour on the house of David and on the inhabitants of Jerusalem the Spirit of grace and supplication [prayer].
>
> – Zechariah 12:10

The key to enjoying the good land is having the mind-set of the Spirit, joined to the believer's spirit. And the key to being in the fellowship of the Spirit is supplication.

"Supplication" in this verse means *prayer*. Prayer means speaking to God in fellowship and making requests of Him. Any time the believer turns their heart to speak to the Lord Jesus, they are praying. There is no "right" way to pray. Just start talking to Him, have a conversation and make any requests known to Him.

The Spirit that has been given to every believer is the Spirit of grace and prayer. The Spirit the believer has received in their spirit, joined together in one, is a praying spirit. Grace and prayer go together. Grace is related to all that the Lord Jesus is, has, has accomplished, and has given freely for the believer's enjoyment. The way to realize this grace is through fellowship in prayer. When believers are in fellowship with the Lord, grace is their reality. Wonderfully, the Spirit in believers is constantly praying to bring them into continual fellowship and grace.

> Pray without ceasing, in everything give thanks; for this is the will of God in Christ Jesus for you.
>
> – 1 Thessalonians 5:17–18

There is only one thing human beings do without ceasing: breathe. A person can be very aware of their breathing; sometimes they may even need to stop and breathe deeply, to calm down or muster up energy to do something. However, most of the time people breathe subconsciously. Praying is like breathing for believers. God's Spirit joined with the believer's spirit is unceasingly praying. However, believers need to recognize and enter into this constant connection of prayer. Yes, sometimes people need to stop everything to pray, but the Christian can be praying constantly as they walk and live out their daily lives.

Many believers consider prayer to be an event; they may even feel they need to go through a certain process before actually praying. If that is the case, it will be impossible to pray without ceasing. Because Christians already have the Spirit in them praying incessantly, whether they are aware of it or not, it is not complicated to "join in" and pray as the Spirit makes one aware. The believer's praying spirit is independent of their behavior and actions. A person may be upright and respectable, or morally deficient. They may be about to fall (or have fallen) into sin. It doesn't matter; any believer can immediately enter into prayer because the Spirit that resides in them is still praying, even when they are not.

Just as it is physically hard for people to hold their breath, it is actually more difficult to have broken fellowship with the Lord. Once a person realizes praying is like spiritual breathing, they will find it is easier to pray and have fellowship, than to not!

Paul also exhorts believers in 1 Thessalonians 5:17 to give thanks in everything. The believer who realizes God has done everything and given everything to them naturally responds in thanksgiving and praise. Throughout the day, consider all the items that can be enjoyed through prayer and thanksgiving through Christ in the good land.

For example, as I sit at my desk and glance at the various items I keep at hand, I might be able to realize: Lord Jesus, you are my real money. You are all the riches that I need in the world. Lord, you are my reading glasses; with you I can see clearly. Lord, as I see this bill, I thank you for paying off all my debt of sin. I am free from debt because of your death on the cross. Lord, you are my real headphones! I want to hear you and not be distracted by the noise of the world. Lord, as I am writing, you are writing in me. Write your Spirit on the tablet of my heart.

In the good land, the believer never becomes exhausted from exploring and enjoying the riches of Christ. This is the will of God.

> …praying always with all prayer and supplication in the Spirit, being watchful to this end with all perseverance and supplication for all the saints.
> — Ephesians 6:18
>
> I desire therefore that the men pray everywhere.
> — 1 Timothy 2:8

Believers are to pray always and everywhere; this is what it means to be joined with the Spirit. Through prayer, believers will also make requests concerning others. Prayer is never self-centered because the Spirit cares for *all* people; when believers are joined with God's Spirit, they spontaneously pray for other's needs. Praying is one of the most powerful ways to care for other people; beautifully, the love of God will instill believers with a love for others as they pray for them.

Practice: Turning Everything to Prayer

Take time to practice turning everything in life into prayer and thanksgiving, enjoying the all-inclusive Christ as the good land. This should not be hard work…it should be as easy as breathing! At home, take pleasure in Christ while completing daily chores — when cooking, washing, or relaxing. Enjoy Him as the good land when together with a spouse, friends, relatives, or taking care of children. Enjoy Jesus as the good land while at school or work, when solving problems, when interacting with others, when deadlines are met, and even when working on the computer!

Jesus, the good land, can be experienced when exercising, commuting, and when entering various environments (good and bad). And this can continue always, even during accidental or willful failures.

Take five minutes right now and look around you. Start applying what you see to a fellowship prayer with the Lord Jesus. Talk to Him and allow the things surrounding you to prompt you to see Jesus as the reality of what you are seeing. Let them be an opening for you to enjoy Him in prayer.

Write down the items that you see and write down how they remind you of Christ:

Item 1:
How applied:

Item 2:
How applied:

Item 3:
How applied:

Item 4:
How applied:

5.

EXERCISING NEEDED TO GROW AND MATURE

Every life needs activities, or exercise. If a person lies in bed day after day without any physical movement, their muscles will soon waste away. Eventually they will die from the absence of activity. Exercise involves pushing against an opposite force, and requires effort. Sadly, that is the reason why most people don't like to exercise, and because of this, they are likely not healthy. A healthy person is active and exercises regularly; the more they are willing to push themselves physically, the more their health will improve over time, and they will become physically stronger. Even though effort is required, exercising can also be fun and enjoyable. Certainly regular exercise will improve a person's quality of life; their efforts will be well rewarded!

What *spiritual* exercise and activity should every believer be engaged in? In this chapter, spiritual exercise and activity is focused on ministering and teaching the Word of Jesus Christ to others. The effort put forth to help others understand the Word concerning Jesus Christ and the ministering of spiritual food and drink to others is "exercise" for believers.

There are all sorts of forces inside and outside of the believer that oppose this ministry of the Word and the Spirit. This is why the believer must put forth effort to push through these contrary forces, and why it is considered exercise. Additionally, living a life without offense — keeping a clear conscience toward God and man — is also an exercise. Without these activities, believers will feel unfulfilled and without purpose.

Most believers today listen passively to the teaching of members of the clergy; because of this, there is a lack of growth. Just as a baby is physically active immediately at birth, something that should continue the rest of his life, new believers need to start learning to teach others and live according to their conscience immediately. This exercise will cause them to grow, enjoy more of Jesus Christ and fulfill what God intended for them. This chapter will explore this topic of exercising for believers.

What Is Spiritual Exercise?

Spiritual exercise is teaching and ministering what has been eaten — learned and enjoyed — of Christ. The writer of Hebrews 5 and 6 says exercise means participating in the priesthood of Melchizedek. God commanded the Aaronic priesthood to make sacrifices for sinners, whereas the priesthood of Melchizedek ministered bread and wine to victorious fighters.

> He [Aaron] can have compassion on those who are ignorant and going astray, since he himself is also subject to weakness. Because of this he is required as for the people, so also for himself, to offer sacrifices for sins. . . . So also Christ did not glorify Himself to become High Priest, but it was He who said to Him: "You

> are My Son, Today I have begotten You." As He also says in another place: "You are a priest forever According to the order of Melchizedek."
>
> – Hebrews 5:2–3, 5–6

In Hebrews 5, the writer compares and contrasts the priesthood of Aaron and the priesthood of Melchizedek. Aaron was the first in the line of high priests in the Old Testament that offered sacrifices to God for sin. These high priests were sinful themselves; therefore, when they offered sacrifices for the sins of the people, they offered sacrifices for themselves as well. What was significant of the Aaronic priesthood was that God commanded sacrifices to be offered continually for sin, a reminder that their sacrifices never permanently took sin away (Heb. 10:2–3).

In contrast, Jesus Christ, who is the Son of God, is now serving according to the priesthood order of Melchizedek. In Acts 13:33 Paul quoted Psalm 2 saying, "You are My Son, Today I have begotten You." This was a declaration referring to the day of the resurrection of Jesus Christ, indicating the ministry of Melchizedek is in resurrection — Jesus entered that priesthood the day of His resurrection. When Jesus Christ died on the cross He was the real sacrifice for sin, a sacrifice that actually took away sins permanently (John 1:29; Heb. 10:11–12). Instead of reminding people of their sins, through Jesus' redemptive death, God remembers sin no more. After accomplishing such a wonderful death, and being perfected through His resurrection, Jesus became the author of eternal salvation which is the ministry of His eternal life. It was only after His resurrection that Jesus became qualified to be the High Priest, according to the order of Melchizedek (Heb. 5:10). The death of the Lord Jesus was to take away sins, and His resurrection is for imparting life.

> So he [Abraham] brought back all the goods, and also brought back his brother Lot and his goods, as well as the women and the people. And the king of Sodom went out to meet him at the Valley of Shaveh (that is, the King's Valley), after his return from the defeat of Chedorlaomer and the kings who were with him. Then Melchizedek king of Salem brought out bread and wine; he was the priest of God Most High. And he blessed him and said: "Blessed be Abram of God Most High, Possessor of heaven and earth; And blessed be God Most High, who has delivered your enemies into your hand." And he gave him a tithe of all.
>
> – Genesis 14:16–20

> For this Melchizedek, king of Salem, priest of the Most High God, who met Abraham returning from the slaughter of the kings and blessed him, to whom also Abraham gave a tenth part of all, first being translated "king of righteousness," and then also king of Salem, meaning "king of peace," without father, without mother, without genealogy, having neither beginning of days nor end of life, but made like the Son of God, remains a priest continually.
>
> – Hebrews 7:1–3

The first time Melchizedek appeared was in Genesis when he met Abraham after Abraham defeated five kings who had captured his brother (nephew), Lot. At that point

Abraham was a victorious fighter, not a defeated sinner. As a sinner, he would have needed Aaron to provide a sacrifice for sins on his behalf.

However, Melchizedek blessed Abraham — the victorious fighter — and ministered to him bread and wine. Unlike the Aaronic priesthood, which reminded people of their sins, the Melchizedek priesthood ministered bread and wine to those in victory.

This is a picture of God's eternal salvation. Jesus Christ has already completed the sacrifice for sins on the cross — sin is now over. Christ's current function is to be the High Priest ministering bread and wine to believers, no longer poor sinners in God's eyes, but victorious in Him. In Jesus Christ, believers are blessed and qualified to partake of Him.

Teaching and Dispensing Food

Sadly, believers often remain babes and become dull of hearing concerning the ministering Christ because they do not teach, or dispense food.

> ...of whom we have much to say, and hard to explain, since you have become dull of hearing. For though by this time you ought to be teachers, you need someone to teach you again the first principles of the oracles of God; and you have come to need milk and not solid food.
>
> – Hebrews 5:11–12

There is much to say about Melchizedek because He is the very Jesus Christ in resurrection, ascension, and outpouring of the Spirit. His ministry as *the* Great High Priest has been continuing for 2000 years. It took Jesus only thirty-three and a half years to complete His earthly ministry — to take away sins and offer forgiveness. But now some 2000 years later, Jesus is still doing the ministry of life. The priesthood of Melchizedek, which is the ministry of eternal life, with all His riches, continues into eternity.

However, though Jesus is unsearchably rich, most believers' hearing has become dull and sluggish. There is little interest in the riches of Christ in resurrection beyond the forgiveness of sins, and believers are bored hearing about Christ's ministry of Himself as bread and wine. Many believers remain in the basic principles of Christ. These basic principles include such things as the forgiveness of sins emphasized through the Aaronic priesthood, as well as foundational doctrines like baptism and eternal judgment (Heb. 6:1–3). Believers who continue to crave instruction in these elementary doctrines will remain with milk. Solid food is for those who move beyond these first doctrines and participate in the priesthood of Melchizedek by ministering bread and wine to others. Their instruction to other believers concerning Jesus Christ, with all of the riches of His person and work, in turn becomes *their* solid food. For those listening to the instructor's teaching, it is milk. But to the one teaching, it is solid food. Once believers begin to teach others instead of remaining a babe, repeatedly hearing the same teaching on forgiveness of sins, their ears will be opened. They will be interested and excited to hear more concerning Christ as the High Priest in resurrection and ascension. Teaching others will strengthen the believer with solid food to grow in the eternal divine life they have received and into a deeper appreciation of Christ.

Just as newborns are immediately active and must use their muscles to grow, new believers should start to teach others immediately, too. Just as toddlers learning to talk cannot speak in full sentences, new believers learning to speak Christ, though without all the scriptural citations, is music to their heavenly Father's ears. What has been learned of Jesus Christ, even though it may seem small, can be taught to those even less informed then they. However little a new believer learns or experiences concerning Jesus Christ is good enough to pass on and teach others. Their teaching may be very elementary and even inaccurate, but it is the best way to start exercising! The new believer will grow and learn more concerning Jesus Christ, and their teaching ability will improve over time.

The Ministry of the Spirit

The beginning of the believer's life in Christ begins with their justification through His death. This is the word of "milk." However, the "word of righteousness" refers to the believer's participation in Melchizedek, through ministering the bread and wine of the New Covenant to others — *the* ministry of Spirit (2 Cor. 3:6). This is solid food, which is the ministry of righteousness.

> ...for everyone who lives on milk is unskilled in the word of righteousness, since he is a child.
>
> – Hebrews 5:13, ESV

> ...who has made us sufficient to be ministers of a new covenant, not of the letter but of the Spirit. For the letter kills, but the Spirit gives life. Now if the ministry of death, carved in letters on stone, came with such glory that the Israelites could not gaze at Moses' face because of its glory, which was being brought to an end, will not the ministry of the Spirit have even more glory? For if there was glory in the ministry of condemnation, the ministry of righteousness must far exceed it in glory.
>
> – 2 Corinthians 3:6–9, ESV

Those that depend on milk year after year are unskilled in the word of righteousness. The word of righteousness, in context, is the ministry of Melchizedek (or the ministry of bread and wine). Scripture reveals that participating in this ministry is the solid food for believers. In 2 Corinthians 3:6–9 Paul told his hearers that God made believers sufficient ministers of the new covenant; Paul made it clear this is *not* the ministry of the letter of the law, which ministers death. Believers are qualified to minister *the Spirit*. Speaking the law will minister death to people. No one can fulfill the law; therefore, everyone who receives this ministry is condemned to death. But the ministry of the new covenant is the ministry of the Spirit, and it is also the ministry of righteousness. When people receive the ministry of the Spirit, the Spirit works within them to produce a life and character that is right with God and man.

This is the true priesthood of Melchizedek: those who minister the bread and wine of the new covenant, which is the Spirit — the word of righteousness.

Exercise to Become Mature

Exercising to become mature means to practice teaching and ministering to others. Doing so will sharpen one's perception; while ministering to others, the believer will be able to discern what is useful or worthless to their listeners.

> But solid food belongs to those who are of full age, *that is,* those who by reason of use have their senses [faculties for perception] exercised to discern both good [useful, precious] and evil [worthless].
>
> – Hebrews 5:14

To better understand how teaching — ministering bread and wine according to Melchizedek — equates with exercising, think of physical exercise. Just as people need to exercise physically in order to grow, spiritual exercise is needed for a person to progress to maturity. This means being more than just a listener of the Word, but also a teacher. Every person needs to exercise, and every believer needs to be a teacher — a minister like Melchizedek. If believers do not exercise in such a way, they will stay a babe and will become dull of hearing. The more believers exercise to teach others about Christ, the more their inward faculties for perception will be able to discern good and evil.

The phrase "good and evil" may be misleading, however. Some might immediately associate it with being either morally upright or depraved. The actual meaning in Greek, and the better translation is, "to be able to discern what is useful or precious and that which is worthless." As the believer exercises to teach and minister Christ to others, they will be able to discern through their ministering what is useful in their teaching and what is not necessary at that time. The more a person ministers Christ to others, the more their inner senses and perception will be sharpened.

First, they will be able to discern for themselves what is precious for food and what teachings are worthless. Not only that, they will be able know what they should teach, how to say certain things, and what to avoid at that particular time. They will better minister and serve the right teaching to each listener at the right time, and in the right way; the listener will partake of bread and wine, and be nourished with Christ. Teaching here does not necessarily mean teaching like a teacher in front of an audience in a big room! The best and the most opportune time is when teaching happens in a group of two or three or in a home assembly.

Leave the Elementary Principles of Christ

Contrary to Paul's request to not linger in the elementary doctrines, it seems this is what most believers are continually taught year after year.

> Therefore, leaving the discussion of the elementary principles of Christ, let us go on to perfection, not laying again the foundation of repentance from dead works and of faith toward God, of the doctrine of baptisms, of laying on of hands, of resurrection of the dead, and of eternal judgment.
>
> – Hebrews 6:1–2

The word "therefore" in Hebrews 6:1 is key to understanding this section. It reveals the writer's next words will be both a continuation of the last chapter, and also a conclusion. Earlier in 5:12, the writer of Hebrews spoke of the first principles being the milk. Hebrews 6 lists out these elementary principles: repentance, faith, baptism, the receiving of the Spirit (laying on of hands), and a future without eternal judgment.

This is basically what most believers are taught over and over again. The problem is not with these teachings, but *lingering* as a student, always listening, instead of moving on to become a teacher. Leaving these things does not mean they are never talked about; leaving refers to progressing on to be a teacher, a minister like Melchizedek. It means turning from being in a state of perpetually being taught.

It is easy to be a passive listener, but it is an exercise to rise up to teach and minister.

> For it is impossible for those who were once enlightened, and have tasted the heavenly gift, and have become partakers of the Holy Spirit, and have tasted the good word of God and the powers of the age to come, if they fall away, to renew them again to repentance, since they crucify again for themselves the Son of God, and put Him to an open shame.
>
> – Hebrews 6:4–6

Once believers have received all these wonderful gifts — once they have "become partakers of the Holy Spirit, and have tasted the good word of God and the powers of the age to come" (Heb. 6:4–5) from their faith in Christ — they need to move on. Even if they "fall away" and backslide, it is impossible to return to the beginning, repent and start all over again as a new believer. Just about every believer has experienced a falling away from the Lord, and many think when this happens they need to be re-taught the basics. They feel the need to hear the gospel and repent again, to participate in another "altar call."

This is not so! Christ's crucifixion is once for all. To repent again is like asking the Lord to die for the believer again. Accepting this deception is why many believers remain babes, and continue to crave milk. Their experience is one of constantly being reminded of their sins, which is a function of the Aaronic priesthood.

Mature believers are not perfect; they can also fall into sin, and they may experience times of falling away from Christ as well. However, they have enough trust in the work of Christ and their own solid foundation of faith to resume moving forward in Christ's victory. Thus, the mature believer continues his journey as a victorious fighter, a priest in the order of Melchizedek who ministers bread and wine to others. This is spiritual exercise.

A mature believer is one like Abraham, who did not linger in his own condition but went out to rescue his brother, returning victorious. Mature believers don't linger in the apathy of being taught! Once the wonderful gifts have been tasted, they start teaching and ministering in the priesthood of Melchizedek, despite repeating failures. Doing so results in seeing and enjoying more of the unsearchable riches of Christ.

Believers should learn higher points of truth beyond the teaching of the basics of Christ. They should also learn such things as the building up of the body of Christ, God's economy for His eternal purpose, the ministry of the Spirit for renewing and transforming believers in His image, the new covenant, and the new commandment of loving one another. But even if they learn some of these things related to the ministry of Melchizedek, they will become dull from repeatedly hearing these things. They will remain a babe if they do not exercise and begin teaching others themselves. Maturity is not about knowing a lot and even understanding what may be the peak of God's revelation, but whether the believer is actually participating in the ministry of Melchizedek by ministering bread and wine.

Cultivating Believers to Produce Food

God's purpose is to cultivate believers with His riches so they produce food that satisfies others, just as Melchizedek did with bread and wine.

> For land that has drunk the rain that often falls on it, and produces a crop useful to those for whose sake it is cultivated, receives a blessing from God. But if it bears thorns and thistles, it is worthless and near to being cursed, and its end is to be burned.
>
> – Hebrews 6:7–8

The writer of Hebrews reveals God's purpose in providing the rich spiritual supply. This specifically refers to verses 4 and 5: receiving a share of the Spirit, and tasting the heavenly gifts, and the good Word. Each of these things is "rain" on the believers (the land). God's expectation for the rain is that it will produce food for those that God intends. God is in the process of cultivating believers who will produce food that will nourish.

There are many people around each and every believer that God wants to feed with Christ as the bread and wine. God wants every believer to participate in the priesthood of Melchizedek, with Jesus Christ the High Priest of this order. If after receiving God's gift of rain, the believer in turn produces something nourishing for others, they are blessed. If they do not minister Christ, they are a barren land with non-edible worthless thorns and thistles. Those are believers that only receive, but never give.

This is a serious warning to all believers. Those that embrace the idea that teaching and ministering is only to be done by trained professionals such as pastors, ministers or priests are making a detrimental mistake. *Every* believer is called to teach — to minister to others the riches of Christ as bread and wine — and each needs to exercise toward this function. Otherwise, they will remain a babe and never mature. Sharing what the believer has learned should begin as soon as a person comes to know the Lord.

John 15 provides this same warning. Here the Lord Jesus warned the branches in the vine to bear fruit, to supply life to others for His multiplication; any branch without fruit is "cast into fire."

Minister to Strengthen and Increase Godliness

It is important to spiritually exercise to be a good minister of the things of God's economy. This will strengthen and increase godliness. Godliness is the entire process of God becoming flesh to be dispensed into His household (the assembly), that it may grow unto glorification.

> But if I am delayed, I write so that you may know how you ought to conduct yourself in the house of God, which is the church [assembly] of the living God, the pillar and ground of the truth. And without controversy great is the mystery of godliness: God was manifested in the flesh, Justified in the Spirit, Seen by angels, Preached among the Gentiles, Believed on in the world, Received up in glory.
>
> — 1 Timothy 3:15–16

Paul's concern was Timothy's conduct in the household of God, the family of God, which is the assembly. This assembly is composed of living members because God is living and moves within His family members, the assembly.

In 1 Timothy 3:16, Paul continues and explains the mystery of godliness: God was manifested in the flesh (His incarnation and His God–man living on earth), justified in the Spirit (His resurrection after crucifixion), seen by angels (His ascension and enthronement), preached among the Gentiles (His outpouring of the Spirit to initiate the dispensing of Himself to man through the gospel), and believed on in the world (the multiplication of the members of His body). Finally, He was taken up in glory (the members of His body transformed and glorified). This description of the mystery of godliness is the truth. It is this truth that the assembly supports and uplifts as the ground and pillar.

The truth, this mystery of godliness, is not just the person of Jesus Christ, but it also includes God's family, the assembly — His body. Godliness comprises God Himself processed through death and resurrection and dispensed into man, resulting in glorification — the manifestation of God and man joined and intermingled into one. God Himself is not separated from His household (assembly), but is intrinsically joined to it; therefore, it is impossible for Him to separate from His assembly. This should be what is manifested when people enter the assembly of believers. This is God's eternal purpose.

Proper Conduct in the Household of God

Upon understanding God is intrinsically joined to His household, how then should believers respond? According to Paul, it should be by dispensing nourishment, or teaching the truth to others.

> Laying these things before the brethren, you will be a good minister of Christ Jesus, nourished with the words of the faith and of the good teaching which you have fully followed up. . . . Enjoin and teach these things. . . . Till I come, give yourself to [public] reading, to exhortation, to teaching. . . . Give heed to yourself and to the teaching. Continue in them; for doing this, you will save both yourself and those hearing you.
>
> — 1 Timothy 4:6, 11, 13, 16, DBY

After exhorting his listeners regarding godliness, Paul charges Timothy to be a teacher, a minister of the truth, and a dispenser of life. This is how Timothy is to conduct himself in the household of God, and thus, it is how every believer ought to behave. On the one hand, they are to be nourished up with the truth, and continue in it. On the other hand, they are to teach: to present the nourishing truth before their brothers and sisters, and to exhort fellow believers to imitate what they are doing — teaching and ministering.

Exercising Oneself toward Godliness

Believers who desire to be good ministers refuse that which is not truth, and exercise themselves toward godliness

> If you instruct the brethren in these things, you will be a good minister of Jesus Christ, nourished in the words of faith and of the good doctrine which you have carefully followed. But reject profane and old wives' fables, and exercise yourself toward godliness.
>
> *— 1 Timothy 4:6–7*

After believers eat and are nourished (1 Tim. 4:6), Paul writes that "exercise" is needed next. In order for life to grow and mature, one must eat; however, exercise must not be neglected. This supports the underlying thought of this chapter that if life is to grow and mature, there is the need to eat, and there is also the need to exercise. It cannot be overemphasized that godliness here in context is not a matter of ethics or morality. Godliness was not defined in this chapter as a matter of ethics or morality, but rather it is truth concerning the joining and mingling together of God with man. Therefore, exercise toward godliness relates to the teaching of the nourishing truth in contrast to fables and other unhealthy teachings that corrupt.

Reject Fables, Endless Genealogies, and Law Teachers

> Even as I begged you to remain in Ephesus, when I was going to Macedonia, that you might charge some not to teach other doctrines, nor to turn their minds to fables and endless genealogies, which bring questionings rather than further God's dispensation, which is in faith. But the end of what is charged is love out of a pure heart and a good conscience and unfeigned faith; which things some having missed, have turned aside to vain discourse, desiring to be law-teachers, not understanding either what they say or concerning what they so strenuously affirm.
>
> *— 1 Timothy 1:3–7, DBY*

Paul's command to reject "profane and old wives' fables" (1 Tim. 4:7) is consistent with charging Timothy not to teach any doctrines that are of the nature of fables, endless genealogies, and law keeping (1:3–7). Rather, believers are to continue with the teaching of truth that furthers God's dispensation (See Chapter 11).

A fable might be considered the adding of undue embellishments and emphasis to someone's testimony or witness of a "miracle," making it into a legend or myth. Endless genealogies may include elevating certain ministers or preachers who have a proper theological lineage, listing the great things they have done. People consider these teachers sound simply because of their genealogy, without questioning what they are teaching to examine if it is true or healthy. Conversely, instructions from teachers without an acceptable genealogy is automatically rejected, regardless of how healthy or true their teaching is.

Then there are the law teachers who bring believers back to the old covenant. These teachings are deceptive because they teach principles and laws from the Bible, but they draw believers back to the old covenant, away from grace. They energize believers' fleshly nature, teaching believers to use their best efforts to keep the law, leading them away from faith. Paul's entire epistle to the Galatians was his effort to expose this evil and recover believers back to freedom in Christ. Any teaching or speaking that distracts believers from the nourishing truth in God's economy should be avoided, and even rejected.

Stand Firm in Truth When Teaching Others

Exercising toward godliness requires remaining in the things of truth while teaching and ministering to others.

> But reject profane and old wives' fables, and exercise yourself toward godliness.
> – 1 Timothy 4:7

In the context of 1 Timothy 4 godliness must refer to the proper teachings that encompass the items previously described as leading to godliness. Also, because Paul contrasts godliness with the profane and fables, godliness must be in the context of proper teachings. For the divine life to mature in believers, exercise (teaching the proper nourishing truth to others) is imperative and necessary for the household (the assembly of God) to grow and be built up.

Not Taking Grace in Vain

Laboring is an exercise, and grace (food) given to believers is in vain if there is no laboring through speaking Christ.

> But by the grace of God I am what I am, and his grace toward me was not in vain. On the contrary, I worked harder than any of them, though it was not I, but the grace of God that is with me. Whether then it was I or they, so we preach and so you believed.
> – 1 Corinthians 15:10–11, ESV

Grace is the supply of the Lord Himself with all of His riches for the believer's enjoyment. It is surprising to read that God's grace towards Paul could possibly be in vain, or for nothing. Why was it not?

The grace to Paul was not in vain because he worked in spreading the good news. Grace was acting like food for Paul, giving him the inward energy to work. Only because of grace was Paul able to proclaim Christ and teach others. If Paul didn't do any of the Lord's work, then grace to him would have been in vain. *Work is exercise.*

This is true for all believers. The more grace believers receive, the more they need to exercise through teaching, ministering, and preaching to dispense Christ to others. The more they exercise, the hungrier they will become and subsequently, the more grace they will receive.

This is just like the act of physically eating food; if people only ate but never exercised or worked, they could die from inactivity. But the more people exercise, the more they need nourishing food. Therefore, for a believer to function normally, grow and mature, he or she needs to eat (be nourished with Christ regularly), and to exercise (labor in preaching or teaching regularly).

This is why the typical clergy/laity system practiced among most churches is detrimental to believers. In this system only a professional class of people teaches and preaches, while the majority of the believers listen.

This is not the scriptural way to build up the body of Christ. Every member needs to rise up, take responsibility, and exercise what the Lord has given them: the grace to speak Christ.

A Good Conscience: Being Led by the Spirit

A person's conscience is like an inner guide that helps them to discern right from wrong. Spiritual exercise involves possessing a *good* conscience, and this, to believers, is related to being led by the Spirit.

> For when Gentiles, who do not have the law, by nature do what the law requires, they are a law to themselves, even though they do not have the law. They show that the work of the law is written on their hearts, while their conscience also bears witness, and their conflicting thoughts accuse or even excuse them.
> – Romans 2:14–15, ESV

Man's conscience (even the nonbeliever's conscience) accuses of guilt for certain actions or excuses from guilt when innocent. God's law actually matches the created human nature. God's law regarding human conduct in society is itemized in the Ten Commandments, but wrapped up in this one commandment: love your neighbor as yourself (Matt. 22:39–40). This single commandment mirrors man's created good nature; a person's conscience will object and accuse when an action may be harmful to themselves or others. When this is about to happen, their conscience will "object" and sound an inner alarm in an attempt to prevent them from going further. The conscience is the innate mechanism God created in human nature for preserving and multiplying life.

> My little children, let us not love in word or in tongue, but in deed and in truth. And by this we know that we are of the truth, and shall assure our hearts before Him. For if our heart condemns us, God is greater than our heart, and knows all things. Beloved, if our heart does not condemn us, we have confidence toward God.
> – 1 John 3:18–21

Believers in Jesus Christ possess a conscience that is strengthened and becomes more sensitive over time. Because the believer's redeemed human nature is lifted up and fused with God's divine nature, so too are the New Testament external laws which are elevated to match the believer's new nature. For example, the Old Testament law says, "do not murder," but the corresponding New Testament law says do not get angry with others and abuse verbally. The old condones hurting someone who has hurt others (an eye for an eye), but the new commands people to love their enemies.

Thus, if believers do not love others in deed as Christ has loved them, their hearts — which includes the conscience — will condemn them. If their conscience objects, surely God also objects since He is even greater. To follow the Lord and live according to the new nature — Christ in the believer — those in Christ must follow the sense of their conscience. They must love others in deed, whether Christians or not. Loving others in this way means much more than not harming others, but doing something good for their benefit.

> Now the Spirit expressly says that in latter times some will depart from the faith, giving heed to deceiving spirits and doctrines of demons, speaking lies in hypocrisy, having their own conscience seared with a hot iron.
> – 1 Timothy 4:1

The conscience leads a person away from that which is harmful, and toward what is beneficial.

Nerve endings in a person's fingers help prevent their fingers from getting seared; however, if those endings are damaged and a person has no sensitivity to heat, their fingers could catch on fire without the person even being aware. In the same way, a person's conscience can be seared so that it has no more sensitivity. When a person denies his conscience for too long, it can become seared. That person becomes susceptible to receiving and accepting all sorts of harmful and evil things. This is true for both believers and unbelievers. A seared conscience will open a person up to demonic spirits and activities; such a person can end up living a lie his entire life or even have an early and untimely death.

A Conscience without Offense

It is important for believers to exercise their conscience so that it is without offense toward God and men.

> ...having hope towards God, which they themselves also receive, that there is to be a resurrection both of just and unjust. For this cause I also exercise myself to have in everything a conscience without offence towards God and men.
> – Acts 24:15–16, DBY

Knowing that there is a resurrection of all men for judgment, Paul exercised (or strove) to have a conscience that was without offense. This should be part of *all* the believers' spiritual exercise. On one hand, they should exercise to teach and minister to others; on the other hand, they should exercise to have a good conscience. Both need the nourishment of the grace of the Lord Jesus, and both are needed if believers are to grow and mature.

A Conscience without Offense toward God

Therefore, brothers and sisters, since we have confidence to enter the Most Holy Place by the blood of Jesus. . . . let us draw near to God with a sincere heart and with the full assurance that faith brings, having our hearts sprinkled to cleanse us from a guilty conscience and having our bodies washed with pure water.

— Hebrews 10:19, 22, NIV

This is the most basic tenant of faith: that by the blood of Jesus Christ the believer has the confidence, the boldness to come into the Holiest Place, God's presence. They do not come to God because of merit, or because they never offend their conscience due to failures and sins, but because they have the redemptive blood of Jesus that fully forgave them of all their sins…past, present and future. Due to this wonderful fact, the believer comes forward to God continually without hesitation. Because of the blood of Jesus, before God, believers do not have a guilty, accusing conscience.

If we confess our sins, He is faithful and just to forgive us our sins and to cleanse us from all unrighteousness.

— 1 John 1:9

The word, "confess" in 1 John 1:9 in the original Greek is the word *homologeō,* which literally means, "to speak the same thing, " or "to assent, accord, agree with" (Vine's Expository Dictionary). With whom is Paul saying believers are to agree? They are to agree *with the Lord* speaking in their conscience. As they are living and walking in the Lord, the Lord in their conscience will point out things that are not according to their inward nature, the divine life in them. Upon hearing this speaking from their conscience, they must agree and speak back to the Lord the sin exposed by His light. By confessing in this way, God is faithful and righteous to forgive the believer's sins and to cleanse them. This kind of confession is simply part of speaking to the Lord throughout the day (breathing prayer). While in conversation with the Lord throughout the day, the believer's conscience will speak here and there; the very moment he or she answers back to the Lord in agreement, the believer receives instant cleansing. For example, the believer might agree, "Lord, my attitude was not right with my wife just now," or "Lord Jesus, I am not loving this person as you." It is not that believers need to confess their sins before they come back to enjoy the Lord, but rather, they confess *while they are already in fellowship* with the Lord.

A Conscience without Offense toward Men

Let all bitterness, wrath, anger, clamor, and evil speaking be put away from you, with all malice. And be kind to one another, tenderhearted, forgiving one another, even as God in Christ forgave you.

— Ephesians 4:31–32

You have heard that it was said, 'You shall love your neighbor and hate your enemy.' But I say to you, love your enemies, bless those who curse you, do good to

> those who hate you, and pray for those who spitefully use you and persecute you,
> that you may be sons of your Father in heaven; for He makes His sun rise on the
> evil and on the good, and sends rain on the just and on the unjust.
>
> – Matthew 5:43–45

The conscience of the believer is more sensitive than the conscience of the unbeliever, because as sons of their Father God, believers are born of Him with the eternal life and divine nature. The unbelievers' created human nature may agree with God's commandments such as, "honor your father and mother," "do not kill," "do not commit adultery," "do not steal," "do not bear false witness," and "do not covet your neighbor's things." But with an uplifted and divine nature, a believer's conscience will object to more than just the negative of harming a person; it will object when the believer doesn't act on the positive. When believers exercise themselves to have a conscience without offense, they live according to their Christ nature in a way that benefits those around them. In other words, their conscience will bother them, when they do not live out Christ.

> Therefore if you bring your gift to the altar, and there remember that your
> brother has something against you, leave your gift there before the altar, and go
> your way. First be reconciled to your brother, and then come and offer your gift.
>
> – Matthew 5:23

When a believer's conscience alerts them to an offense, especially if it is causing a rift in a relationship, it is important to attempt to reconcile quickly with the offended person. The believer may need to admit wrongdoing or apologize. They may even need to offer some sort of financial restitution, if necessary. In any case, believers are charged to reconcile; not choosing to reconcile could become a hindrance in fellowship with the Lord. It is actually easier to possess a conscience without offense to God, than to men. To appease men, material restitution might be necessary. Therefore, it is important that believers follow their conscience in dealing with others. Paul teaches an important guideline for this in Romans 12:18: "If it is possible, as much as depends on you, live peaceably with all men."

Those with a Good Conscience Are Led by the Spirit

> I tell the truth in Christ, I am not lying, my conscience also bearing me witness
> in the Holy Spirit.
>
> – Romans 9:1

A believer's conscience is connected with the Holy Spirit. It is because of the indwelling Holy Spirit that they have an uplifted conscience able to sense whether they are living according to their human and divine nature. Whether acting positively (speaking truth in Christ) or negatively (lying), their conscience constantly reacts as the believer moves about their daily life; this reaction reflects the thoughts and feelings of the Holy Spirit.

> For as many as are led by the Spirit of God, these are sons of God.
>
> – Romans 8:14

> But if you are led by the Spirit, you are not under the law.
>
> – Galatians 5:18

When believers live and act according to their conscience, they are "led by the Spirit" (Gal. 5:18). The word "led" in Galatians 5:18 in the original Greek is the word *agō*, which communicates compulsion. Paul states there is no option for believers but to follow the Spirit's leading; they are being brought, or are compelled, to go a certain direction. This is the believer's conscience: completely one with and led by the Holy Spirit. Of course, each follower of Jesus still must choose whether to follow the feelings of their conscience.

The more believers exercise to live according to their conscience, the more they will manifest the divine nature as sons of God. God's law as contained in the Ten Commandments demands men and women live in a way that corresponds to their created nature. Believers led by the Spirit – those who live according to their conscience – will exceed the law given by God. Their life will be lived according to the natural law of the divine life in them.

Most believers liken being led by the Spirit to the way of the Old Testament, where God told His people what to do or not to do. For example, a Christian might ask, "Shall I visit this place? Shall I buy this car? Shall I buy this house?" Though the Lord can absolutely answer this type of request, in the New Testament, such cases are rare. God didn't tell believers or apostles to do or not to do something.

Under God's new covenant, believers are filled so that their minds are transformed; they have His mind. His law of life becomes a very part of their nature, their being. How they think and what they feel is one with the Lord, and they live accordingly. Believers become one with the Lord; He is in them, and they are in Him. That is why it is so important to know the truth in His Word, so that the mind is transformed to His mind, and believers are filled in Spirit to walk according to their conscience.

Practice: Teaching a Verse or Two

Practice teaching others the "unsearchable riches" of Christ in His person and work. Each week, explain a verse from a section of Scripture to another person. Teach to make sure they understand, and check to make sure one truth impresses them in the Word. It is important that people learn to read and understand the Bible for themselves.

Make sure to simply pass along the good news from the Word. Try not to argue to convince people in an attempt to convert them. Finally, avoid sounding "preachy."

There are many ways to teach the Scriptures, but here is a way that you can practice. Let's use the second part of John 10:10 to demonstrate a teaching conversation with your friend, Bob:

You: Bob, let's turn to this wonderful verse in John 10:10. Here – why don't you read this portion out loud to me.

Bob: I have come that they may have life, and that they may have it more abundantly.

You: This is a wonderful verse speaking of the purpose for which Jesus came to earth. Do you know who the "I" is referring to?

Bob: Jesus?

You: Yes, you are absolutely correct. So according to this verse why did Jesus come?

Bob: To save me from sin?

You: That is true, but is that what the verse says? Here, read it again (pointing to the phrase).

Bob: I have come that they may have life.

You: So why did Jesus come?

Bob: That they may have life?

You: Yes, correct. Now who do you think "they" is referring to?

Bob: I don't know.

You: "They" there refers to people including you and me, all people including sinners. So now read again and replace "they" with "Bob," and say Jesus for the "I" in the beginning.

Bob: Jesus has come that Bob may have life.

You: Isn't that great! Jesus came to give you life, life abundantly. So again why did Jesus come?

Bob: To give me life.

You: Amen! Isn't that something that the reason Jesus came is to give you life? Now what kind of life is that? Aren't you alive now? Why does He have to give us life if we are already alive?

Bob: I don't know.

You: Do you have God's eternal life?

Bob: No.

You: That is what Jesus wants to give you — God's eternal divine life. He came to give you this wonderful life. Do you understand this verse now? Explain to me again.

Guiding people through the Word like this may seem slow at first, but after a short while they will start to understand more and more. There is a point in their reading where they will start understanding for themselves, and it is in the understanding of the Word that the Spirit works to either bring salvation to the unbeliever or nourishment for growth for a believer.

6.

SLEEPING: RESTING IN THE DEATH OF CHRIST

As life grows and matures, that life will spontaneously and innately become what is encoded in its DNA. Consider the life of an apple tree. Through growth, apples will be produced. If the life is a dog, the little tiny puppy at birth will grow into a chasing, barking and biting dog. If the life has human DNA, it would be impossible for that embryo to develop and grow into anything else but a human person. As long as the four ingredients necessary for life to exist and grow are present, there is absolutely no doubt that life will mature, and function and express the DNA of that particular life.

One of the essential characteristics of the life of Christ in the believer is sacrificial love. Those that are mature in this life will manifest this divine love that serves others as one who washes others' feet. Those that have such a love as their nature are surely one with all believers. They are ones that express God as their Father, bearing the Father's name. This is the oneness in the Father's name.

It is critical for believers to grow in the life of the Father; this is the divine life growing in them. Four essential ingredients are needed for this to happen: nutrients (eating and drinking), air (breathing), exercise, and sleep. When these four items are consistent and regular, life will grow and bear fruit. This is the natural law of life. Let's now explore the fourth essential ingredient for life: spiritual sleep.

Sleep is essential for life. Sleep deprivation is torture. In fact, a person can die from lack of sleep. When a person goes to sleep, they experience rest physically and psychologically; they receive a break from labor and a hiatus from anxiety. A person may worry about a lot of things or be angry or disappointed, but when he or she sleeps, they receive both physical and psychological rest. While a person is asleep, disappointment, worry, anger, and anxiety vanishes.

If a believer does not know and experience *spiritual* sleep, then his or her spiritual life will not last. He will not be a happy believer. Enjoying sleep is key to a joyful, healthy, and productive spiritual life.

However, what exactly is *spiritual* sleep?

Biblically, Sleep Refers to Death

Our friend Lazarus sleeps, but I go that I may wake him up. . . . However, Jesus spoke of his death.

– John 11:11, 13

> And they stoned Stephen as he was calling on [God] and saying, "Lord Jesus, receive my spirit." Then he knelt down and cried out with a loud voice, "Lord, do not charge them with this sin." And when he had said this, he fell asleep.
> – Acts 7:59–60

> But I do not want you to be ignorant, brethren, concerning those who have fallen asleep. For if we believe that Jesus died and rose again, even so God will bring with Him those who sleep in Jesus.
> – 1 Thessalonians 4:13a–14

In the Bible, "going to sleep," describes death. In John 11, Lazarus died, but Jesus said that Lazarus had only gone to sleep and that He would go and wake him up. The story continues with Lazarus actually dying and Jesus resurrecting him from death. To Jesus, death means going to sleep and resurrection means waking up. While being stoned to death Stephen called on the Lord and prayed for his persecutors; then Scripture says he "fell asleep" (Acts 7:60). What a wonderful picture! Stephen's persecutors were stoning him to death, and he was suffering terribly; being stoned to death is one of the worst ways to die. When Stephen "went to sleep," the suffering ended. His pain was over, and he rested. It is appropriate to say, "rest in peace" (RIP) for those that have died in Christ, because when a person "sleeps," they experience true rest.

In Thessalonians 4, Paul referred to all the believers who have died, saying there was no need to sorrow for those who had passed away because they had only fallen asleep; one day, they will all wake up in resurrection. Death is the ultimate rest. There is no more suffering, pain, anxiety, unhappiness, sorrow, or labor. Everything negative ends and the person is simply resting in death. For believers, death is therefore the *real* rest and sleep.

This does not mean believers should actually seek physical death. In fact, it is much better for believers to remain alive physically as long as possible until they have finished the course God has laid out for each one (2 Tim. 4:6–7). Believers should not have the thought to die prematurely, nor attempt to do so; it is important to stay alive physically and work out the course of living.

If that is the case, what is spiritual rest for believers *while they are still physically alive?*

Sleep and Rest: Experience Christ's Death

For believers, to "sleep" and rest is to experience the death of Christ.

> Or do you not know that as many of us as were baptized into Christ Jesus were baptized into His death? Therefore we were buried with Him through baptism into death, that just as Christ was raised from the dead by the glory of the Father, even so we also should walk in newness of life.
> – Roman 6:3–4

Baptism is a symbol of being immersed into Christ's death. Actually, when a person believes into Christ, that faith joins him into Christ and all that Jesus is and has accomplished.

One of His accomplishments is death; therefore, the believer's faith joins him or her to His death — His wonderful and powerful death. Baptism is the symbol of that union, of the joining together with Christ in His death.

Believers are even buried with Him — dead and buried. Their death with Christ is final, terminal, and eternal, just as Christ died once, never to die again. Through faith, believers are joined to Christ's death, dying to their old man spiritually once for all. This is really wonderful news! Consider the peaceful rest believers have in the death of Christ, according to these verses:

> Therefore put to death your members which are on the earth: fornication, uncleanness, passion, evil desire, and covetousness, which is idolatry. Because of these things the wrath of God is coming upon the sons of disobedience, in which you yourselves once walked when you lived in them. But now you yourselves are to put off all these: anger, wrath, malice, blasphemy, filthy language out of your mouth. Do not lie to one another, since you have put off the old man with his deeds.
>
> – Colossians 3:5–9

The "old man" is dead. The old man refers to the fallen man, the man without God. When Adam ate of the tree of knowledge of good and evil, he and all of his offspring became the "old man." All of Adam's offspring are alienated from God. They possess the natural life from birth, but they do not yet possess God's divine eternal life. Even a newborn baby is part of the "old man." Attached to the old man is sin and death, the very nature of the old man.

Greediness, pride, anxiety, lust, discontent, the desire for revenge, and all other negative attributes within a person, are attached to this nature. All of man's problems stem from this old man. Thankfully, the old man is dead and buried through crucifixion and burial providing rest from these problems. This is not so for the unbeliever; when bothered and troubled by the old man, he or she has nowhere to go for relief. Many unbelievers try to fix their problems themselves. They may seek self-improvement regimens or religion to strengthen their moral character. They may degenerate to abusing drugs or alcohol, or drown themselves with material riches or achievements. These people have no rest, no sleep.

For believers, it is completely different. Believers can rest and sleep in the death of Christ; the old man is dead, and all troubles related to their sin nature become distant history. They can rest in peace in the death of Christ, by putting off the old man.

Freedom from the Slavery of Sin

> For I know that in me (that is, in my flesh) nothing good dwells; for to will is present with me, but *how* to perform what is good I do not find. For the good that I will *to do,* I do not do; but the evil I will not *to do,* that I practice. Now if I do what I will not *to do,* it is no longer I who do it, but sin that dwells in me.
>
> – Romans 7:18–20

A slave has to do his master's bidding. Every human is born fallen and a slave to sin. How awful a life under slavery! People who are slaves of sin don't want to be angry, but they can't help it. They want to forgive, but they can't. They want to be content, but they are not. They don't want to hurt anyone, but they do. When these experiences are present, the person is a slave to sin.

Freedom from sin comes only through the death of Christ. What a rest in the death of Christ when man is no longer a slave to sin. Everyone (especially most Christians) tries his or her best to avoid sin. However, their focus tends to be on expending effort to not sin. This will be a losing battle every time. Though a person may never commit more external and visible sins like murder, adultery or debauchery, they can never escape the more hidden sins of anger, greed or the desire for revenge. Therefore, instead of struggling through the effort of the old man to be a good person, the secret to freedom is focusing on Christ. Those who do so enjoy Christ, because only through the death of Christ can a person truly sleep and experience the joy of comfortable, peaceful rest.

Death Has No More Dominion

> For the wages of sin is death, but the gift of God is eternal life in Christ Jesus our Lord.
> – Romans 6:23

> O wretched man that I am! Who will deliver me from this body of death?
> – Romans 7:24

> ...and release those who through fear of death were all their lifetime subject to bondage.
> – Hebrews 2:15

At the fall of man, sin entered mankind resulting in death; Scripture is clear that the payment for sin is death. The more a person sins, the closer he is to death.

This death, however, is completely opposite to the death of Christ. The death of Christ brings freedom, while death from sin dominates and will not release man (male and female) from its clutches. Eventually every person will succumb to physical death. But even before physical death, the power of death dominates, evidenced in sicknesses, weaknesses, aging, deterioration, depression, and hopelessness. Each is an indicator of death's control over man, its dominion that starts at the moment of birth and continues until physical death. How pitiful are those dominated by death who have no way out!

Even when everything seems okay, bondage still exists in the form of *the fear* of death. Most everyone is afraid of death. Though this fear can be drowned out for a period of time, it often rears its head and grips its victim. This fear is real and the bondage is powerful. There is no escape. What misery and torment to be in such a state through life!

Even when a man dies, he still cannot escape death because there is a death worse than physical death: the second death (Rev. 21:8; see also 2:11, and 20:6, 14). The second death is the eternal lake of fire from which there is no escape. It will be like having a perpetual nightmare and never waking up, because the nightmare is real. Truly, death is dreadful and horrible.

Believing into Jesus Christ and participating in His death and resurrection frees believers from this dominating, eternal death. Victory over death begins immediately and can be the believer's daily experience. This is the reality for all those that have believed into Christ and into His death and resurrection. It is in this rest that believers are free from the dominion of death. Contrary to most Christians' concept of experiencing the death of Christ as a suffering, the believer who experiences the death of Christ does not suffer; the death of Christ actually terminates suffering.

Types of Sufferings Believers May Experience

For many people, when difficulties surface in life, they just want to go to sleep. At least when they fall asleep, they receive temporary respite from the bad things weighing them down. Of course, when they wake up, whatever rough situation they wanted to escape from is still there. Many times, suffering is what causes unbelievers and believers alike to turn to God for relief; true relief is to rest in the death of Christ.

There are two "types" of sufferings: involuntary and voluntary. Involuntary sufferings are those negative experiences a person doesn't seek out. Voluntary sufferings, on the other hand, are those that believers sign up for by choice.

Involuntary Sufferings Result from Sinful Man and the Corruption of God's Creation

> And since they did not see fit to acknowledge God, God gave them up to a debased mind to do what ought not to be done. They were filled with all manner of unrighteousness, evil, covetousness, malice. They are full of envy, murder, strife, deceit, maliciousness. They are gossips, slanderers, haters of God, insolent, haughty, boastful, inventors of evil, disobedient to parents, foolish, faithless, heartless, ruthless.
>
> – Romans 1:28–31, ESV

Many people have asked, as a challenge to God: if God is real and God is love, why is there so much suffering in the world? Why doesn't God stop the suffering?

The problem is that much of the suffering in the world is due to man himself and not God. Consider the following: war causes suffering to untold millions of people; theft causes suffering because of covetousness; and murder and maliciousness result from anger. How many children suffer at school because of a schoolmate's deceit or bullying? How many parents suffer because of disobedient children? How much suffering results from even two or three of things listed above, committed by virtually every human being regularly?

It is highly unfair and illogical to blame God for all the suffering man causes, unless man also expects God to immediately judge and execute anyone who has ever caused someone to suffer or turn everyone into a robot. Every person alive has both received and caused another person's suffering because of their sin nature.

> For I consider that the sufferings of this present time are not worth comparing with the glory that is to be revealed to us. For the creation waits with eager longing for the revealing of the sons of God. For the creation was subjected to futility, not willingly, but because of him who subjected it, in hope that the creation itself will be set free from its bondage to corruption and obtain the freedom of the glory of the children of God. For we know that the whole creation has been groaning together in the pains of childbirth until now.
>
> – Romans 8:18–22, ESV

As a result of man's fall in Genesis, all of creation was cursed and is now in bondage to corruption. This includes animals, plants, the earth, the oceans, and the atmosphere; everything is subject to futility, or vanity. Because harmony does not exist in creation today, earthquakes, hurricanes, diseases, drought, and pestilence result. Therefore, God's entire creation "groans," or suffers, but man in particular experiences the weight of creation's corrupt state. Creation is groaning to be set free at the revealing of the sons of God, when the believers are matured to be glorified.

Today, believers have Christ in them as the hidden hope of glory. One day, this glory will break forth into a manifested glory at the second coming of Jesus Christ. At that time, the entire creation will be happy, as mountains "sing" and the trees "clap their hands" (Isa. 55:12). It can be said that believers seeking to grow and mature are the real environmentalists! Only through their glorification will the entire creation be healed. In the meantime, corruption continues to bring suffering to humankind.

Involuntary Sufferings Result from A Person's Own Destructive Choices

> Let no one say when he is tempted, "I am tempted by God"; for God cannot be tempted by evil, nor does He Himself tempt anyone. But each one is tempted when he is drawn away by his own desires and enticed. Then, when desire has conceived, it gives birth to sin; and sin, when it is full-grown, brings forth death.
>
> – James 1:13–15

> But let none of you suffer as a murderer, a thief, an evildoer, or as a busybody in other people's matters.
>
> – 1 Peter 4:15

People bring on much of their own suffering. Rampant substance abuse is a huge source of suffering, often resulting in death. Uncontrolled lust destroys families and affects untold numbers of children. Poor personal diet impacts people's health.

God cannot be blamed for each person's personal actions; yet these things have caused the most suffering on a personal level. It seems that what people want is freedom of choice to live how they want, without the consequences or the result.

Yet, the consequences of these poor choices are still involuntary. Just because one may choose to drink and drive, for example, doesn't mean they volunteered to suffer the consequences of a crash.

Involuntary Consequences from Satan's Attacks Allowed by God

> And the LORD said to Satan, "Behold, he is in your hand, but spare his life." So Satan went out from the presence of the LORD, and struck Job with painful boils from the sole of his foot to the crown of his head.
>
> – Job 2:6–7

> And lest I should be exalted above measure by the abundance of the revelations, a thorn in the flesh was given to me, a messenger of Satan to buffet me, lest I be exalted above measure.
>
> – 2 Corinthians 12:7

The first two types of suffering due to sinful nature of man and the corrupted environment are indiscriminate and can happen to anyone on earth. Any citizen of this world — believer or not — can experience those sufferings. The third type of suffering, however, only seems to target God's people.

God allows Satan to do the "dirty work" to test His people. In Job's case, Satan can be seen marshalling his power over health, the weather, and ungodly people, and causing God's people to suffer. But before Satan could do any of those terrible things, he needed God's permission. God *allowed* Satan to test Job, for example, because He knew Job would come out stronger and better because of the testing. It is the same for all of God's people.

After Job's testing, Job saw and knew God differently. Job received back much more than he lost during the testing. Paul (who will be highlighted later in this chapter) also gained much through intense trials.

Even after Satan rebelled against God, he remained God's servant; when he tried to humiliate God, Satan was actually still serving Him. God remained, ultimately, in control of Satan's actions and used them for His purpose.

Voluntary Sufferings For the Ministry of the Word and the Building Up of the Assembly

Believers should participate in Christ's afflictions by being a minister of God's economy.

> Now, I rejoice in sufferings for you, and I fill up that which is behind of the tribulations of Christ in my flesh, for his body, which is the assembly; of which I became minister, according to the dispensation of God which [is] given me towards you to complete the word of God.
>
> – Colossians 1:24–25, DBY

The apostle Paul didn't have to suffer. If he refused God's call to carry out his mission, Paul likely would have become a respected lawyer in the upper class of society. But instead, he rejoiced in being able to suffer in order to minister to the assembly, to complete the Word of God to them. This is called "voluntary suffering."

Paul continued in the sufferings and tribulations of Christ in order to serve people for the assembly. He knew what he was getting into, he knew the sufferings he would experience, and he knew why tribulations would come. In spite of these things, Paul chose to accept and carry out his mission with joy.

Suffering and Enduring as a Soldier, Athlete and Farmer

Paul, writing to his young co-worker Timothy, encouraged him to be strengthened in serving the Lord due to the various difficulties he knew a servant of the Lord would encounter. He gave Timothy three analogies — serving the Lord as a soldier, an athlete, and a farmer — in order to inspire him to be a faithful servant.

> You then, my child, be strengthened by the grace that is in Christ Jesus, and what you have heard from me in the presence of many witnesses entrust to faithful men who will be able to teach others also. Share in suffering as a good soldier of Christ Jesus. No soldier gets entangled in civilian pursuits, since his aim is to please the one who enlisted him. An athlete is not crowned unless he competes according to the rules. It is the hard-working farmer who ought to have the first share of the crops. . . . Remember Jesus Christ, risen from the dead, the offspring of David, as preached in my gospel, for which I am suffering, bound with chains as a criminal. But the word of God is not bound! Therefore, I endure everything for the sake of the elect, that they also may obtain the salvation that is in Christ Jesus with eternal glory.
>
> – 2 Timothy 2:1–7, 8–10, ESV

Making disciples is no easy task. It is a lifelong mission that guarantees much opposition and disappointment; therefore, Paul charged those that follow in his footsteps to be strengthened by grace and be prepared to take part in suffering.

Again, this type of suffering is voluntary. The believer is not forced to serve as a soldier. Many believers are satisfied with simply knowing they are saved from eternal damnation. They have become complacent believers with little to no focus on the mission of the gospel or on the making of disciples. Therefore, they will bypass suffering reserved for the soldiers of Christ. Because so few believers today are willing to suffer the challenges of being a minister of Christ, the Lord's move in the gospel and the building up of the genuine assembly is slow.

Paul reaffirmed again that he was suffering for the gospel. Although he was in prison for the gospel, the gospel was not hindered by his captivity. Instead, it spread and multiplied. Paul was truly transformed from being a persecutor of the saints to a passionate disciple with the heart of Jesus Christ, so much so that Paul would endure all sorts of sufferings that others might receive salvation. It takes this kind of willingness to suffer for salvation to spread and for disciples to be produced.

What were the sufferings for which Paul was preparing Timothy? Paul was not preparing Timothy to do something purposely to hurt himself in order to suffer; rather, as a soldier, Paul knew Timothy would not be entangled with the things of the worldly life. As an athlete, Timothy would serve by the law of the Spirit of life. And as a farmer, Timothy would be faithful and diligent in taking care of his crop in order to bear fruit. The believer who stands firm as a soldier in the warfare of the gospel will automatically forego many of the worldly pleasures. One competing as an athlete cannot freely live according to their old fallen life, but will have to be led by the Spirit's law of life. Finally, the "farmer" who makes disciples by bearing remaining fruit has to be diligent and faithful to plant and water on schedule, without the freedom to serve only when he or she feels like it.

Suffering for the Word and His Testimony

Believers will naturally participate in tribulation, because of the Word and Christ's testimony.

> John, your brother and partner in the tribulation and the kingdom and the patient endurance that are in Jesus, was on the island called Patmos on account of the word of God and the testimony of Jesus.
>
> – Revelation 1:9, ESV

The apostle John also suffered voluntarily on account of the Word of God and the testimony of Jesus. John was not enjoying an island vacation while on Patmos; he was a prisoner, exiled by the Roman government because he would not stop preaching the gospel. John was a partner in the tribulation in Jesus Christ. According to the New Testament, all believers should be partners in tribulation and the kingdom, with the patient endurance of those that are in Jesus Christ.

Believers Voluntarily Bear the Cross of Christ

This voluntary suffering of the cross of Jesus Christ is what Jesus asks His disciples to bear. It is voluntary suffering for the sake of others — for their salvation and growth. Jesus didn't *have* to bear the cross for man; he willingly accepted this mission.

Many Christians mistakenly assume that any kind of suffering is the cross for them. Even some worldly unbelievers say, "That is my cross" when going through difficulties. Some may say, "My wife is mad at me; she is my cross that I am bearing." No, she might be mad because her spouse is lazy and neglects caring for her, but that is not the cross. Others may say, "I am bearing the cross because the drought really hurt my business." No, that is not the cross either; that is making light of the cross and misapplying its meaning. Involuntary sufferings are not the cross, because the cross is only for believers who volunteer. More serious and "spiritual" Christians may think that a form of asceticism (severe self-discipline) is the cross. That means a denial of any enjoyment for their physical and psychological self. They consider the cross to be denial of any pleasure. For example, if they like to look attractive, they should make themselves as plain as possible; if they like gourmet food and drink, they should avoid it at all cost. This kind of Christian will even feel guilty if they find themselves having fun in the world's amusement. Their view of the cross is to voluntarily place themselves in situations where they are devoid of any worldly pleasure. This is not the cross of Christ as described by the Lord in the Bible.

Any suffering that causes the believer to be downcast or to complain about suffering, even if it is for others, is also not the cross of Christ. Bearing the cross of Christ is a matter of joy, rejoicing and hope; it is in the power of the Lord's Spirit for accomplishing the eternal mission of building His eternal dwelling place.

Sufferings Often Causes Believers to Turn to God

Any trials and sufferings, whether involuntary or by choice, often cause believers to turn to God and away from sin and distractions.

> Since therefore Christ suffered in the flesh, arm yourselves with the same way of thinking, for whoever has suffered in the flesh has ceased from sin, so as to live for the rest of the time in the flesh no longer for human passions but for the will of God.
>
> — 1 Peter 4:1–2, ESV

When unbelievers undergo any kind of suffering, there is no hope of any redeeming value. What will they gain from sickness? Or from being cheated of their wealth? Some philosophies may bring comfort in the immediate, such as, "This is an opportunity, think positively!" or "Look for the silver lining." But if sufferings pile up one after another, the unbeliever will become depressed sooner or later.

For believers, however, it is different. Believers have a weapon: *the mind of Christ.* Believers can arm themselves and be prepared for all kinds of suffering. There is only one way to possess the mind of Jesus, and that is for the believer to turn to Him and let Him live in them. Jesus Christ today is not just in the heavens, but He is also in the believers. He is in every part of them, including their minds.

To prepare for future unexpected sufferings, believers need to abide in Christ and let Him abide in them. Then, when suffering comes, they will be able to turn to Jesus immediately in prayer, praise, song, and fellowship.

All sufferings — even involuntary ones — can work out positively to the believer's eternal benefit if they turn to the Lord through them. Even if the believer caused his or her own suffering, turning to the Lord can bring positive results. That is why many have found Christ in prison, though they have committed a crime to be there. Believers armed with the mind of Jesus will be sanctified through suffering. They will cease from sin and live for God. Something so negative will be turned into something positive — and the hinge for this is turning to Jesus Christ, to have *His* mind. While unbelievers dread the thought of calamities befalling them, while they fear evil people bringing pain to their families, while they are anxious about sickness or any kind of pain, believers are ready. They know suffering will help them cease sinning and live the rest of their lives for God. The suffering will turn them to Jesus Christ, to rest in Him. This is spiritual sleep, and every believer needs to experience it regularly. Good sleep and rest in Christ puts everything in the proper perspective, turning the negative into positive.

Proving that Faith Works

> In this you rejoice, though now for a little while, if necessary, you have been grieved by various trials, so that the tested genuineness [or proving] of your faith — more precious than gold that perishes though it is tested by fire — may be found to result in praise and glory and honor at the revelation of Jesus Christ.

> Though you have not seen him, you love him. Though you do not now see him, you believe in him and rejoice with joy that is inexpressible and filled with glory.
>
> – 1 Peter 1:6–8, ESV

> Count it all joy, my brothers, when you meet trials of various kinds, for you know that the testing [proving] of your faith produces steadfastness.
>
> – James 1:2–3, ESV

As previously stated, faith is the ability to substantiate the unseen. Faith can be likened to a sixth sense with which believers can enjoy and realize all that Jesus Christ is and has accomplished in the spiritual realm. In other words, believers are already sitting in the heavens with Christ, and Satan is already defeated; the old creation is dead and buried. To a human being's five senses, this cannot be true; but when faith is activated, a person's presence in the heavens is truer than their presence on earth. That is reality. So, faith is the ability to see and realize the unseen realm of the Spirit.

This is the reason that in the midst of suffering the revelation of Jesus Christ exists, and because of this, the believer's suffering fades. They rejoice in seeing the One they love. Though they cannot see Him with their eyes, Jesus is revealed to them through faith (belief), and they are filled with inexpressible joy and glory.

The believers' faith is really the faith of Jesus Christ. He originated this faith in the believers, and it is a gift of God. Faith is not something that a person can muster up and generate on his or her own. Since faith is something of Christ from God, it does not need testing. It will pass any test all the time, any time. Yet, James writes, "the testing [proving] of your faith produces steadfastness" (James 1:3), and Peter writes about the "tested genuineness [or proving] of your faith" (1 Pet. 1:6).

What, then, does it mean to be tested?

The Greek word used in both "tested genuineness" and "testing" in these verses is the same word, and it is better translated "proving." This means believers are to prove to themselves that their faith works. They may not know how genuine and precious their faith is until they face trials and sufferings. Instead of being depressed and grumbling, they are able to persevere with joy. Their faith is activated in the midst of difficulty, and they see Jesus. They are substantiating that which is real in their environment; therefore, their trials become nothing to them. They received proof of their faith. They now know by experience the genuineness of their faith.

Of course faith is precious, but to the believers that are suffering, the "proving out" or the experience of this faith is more precious than gold. They actually experience being transferred from the worldly to the spiritual, heavenly realm where they see Jesus, resulting in praise, glory and honor. They are no longer in the realm of suffering, but in the realm of glory where they respond with song and praise.

This is what happened with Paul and Silas when they were in prison. They were beaten and chained down in the dungeon of a prison; yet, they were singing and praising God (Acts 16:22–34), and even comforting and caring for a jailer about to kill himself. In the earthly realm, this appeared to be two men of God suffering in prison. But in the realm of faith, Paul and Silas were in the heavens caring for those that were *really* suffering.

Young and new believers may not have the experience of proving their faith and may encounter trepidation when facing any form of suffering. More mature believers have proven the faith of Jesus more and more and have joy in the face of suffering, because they know they can have a good rest and sleep through it. Knowing how to experience Christ's death as spiritual sleep produces steadfastness in the believers. No matter what is thrown at them, they will not tire nor be discouraged, because they are resting in Jesus. *Sleep, then, is being dead to the world and alive to Christ, and experiencing the reality of the crucified and resurrected life of Jesus Christ.*

The Simultaneous Experience of Christ's Death, Resurrection and Ascension

Many believers isolate the various stages of Christ as separate experiences. True, Jesus did die first before resurrecting, and then forty days later ascended. In His experience, these were separate sequential events. But to believers today, they are now part of who Jesus is in His Spirit. Isolating and separating these experiences may cause some to say, "What I need now is Christ's resurrection because I am down." Others may say, "I am troubled by a hard situation; I need to experience Christ's death."

However, *all* aspects of Christ — his death, resurrection and ascension — are a part of Him; when the believer has Christ, they experience each stage simultaneously. This simplifies the experiences for believers, and also puts the focus on Christ rather than an aspect of His work. These stages of Christ are for the believer's experiences; they are distinct, but not separate.

Know Jesus Christ Experientially

> ...that I may know Him [Jesus Christ] and the power of His resurrection, and the fellowship of His sufferings, being conformed to His death.
> – Philippians 3:10

Paul's aspiration was to know Jesus Christ in a way that was experiential to Him. This did not mean simply knowing facts about Him, but *knowing* Him in the way of experience. For example, one may understand the ingredients that go into making a dish, but knowing about the ingredients is much different from experiencing the food by tasting it. Paul aspired to know Jesus Christ by tasting all His goodness. Knowing Him means knowing the power of His resurrection. Paul didn't just know *about* the power of resurrection; he experienced it in the midst of tribulation. Since that was Paul's own experience, nothing could hold him down no matter the opposition. Paul also participated in Christ's suffering through his care for the assembly. He rejoiced in having the privilege of experiencing the same sufferings of Christ as He did for His body. This is what it means to "take part" in His death, the spiritual "sleep" that believers need.

Physically, people go to sleep when they are tired and wake up to start a new day, refreshed. But in the spiritual realm, believers live in the state of being conformed to His death. In other words, believers are always resting. They should never depart from resting in Christ. Whether working or going through trials, they are still resting.

Resting, or living in the reality of death to the old man (the self), should be the believer's daily, moment-by-moment experience. It is in this position of rest — of death — that believers know Jesus experientially. It is in this position they know His resurrection power and participate in the suffering of Jesus for the sake of His body.

The Fruit of the Spirit in Resurrection through Death in Christ

> I have been crucified with Christ; it is no longer I who live, but Christ lives in me; and the [life] which I now live in the flesh I live by faith in the Son of God, who loved me and gave Himself for me.
>
> – Galatians 2:20

> But the fruit of the Spirit is love, joy, peace, longsuffering, kindness, goodness, faithfulness, gentleness, self-control. Against such there is no law. And those [who are] Christ's have crucified the flesh with its passions and desires. If we live in the Spirit, let us also walk in the Spirit.
>
> – Galatians 5:22–25

The "I" that is crucified with Christ that Paul speaks of in Galatians is the "I" before the new birth in Christ. This is the old "I," the "I" without the life of Christ. Since the old "I" is dead, who is the "I" that is now living in the flesh?

That is the new "I" with Christ living in him. The new "I" is the believer living in faith, and Christ living in him. It is a mingled living between the believer and Jesus Christ. Such a person expresses Christ's life through love for people around him, joy that's unquenchable, peace with God and man, and the ability to suffer through all difficulties. Those believers are kind in their actions toward all of creation, and don't have to *put forth effort* to act this way because that is their normal, divinely natural character. It is the fruit of the believer's new life in Christ, the fruit of the Spirit in them. They are not putting up a front; they are living Christ.

A believer that does not "sleep" or live in Christ's death will always try to fulfill God's requirements in his own efforts. He or she will use the natural life of their old man to live out God's requirements. This believer will be exhausted and become a failure in a short time. When a believer finds himself worn-out from being a Christian, depressed by his environment, irritated by people around him or wanting to give up, it is a sign affirming he is not sleeping. If he will just "sleep" in Christ, Christ will live in him and his experiences will return to the positive immediately.

Experiencing the Killing of Jesus that Others May Receive Life

Paul described the death and life of Christ acting simultaneously in 2 Corinthians 4:10–12:

> ....always carrying about in the body the dying of the Lord Jesus, that the life of Jesus also may be manifested in our body. For we who live are always delivered

> to death for Jesus' sake, that the life of Jesus also may be manifested in our mortal
> flesh. So then death is working in us, but life in you.
>
> – 2 Corinthians 4:10–12

Paul didn't bear the death of Christ for a certain period of time before he started to serve Christ to others; rather, while he was experiencing the death of Christ, others were experiencing the life of Christ through Paul. Paul ministered to them in ascension.

As ministers of Christ, Paul and his co-workers experienced tribulation and persecution, but those sufferings did not deactivate or destroy them; rather, they rested in the death of Christ. The life of Christ was manifested, giving life to those that they spoke to. The "death" that was working in them was not the negative death of Satan, but the positive death of Christ. Satan's death is crippling, hopeless, crushing, destructive, and utterly despairing. On the other hand, the death of Christ is restful, comforting, hopeful, and life giving. So while Paul and his co-workers were "sleeping" in Christ's death, Christ's life was working in those to whom Paul was ministering. Although Jesus Christ died 2000 years ago, His death is still active, effective and experiential today.

Being Comforted in Affliction to Comfort Others

> Blessed *be* the God and Father of our Lord Jesus Christ, the Father of mercies
> and God of all comfort, who comforts us in all our affliction, so that we may be
> able to comfort those who are in any affliction, with the comfort with which
> we ourselves are comforted by God. For as we share abundantly in Christ's
> sufferings, so through Christ we share abundantly in comfort too. If we are
> afflicted, it is for your comfort and salvation; and if we are comforted, it is
> for your comfort, which you experience when you patiently endure the same
> sufferings that we suffer.
>
> – 2 Corinthians 1:3–6, ESV

Once again, Paul describes the death, resurrection and ascended life of Christ working simultaneously, so much so that the word "comfort" can be substituted for both His death and the impartation of life. Comfort in the midst of suffering is a much more experiential and identifiable word than even "death" or "life." Just as in the previous example in 2 Corinthians 4:10–12, Paul said in 2 Corinthians 1:3–6 that the experience of Christ's death brings comfort, as does His life released.

In these verses, the God of all comfort is active in the believers' affliction, and in turn becomes a comfort for others as well. God's comfort is eternal; once given, His comfort continues to be passed on from person to person, and generation to generation, to this very day. Believers are presently being comforted by the comfort that was given to Paul. Whatever comfort believers receive today is to be passed on to someone else tomorrow. These are the experiences of the crucified, resurrected and ascended Christ.

A Portrait of a Minister Who Knows How to "Sleep"

> But in everything commending ourselves as God's ministers, in much endurance, in afflictions, in necessities, in straits, in stripes, in prisons, in riots, in labours, in watchings, in fastings, in pureness, in knowledge, in longsuffering, in kindness, in [the] Holy Spirit, in love unfeigned, in [the] word of truth, in [the] power of God; through the arms of righteousness on the right hand and left, through glory and dishonour, through evil report and good report: as deceivers, and true; as unknown, and well known; as dying, and behold, we live; as disciplined, and not put to death; as grieved, but always rejoicing; as poor, but enriching many; as having nothing, and possessing all things. Our mouth is opened to you, Corinthians, our heart is expanded.
>
> – 2 Corinthians 6:4–11, DBY

A person that knows how to sleep spiritually is a mysterious and wonderful person. He or she becomes like Jesus, a person hard to describe, and one who cannot be put into a box. Although hard to understand and figure out, at the same time, this person is an absolute delight to be around. There is something "attractive" about him or her.

In 2 Corinthians 6:4–11, Paul's description of God's ministers almost seems contradictory and impossible…even out of this world. This is because Paul was describing people living in another realm — the realm of the death, resurrection, and ascension of Christ. Such a person's heart is expanding and enlarging to include more and more people with their blessings. They pour out life and make those around them spiritually rich. All believers should be this kind of person, and can be, by being with Jesus and experiencing His death, resurrection, and ascension.

Practice: "Voluntary suffering"

Consider someone whom you want to reach either for the gospel or someone that needs ministry. What might you not want to do in order to gain this person for Christ? Maybe it is as simple as taking some time out to spend with this person, or to give this person something that you don't want to give up, or maybe to forgive this person of some offenses. As you pray for this person, you will realize that you will have to "deny yourself" in order to be effective in reaching this person. Take the resting and empowering Christ through prayer and take action to "voluntarily suffer" for the sake of Christ in reaching this person.

Write down a person's name:

What is the Lord teaching you that you have to deny in order to reach this person?

Part 2

ONE IN TRUTH, HIS WORD

(Chapters 7–14)

I have given them Your word.

> Sanctify them by Your truth. Your word is truth.
>
> . . . that they all may be one, as You, Father, [are] in Me, and I in You; that they also may be one in Us, that the world may believe that You sent Me.
>
> —John 17:14, 17, 21

For the next eight chapters starting from this chapter, the gift of the truth shall be expounded. God's Word is truth, and that is what He has given to the believers that they may be one. Therefore, it is critical to know truth, and to understand truth.

Who (or What) Is the Definition of Truth, according to the Bible?

First and foremost, God as the Word is truth. "In the beginning was the Word and the Word was with God, and the Word was God…and the Word became flesh…full of grace and truth" (John 1:1, 14).

Second, Jesus Christ who is God in the flesh is truth. Truth was revealed in Jesus Christ. Jesus said, "I am the truth" (John 14:6), and Paul declared that "the truth is in Jesus" (Eph. 4:21).

Third, the Spirit is truth. The Scriptures declare the Spirit of truth (John 14:17, 15:26, 16:13; 1 John 4:6), and that the Spirit is truth (1 John 5:6). The Spirit of truth guides believers into all truth by declaring and infusing the reality of all that the Father and the Son are into believers (John 16:13–15).

Fourth, all that the Father, the Son and Spirit have accomplished for His eternal purpose is truth. This includes the death of Jesus Christ on the cross, His resurrection, His ascension and enthronement, and His work of redemption for the forgiveness of sins, justification, the believers' regeneration (new birth) and future glorification. Therefore, the person of the triune God dwelling bodily in Jesus Christ (Col. 2:9) and His work of redemption and regeneration is the Word of truth — that is, the gospel of salvation. It is through believing the truth that people are saved and sealed by the indwelling Spirit (Eph. 1:13). Believers in God's eternal purpose become members of His body — the new man spoken of in Ephesians 2:15. This corporate entity is created and built up into maturity in truth (Eph. 4:24).

Finally, the Word as recorded in the Bible is truth. The Bible conveys the truth, and truth is understood when the Word is made real to a person. The Word, the logos, speaks to people and communicates to their reasoning. When the Word is received, understood, and becomes real to a person, then it is truth. That is why people need to know and come to the full knowledge of the truth (2 Tim. 2:25, 3:7; 1 Tim. 2:4). For example, the Bible says Jesus Christ is God who became man, died for mankind's sin and was resurrected on the third day. Many unbelievers have heard this, but it is not truth or real to them. One day as they consider this word, they will hopefully open their heart and connect with Jesus through faith. At that very moment, the Spirit of truth will enter them and make the word of God that they heard real; they will understand with a living knowledge, and then, that will be truth to them.

Taken together within the New Testament revelation, the meaning of truth is rich and deep. It is God in Jesus Christ as the Spirit with all that they have accomplished for man and in man, which includes the eternal purpose of God's assembly fulfilled in Jesus Christ. Therefore, truth is God Himself, with His life, nature, and essence, intrinsically joined, mingled or blended with humankind. The truth is eternal (2 John 1:2). If it is only temporal and has no effect in eternity, then it is not truth.

What Is __Not__ Truth?

Jesus prayed in John 17 that it is in the truth that believers are made one. Thus, anything that divides believers — things that Christians argue over and become sectarian over — is not truth. Most Christian groups agree that truth is what was outlined above. Any doctrines not defined as truth are non-essential. What have divided Christians are non-essential doctrines, various Christian practices, or worldly causes. Christians have been divided, have fought over, and have rejected each other over some of the smallest things such as musical style in worship, whether women should have their head covered, whether the rapture is pre-, mid-, or post-tribulation, methods of baptism, and even methods of leadership. There are literally thousands of such things that have divided Christians; yet, the truth remains the same. A believer that has a growing understanding of the truth stays anchored in the truth and will not be distracted by positioning themselves in the non-essentials; they will remain one with all believers.

The tactic of the enemy (Satan) is to use men and women — specifically Christian men and women — to elevate non-essential doctrines and practices and eventually form groups and churches around those doctrines. For example, a major dividing doctrinal point among Christians is centered on the debate over predestination or free will. Churches have been grouped together on one side or the other. Both sides can show supporting Bible verses and speak of how their doctrine is better for Christians, but the fact is, neither of those doctrines died for humankind or was resurrected! Nowhere in the Scriptures does it say that in order to receive eternal life a person needs to believe in one of these doctrines. And ultimately, it does not matter in eternity which doctrine is correct. Therefore, neither doctrine is truth, and certainly not worth dividing over. Whether a person espouses one side or the other, or even both, is not a problem unless it becomes a condition for fellowship — and a rejection of those with contrary views.

Another major point of division is whether the Holy Spirit is still doing works of power as in the days of the early apostles, or if these works of power have ceased. Again, using the measurement above, this belief is not truth either way. A person who is established in the truth will be able to have fellowship and receive believers no matter their doctrinal position or preference. Those who are not standing in truth may be so biased with their personal doctrinal stance that they end up taking an extreme stand. For example, some may not acknowledge that a genuine miraculous healing today can be from God; others may belittle believers for not receiving any manifestation of the Holy Spirit.

Practices are much more common than doctrinal differences in dividing believers. For example, the moment a person believes in Christ and receives salvation, that person is regenerated in Christ; this is biblical truth. It is faith that brings a person into Christ. Baptism is a physical symbol declaring the truth of being in Christ. While every believer agrees with the truth that it is uniquely faith that brings a person into Jesus Christ, many sectarian groups have formed over the physical symbol of baptism. Some insist on water baptism, while others insist baptism has to be by immersion and not by sprinkling. Still others within the same immersion camp, insist that the following phrase has to be recited at baptism: "In the name of the Father and of the Son and of the Holy Spirit." Others insist that the wording should be: "In the name of Jesus Christ." All of the above are various ways to practice baptism, but not the truth of being immersed into Jesus Christ, the triune God. Different teachings on baptism use different scriptural verses as their foundation, and many believers are helped by their way of baptism. However, it is against the truth to use any of these particular practices to build up an entire sectarian group that hinders believers in that group from accepting and having fellowship with other believers if they do not hold to the same practice.

I was with a group of believers that were confident of their knowledge of the truth, who declared they sought to build the one body of Christ. Though they were zealous for this oneness of the body, their practice of this oneness involved a single leadership structure. When I didn't agree with such a structure, the leadership told believers not to participate in the fellowship in my home. So their way of practicing became sectarian. This personal experience magnified the difference between truth and practices. Just about all Christian practices stem from some verse or principle in the Bible; undoubtedly, many people receive help from various practices, but no matter how helpful they are, they should not evolve into a sectarian system. What subtlety in damaging the body of Christ.

Easy to Be Distracted Away from the Truth

At this juncture, let's consider the story in Matthew 17 because it shows how easily and quickly the Lord's disciples forgot the revelation that they received just eight days earlier. Here, Jesus brought a few of His disciples up to a high mountain, and Peter was included — one who recently received the revelation concerning Jesus being the Christ, the Son of God (in chapter 16). On this mountain, Jesus was transfigured before them; He became shining as the sun. Together with this glorious Jesus were Moses and Elijah also standing there talking with Jesus. Peter grew excited and immediately said that they should make three tabernacles, one for each of them. Moses represented the law given by God since Moses gave the law (John 1:17); therefore, many times the law was associated with Moses throughout the Bible. After Moses, the major prophet who did many works of miraculous power was Elijah. He was the only prophet prominently named in the New Testament, twenty-nine times; therefore, Elijah represents the prophets with God's supernatural power.

When encountering all three, Peter viewed them the same: Jesus, Moses, and Elijah. Since he wanted to build three tabernacles, one for each, this showed that Peter considered them with equal standing, requiring equal reverence. But then the Father spoke from a cloud and said, "This is my beloved Son, hear Him." The disciples fell down in fear of such a voice. When Jesus came to lift them up, and when they looked up, they saw "no one, but Jesus alone." Both Moses and Elijah were gone; only Jesus was left for them to look at.

This is the experience of most Christians. They are saved by a wonderful revelation concerning Jesus being the Christ, the Son of the living God. They then immediately view the law and so many other items on an equal level as Jesus. "Now that Jesus saved me," they think, "I have to learn these doctrines, keep these laws, pursue these spiritual gifts, do these works, and on and on." Even though Jesus is the shining One, from their perspective, Jesus is now just another item among a long list of things. No, no, no! Another revelation is needed after believing — that there is no one else other than Jesus. It is not Jesus plus this and that. It is Jesus Himself alone! The goal for Part 2 is to focus believers back to Jesus Christ — who He is, what He has done, and what He is doing.

It is unfortunate that most believers, when they study the Bible, consider it elementary to stay on Jesus Christ. There is a thought that the "deeper truth" is to understand how to behave as a Christian, understand the end times, learn self-denial, obtain a special gift from God, or many other topics. Some think, "I already know that Jesus Christ died and resurrected; lets learn about all the other things in the Bible." One can study, know, and discuss the many topics in the Bible, and it is advisable to read the Bible from cover to cover thoroughly, but a mature believer is one who can only be satisfied with the excellence of the knowledge of Jesus Christ (Phil. 3:8–15). This person has lost the taste for all peripheral topics other than Jesus Christ, and His pursuit of the truth is to see and know how Jesus Christ's person and work is revealed in the pages of the Bible. There is a recognition and appreciation that Jesus is unsearchable and unlimited in His riches; therefore, it is an eternal pursuit to come to the full knowledge of the Son of God.

What will be covered in these chapters are major points that affect the general understanding of the truth. The peripheral points outside this sphere (or the truth) may be considered healthy teachings and practices for living and relationships, depending on whether they help believers to seek the Lord Jesus or function in the body. These "healthy teachings and practices" are conditional based on environment, culture, and individual needs at the time. For example, a teaching concerning head-coverings for women was clearly helpful during Paul's environment, but may not be in some cultures today. Certainly any such teachings and practices should not be points of contention that break fellowship among believers. Even disagreements concerning the deeper and richer points of truth such as the triune nature of God should never break fellowship. Only the essential faith that brings salvation determines whether one is in the fellowship of Jesus Christ, and this faith is the only item that believers should contend for or insist on.

An Overview of the Points of the Truth

The points below will be covered in this chapter. However, not every point is considered to be truth according to the definition given in previous pages. Some of the points would be classified as healthy teachings. Within this sphere of truth is the essential faith concerning Jesus Christ that brings man salvation and the knowledge of the Son of God—the nourishment for building up. This was explained in Chapter 2 concerning Ephesians 4:13–15. Saving faith is simple: Jesus is God who became man to die on the cross for man's sins; He was resurrected on the third day with a spiritual form that can indwell His believers. The knowledge of the Son of God is the entire truth that is unsearchably rich. His riches cannot be exhausted. Therefore what is presented can only be a framework of the truth for believers to appreciate so that their pursuit of the truth has a clear direction.

1. Jesus Christ, His person—He is both God and man. This point is essential to a believers' faith. This is what a person must believe in order to have salvation and be born of God.

2. Jesus Christ, His work—Jesus died on the cross for man's sin, resurrected on the third day, and ascended to be Lord of all. As the Spirit, He is now indwelling His believers, His one body. These matters are also essential: One cannot claim to be a follower of Christ, a believer in Him, without clearly accepting this sequence of events as the work of Jesus Christ.

3. Man, His creation and fall—This chapter would not be considered as truth. There can be disagreement among believers whether human beings possess original sin, what the makeup of man is, or whether his spirit is the same as his soul. However, this chapter offers Scripture that will open up the reader's understanding (or consideration) concerning humankind; each person can then come to their own conviction.

4. God's redemption and salvation—This chapter unveils the effect of the work of the Lord Jesus when applied to humankind. How this chapter slices and dices various words may result in differing opinions among believers, but the overall effect on man's sins is forgiveness resulting from Christ's redemption and man's salvation through the work of Jesus Christ. This is truth.

5. God's economy—Although this point is infrequently mentioned among Christians, it is God's purpose and method of accomplishing His eternal goal through Jesus Christ. Therefore, it is truth. The more believers understand and enjoy God's economy, the more they can and will be one with other believers. God's economy is a description of how Jesus Christ is working out God's plan.

6. The assembly (ekklesia) is one—This is also truth. The assembly is not essential for salvation, in the sense that a person does not have to believe this point in order to be saved. However, it is the result and goal of the person and work of Christ.

It is for the one assembly that He died and for which He continues to minister in resurrection until the oneness of the assembly is manifested for eternity.

7. The practical assembly — This was the early apostles' practice, as shown in the Scriptures of the building up of the one assembly. Believers should give allowances liberally to each believer's practices. Differing practices of assembly should not break the bond of the one fellowship in the body of Christ. However, when believers practice and function closer and closer to the truth of the one body, they will have a practical and manifested oneness.

8. The new covenant — This is also truth. It is for the enacting of the new covenant that Jesus Christ died and resurrected. Additionally, the essence and power of the new covenant is the indestructible life of the Lord Jesus Christ. It is in the new covenant that believers are made one.

7
JESUS CHRIST – HIS PERSON

Jesus Christ: The Topic of the Entire Bible

First, let's consider the person of Jesus Christ. *Who is He?* When people read the Bible, they read for various reasons and often come away with different impressions. A person could read the Bible for the intriguing stories. Another might read to learn morality and ethics, while still others read to learn law and history. However, what is the real goal of the Bible?

God's intention is to reveal His purpose — hidden and fulfilled in the person and work of Jesus Christ. If a person reads the Bible and misses Jesus Christ, it is like they never read the Bible. It would be like reading a book on American History, and, at the end, knowing nothing about the United States. Let's look at the Bible itself, to see what it reveals as the main topic in its pages.

The New Testament Starts and Ends with Jesus Christ

> Book of the generation of Jesus Christ, Son of David, Son of Abraham.
> – Matthew 1:1, DBY

The very first verse of the gospel of Matthew, the first book of the New Testament, says it is the book of the generation of Jesus Christ. Some translations use the term "historical records" of Jesus Christ. Some believe the word "book" in this verse only refers to Jesus' genealogy, those who came before Him; but the point of any person's genealogy is to bring focus on that person based on history. God in His sovereignty designed this to be the first verse for the entire book of the New Testament. This verse can then be applied to the entire New Testament, *the* book that is about Jesus Christ. It is a book about where He came from, what He did, what He is doing, and who He is in eternity.

The New Testament begins with Jesus' ancestry spanning back to King David and Abraham, and continues with His birth, His youth, His work, His teachings, His life, His death, His resurrection, and His continuation with His disciples through His Spirit. In another section of the New Testament, in a section written by John, the apostle says that Jesus Christ is God without a beginning. Jesus created all things, and He put on flesh to become a man. In yet another section of this book, the writer describes Jesus living in His disciples. As a result of their preaching about Jesus Christ, those disciples were multiplied. Believers in Him became His enlargement, His body — His assembly.

Also recorded in this book are various letters written by apostles to woo believers back to Jesus Christ, since many were becoming distracted and turning away to other things such as laws and meaningless philosophies. Satan, the enemy, did his best to confuse believers, distract them, and pull them away from the simplicity that is in Jesus Christ. The apostles, on the other hand, made it their life's work to keep believers focused on *Christ*.

Revelation: The Unveiling of Jesus Christ

Revelation, the last book of the Bible, is the conclusion of this book of the New Testament of Jesus Christ.

> The Revelation of Jesus Christ, which God gave Him to show His servants —
> things which must shortly take place. And He sent and signified [it] by His angel
> to His servant John.
>
> – Revelation 1:1

> He who testifies to these things says, "Surely I am coming quickly." Amen. Even
> so, come, Lord Jesus! The grace of our Lord Jesus Christ *be* with you all. Amen.
>
> – Revelation 22:20–21

In fact, Revelation is the end for the *entire* Bible, both the Old and the New Testaments. In this last record written by John, the apostle begins by saying that it is "the revelation of Jesus Christ" (Rev. 1:1). Yes, Revelation includes graphic descriptions of the end times in the form of signs and wonders, but if the reader misses the unveiling of Jesus Christ, then they miss the actual revelation. The purpose of the entire book of the New Testament from Matthew to Revelation is to unveil Jesus Christ — His person and His work.

Finally, the last two verses of this book conclude with Jesus Christ coming again, and the joy and rejoicing of Jesus Christ dwelling physically and visibly with all the saints, His believers.

Jesus Christ is the subject and focus of the entire New Testament.

The Old Testament Speaks of Jesus Christ in Prophecies, Types and Allegories

> You search the Scriptures, for in them you think you have eternal life; and these
> are they which testify of Me. But you are not willing to come to Me that you may
> have life.
>
> – John 5:39–40

> Then He said to them, "These *are* the words which I spoke to you while I was
> still with you, that all things must be fulfilled which were written in the Law of
> Moses and *the* Prophets and *the* Psalms concerning Me." And He opened their
> understanding, that they might comprehend the Scriptures.
>
> – Luke 24:44–45

During Jesus' time on earth, the Pharisees (can be considered the religious people of the day) were persecuting Jesus and sought to kill Him. These Jews were very familiar with the Scriptures, which, at the time, included only the Old Testament. As religious people, they searched and studied the Scriptures diligently, but focused intently on the Law. They used God's command to keep the Sabbath as a reason to persecute Jesus; in their minds, they believed He had broken this religious law by healing on the Sabbath (Luke 13:14).

Jesus told the Pharisees, however, that they got it completely wrong. Instead of drawing laws from the Scriptures that cannot give life, they should have realized the purpose of the Scriptures was to testify concerning Jesus Christ. If they knew this, they would have come to Jesus for eternal life. Everything in the Old Testament Scriptures, which were written hundreds of years before the birth of Jesus Christ, pointed to the person and the purpose of Jesus. When a person reads the Scriptures in this way, as originally intended, they will come to Jesus Christ for eternal life.

The gospel of Luke reveals how a person's mind may be opened to understand the Scriptures: by looking for and seeing Jesus in the Law, in the prophets and in the psalms. These three sections comprise the entire Old Testament and each makes Jesus Christ known through types, allegories and prophecies. When someone looks for anything other than Jesus when reading the Scriptures, their mind will remain closed, and they will not truly understand Scripture. May the readers of *this* book be directed to Jesus Christ with an open mind to really understand the Bible!

Let's consider a few examples of how the Old Testament speaks of Jesus Christ.

Adam, the First Man Created by God

Genesis begins with creation. Adam, the first man, completed God's creation. Paul wrote in Romans 5:14 that Adam was a type of Jesus Christ. Jesus was referred to as the last Adam in 1 Corinthians 15:45. That means that the real man was not Adam, but Jesus; He is the man that actually fulfills God's purpose which the first Adam failed to do. As the real man, Jesus Christ both expresses God and subdues God's enemies completely.

The Tree of Life in Genesis

In Genesis, man was given to eat of the Tree of Life. Eating of the Tree of Life would have given man eternal life (Gen. 3:22). The Tree of Life in Genesis is a picture of Jesus Christ, the real Tree of Life for man to eat to have eternal life. Since Jesus is life (John 14:6), and He is also the vine tree (John 15:1; Rev 22:2), He is, therefore, the Tree of Life for man to eat to have eternal life.

The Passover Lamb in Exodus

In Exodus, before the tenth plague was to come on Egypt to kill the first born of the land, God told Moses to instruct each family to kill a lamb. They were to then paint its blood on the outside of the house on the doorposts, and eat the lamb. This lamb was called the "Passover" lamb because God's judgment "passed over" the houses when He saw the lamb's blood.

Jesus is the *real* Passover Lamb of God (John 1:29) that was slain to take away the sins of the world. His blood satisfied God's judgment on mankind, and His flesh is for man to eat (John 6:53).

Manna in Exodus

During Israel's journey through the wilderness for forty years, the Israelites received bread from heaven six days each week to sustain them. This bread was called "manna." This manna in the Old Testament, however, was not the real bread from heaven. When Jesus came He declared He is the real bread from heaven; those who ate manna died in the wilderness, but anyone that eats Him as the bread of life shall have eternal life (John 6:32–35).

The Tabernacle and the Temple Built by Israel

A major portion of the story of Israel surrounds the tabernacle and temple. Jesus is the real tabernacle where God dwells among men (John 1:14), and the true temple that was destroyed and raised up in three days (John 2:19). In resurrection, Jesus as the real temple was enlarged to include all believers in Jesus (Eph. 2:21–22). He is the real temple God wanted in the Old Testament.

These are just a few examples that show how Jesus Christ is the focus of the entire Old Testament. There are volumes of books available today that discuss the various types, figures, and prophecies of Jesus Christ. The hidden riches of Christ will continue to be discovered by those who seek Him while reading the Old Testament.

Witness to See Jesus in the "Things"

> But rise and stand upon your feet, for I have appeared to you for this purpose, to appoint you as a servant and witness to *the things* in which you have seen me and to those in which I will appear to you.
>
> – Act 26:16, ESV (emphasis added)

The Lord appeared to Paul and called Him to be a servant and a witness of Jesus Christ. The Lord showed him many things, and in each he was to see Jesus. A few of these "things" included:

- Adam is Jesus Christ, the real man (Rom. 5:14)
- Husband and wife is Jesus Christ and His body, the wife, the assembly (Eph. 5:23–32)
- The good land is the expansive and all-inclusive Jesus Christ (Col. 1:12)
- Melchizedek is Jesus Christ who is ministering bread and wine (Heb. 5)
- Sarah and Hagar is the grace of Jesus Christ versus the enslaving law (Gal. 4:24)

Paul saw many things when caught up in the "third heaven" into paradise (2 Cor. 12:2–4). Imagine how many books might have been written about this experience had it happened to someone else! However, Scripture says Paul didn't have the heart to talk about it; he was called to be a witness to Jesus alone, and no other thing. When something was not about Jesus, Paul doubted if it was necessary to talk about it at all (see the example of marriage in 1 Cor. 7:25–40).

Today, Christians have seen and heard many things on various topics, or read books about such things as the end times, Christian marriage, raising children, Christian finance, leadership, miraculous gifts, predestination and so on. However, how much is Jesus unveiled in these topics? If Jesus is not unveiled and witnessed, those topics do not bear much spiritual value. In fact, the things themselves can divert people away from Jesus Christ.

Many things can distract believers. It is time to come back to see and witness Jesus Christ.

Who, or What, Is God?

God Is the Self-Existing One

'The God of your fathers has sent me to you,' and they say to me, 'What is His name?' what shall I say to them?' And God said to Moses, 'I AM WHO I AM.' And He said, 'Thus you shall say to the children of Israel, 'I AM has sent me to you.'

– Exodus 3:13–14

Therefore I [Jesus] said to you that you will die in your sins; for if you do not believe that I am *He*, you will die in your sins.

– John 8:24

When Moses asked God to reveal His name, God answered, "I AM." The word "I AM" in Hebrew means, "be" or "existing."[11] God simply *is*. He is self-existing, but He also *existed*. The Hebrew word Jehovah (or Yahweh) is derived from "the existing one"; therefore, "Jehovah" or "Yahweh" means the same as "I AM," or "the existing one."[12] The self-existing one without a beginning or ending is the very name of God. That is who God is. He is the "I AM."

Jesus said in John 8:24 that men must believe that He is the "I AM" in order to be saved. In the translation above, the "He" was added; it was not there in the original Greek. Jesus said that *He is the I AM*. He is the same I AM as the I AM in the Old Testament. There is only one I AM. In the Old Testament the I AM is called Jehovah. In the New Testament, He is called Jesus. Jesus is the very self-existing God. Unless men believe that Jesus is the I AM, they will die in their sins.

"Jesus" is the transliteration of the name "Joshua" in Hebrew. The etymology of the word Joshua comes from two words: "Jehovah" and "save." Thus, Jesus literally means, "Jehovah saves."[13] Jesus is the very Jehovah, the name of God in the Old Testament, the I AM, who came to save. Jesus is not another person sent by God to save, but *He is God Himself* who came to save.

God Is the Creator and Source of All Things

In the beginning God created the heavens and the earth.

– Genesis 1:1

---

11   Gesenius' Hebrew-Chaldee Lexicon for "I am"
12   Gesenius' Hebrew-Chaldee Lexicon for "Jehovah"
13   Vine's Expository Dictionary for "Jesus"

> Thus says God the LORD, Who created the heavens and stretched them out, Who spread forth the earth and that which comes from it, Who gives breath to the people on it, And spirit to those who walk on it.
>
> — Isaiah 42:5

God, as the always-existing one with no beginning or ending, created. God is the Creator. He created the heavens and the earth, and gave breath (life) to all those living on the earth. This is the second characteristic of God: He is the Creator. Without Him, nothing would exist. God existed on His own and through Him all things came into existence. This is a definition of God.

> In the beginning was the Word, and the Word was with God, and the Word was God. He was in the beginning with God. All things were made through Him, and without Him nothing was made that was made.
>
> — John 1:1–3

The Word — Jesus — was God. Since God is both singular (one) and plural (three), the Word was both *with* God and *is* God. The Word as God was the Creator. All things were made through Jesus as the Word, and without Him, nothing exists. These and other verses (see Col. 1:15–16) make it clear that Jesus Christ is the Creator, since He is God.

God Is the Source of all Life

> Nor is He [God] worshiped with men's hands, as though He needed anything, since He gives to all life, breath, and all things.
>
> — Act 17:25

> (as it is written, "I have made you [Abraham] a father of many nations") in the presence of Him whom he believed — God, who gives life to the dead and calls those things which do not exist as though they did.
>
> — Romans 4:17

God is the one who refers to things that do not exist "as though they did" (creation), but also gives life to all things — even life to the dead. God is the author and giver of life. He initiated life, and He sustains it. Satan, God's enemy, is death. His mission is to kill — to end life.

> For as the Father raises the dead and gives life to them, even so the Son gives life to whom He will.
>
> — John 5:21

Jesus, the Son of God, does the same. As God, Jesus has the same life giving ability, and grants life to whomever He desires. The Son and the Father are one God. Jesus is the self-existing and ever existing I AM. He is the Creator and gives life. Jesus is nothing less than God Himself.

God Is Omnipotent, Omnipresent and Omniscient

"I am the Alpha and the Omega," says the Lord God, "who is and who was and who is to come, the Almighty."

– Revelation 1:8

I am [Jesus Christ] the Alpha and the Omega, the Beginning and the End, the First and the Last.

– Revelation 22:13

"Omnipotent" means "all-powerful" or "all-dominion." That God is omnipotent means He has power, authority and dominion over all things. The word "almighty" in the original Greek literally means all-powerful or omnipotent.[14] God is omnipotent, and so is Jesus Christ. It is not clear from Revelation 1:8 who God was referring to, but Revelation 22:13 answers that question: *Jesus* is the Alpha and Omega declared in Revelation 1:8. Jesus as God is the almighty, omnipotent one.

Can anyone hide himself in secret places, So I shall not see him?" says the LORD; "Do I not fill heaven and earth?" says the LORD.

– Jeremiah 23:24

For where two or three are gathered together in My name, I am there in the midst of them.

– Matthew 18:20

God's omnipresence means He is everywhere, even throughout time and space. There is not one place in the entire universe, or time period, that God's presence does not occupy. There is nowhere to hide from God. In space, on earth, or even under the earth, God is there.

Jesus is also omnipresent. Two thousand years after His birth, death and resurrection, Jesus is still everywhere. There is not a place in the universe where He is not. Anyone who calls on the Lord Jesus will find Him, wherever the caller's location.

Declaring the end from the beginning, and from ancient times [things] that are not [yet] done; saying, 'My counsel shall stand, and I will do all My pleasure.'

– Isaiah 46:10

But Jesus, knowing their thoughts, said, "Why do you think evil in your hearts?

– Matthew 9:4

God is also omniscient. This means He knows all things, before things even take place or exist. He knows what is in the hearts of man, and He knows their thoughts. There is no place for mankind to hide physically, and even the thoughts of men cannot be hidden from Jesus Christ.

14   Strong's Definition for "Almighty"

God Is One–Three: The Trinity, or Triune God
God Is One (Singular)

> ...and that there is no other God but one.
>
> – 1 Corinthians 8:4

I am the LORD, and there is no other; There is no God besides Me. I will gird you, though you have not known Me.

– Isaiah 45:5

The Bible teaches there is only one unique God in the universe. The word "one" in 1 Corinthians 8:4 in the original Greek is *heis,* the word for the numeral "one."[15] It is a singular word, indicating there is no other God besides the one God. This is what "monotheist" means: one God.

God Is Three, Existing at the Same Time

> Then God said, "Let Us make man in Our image, according to Our likeness..." So God created man in His own image; in the image of God He created him; male and female He created them.
>
> – Genesis 1:26a–27

> Also I heard the voice of the Lord, saying: "Whom shall I send, and who will go for Us?" Then I said, "Here am I! Send me."
>
> – Isaiah 6:8

Although Judaism does not believe that God is both one and three, the Jewish Bible or the Torah (the Old Testament) gave clear indications that God is indeed one and yet three. The very first chapter of Genesis says, "Then God (singular) said, 'let Us make man in Our image according to Our likeness'" (Gen. 1:26a). The words "Us" and "Our" are both plural in number. Then in verse 27, Genesis reverts back to using the singular pronoun "His": "So God created man in His own image." The mystery of God as both singular and plural was revealed in the very first words of the Bible! This conflict of pronouns used for deity also occurs in Isaiah 6:8: "Whom shall *I* send, And who will go for *Us*?" Did Isaiah mean "I," or "us"?

The revelation of the Bible shows Isaiah meant *it is both*. If God is purely one, there is no ground for plural pronouns, but the Old Testament does not clarify how many are included.

This, however, is revealed and affirmed in the New Testament. The number THREE is clearly defined within the singular God:

> "Go therefore and make disciples of all the nations, baptizing them in the name of the Father and of the Son and of the Holy Spirit.
>
> – Matthew 28:19

---

15   Vine's Expository Dictionary

The one God who is also three is clearly referenced in Matthew 28. In fact, this is a foundational concept that runs throughout the New Testament from the beginning of Matthew to the last words of Revelation: the one–three God is clearly defined and interwoven throughout. The three are the Father, Son, and Holy Spirit. The words "Trinity" or "triune God" have been coined to describe the God who is both one and three. God being triune is a mystery that cannot be fully explained, but can be enjoyed, appreciated, and experienced by all believers.

Matthew refers to a singular name for three in 28:19: the Father, Son, and the Holy Spirit…three persons, so to speak, but only *one* name. When a person calls on His name, they receive all three. When baptized into His name, people are immersed into all three. Believers are in the Father, in the Son, and in the Holy Spirit. This is truly a wondrous mystery!

The name of God, the "I AM," always existed with no beginning or ending, and it applies to all three. The Father, the Son, and the Holy Spirit existed from eternity to eternity and each existed simultaneously. They existed within each other — never in conflict but in perfect harmony — because they are in fact, one God. Believers cannot fully explain how this works, but they can accept their one God is also three.

Though distinct, the three are not separate. If a person focuses on "three" too much, they, in reality, worship three gods or are a "tri-theist." If a person emphasizes "one" too much, they may lose God's distinction of being three. The Bible does not teach that the one God is sometimes the Father, switching at times to the Son, and becoming another mode of the Spirit at other times. This is called *modalism*,[16] and it is not the description of the Trinity in the Bible. Both errors are because of the limits of the human mind. People try to logically define the mystery of the one–three God, who is not able to be logically defined! Believers need to accept by faith that God is one and three, existing simultaneously from eternity to eternity, but never separate the three; they exist within one another.

> The grace of the Lord Jesus Christ, and the love of God, and the communion of the Holy Spirit be with you all. Amen.
>
> – 2 Corinthians 13:14

In the Old Testament, where there is a clear separation between God in heaven and man on earth, God in the singular is fully unveiled. In the New Testament, where God's intention of being joined with man is realized, the three are unveiled and emphasized. Paul unveiled the three in 2 Corinthians 13:14; man can now apply and experience the triune God, who was not seen as nor was available as three in the Old Testament.

The love of God the Father, the grace or enjoyment of the Son, and the fellowship of the Holy Spirit are practical and experiential for all situations now.

In the Old Testament the focus of the relationship between God and man was evidenced through the Law; God was seen primarily as either a judge or a giver of physical and material blessings. While man was either keeping or breaking God's Law on earth, God in heaven

16   http://www.theopedia.com/modalism

was judging or blessing man based on one or the other. This relationship is codified by what is known as the old covenant.

In the New Testament, however, God's purpose is revealed: to have a life relationship directly with man. God desires to participate in human life, and He longs for man to participate in His divine life. God wants to be in man and wants man to dwell in Him in perfect, inseparable unity.

For this purpose, the one God is unveiled as three: Father, Son, and Holy Spirit. God's desire to be one with man originated out of His love — the love of the Father for many sons. God as the Father was rarely mentioned in the Old Testament, whereas the Father God is prominently revealed throughout the New Testament. The Son as the Lord was sent to solve man's problem of sin through His redemption and to give the divine eternal life to man. This is grace.

Finally, the Holy Spirit brings man into this same fellowship within the Trinity. Believers participate in all that the Father's love entails and the Lord's grace provides. This fellowship is available for believers 24/7 wherever they are, and in whatever circumstances they find themselves. Through this fellowship, God as the Father fulfills His joy of having many sons within the sphere of the triune God (Eph. 1:5).

"Love," "grace" and "fellowship" are wonderful words describing the experiential relationship between God and man. In order for man to be included within the Trinity, all three — love, grace and fellowship — work together to fulfill God's awesome purpose. Without the love of the Father God, there would be no such purpose. Without the coming grace of the Son, the Father's plan would not be realized. And without the fellowship of the Spirit, there would no way for man to be included and brought into the participation of all the divine riches contained in God's divine life and nature. God, one and yet three, cannot be fully analyzed, understood, or explained. But because He is one–three, God can be enjoyed and experienced through the deepest union that exists: the oneness between God and man.

Recall again the focus of John 17 — *Jesus' prayer that believers be one.* The foundational concept of John 17 is the Trinity, the source of oneness among all believers. The first gift discussed in John 17 was eternal life, the Father's name; the second gift was the Son who exists as the Word, the truth; and the third gift was His glory through the Lord's Spirit (2 Cor. 3:18). The first gift does not need any explanation: The name to be kept in is clearly the Father. The second gift is the Word. John 1:1 clearly reveals the Son, Jesus, is the Word. The third gift is the Lord Jesus' glory manifested through service, or ministry. Paul discussed the apostles as ministers of the new covenant, or ministers of the Spirit, in 2 Corinthians 3. The chapter ends with the apostles being transformed into the same image as the Lord Jesus, from glory to glory. It is through ministering to people that believers behold the Lord and receive His glory through the Spirit.

Therefore, the source and the structure of oneness among believers occur through knowing the triune God in a real and experiential way.

Jesus Christ Is the Embodiment of God

> For in Him [Jesus Christ] dwells all the fullness of the Godhead bodily.
>
> – Colossians 2:9

> To them belong the patriarchs, and from their race, according to the flesh, is the Christ, who is God over all, blessed forever. Amen.
>
> – Romans 9:5, ESV

Jesus, who is I AM, came in a bodily form. Colossians 2:9 reveals the entire Godhead — the fullness of deity (Father, Son and Spirit), dwells inside the body of Jesus. It is too wonderful to even attempt to explain this awesome reality. Jesus Christ contains the entire triune God because He *is* God. He is not just a part of God, or even a third of God. He is the entire fullness of God. There is no other God outside of Jesus Christ.

As shown earlier, Jesus Christ is the subject, center, and focus of the whole Bible but especially the New Testament. He is unveiled in plain words. As the focus, Jesus Christ is God in fullness and in His entirety.

Jesus Is the Son, He Is the True God, and He Is Equal to God

> And we know that the Son of God has come and has given us an understanding, that we may know Him who is true; and we are in Him who is true, in His Son Jesus Christ. This is the true God and eternal life.
>
> – 1 John 5:20

The Son of God, who is Jesus Christ, came that believers might not only know Him but also be in Him. The apostle John affirms in 1 John 5:20 that Jesus Christ is the Son of God, and the Son of God is the true God. The true God means there is no other God beside Him.

> Therefore the Jews sought all the more to kill Him, because He not only broke the Sabbath, but also said that God was His Father, making Himself equal with God.
>
> – John 5:18

When hearing that Jesus is the Son of God, most people, including some Christians, think Jesus as the Son of God is somehow less than the Father. They misunderstand the Trinity, and think the Father must be higher in rank and have more authority than the Son since the Father should have existed before the Son. However, John 5:18 says Jesus made himself completely equal with God by calling God His Father. He is not less than God, or inferior; He is equal, the same as God.

In the Bible, the relationship between God the Father and God the Son is not one of birth; this would mean the Father existed first and gave birth to the Son. Rather, the Father may be considered as the invisible source, and the Son is the expression, or the image of that which is invisible (John 1:18).

Jesus, the Expression of the Father

Jesus is the expression of the Father, and is even *called* the Father, because He and the Father are one.

> Jesus said to him, "Have I been with you so long, and you still do not know me, Philip? Whoever has seen me has seen the Father. How can you say, 'Show us the Father'?
>
> – John 14:9, ESV

It is impossible to see the Father. However, because Jesus is the manifestation of the Father, seeing Jesus is the same as seeing the Father. Searching for the Father outside of Jesus is a complete waste of time and energy, but when the believer sees Jesus, he sees the Father fully expressed.

> For to us a child is born, to us a son is given; and the government shall be upon his shoulder, and his name shall be called Wonderful Counselor, Mighty God, Everlasting Father, Prince of Peace.
>
> – Isaiah 9:6, ESV

Tucked away in Isaiah 9:6 is a wonderful prophecy concerning Jesus. A child, born of a human virgin, is the unique mighty God of the universe. This is the faith of Jesus Christ: He was born of a virgin, yet He is the *mighty God.* Jesus is also, "Immanuel," which is translated, "God with us'" (Matt. 1:23).

Believing this gives man life, but one should also believe the rest of the verse: the Son is called the *everlasting Father.* Just as the child (Jesus) is God, the Son (Jesus) is the Father. He is truly wonderful! He came as a child, but He is called the mighty God. He came as the Son, but He is called the everlasting father. Therefore, He is a child and God, the Son and the Father.

> I [Jesus] and the Father are one.
>
> – John 10:30, ESV

> Believe me that I am in the Father and the Father is in me, or else believe on account of the works themselves.
>
> – John 14:11, ESV

The Son and the Father are inseparable from one another; though two, they are really only one. The word "one" in John 10:30 is, again, the *number* one. Jesus and the Father are literally only one person. Within this one person dwells the Father and the Son, and this one person is Jesus Christ. Jesus Christ is the Son with the Father. Jesus, the "I AM" and "Jehovah saves," is the complete God, the Son and the Father.

Men Are Saved by Believing that Jesus Christ Is God

> But these are written so that you may believe that Jesus is the Christ, the Son of God, and that by believing you may have life in his name.
>
> – John 20:31, ESV

Believing that Jesus Christ is the Son of God is the very essence of the Christian faith. To believe that Jesus is the Son of God means that He is God — not a third of God, but the complete God. This is an essential part of the faith in order to have eternal life.

Jesus Christ Is a Genuine but Sinless Man

His Incarnation – God Put on Flesh to Become Man

> Now the birth of Jesus Christ took place in this way. When his mother Mary had been betrothed to Joseph, before they came together she was found to be with child from the Holy Spirit. . . .behold, an angel of the Lord appeared to him in a dream, saying, "Joseph, son of David, do not fear to take Mary as your wife, for that which is conceived in her is from the Holy Spirit. She will bear a son, and you shall call his name Jesus, for he will save his people from their sins." . . . Behold, the virgin shall conceive and bear a son, and they shall call his name Immanuel (which means, God with us).
>
> – Matthew 1:18, 20b–21, 23, ESV

Here Matthew records the birth of Jesus Christ. Mary was found to be with child from (or out of) the Holy Spirit. The source of this child is the Holy Spirit. Jesus was produced from a combination of the divine source and a human vessel. His divinity is from the Holy Spirit, and His humanity was from Mary. Since He was born of Mary, He is a man; but, since He is also born of God, then He is God. Thus, He is both human and divine.

Matthew focuses on the fact that Jesus is a genuine man, born of a real human virgin. This is also essential to the Christian faith: Jesus Christ is a man, but He is God in man. He is the God–man who came to save. He is "Jehovah saves."

His name is Jesus.

The fact that God can be joined to a human virgin to produce Jesus corroborates Genesis 1, where God said that He made man in His own image and likeness. Everything else God created was after its own kind, after a certain species of creatures. But when it came to man, the "kind" or "species" He created man after was Himself! Man was fashioned after God's kind. Biologically, cross species cannot mate and give birth; this is a well-understood fact. However, mankind is so closely aligned to God, with His same image and likeness, that God can impregnate a human virgin by the Holy Spirit. Jesus is the product of the joining of God and man. How wonderful!

> In the beginning was the Word, and the Word was with God, and the Word was God... And the Word became flesh and dwelt among us, and we have seen his glory, glory as of the only Son from the Father, full of grace and truth.
>
> – John 1:1, 14, ESV

God, who was in the beginning and ever existing, became flesh. This is truly a great mystery. God became a man to have a dwelling place among man. The word for "dwelt" in the Greek literally means, "to pitch a tent" for residing. This word is a clear reference to the tabernacle in the Old Testament. God had commanded Moses to build a tabernacle, where He dwelt on earth for forty years. The temple replaced the tabernacle after Israel entered the good land. In John 1, the apostle referred to Jesus in the flesh as the reality of the tabernacle. Jesus is God residing in the flesh. Wherever the flesh of Jesus goes, God goes. This verse doesn't say "and the Word became *man. . .*" but "the Word became flesh" (John 1:14, emphasis added). The word *"flesh"* is used to denote that man is fallen, corrupt, and sinful. Jesus didn't become like the original Adam created by God; rather, He became associated with fallen man, putting on flesh. This flesh described by Paul is "where nothing good dwells" (Rom. 7.18), and it is sinful (Rom 8:3).

Just as the tabernacle (where God resided) in the Old Testament was full of God's glory, Jesus, who is the real tabernacle of God, is full of God's glory. Inside His flesh, a fallen body of man, is the glory of God; therefore, Jesus is full of grace and truth. The incarnation of God, Jesus Christ, is full of grace and truth for man's enjoyment and participation. This is a mystery that cannot be fully explained.

God became a real man, had a real birth, and had a real, physical body. This is an essential point of the Christian faith.

Yet without Sin...

> For we do not have a high priest who is unable to sympathize with our weaknesses, but one who in every respect has been tempted as we are, yet without sin.
> – Hebrews 4:15, ESV

> For what the law could not do in that it was weak through the flesh, God [did] by sending His own Son in the likeness of sinful flesh, on account of sin: He condemned sin in the flesh.
> – Romans 8:3

Because Jesus put on a flesh that is similar to man with all its weaknesses and temptations, He can fully sympathize with fallen man. He experienced the same temptations as any man, because of His fallen body — the flesh — that He put on as a man. But Jesus didn't succumb to any of its temptations. He was without sin in the core of His nature; He lived His entire life on earth without sin.

That Jesus was without sin is paramount. If Jesus Himself possessed sin, He would have needed to die for His own sin. Jesus cannot be a substitute to die for man's sin. Man was judged by God to die for sin. If Jesus as a man had sin, then He would be under the same judgment of death as every other person who has lived on this earth. The only reason that Jesus could die for man's sin was because *He was sinless.*

Romans 8:3 states Jesus put on the "likeness of sinful flesh." The flesh that Jesus put on was somehow the same as man's sinful flesh, but also something different. It was "like" the sinful flesh in every way, yet, without sin. If it was exactly as man's sinful flesh, that would mean Jesus also possessed sin; therefore, what Jesus put on was *in the likeness of* sinful flesh — somehow very close, but not exactly. Although He didn't have sin, still as a man with the flesh, Jesus aged and he grew tired. He needed to sleep, eat, drink, and breathe, and like any human being, He could die...*and He did.*

A good picture of the likeness of the sinful flesh is the story of the brass serpent in Exodus 21:4–9. The Israelites were bitten by poisonous serpents and were dying because of the poison the snakes injected into them. Moses prayed to God to save them. God answered by telling Moses to make a serpent out of brass and lift it up on a pole. Whoever would just look at the brass serpent on the pole would be saved.

John interpreted the brass serpent in Exodus to be Jesus in John 3. Jesus has had the likeness and form of the serpent that bit the Israelites, but He didn't possess the nature and the poison of the serpent. This is a good example of a type of Christ. Although Jesus put on flesh, it was only in the "likeness of sinful" flesh. His nature was not one of sin; He was sinless.

A Common, Everyday Man

Jesus grew up living a common human life with parents and siblings, and worked as a carpenter.

> And the Child grew and became strong in spirit, filled with wisdom; and the grace of God was upon Him.
>
> – Luke 2:40

> Is this not the carpenter, the Son of Mary, and brother of James, Joses, Judas, and Simon? And are not His sisters here with us?" So they were offended at Him.
>
> – Mark 6:3

As a man, Jesus experienced birth, was a baby, had a childhood, and grew up with half-brothers and sisters. He worked in His trade as a carpenter. He had to obey human parents, and when he was about to die, He expressed concern for them. Jesus lived and experienced humanity in every way, yet, without sin.

The Bible does not record much concerning Jesus' life before He started His ministry at age thirty. It was likely uneventful, but He probably experienced every facet of humanity since He is man. Why didn't God just come to earth as a full-grown man from the outset? He could have arrived in the form of a man like He did multiple times in the Old Testament. However, He needed to be born of a human virgin to be an authentic man with a genuine human nature. This was God's desire and purpose from the very beginning: to join Himself to man, to be part of man and be one with man.

Jesus Died as a God–Man

> . . . who, being in the form of God, did not consider it robbery to be equal with God, but made Himself of no reputation, taking the form of a bondservant, and coming in the likeness of men. And being found in appearance as a man, He humbled Himself and became obedient to death, even the death of the cross.
>
> – Philippians 2:6–8

> "And I, if I am lifted up from the earth, will draw all peoples to Myself." This He said, signifying by what death He would die.
>
> – John 12:32

These verses speak of God becoming man, and dying as a man. Jesus Christ did not use His supernatural power to escape death; rather, he suffered the most excruciating death: crucifixion. God's judgment on mankind was death; therefore, only the death of a sinless man could redeem man from God's judgment. God didn't just take away sin or forgive man's sin without requiring payment for sin. God's demand on man was fully satisfied by the death of the sinless man, Jesus Christ.

His death is referred to as a vicarious death (done for another) because Jesus became a substitute for man: Jesus died instead of man. As a result of the death of the Son of Man, Jesus can draw all people to Himself. Without His death, man cannot come to God. But with His death, humanity can all be drawn and come to God.

> ...to shepherd the church [assembly] of God which He purchased with His own blood.
>
> – Acts 20:28

> How much more will the blood of Christ, who through the eternal Spirit offered himself without blemish to God, purify our conscience from dead works to serve the living God.
>
> – Hebrews 9:14, ESV

Although He died as a man, Jesus is also God; therefore God shed His own blood. God is not flesh and blood, so it is not possible for Him to shed His blood *unless* that blood is the blood of Jesus. When Jesus shed His blood, God shed His blood. Jesus Christ as a man offered Himself up to God by the shedding of His blood. He did this through the eternal Spirit within Him, as God; therefore, His blood is eternally effective. His blood's eternal value has redeemed every person from sin throughout time and space — past, present and future.

Jesus Is the God–man for Eternity

After Jesus' resurrection and ascension, He remained a man and will be the God–man for eternity.

> But he, being full of the Holy Spirit, gazed into heaven and saw the glory of God, and Jesus standing at the right hand of God, and said, "Look! I see the heavens opened and the Son of Man standing at the right hand of God!"
>
> – Acts 7:55–56

When Stephen was being stoned to death, the writer of Acts says he was "full of the Holy Spirit" and that he "saw the glory of God in heaven." Stephen saw Jesus, the "Son of man standing at the right hand of God."

The right hand of God is figurative, alluding to power and authority. It symbolizes the one with God's power and authority to carry out His plan: Stephen saw a man while he was being stoned. This echoes Peter's sermon in Acts 2:36, where Peter proclaimed Jesus in resurrection and ascension was made Lord and Christ.

Since Jesus' resurrection and ascension, He has remained bodily in the heavens; He is still a man. He didn't give up His humanity after His crucifixion; rather, He brought humanity into the Godhead for eternity. God is no longer only divine, but also human. Jesus Christ is the Son of Man with all of God's authority and power.

> And he showed me a pure river of water of life, clear as crystal, proceeding from the throne of God and of the Lamb.
>
> – Revelation 22:1

In this last chapter of the entire Bible unveiling a scene in eternity, there is one throne of God and the Lamb. The Lamb refers to Jesus, who came as a man to be the Lamb of God to take away the sin of the world.

Jesus will continue to be the Lamb for eternity. The Lamb indicates His humanity and that Jesus came to be man. Jesus with humanity will continue on in eternity. Just as it would be silly to actually see a literal lamb on the throne, neither should believers picture two persons with two bodies occupying one throne. God and the Lamb are one person, both divine and human. God and man, divinity and humanity, are fused together in the Godhead for eternity. God is on the throne of the universe, but man also is now on the throne, for eternity.

Today's world tends to depreciate humankind, making man the enemy of the environment and the cause of all problems. If given a choice, it seems worldly people today would prefer the existence of animals, or even plants, even if detrimental to man! But the reality is man is uplifted to the highest position in the universe. God loved humanity to the point of coming into complete, inseparable union with humanity. God Himself became man and brought man into God.

> For He has not put the world to come, of which we speak, in subjection to angels. But one testified in a certain place, saying: "What is man that You are mindful of him, Or the son of man that You take care of him? You have made him a little lower than the angels; You have crowned him with glory and honor; and set him over the works of Your hands. You have put all things in subjection under his feet." For in that He put all in subjection under him, He left nothing [that is] not put under him. But now we do not yet see all things put under him. But we see Jesus, who was made a little lower than the angels, for the suffering of death crowned with glory and honor, that He, by the grace of God, might taste death for everyone.
>
> – Hebrews 2:5–9

The writer of Hebrews states the coming kingdom is not subjected to angels, but to man. Though man was created in his physical make up to be lower than the angels, God ordained man to have dominion—to have everything subject to him—in the coming kingdom. Though this does not seem to be the situation presently, "but we see Jesus."

He is the man that has everything subjected under His feet. He is the man that went through death and is now crowned with glory and honor. Jesus Christ who was made in His physical being lower than the angels so that He could suffer death, was in resurrection crowned with glory and honor. He is the fulfillment of God's original intent in creating Adam: that man would have dominion over the whole earth. Jesus is the man ruling and reigning for eternity according to God's eternal purpose.

The Importance of Believing Jesus Is a Man

Believing that Jesus is a man is an essential part of faith; otherwise, it is a spirit of the antichrist to reject that God has put on flesh.

> By this you know the Spirit of God: Every spirit that confesses that Jesus Christ has come in the flesh is of God, and every spirit that does not confess that Jesus Christ has come in the flesh is not of God. And this is the spirit of the Antichrist, which you have heard was coming, and is now already in the world.
>
> – 1 John 4:2-3

The spirit within any man that confesses with the Spirit of God that Jesus Christ came in the flesh, that He is a real man, is of God. Denying that Jesus is God in the flesh reflects the spirit of the antichrist. This is a clear, essential tenet of the Christian faith — belief that Jesus is a man and continues to be a man. If Jesus is not a man, no virgin birth could have occurred, and therefore no shedding of blood for redemption. Union with God for any man would not be possible, and no fulfillment of God's eternal purpose for man to have dominion.

Let's now circle back to the question at the beginning of this chapter: *Who is Jesus?* Jesus is in every way God and in every way man. He is the complete God and a perfect and genuine man for eternity. God and man are united, mingled in a perfect union in one person for eternity. This joining together did not produce a third nature; rather, God is still God and man is still man. However, they now live and abide within one another, a wonderful mystery!

> At that day you will know that I am in My Father, and you in Me, and I in you.
>
> – John 14:20

> ...that they all may be one, as You, Father, are in Me, and I in You; that they also may be one in Us, that the world may believe that You sent Me.
>
> – John 17:21

Since Jesus is a man that has been accepted into the Trinity, every believer is now also included. It is in the Trinity — the Father, Son and Holy Spirit — that all believers are made one.

Practice: Teaching

Write down something new that you learned from this lesson:

Describe what you can practically apply in your life:

Think of a person, and write out what you want to teach that person from this lesson:

8

JESUS CHRIST – HIS WORK TO FULFILL GOD'S PLAN

Jesus is the name of the person who is God who became man. Christ, the anointed one, is commissioned by God to do God's will and fulfill God's eternal purpose.

This chapter will consider His work of crucifixion, resurrection, and ascension. Although these three events happened almost 2000 years ago, the understanding of these events will affect people tremendously in this day, and the result of understanding can wonderfully affect believers' daily experiences. The believer's proper experience depends completely on what Christ has accomplished and not on their own effort.

Overview of His Major Work

His Crucifixion

For most people of this world, death is tragic, sad, and terminal. But the death of Jesus Christ on the cross was the beginning of a new creation. Believers celebrate His death. The work of the cross is the power of God to deliver mankind from all that is negative in the universe. It is ultimate freedom for those who truly understand and believe Christ's full accomplishment on the cross; it brings believers forgiveness of sins, destroys the devil, releases believers from a life of self that keeps them in bondage, and releases Jesus' reproducing life.

His Resurrection

Two major tenets of faith that give salvation are the death and resurrection of Jesus Christ. When Jesus resurrected He didn't just come back with the same physical body; He came back with a wonderfully physical and *spiritual* body that can indwell all His believers. After the resurrection, the disciples could touch him, and He even ate food affirming he was physical. He also appeared and disappeared at will. Though physical, he is also the Spirit that can indwell His believers. What's more, something amazing happened when He resurrected. Jesus brought humanity into divinity; man was brought into God. At that point, Jesus was more than the only begotten Son of God, He also became the firstborn among many brothers. It is important to embrace the richness of this miracle, to be able to appreciate greatness of Jesus' resurrection.

His Ascension and Outpouring

To most Christians, the ascension of Jesus Christ was just a historical fact. Not many realize how this work of Christ affects them today. His ascension — together with the outpouring of the Spirit — is what makes all His believers a part of the Christ, that they might share in His anointing and commission to fulfill God's purpose on earth. Today, Christ as the Head is on the throne in the heavens praying for believers, and Christ as the body is on earth with His authority and power continuing and finishing His gospel and building work. How wonderful that the believers are the continuation of Christ on earth!

Jesus Christ Crucified on the Cross

> Then he released Barabbas [a murderer] to them; and when he had scourged Jesus, he delivered *Him* to be crucified.
>
> – Matthew 27:26

Crucifixion refers to Jesus Christ's death by the cross. At His crucifixion, Jesus literally died as a substitute for a murderer who deserved death; the murderer was freed and Jesus died in his place. Through the eternal Spirit, all believers that are deserving of death are released as a result of Jesus Christ's substitutionary death.

> For Jews request a sign, and Greeks seek after wisdom; but we preach Christ crucified, to the Jews a stumbling block and to the Greeks foolishness.
>
> – 1 Corinthians 1:22–23

Christ's crucifixion was a stumbling block to the Jews, possibly because Jesus did not perform any miracles to save Himself. Jews in the first century liked to see miraculous signs. Thus, they concluded Jesus could not possibly be the Son of God, because He let Himself die by such an excruciating death. The Greeks, priding themselves in rhetoric, considered Jesus foolish for not being wise enough to talk Himself out of crucifixion; therefore, to the Greeks, Jesus' crucifixion was "foolishness."

Jesus, a Qualified Substitute

Jesus was able to die as the Lamb of God to take away the sins of the world (John 1:29), because He was without sin (Heb. 4:15). He was qualified to be an adequate substitute so mankind doesn't have to die (1 Pet. 3:18), but instead can receive the forgiveness of sins (Matt. 26:28).

> The next day John saw Jesus coming toward him, and said, "Behold! The Lamb of God who takes away the sin of the world!"
>
> – John 1:29

What wonderful news! Men no longer need to be under the weight of guilt and the condemnation for sin by God. Jesus Christ took away the sins of the entire world. At the time of His crucifixion, though it was noon, the sky became dark as God forsook Jesus who came under judgment for all the sins of mankind. The sin of the world was laid on Jesus Christ when He was crucified; therefore, God judged Him and departed from Him. Jesus Christ took on the sins of humankind, and thus God's judgment came upon Him for all of man's sins; therefore, man (male and female) is delivered from God's judgment and the guilt of sin. Guilt and shame can be debilitating and unbearable to a person to the point where psychotherapy is needed. But one who believes in the death of Christ for his or her sins will experience release from the depression of guilt and shame.

> For we do not have a High Priest who cannot sympathize with our weaknesses, but was in *all points* tempted as *we are, yet* without sin.
>
> – Hebrews 4:15

Jesus Christ could die instead of man because He was sinless. As a man without sin, He was not under the judgment and condemnation of God. If Jesus had also committed sin and broken God's law, then He Himself would have needed to die according to God's righteous judgment. He would not have been able to die for man's sin. But because He was without sin, He could die on behalf of sinful man. This is called "vicarious death" for man.

> For Christ indeed has once suffered for sins, [the] just for [the] unjust, that he might bring us to God; being put to death in flesh, but made alive in [the] Spirit.
>
> – 1 Peter 3:18, DBY

> For this is My blood of the new covenant, which is shed for many for the remission of sins.
>
> – Matthew 26:28

Due to Jesus Christ's vicarious death, men with the faith of Jesus Christ who were once unrighteous are now made righteous. They have the boldness to come to God. Unrighteous men would be afraid and ashamed to come before God, but believers can have full confidence to be in God's presence to build a relationship with God. The death of Jesus Christ is full payment to God's righteous demand; therefore, God is obligated to forgive all of man's sins. He is obligated because man no longer owes Him for its sin, and His demand for justice has been executed and satisfied.

Jesus' Death Destroyed the Devil

> Inasmuch then as the children have partaken of flesh and blood, He [Jesus Christ] Himself likewise shared in the same, that through death He might destroy him who had the power of death, that is, the devil.
>
> – Hebrews 2:14

What wisdom that the Lord used death, the very power of His enemy, to destroy the devil. God did not taint His holy hands to destroy a being He created; rather, He used the devil's own schemes and power to crucify Jesus, which ultimately destroyed him. Satan is destroyed not in the sense that he no longer exists, but rather that his power is rendered ineffective. The word in the Greek is *"katargeo"* which means, "to be idle, inactive, or inoperable." Satan has been defanged. He is harmless to the believers because his power is no longer active or operable. Even though he still exists, all he can do now is deceive and accuse. It is all smoke and mirrors. If a person falls under Satan's deception or accusation, it would affect their lives; once that person exercises his faith in Jesus Christ, the smoke retreats, and everything becomes clear: He is already victorious in Christ, and Satan is just a liar.

Jesus Terminated the Old "I" with All of Its Problems

> Knowing this, that our old man has been crucified with [Jesus Christ], that the body of sin might be annulled, that we should no longer serve sin.
>
> – Romans 6:6, DBY

The old man is the fallen sinful man — the cause of all man's problems such as anxiety, jealousy, greed, depression, hate toward others, and the inability to forgive. Most of the problems in the world today are not because of Satan, but man's own actions expressing his fallen character. There is no need to look further than oneself. A person may ask himself, "How many people did you hurt or deprive of what is rightfully theirs in the last year?" Maybe this person didn't commit murder, but he might have wished a particular person would disappear. Multiply that by six billion people on earth, and it becomes obvious why the corrupt world situation is what it is today.

The good news is that as a result of Christ's death, this old man with all of its difficulties died with Him. The reality is believers are no longer bound as slaves to serve sin. The old man is dead, and there is no more need for the body of sin. Believers are no longer enslaved to their fallen character or nature — the old man. There is freedom from the fallen man because he is dead and buried. The body of sin is annulled. The Greek word for "annulled" is the same word that refers to Satan's destruction: *katargeo*. The body of sin is unemployed, inactive, or no longer needed because the person needing that body is dead and buried with Jesus Christ.

> I have been crucified with Christ; it is no longer I who live, but Christ lives in me; and the life which I now live in the flesh I live by faith in the Son of God, who loved me and gave Himself for me.
>
> – Galatians 2:20

The "I" who was crucified with Christ is the old man in Romans 6:6. The old "I" no longer lives, but instead a new "I" lives with the indwelling Christ. When believers are born anew, Christ comes into them to live *in* them, and the life they used to live without Christ is over. They are now completely freed from all the problems that were attached to the old "I" that was without Christ. They and Christ now live as one, a new creation.

The life that believers live today is by or in the faith of the Son of God. Without faith, it might seem that the old man is fully alive and Christ is not living in the believer. But with the eyes of faith, the truth can be realized that the old "I" is no more, but Christ is the One living in the believers. The life that believers live in their physical body today is a life that is together with Jesus Christ. Jesus Christ and the believers have the same life lived out and expressed in their living. Faith that can realize this is strengthened whenever believers appreciate the love of the Lord who died for them. Whenever a believer sincerely says to the Lord, "Lord Jesus, thank you for your love and thank you for dying for me; I love You, Lord," immediately, in their experiences, the Lord living in them is real and the old "I" is gone.

Jesus' Death Released His Generating Life to Bear Much Fruit: The Believers

> But Jesus answered them, saying, "The hour has come that the Son of Man should be glorified. Most assuredly, I say to you, unless a grain of wheat falls into the ground and dies, it remains alone; but if it dies, it produces much grain."
>
> – John 12:23–24

Jesus Christ's death was a wonderful death, likened to the death of a seed. A seed's life is within its kernel. "Life" in a seed cannot be released unless it has gone through death. The result of the release of life in the seed is the reproduction of many more seeds; those seeds duplicate the original that died. A seed is the best analogy of resurrection life. Anything other than a seed will die once buried, and its death is terminal. But because there is resurrection life in a seed, the only way for it to grow, flourish, and reproduce is through burial and "death." Amazingly, that is exactly what resurrection life needs…death. Through death, there is more life…*abundant* life.

Like physical plants, Jesus' death reproduced His believers who bear His exact image and likeness. The reproduced seeds are exactly the same in form, shape, function and even DNA as the seed (Jesus) that was buried. Jesus is no longer the only divine and human person. Now believers are like Him, human and divine, the sons of God. This is why the Bible can say that being in the image of Christ is the destiny of every believer (Rom. 8.29), and that they will be like Jesus Christ when they see Him again at His second coming (1 John 3:2).

This is the positive goal of the Lord's death. As a seed, the Lord did not only die for sin or to destroy Satan. He died to bear much fruit. He died to reproduce Himself in millions and millions of people, so that God the Father would have many sons.

> Foolish one, what you sow is not made alive unless it dies.
>
> – 1 Corinthians 15:36

Unbelievers are skeptical of the Lord's resurrection. They foolishly question how a person can die and come back in resurrection. But the fact is, nature has been declaring resurrection in the form of the sowing of seeds and the growth of plants and trees from the beginning of time. Humanity has been enjoying and daily benefiting from the physical death and resurrection of plants through the supply of food, through useful material such as lumber, and through the beauty of the botanical kingdom.

Jesus said in John 11:25, "I am the resurrection and the life." Jesus is the real resurrection life. Plants are a physical picture of the real resurrection life in the universe. God wants to manifest resurrection life everywhere to benefit mankind for His physical sustenance and enjoyment, so that man may know and receive the real resurrection life of Christ. Every time men and women look at the beauty of the botanical kingdom or take a bite of their favorite bread, they should remember to receive Jesus Christ in resurrection.

Jesus' Death Abolished the Ordinances that Divided People

> For He is our peace, who has made both one, and has broken down the middle wall of enclosure, having annulled the enmity in his flesh, the law of commandments in ordinances, that He might form the two in himself into one new man, making peace; and might reconcile both in one body to God by the cross, having by it slain the enmity;
>
> – Ephesians 2:14–16, DBY

The Jews and the Gentiles were not at peace. The main reason for this enmity or hostility between the two people was because of "the commandments in ordinances." These ordinances refer to the way of living that the Jews were to abide by according to the law. These ordinances included such major items as keeping the Sabbath day (cannot work on that day), having a diet that consisted of "clean" foods (as an example, pork and shrimp are "unclean"), and rituals surrounding religious "feasts." It is because of these ordinances that Jews were distinct and kept separate from the Gentiles and experienced hostility. Peter even said that it was unlawful for a Jew to come near a non-Jew (Acts 10:28).

Under such circumstances, it is not possible for the Lord to have His one body consisting of all people. Therefore, in order to have one body of all people, specifically a coming together of Jews and Gentiles, He needed to abolish all the ordinances that kept the two people separate. On the cross He slew all the ordinances of the law relating to lifestyle, ritualistic, and ceremonial observances for the sole purpose of joining the two people (Jews and Gentiles) into one new man, one body. By nailing these ordinances to the cross, He eliminated the enmity or hostility and brought peace so that people can be joined together in His one body. This is clearly needed for the fulfillment of His prayer in John 17.

In John 17:20 and 21, the Lord prayed not just for His disciples, who were all Jews, to be one, but for all those who believe through their words, that they all may be one. Those that believe through their words clearly include Gentiles. So in the Lord's Prayer he already foretold of Jews and Gentiles becoming one in order that the world will believe in Jesus. After that prayer, Jesus went to the cross to nail and abolish all the ordinances in the law that kept the Jews separate so that all His people may become one according to His prayer. Religious strife can be considered the most hostilely divisive matter among peoples, since how a person acts and lives is considered to be "God given" commands (even Islam, Buddhism, Hinduism are all divided). Therefore, if Jews and Gentiles can be one, then it is an easier matter for the other races with all their other differences to be one in Jesus Christ. The topic of the law will be discussed in more detail in Chapter 14.

Jesus Christ Resurrected

> But the angel answered and said to the women, "Do not be afraid, for I know that you seek Jesus who was crucified. He is not here; for He is risen, as He said. Come, see the place where the Lord lay. And go quickly and tell His disciples that He is risen from the dead.
>
> – Matthew 28:5–7

Jesus' Death and Resurrection Are the Basis of the Gospel

The death and resurrection of Christ are foundational elements of the gospel; receiving both by faith is both essential and necessary for salvation.

> Moreover, brethren, I declare to you the gospel which I preached to you, which also you received and in which you stand, by which also you are saved, if you hold fast that word which I preached to you — unless you believed in vain. For I delivered to you first of all that which I also received: that Christ died for our sins according to the Scriptures, and that He was buried, and that He rose again the third day according to the Scriptures.
>
> — 1 Corinthians 15:1–4

> That if you confess with your mouth the Lord Jesus and believe in your heart that God has raised Him from the dead, you will be saved.
>
> — Romans 10:9

Paul in 1 Corinthians 15:1–4 presents the gospel in a nutshell: Jesus Christ died for the sins of all people, He was buried, and He resurrected on the third day. This is the faith of Jesus Christ that saves people. What simplicity! Believers trust that Jesus is both God and man, and that he died for their sins and was raised from death. This alone is what saves people, and it is the uniting faith of all believers. Why should there be so much arguing and infighting among Christians, when there is such simplicity of faith? The human mind has a tendency to complicate things, and it is in these unnecessary complications that division surfaces among believers. In both of the above portions of Scripture, what it means to be "saved" is simply defined: believing the message of Jesus Christ, who died for man's sins and was resurrected.

Jesus, the Life-Giving Spirit

Jesus breathed into His believers in order to minister the indestructible life within His believers.

> Thus also it is written, "The first man Adam became a living being; the last Adam [Jesus Christ] *became* a life-giving spirit."
>
> — 1 Corinthians 15:45

The phrase, "The first man Adam" in 1 Corinthians 15:45 referred to the Adam God created in Genesis. However, Paul also referred to the "last Adam," Jesus Christ. As the "last," Jesus ended the old creation in Adam. In His resurrection, He became a life-giving Spirit to give His believers the divine, eternal, and indestructible life, thus making them a new creation. In resurrection, Jesus Christ took on a wonderful, spiritual form. In this form, He can enter into the believers and give life to them. Life is something within a person and not outside a person. For Jesus to indwell a person, He has to be the life-giving Spirit.

> And having said this, He [Jesus Christ] breathed into [them], and says to them, Receive [the] Holy Spirit.
>
> — John 20:22, DBY

This is the fulfillment of the promised Spirit, the Comforter mentioned in John 14, and the Living Water in John 7. Before resurrection, Jesus could only be *with* people, but after resurrection Jesus could breathe Himself *into* His believers. They, in turn, could receive the Holy Spirit.

The Greek word for "Spirit" is *pneuma,* which is the word for air. The Holy Spirit became the breathable air to the believers. Jesus could breathe the Spirit into them, and they could in turn receive the Spirit as breath. This mirrors the record in Genesis when God created Adam and animated him by breathing into his nostrils. Here, the new creation came into being and the corporate new man was generated by another breath. This time in John 20:22, believers breathed and received the actual Holy Spirit.

> ...who [Jesus Christ] has been constituted not according to law of fleshly commandment, but according to power of indissoluble life.
>
> – Hebrews 7:16, DBY

The life that He is ministering to His believers as the Priest of God is the "indissoluble," or indestructible life. No matter the obstacle, even death, nothing can destroy this life in the believer. The greater the challenges and the deeper the problems, the more victorious this indestructible life shines forth. Resurrection is not just an event that happened to Jesus Christ 2000 years ago. The same resurrection life is now in the believers. If that is their life, how can any difficulties cause them to lose heart or depress them? Since resurrection life overcomes the ultimate difficulty — death — believers can rely on the resurrection life in them to go through trials with strength and joy.

> Examine yourselves as to whether you are in the faith. Test yourselves. Do you not know yourselves, that Jesus Christ is in you? — unless indeed you are disqualified.
>
> – 2 Corinthians 13:5

Being "in the faith" means to believe that Jesus Christ is both God and man who died for sin and resurrected on the third day. By this simple faith, believers are approved by God. And not only this: Jesus Christ Himself also comes in to indwell man. Even while this is true, it is "unbelievable." No wonder man (male and female) needs to have the gift of faith from God in order to believe! Notice that 2 Corinthians 13:5 does not say the Spirit is in the believer, but the *very person Jesus Christ* is in them! Jesus Christ Himself is in each one of the believers, because He and the Spirit are one in the same person.

Jesus Became the Indwelling Comforter

As the indwelling Comforter (the Spirit of truth), Jesus makes real to believers all things of Christ.

> And I will beg the Father, and He will give you another Comforter, that He may be with you for ever, the Spirit of truth, whom the world cannot receive, because it does not see Him nor know Him; but you know Him, for He abides with you, and shall be in you. I will not leave you orphans, I am coming to you.
>
> – John 14:16–18, DBY

The phrase "another Comforter" in John 14:16 is referring to the "Spirit of truth" in 14:17. As the Comforter in the flesh, Jesus abides *with* His disciples physically, but as "another Comforter," He abides *in* them. The Spirit of truth is simply Jesus coming in another form. That is the reason He said, "I am coming to you."

Today through His death and resurrection, no matter the time or place, Jesus continually comforts believers as the Spirit within them. The world is full of conflicts. It seems that wars and unprovoked attacks are increasing globally, even in the name of religion. Individually, it seems that people today experience more anxiety, uncertainty and unrest within their souls. Truly, the Comforter is needed; He needs to be present and available. The good news is that Jesus Christ, as the reliable Comforter, brings true comfort and He exists within every believer. Whenever comfort is needed, all believers need to do is turn to Him. He is never far away. He is available 24/7 to comfort each and every one of His believers from within them.

> But when He is come, the Spirit of truth, He shall guide you into all the truth: for He shall not speak from himself; but whatsoever He shall hear He shall speak; and He will announce to you what is coming. He shall glorify Me, for He shall receive of mine and shall announce it to you. All things that the Father has are mine; on account of this I have said that He receives of mine and shall announce it to you.
>
> –John 16:13–18 DBY

Truth in John 16:13–18 is God (Jesus Christ, the Spirit) and all His attributes such as love, light and mercy. This is the eternal and universal truth.

This truth also includes everything that Jesus obtained, attained, and accomplished through His incarnation, crucifixion, resurrection and ascension. These wonderful life elements include such things as redemption, forgiveness of sins, and justification; they transform believers into the image of Jesus Christ, as God and man, who became both Lord and Christ. This is the unsearchable riches of Christ that the Spirit of truth is guiding believers into. It is the Spirit of truth that makes all that Christ is, including all the things of the Father, true or real to believers in their understanding and experiences.

It is a fact that the crucifixion of Jesus Christ has solved all problems. The old man, which is the source of man's troubles, has been nailed to the cross and buried with Christ. But in the believers' daily situations, they may not have such experiences. They may feel very much trapped in negativity and in the "death" of the world. It is at such a time that they need the Spirit of truth (reality) to intervene. If they would start to pray and call out the name of the Lord Jesus, the Spirit of truth in them would be activated. He would guide them into the reality of their old man's crucifixion and burial and into the reality of being in the resurrection and ascension in Christ. It is the Spirit of truth that makes all the unseen realities that Jesus Christ accomplished real to believers, guiding them into all truth. This is reality.

It is unimaginable how rich and how wonderful are the many items of the truth the Spirit desires to guide believers into. The Spirit's job is to be such a guide. Believers only need to be open to Him and turn to Him.

Jesus Brings Humanity into God

Through these things, Jesus brought humanity into God, that mere men could become sons of God. As a result, they became His duplication.

> ...concerning His Son Jesus Christ our Lord, who was born of the seed of David according to the flesh, and declared to be the Son of God with power according to the Spirit of holiness, by the resurrection from the dead.
>
> – Romans 1:3

The reference to "His Son" in Romans 1:3 refers to Jesus' divinity as the Son of God. The phrase "born...according to the flesh" refers to His humanity. In His resurrection, Jesus — not just in His divinity but also in His humanity — was declared (appointed, or marked out as) the Son of God. Romans 1:1 references this as the gospel of God: It is concerning such a One. He is the gospel, the good news.

> Now when they had fulfilled all that was written concerning Him, they took Him down from the tree and laid Him in a tomb. But God raised Him from the dead. And we declare to you glad tidings — that promise which was made to the fathers. God has fulfilled this for us their children, in that He has raised up Jesus. As it is also written in the second Psalm: 'You are My Son, Today I have begotten You.'
>
> – Acts 13:29-33

It is abundantly clear that at Jesus' birth He was *already* the Son of God. He didn't need resurrection to be begotten of God. He was already the "only begotten Son" (John 3:16). He existed in eternity as the Son with the Father (see Chapter 7 concerning His person).

However, in verse 33, Luke (the writer of Acts) says that it was at the day of resurrection that Jesus was begotten of God. Something transpired within Jesus on that day of resurrection! Before resurrection, Jesus' humanity was still flesh, susceptible to weakness, hunger, thirst, and even death. On the day of resurrection, however, His humanity was uplifted to the highest place. As a man, He was begotten of God. By incarnation, God was brought *into man*. By resurrection man was brought *into God*. Now, Jesus' divinity and even His humanity exist in God. Divinity and humanity are now joined, mingled, and blended in a perfect union in the same person. How wonderful!

> For whom He foreknew, He also predestined to be conformed to the image of His Son, that He might be the firstborn among many brethren.
>
> – Romans 8:29

Before death and resurrection, Jesus was the "only begotten" (John 1:18; 3:16), but after resurrection, He became the "firstborn" (Rom. 8:29). The word "only" in John 1:18 and 3:16 is derived from the Greek word *monogenēs* and means that Jesus is unique and there is no other. "Firstborn" in Romans 8:29 comes from the Greek word *prōtotokos,* derived from the root word *prōtos* meaning, "first in any succession of things or persons." Thus, "firstborn" indicates there are others to follow. Many brothers will come after Jesus. At His resurrection, all of Jesus' believers were begotten in resurrection with Him (1 Pet. 1:3).

When Jesus' humanity was begotten of God at resurrection, believers were included with Him. Today, just as He is the firstborn Son of God with divinity and humanity, His believers too are sons of God with humanity and divinity. This is God's purpose: to reproduce many sons "to be conformed to the image of his son" (Rom. 8:28–29; see also Eph. 1:5).

> Most assuredly, I say to you, unless a grain of wheat falls into the ground and dies, it remains alone; but if it dies, it produces much grain.
>
> – John 12:24

Christ is the "grain of wheat" that fell to the ground and died, albeit on the cross. The "much grain" is Christ's increase in resurrection. The believers are the grains that were produced through His death and resurrection. The many grains that were produced in resurrection are exactly the same as the first grain (Jesus) that was planted through death. How amazing that the many brothers produced through Christ's death and resurrection, exactly like Him, are the believers — the very image of the firstborn Son of God in both His humanity and divinity.

Jesus Christ Ascended

> Now when He had spoken these things, while they watched, He was taken up, and a cloud received Him out of their sight. And while they looked steadfastly toward heaven as He went up, . . . this same Jesus, who was taken up from you into heaven, will so come in like manner as you saw Him go into heaven."
>
> – Acts 1:9–10a, 11

The Crucified Jesus Made Lord and Christ

> Let all the house of Israel therefore know for certain that God has made him both Lord and Christ, this Jesus whom you crucified.
>
> – Acts 2:36, ESV

At birth, Jesus was already both Lord and Christ (Luke 1:43, 2:11). As the Son of God, surely He was the Lord. And as Christ, He was appointed to fulfill God's purpose through incarnation and crucifixion. Why then was it necessary for Jesus to be made *both* Lord and Christ after His ascension? The reason is that just as His humanity was declared the Son of God, in ascension His humanity was made both Lord and Christ. He is both Lord and Christ not only as God, but also as a man. There is a man today that is Lord over all! And God needs man, and anointed this Man for the ultimate fulfillment of God's eternal purpose.

> ...who, being in the form of God, did not consider it robbery to be equal with God, but made Himself of no reputation, taking the form of a bondservant, and coming in the likeness of men. And being found in appearance as a man, He humbled Himself and became obedient to death, even the death of the

> cross. Therefore God also has highly exalted Him and given Him the name
> which is above every name, that at the name of Jesus every knee should bow,
> of those in heaven, and of those on earth, and of those under the earth, and
> that every tongue should confess that Jesus Christ is Lord, to the glory of
> God the Father.
>
> *– Philippians 2:6–11*

In Philippians 2:6–11, Paul presented a clear narrative concerning Jesus' incarnation, crucifixion, resurrection and ascension. It was after this process, as a man, that Jesus was exalted above all names. It is this divine and yet lowly human who is now ascended that believers confess: "Jesus Christ is Lord." Jesus, at the end of this process (starting from Philippians 2:6), is different from when He started. In the beginning of this process He was God that became man. At the end this process, He was (and currently is) a man that is called Lord with everything under His feet. The One that was exalted by God is not exactly the One that was equal with God; otherwise, Jesus didn't need God to exalt Him. It was the lowly man in resurrection that was highly exalted by God.

Jesus Intercedes and Saves Believers to the Uttermost

> Now He who searches the hearts knows what the mind of the Spirit [is], because
> He makes intercession for the saints according to [the will of] God.
>
> Who is he who condemns? It is Christ who died, and furthermore is also risen,
> who is even at the right hand of God, who also makes intercession for us.
>
> *– Romans 8:27, 34*

How wonderful for believers to have Jesus at the right hand of God interceding for (or praying strongly for) them through every trial and circumstance. This is one of Jesus' full-time jobs; through His intercession, believers will be saved to the uttermost through each trial (Heb. 7:25), and God's purpose will be fulfilled in them. When the Lord prays for His people, He may not be praying for what they think they need. Typically, when believers pray they are praying for their own interests at heart, but Jesus prays for His people according to the will of God. Should God listen to prayers of the believers according to their own interest or listen to the prayer of Jesus according to God's will? Many times when Christians' prayers are not answered, it is because their prayers are conflicting with the will of God. Believers should thus "amen" all His intercessory prayers on behalf of all His followers and submit to God's will. It is certain God's will is that each and every one of His people is saved to the uttermost.

Jesus Was Made Head to Transmit to His Body (to Believers) All He Is, All He Has Obtained and All He Has Attained

> ...and what the surpassing greatness of His power towards us who believe,
> according to the working of the might of His strength, [in] which He wrought
> in the Christ in raising Him from among [the] dead, and He set Him down at

> His right hand in the heavenlies, above every principality, and authority, and power, and dominion, and every name named, not only in this age, but also in that to come; and has put all things under His feet, and gave Him [to be] head over all things to the assembly, which is His body, the fullness of Him who fills all in all.
>
> – Ephesians 1:19–23, DBY

The power of Jesus is toward those who believe. This power toward believers is the same power that raised Christ from the dead — resurrection power. This all-transcending power also raised Jesus to the heavens, to the highest position in the universe. Everything is subdued under his feet by this all-subduing power.

Believers' eyes need to be opened to see what tremendous and wonderful power has been given to them. Now Jesus is the Head of the assembly, the body of Christ. As His body, all His believers are certainly under the constant supply and transmission of this power. Under and attached to the assembly's ascended Head, how can believers create excuses to be weak?

Satan is a liar. All the power of Christ is at the believer's disposal for their experiences.

His Spirit Outpoured to Continue His Work on Earth

By pouring out His Spirit, Jesus gives believers the power and authority to speak His words to continue His life-giving ministry.

> When the day of Pentecost had come, they were all together in one place. And suddenly a sound came from heaven like the rush of a mighty wind, and it filled all the house where they were sitting. And there appeared to them tongues as of fire, distributed and resting on each one of them. And they were all filled with the Holy Spirit and began to speak in other tongues, as the Spirit gave them utterance.
>
> – Acts 2:1–4, RSV

> Being therefore exalted at the right hand of God, and having received from the Father the promise of the Holy Spirit, he has poured out this which you see and hear.
>
> – Acts 2:33, RSV

In John 20:22, after Jesus' resurrection, He breathed into his disciples. At that point, the believers had already received the Holy Spirit as the breath within. However, on the day of Pentecost, the Spirit was described as a "mighty wind" (Acts 2:2). A mighty or rushing wind is very different from a breath. A "breath" is necessary for life, whereas a mighty wind can accomplish a lot of work. Wind can move a ship and generate electricity through a turbine. Therefore, the outpouring of the Spirit on the day of Pentecost was to empower the believers for the working of His ministry to spread the gospel for the building up of His body.

This is the fulfillment of the promise given by the Lord in Luke 24:49, when He told His disciples to wait to be clothed with "power from on high" so that they could go forth to all nations and preach in His name.

Then, Luke spoke of "tongues as of fire" in Acts 2:3. Tongues are a symbol of speaking and indicate that God's work of preaching the gospel to all nations and spreading the truth for building up the body will be mainly accomplished through *speaking*. Jesus is the speaking Spirit. Just as the apostles started to speak the gospel immediately after receiving the outpoured Spirit on the day of Pentecost, this same poured-out-Spirit has reached all His believers enabling each and everyone to go forth to speak with power and authority — and thus fulfill the assembly's commission.

> And Jesus coming up spoke to them, saying, All power has been given Me in heaven and upon earth. Go therefore and make disciples of all the nations, baptizing them to the name of the Father, and of the Son, and of the Holy Spirit; teaching them to observe all things whatsoever I have enjoined you. And behold, I am with you all the days, until the completion of the age.
> — Matthew 28:18–20, DBY

According to Matthew, believers are to spread the good news to minister Christ to people in order that many may be immersed and be brought into the entire triune God. Then they are to continue to teach these new believers the entire counsel of God (Acts 20:26–27) as unveiled in the Scriptures.

The Lord with all His authority is surely with believers as they go, stepping out in faith to do this. Believers are to continue this ministry until the end of this age when the Lord returns. As believers go, the Lord is with them, with all the power that He has obtained and attained. Only by going to fulfill such a commission are believers in the position to experience "all power" that has been given to the Lord. If believers just stay home and care for their own interests, they will not experience this power because this power is specifically for the carrying out of God's eternal purpose.

Believers Share in His Anointing to Be the Continuation of Christ on Earth

> Now He who establishes us with you in Christ and has anointed us is God,
> — 2 Corinthians 1:21, DBY

When people heard and received the gospel from the first apostles, they were immediately established together in Christ. Initially, some apostles were specifically sent to preach the gospel. However, whenever anyone hears and believes the gospel, even today, those new believers become the same group of believers as the apostles, established in Christ.

Not only so, but God has anointed the *entire group* in Christ. This anointing is the commissioning by God to fulfill His purpose on earth. Since believers are in Him, they presently share the same anointing as Jesus Christ to carry out His ministering work. Anyone who believes into Christ through the preaching of the gospel will join all other believers as they unite with the early apostles into one, in Christ. No matter how new the believer, upon belief, this person immediately receives the same anointing or commission as the early apostles to preach the gospel and teach the truth for the accomplishing of God's purpose. No Bible school, seminary, or special calling is necessary to have this anointing; rather, this anointing comes with the initiation of faith in Jesus Christ.

> For as the body is one and has many members, but all the members of that one body, being many, are one body, so also is Christ.
>
> – 1 Corinthians 12:12

"Christ" in 1 Corinthians 12:12 does not just refer to Jesus, but also His one body. According to most Christians' understanding, this verse should say, "so also is the church," where there are many members. They would associate the many members to the church or assembly, and not to Christ. The Scriptures reveal it is Christ who has many members. This cannot refer to the individual Jesus Christ, but rather the corporate Christ — with Jesus as the Head and the believers as the many members.

Again, Christ means "the anointed one," intended to fulfill God's purpose. Since believers are now members of the Christ and share in the same anointing as Jesus Christ as the Head, they naturally also share in His commission to accomplish God's purpose. As His body in this day, believers are the continuation of Christ on earth commissioned to do God's will, mainly by speaking — ministering Christ to others. This results in salvation for sinners and growth and building for other believers.

Practice: Open Your Home For Fellowship

Azzs you continue into this book, you will see that in order to further Christ's commission, it is critical that there are open homes for fellowship and assembling. Therefore, if you are to participate in Christ's anointing for fulfilling of His purpose, it is a good practice to invite Christians to your house for fellowship, or some unbelieving friends or relatives, for the sake of speaking the gospel to them. Inviting people into your house means that you are open to them, that you have nothing to hide from them, and that they are welcomed to be comfortable around you.

Start immediately to pray and consider whom you can invite to your house; then take action and invite them. It can be for a meal, it can be for a Bible reading and discussion, it can be for a snack — it can just be to hang out so that an opportunity for the Word can be spoken.

You can start this occasionally, or better yet, do it regularly. It is not hard to make a decision to do this once a month; eventually it may be once a week. Ideally, you can host the assembly in your house once a week according to the pattern set up by Paul in 1 Corinthians 14. This will be discussed in detail in later chapters. For now, it is excellent to start participating in Christ's anointing by beginning to open your home for fellowship.

I will have someone over to my house on before this date: _____

Potential people that I can invite: _____

_____

9
GOD, MAN, AND SATAN

God created man, male and female, with the ultimate purpose of man becoming His sons with His image and likeness, having His eternal life and divine nature. Equally as important, man would defeat His enemy, Satan. This was God's purpose and pleasure. Satan came to deceive man so that instead of eating of the Tree of Life, man ingested the tree of the knowledge of good and evil. Man thus became one with Satan and Satan's desire to be God — to exist without God or in place of God. Man became utterly corrupted and fallen, so much so that God even regretted creating man. This chapter technically would not be considered truth since the focus of this chapter is concerning man and not Jesus Christ. However, it may be considered healthy teaching since understanding the fallen state of man should cause a person to turn to Jesus Christ for salvation.

Satan Wanted to Overthrow God and Be God Himself

Lucifer, which means, "light bearer," was the highest angel leading worship to God. Though he was God's top angel, he wanted to overthrow God to *be God himself* — thus becoming God's enemy. The prophets Isaiah and Ezekiel reveal how Lucifer fell from God's favor:

> How you are fallen from heaven, O Lucifer, son of the morning! How you are cut down to the ground, you who weakened the nations! For you have said in your heart: 'I will ascend into heaven, I will exalt my throne above the stars of God; I will also sit on the mount of the congregation On the farthest sides of the north; I will ascend above the heights of the clouds, I will be like the Most High.'
> — Isaiah 14:12–14

> Thus says the Lord Jehovah: Because your heart is lifted up, and you have said, I *am* a god, I sit in the seat of God, in the heart of the seas, and you set your heart as the heart of God.
>
> . . .Thus says the Lord Jehovah: You, who seal up the measure of perfection, full of wisdom and perfect in beauty, you were in Eden, the garden of God. Every precious stone was your covering: . . . The workmanship of your tambours and of your pipes was in you: in the day that you were created were they prepared. You were the anointed covering cherub, and I had set you so: you were upon the holy mountain of God; you did walk up and down in the midst of stones of fire. You were perfect in your ways, from the day that you were created, till unrighteousness was found in you By the abundance of your traffic they filled the midst of you with violence, and you have sinned; therefore have I cast you as profane from the mountain of God, and have destroyed you, O covering cherub,

> from the midst of the stones of fire. Your heart was lifted up because of your
> beauty; you have corrupted your wisdom by reason of your brightness.
>
> – Ezekiel 28:2b, 12b–17, DBY

Lucifer was the only angel whose beauty was described in detail in the Bible — as one covered in precious stones (Ezek. 28:13). He was in utmost measure of perfection, full of wisdom and perfect in beauty (28:15). There was nothing in the universe like him. He had and still has authority to roam freely through the very inner sanctum of God. He may even have been more beautiful than God in appearance.

For certain Lucifer considered himself wiser than God. This would be the assumed reason why he thought that he should be on the throne of God. On top of this, he was crowned the highest of angels with a musical celebration. He was the anointed cherub — the head of the angels who protected God's glory and led creation in adoration, or worship of God (Rev. 4:8). At a certain point (perhaps as he was considering God's glory and leading the adoration of God), he began to compare himself with God. Lucifer looked at his own beauty and wisdom and thought that he should replace God. In fact, he should *be* God. He then rebelled with a large contingent of angels under his authority, and he became Satan — an adversary and enemy to God.

Man Was Created to Fulfill God's Purpose and to Give God Pleasure

God's will and pleasure was to produce many sons that would be the fullest expression of Himself. Unlike all other creatures fashioned after their own kind, man is fashioned after God's kind.

> …having predestined us to adoption as sons [sonship] by Jesus Christ to Himself, according to the good pleasure of His will.
>
> – Ephesians 1:5

In the beginning, in eternity past, hidden within God, is His will to produce many sons. His pleasure was not just to have the only begotten Son within Himself, but as the eternal Father, to also reproduce many sons for His glory and pleasure.

The English word "adoption" does not accurately translate the original Greek word *huiothesia* that Paul used in Ephesians 1:5. The Greek word *huiothesia* is a compound word made up of "son," an offspring by birth, and "appoint" or "set in place."

The English word "adoption" is merely a legal procedure, without the actual birth of a son. *Huiothesia,* however, clearly indicates believers are indeed sons by birth. With God's life, they *also* have a place in maturity — a legal standing — to be God's appointed sons. This is the Father's will. How great and wonderful God is, who has begotten millions upon millions of sons who are not just babies, but have the maturity to take their appointed place for the entire universe to behold and glorify the Father in his many sons. This is God's pleasure and glory. A human father can identify with this in a minuscule and limited scale.

Let me share a personal testimony. I (the author) am a father of four children, and they were definitely my pleasure. It was enjoyable to be with them and do things with them as they were growing up. Now that they are grown and are all married with careers that are contributing to society, I am proud of them. They are my glory displaying my achievement. Magnify this by infinity, and a sense of the immensity of God's pleasure and glory in His many mature sons can be appreciated.

> And God made the beast of the earth according to its kind, cattle according to its kind, and everything that creeps on the earth according to its kind. And God saw that *it was* good. Then God said, "Let Us make man in Our image, according to Our likeness; let them have dominion over the fish of the sea, over the birds of the air, and over the cattle, over all the earth and over every creeping thing that creeps on the earth."
>
> – Genesis 1:25–26

Genesis 1:25–26 describes every creature in the water, in the air, and on land as made according to "its kind" (1:25). Each was fashioned according to its own species. However, when it came time for God to make man He said, "Let Us make man in Our image and according to Our likeness" (1:26).

When God fashioned man, His three-oneness (His triune nature, or the Trinity) was revealed; this is reflected in the use of the pronoun "Us" in Genesis 1:26. It seems that creating man was of such utmost importance that there was a conference within the Godhead to make a joint decision. Man was not made *according to "its kind" but according to God's own image and likeness,* according to *God's kind.* Man was made very distinct and different from all the other creatures. Clearly before man there was nothing like man. Man was uniquely formed at that point, after God Himself.

> So God created man in His own image; in the image of God He created him; male and female He created them.
>
> – Genesis 1:27

God's character and nature are clearly expressed in the vast expanse of the universe and in the minute details of creation. However, human beings express God on a much higher plane.

Man's ability to be inventive (to imagine and to create), along with his ability to express sacrificial love, and to set goals and to have purpose beyond just existence, clearly expresses God in man in a much more specific and excellent way than the rest of creation. Man expresses God's very inner being, His attributes and even His personality; other creatures cannot do this. Although scientists have concluded that human-like creatures were in existence for hundreds of thousands of years (or longer) before man, most anthropologists and scholars agree language and culture that is associated with modern man have only been in existence within the last 10,000 years. Interestingly, this matches the Biblical record.

Man is special. Man has a unique purpose that took a conference within the Godhead of the Father, Son, and the Spirit to design. This was indicated when God said "let Us make man in Our image." It is also important to recognize that "man" is both "male and female." In God's view man is a pair including both male and female. He does not have a preference between the sexes. Just as God consists of Father, Son and Spirit with distinct roles, but not one more important than the other, so too when God created man, He viewed male and female together as "man." Therefore, this should be kept in mind throughout this book that whenever "man" or even "sons of God" is mentioned, it includes both male and female.

> Beloved, now we are children of God; and it has not yet been revealed what we shall be, but we know that when He is revealed, we shall be like Him, for we shall see Him as He is.
>
> – 1 John 3:2

If man with God's image and likeness would have eaten the Tree of Life, signifying the very life and nature of God, then man (men and women) would literally have become God's children. Man would have the psychological faculties and the physical ability to express the life and nature of God.

In the New Testament, when men receive Jesus Christ, they are born of God to be His children (John 1:12–13). Right now, believers do not *appear* like children of God, but one day everyone will see that the believers revealed in the glory of their Father God. Their physical body will even be a body of glory like the Lord Jesus' body in resurrection. In eternity, all creation will recognize that man has become sons of God. Man with God's divine eternal life and nature expresses God's attributes, fullness, and glory.

God's Purpose: Man Would Be the One to Defeat His Enemy, Satan

> Then God said, "Let Us make man in Our image, according to Our likeness; let them have dominion over the fish of the sea, over the birds of the air, and over the cattle, over all the earth and over every creeping thing that creeps on the earth."
>
> – Genesis 1:26

In Genesis 1:26 God declares created man will have dominion "over all the earth." This means dominion should already include all earthly creatures. However, God then says, "and over every creeping thing." What would be the reason that God singled out "every creeping thing," distinct from all the other creatures already included on earth? It seems that they are not part of the earth, but an addition to other creatures on the earth; Genesis 1:26 is referring to Satan with all his followers, the fallen angels and demons.

> And the LORD God said to the woman, "What is this you have done?" The woman said, "The serpent deceived me, and I ate." So the LORD God said to the serpent: "Because you have done this, you are cursed more than all cattle, and more than every beast of the field; On your belly you shall go, and you shall eat dust All the days of your life. And I will put enmity between you and the woman, and between your seed and her Seed; He shall bruise your head, and you shall bruise His heel."
>
> – Genesis 3:13–15

Even after man ate of the forbidden fruit, God still prophesied that a man born of a woman would defeat Satan (the serpent), with a terminal blow to the head. Even though the Devil did his best to cause man to sin and brought man to a fallen state, God never gave up His purpose: to use lowly man to defeat His enemy. This also means that God will do something to preserve man and not let him become extinct due to sin. Remember, God said that when man eats of the tree of the knowledge of good and evil, "you shall surely die." It was after God made this promise that Adam named his wife "Eve," which means, "life" or "living," because he understood that she would live.

Satan Is Not Afraid of God, but Is Terrified of Man

Satan walks freely in God's presence, according to Scripture, and unafraid. He challenges God and accuses God's people, as in the example of Job:

> Now there was a day when the sons of God came to present themselves before the LORD, and Satan also came among them. And the LORD said to Satan, "From where do you come?" So Satan answered the LORD and said, "From going to and fro on the earth, and from walking back and forth on it." Then the LORD said to Satan, "Have you considered My servant Job, that *there* is none like him on the earth, a blameless and upright man, one who fears God and shuns evil?" So Satan answered the LORD and said, "Does Job fear God for nothing? "Have You not made a hedge around him, around his household, and around all that he has on every side? You have blessed the work of his hands, and his possessions have increased in the land. "But now, stretch out Your hand and touch all that he has, and he will surely curse You to Your face!" And the LORD said to Satan, "Behold, all that he has *is* in your power; only do not lay a hand on his *person*." So Satan went out from the presence of the LORD.
>
> – Job 1:6–12

Satan was free to come and go before God. He was bold to even challenge God concerning Job. Because Satan wrongly accused God of "buying" Job's love and worship by providing Job with many physical blessings, God allowed Satan to cause Job to suffer much loss.

> So the great dragon was cast out, that serpent of old, called the Devil and Satan, who deceives the whole world; he was cast to the earth, and his angels were cast out with him. Then I heard a loud voice saying in heaven, "Now salvation, and strength, and the kingdom of our God, and the power of His Christ have come, for the accuser of our brethren, who accused them before our God day and night, has been cast down."
>
> – Revelation 12:9–10

Until the time of the Lord's second coming when he is cast out from God's presence, Satan will continue to wander freely before God, and accuse God's people day and night. It seems that has been his full-time job since his power was destroyed through the cross of Christ. The condemnation within believers that speaks failure, or lies that God has given up on them, causes weakness, discouragement, and even depression. But these condemnations are actually accusations from the Devil. In those moments believers should look to the blood of Christ shed for them and testify of their faith in Christ in order to overcome the accuser (Rev. 12:11).

God Ordained Man to Be the One to Destroy Satan

> Now when the tempter came to Him, he said, "*If You are the Son of God,* command that these stones become bread." But He answered and said, "It is written, 'Man shall not live by bread alone, but by every word that proceeds from the mouth of God.'" Then the Devil took Him up into the holy city, set Him on the pinnacle of the temple, and said to Him, "*If You are the Son of God,* throw Yourself down. For it is written: 'He shall give His angels charge over you,' and, 'In [their] hands they shall bear you up, lest you dash your foot against a stone.'" Jesus said to him, "It is written again, 'You shall not tempt the LORD your God.'"
>
> — Matthew 4:3–7, emphasis added

When Satan came to tempt Jesus Christ, his first two attempts aimed at seducing Jesus to do something miraculous — like God. Notice both of these temptations started with the phrase, "If you are the Son of God."

Even though Jesus IS the Son of God, He was ordained to defeat Satan *as a man*. Jesus replied to Satan remaining in the position of a man, stating that man lives by God's Word and should not tempt God. Jesus didn't fall for Satan's temptations. He resisted doing anything supernatural, as God can.

It is interesting that Satan tempted Adam and Eve by telling them the same thing: They would "be like God" if they ate of the tree of knowledge of good and evil. Similarly, Satan attempted to tempt Jesus into taking a stand to demonstrate that He is God. Adam and Eve failed, but Jesus succeeded by staying in the position of man to defeat God's enemy, Satan. Adam, though man, was defeated by his desire to be God, to be independent from God. Jesus, though God, was victorious by depending on God as a man.

> But we see Jesus, who was made a little lower than the angels, for the suffering of death crowned with glory and honor, that He, by the grace of God, might taste death for everyone. . . . Inasmuch then as the children have partaken of flesh and blood, He Himself likewise shared in the same, that through death He might destroy [inoperative] him who had the power of death, that is, the Devil.
>
> — Hebrews 2:9, 14

In his physical attributes and mental capabilities, man was created lower than the least of the angels. Angels are much more powerful than man; while the top angel's rebellion was an attempt to become God and rule over everything, *God's* desire is that the lowly man defeat Satan and be placed in the very position Satan coveted. In his opposition to God's plan, Satan detested man. Satan's goal is to kill every man on earth if possible. He used the ultimate weapon he possesses — death — to crucify Jesus. Satan must have thought he had won, putting to death God Himself!

Apparently, he didn't know that the death of this sinless God–man would be his very undoing. He didn't know the power of the true resurrection life of God. Resurrection life cannot be tested and proven, until it is put to death. God needed Satan's power of death to manifest His resurrection life.

Jesus Christ came as the lowliest of men, was put to death by the Devil, and subsequently resurrected and ascended. He was crowned with glory and honor *as a man*. The Devil was made inoperative, defeated by his own schemes and weapons, while the man that he killed became the One at the pinnacle — the position that Satan desired. This is the universal "poetic justice."

Man – A Vessel to Ultimately Contain and Become One with God

> Does not the potter have power over the clay, from the same lump to make one vessel for honor and another for dishonor? What if God, wanting to show His wrath and to make His power known, endured with much longsuffering the vessels of wrath prepared for destruction, and that He might make known the riches of His glory on the vessels of mercy, which He had prepared beforehand for glory, even us whom He called, not of the Jews only, but also of the Gentiles?
>
> – Romans 9:21–24

A beautiful image throughout Scripture is that of God as the master potter, and His people as clay. For example, the Old Testament prophet Isaiah declared, "You are our Father; We are the clay, and You our potter; And all we are the work of Your hand" in Isaiah 64:8. Paul draws from this potter–clay imagery in Romans 9:20–24. God created man to be a vessel, to contain the "riches of His glory" (Rom. 9:23).

"Glory" is the very expression of who God is. When a "clay vessel" contains the riches of His glory, the vessel itself will also *express* God's glory. What a waste if a vessel does not contain what it was made to contain! What mercy, that believers have received the riches of God's glory in Christ Jesus. God is still enduring and waiting for more vessels to be filled with His riches. These riches can't be earned, and no one deserves them. Believers only need to be open to hear, receive, and be filled.

> For we do not preach ourselves, but Christ Jesus the Lord, and ourselves your bondservants for Jesus' sake. For it is the God who commanded light to shine out of darkness, who has shone in our hearts to give the light of the knowledge of the glory of God in the face of Jesus Christ. But we have this treasure in earthen vessels, that the excellence of the power may be of

> God and not of us. We are hard-pressed on every side, yet not crushed; we are
> perplexed, but not in despair.
>
> – 2 Corinthians 4:5–7

As believers hear the good news of Jesus Christ, God's light shines into their darkened hearts and they receive light from the knowledge of Jesus Christ. At that very moment, Jesus Christ Himself becomes the treasure indwelling these earthen "vessels." Without this treasure, earthen vessels are almost worthless. One day they will become dirt again. The highest treasure in the universe cannot be bought or earned, but He can come inside and make the vessel glorious. Possessing this treasure provides an unlimited supply of God's energy and power within the believer. When believers are hard-pressed, or perplexed by challenges, they can draw from this power to continue triumphantly. Not only so, but in the midst of their own problems, they can still provide love, support, and eternal life to those around them.

This Human Vessel, or "Container" Has Three Parts – Body, Soul and Spirit

- Body – To contact and contain the physical world
- Soul – Composed of the mind, emotions and will, to contact the psychological world
- Spirit– To contact and to contain God

> And the LORD God formed man of the dust of the ground, and breathed into
> his nostrils the breath of life; and man became a living soul.
>
> – Genesis 2:7, KJV

> And the very God of peace sanctify you wholly; and I pray God your whole spirit
> and soul and body be preserved blameless unto the coming of our Lord Jesus
> Christ.
>
> – 1 Thessalonians 5:23

The whole, human person consists of three distinct parts: body, soul and spirit. It is clear that the body is composed of the elements of the earth. The physical body is able to relate to the physical world, and is a vessel that needs to consume material food in order to live. The food that is ingested provides energy and becomes the very constituent of the human body.

Man, then, became a living soul. The word soul in Greek is *psyche,* which is the origin for the English word "psychology." Knowledge, consideration, love and hate, purpose, and the need for accomplishment—these are things of the psychological world. The human soul is hungry for these things. Therefore, for the soul to "eat" is to ingest such things as knowledge and various causes in the world. What was once outside a person becomes part of that person's soul, their personality. Whether knowledge of football or engineering, environmental or social causes, once ingested, this external knowledge will energize and bond with the person's soul. As a result, it becomes hard to distinguish whether the person's thoughts, loves, and purposes reflect who they really are, or whether he or she is emulating someone or something else.

The essence that animates the soul is from the breath of God. The original word for "breathe" and "breath" is also translated "spirit." Therefore, it was the very breath of God that formed the spirit within man to animate man. Thus, the spirit of man was derived from the breath (or spirit) of God. Although man did not actually receive God the Spirit into himself at creation, the spirit of man was attuned to and akin to God's Spirit, such that a connection — a relationship, a receiving, or a union — could be made with God. Man's spirit was formed at creation as a vessel to have a relationship and contain God.

The human spirit is the innermost hunger, even when men or women is well fed both physically and psychologically, and though they may continue learning, accomplishing goals and experiencing loving relationships, there will remain a sense of emptiness, a "void." This is the hunger for a connection with God. Not understanding this yearning, men and women are driven to abusive behaviors or insatiable cravings in an attempt to fill the void that can only be filled by God Himself.

Man Fell by Eating the Wrong Tree, and Became Joined with Satan.

Man chose to eat the tree of the knowledge of good and evil, and was therefore rejected from the Tree of Life.

> Then the serpent said to the woman, "You will not surely die. For God knows that in the day you eat of it your eyes will be opened, and *you will be like God, knowing good and evil.*" So when the woman saw that the tree was good for food, that it was pleasant to the eyes, and a tree desirable to make one wise, she took of its fruit and ate. She also gave to her husband with her, and he ate. Then the eyes of both of them were opened, and they knew that they were naked; and they sewed fig leaves together and made themselves coverings.
>
> – Genesis 3:3–7, emphasis added

Satan raised doubt within man, that God was withholding something good from him. Satan tempted man, deceiving him to believe that if he ate of the tree of the knowledge of good and evil, "[he would] be like God" (Gen. 3:4).

The truth is, God *did* want man to be like Him, but not in that way! God wanted man to depend on Him for life. He wanted man to be like Him, not just in image and likeness, but also with His life and nature. Satan wanted to be like God but *without* God and *independent* from God. He wanted to replace God. Satan's deceptive goal was to actually make man like himself: like God, but *without* God.

Satan wanted man to do this without eating the Tree of Life — without depending on God by ingesting Him. Man fell to this temptation and ate of the tree of knowledge of good and evil. This tree, encompassing such positive words as "knowledge" and "good," is actually a deceptive cloak for death, or the satanic nature. By ingesting this tree, what constituted Satan (such as sin and death) became man's constitution.

> Then the LORD God said, "Behold, the man has become like one of Us, to know good and evil. And now, lest he put out his hand and take also of the tree of life, and eat, and live forever."
>
> So He drove out the man; and He placed cherubim at the east of the garden of Eden, and a flaming sword which turned every way, to guard the way to the tree of life.
>
> – Genesis 3:22, 24

Though man's life and nature became corrupted with sin and death, God could not allow man to continue in such an infected state forever; therefore, God kept man away from the Tree of Life. Man was no longer able to partake of God in this fallen corrupted state. Man was driven away and guarded from the Tree of Life.

Sin Entered One Man, Causing Death to *All* Men

> Therefore, just as *through one man* [Adam] sin entered the world, and death through sin, and thus death spread to all men, because all sinned —
>
> For if by the *one man's offense* death reigned through the one…
>
> For as by *one man's disobedience* many were made sinners.
>
> – Romans 5:12, 17a, 19, emphasis added
>
> For *as in Adam* all die.
>
> – 1 Corinthians 15:22, emphasis added

When Adam ate of the tree of knowledge of good and evil, what he ingested was actually sin and death, something of the satanic life and nature. It was like the DNA of man became transmuted and corrupted. Subsequently, sin and death passed on from one generation of men to another.

What is sin? The original Greek word for "sin" is *hamartia,* which literally means, "missing the mark." The "mark" was the Tree of Life — God, to be life in man. By missing this mark man partook of the tree of death, which includes sin. Satan set up a false dichotomy: good and evil. Satan entices man to focus on good and evil. Whether man actually *does* good or evil, he nonetheless bounces back and forth within the tree of death, totally missing the real mark, which is life. The real choice is not between good or evil, but between life and death.

The result of the sin of eating the wrong tree is death.

Man Became One with God's Enemy, Possessing His Life, Nature and Expression

> You are of your father the devil, and the desires of your father you want to do. He was a murderer from the beginning, and does not stand in the truth, because there is no truth in him. When he speaks a lie, he speaks from his own resources, for he is a liar and the father of it.
>
> – John 8:44

> Serpents, brood of vipers! How can you escape the condemnation of hell?
>
> – Matthew 23:33

> In this the children of God and the children of the devil are manifest: Whoever does not practice righteousness is not of God, nor is he who does not love his brother.
>
> – 1 John 3:10

In both John 8:44 and Matthew 23:33, the Lord Jesus condemns fallen people, speaking particularly the Pharisees (the religious people of Jesus' time). He declares their father to be the Devil. In Matthew 23:33, Jesus actually called the Pharisees "vipers," alluding back to Satan, the chief serpent. Satan was the first murderer, and deception is his nature.

In 1 John 3:10, the apostle notes there are only two groups of people: the children of God (those with God's life and nature), and the children of the Devil (those with Satan's life and nature). Today men express this nature in many ways: selfishness, anger, violence and covetousness. This is the sin nature in humankind today. Parents all over the world consistently teach their young children to be honest, to share, and not be selfish. But no matter how much parents try, children growing up all over the world get angry, become deceptive, and are selfish. This is the sin in humankind developing from within them as they grow and mature. When sin is expressed by hurting others or oneself, those *actions* are recognized and called "sins" (Rom. 4:7).

Man's Entire Condition Became Hopeless

> ...in which you once walked according to the course of this world, according to the prince of the power of the air, the spirit who now works in the sons of disobedience, among whom also we all once conducted ourselves in the lusts of our flesh, fulfilling the desires of the flesh and of the mind, and were by nature children of wrath, just as the others.
>
> ...that at that time you were without Christ, being aliens from the commonwealth of Israel and strangers from the covenants of promise, having no hope and without God in the world.
>
> – Ephesians 2:2–3, 12

This portion of Scripture refers to believers before having faith in Christ. Prior to belief, those in Christ were a real mess, completely under the satanic influence. Their nature had degenerated to one born under God's judgment; they were people truly without hope. Their destiny was (and continues to be today) God's wrath and judgment.

Man's Spirit Is Deadened and Has No Contact with God

> Jesus said to him, "Let the dead bury their own dead, but you go and preach the kingdom of God."
>
> – Luke 9:60

> And you He made alive, who were dead in trespasses and sins...even when we were dead in trespasses, made us alive together with Christ (by grace you have been saved).
>
> – Ephesians 2:1, 5

"The dead" in Luke 9:60 obviously did not refer to those who were physically or psychologically dead. Thus, if people were not dead in body and soul, the only thing Luke could have been referring to was to man's spirit. As a result of the fall, the spirit of man became dead. In God's eyes, fallen man was *already* dead and one with His enemy: death.

Faith in Christ makes believers' spirits alive. This concept is referenced in other places in Scripture, in phrases such as "the new birth," "being born again," or "being regenerated." This new birth (enlivening) happens in the spirit of man with the receiving and entering of the Spirit of God.

Man's Soul Is Vain and Darkened, Driven by a Perverted Love

> This I say, therefore, and testify in the Lord, that you should no longer walk as the rest of the Gentiles walk, in the futility [vanity] of their mind, having their understanding darkened, being alienated from the life of God, because of the ignorance that is in them, because of the blindness of their heart.
>
> – Ephesians 4:17–18

> For men will be lovers of themselves, lovers of money, boasters, proud, blasphemers, disobedient to parents, unthankful, unholy, unloving, unforgiving, slanderers, without self-control, brutal, despisers of good, traitors, headstrong, haughty, lovers of pleasure rather than lovers of God.
>
> – 2 Timothy 3:2–4

Man's soul, due to the fall, was damaged. People's minds — the leading part of their psychological being — became darkened and full of vanity. Though men can be very intelligent, but in relation to God, they are ignorant and blind. Additionally, fallen man's love is self-centered and focused on ego. Even when doing something good, man's love is tainted with a selfish motive. He (or she) is ready to cause harm to others for self-gratification. Man's entire being is alienated and separated from God.

Man's Body Is the Corrupted Flesh Where Sin Dwells

> But now, *it is* no longer I who do it, but sin that dwells in me. For I know that in me (that is, in my flesh) nothing good dwells; for to will is present with me, but *how* to perform what is good I do not find. For the good that I will *to do,* I do not do; but the evil I will not *to do,* that I practice.
>
> I find then a law, that evil is present with me, the one who wills to do good. For I delight in the law of God according to the inward man. But I see another law in my members, warring against the law of my mind, and bringing me into

> captivity to the law of sin which is in my members. O wretched man that I am! Who will deliver me from this body of death?
>
> — Romans 7:17–19, 21–24

Man's body, once created pure and good, became the dwelling place of sin and death. In God's eyes the body became flesh — a derogatory word for the body — where nothing good dwells. It is like the original God-created DNA became corrupted with sin and death through the ingestion of the tree of death. The human body became a body of sin and death (flesh) forcing man to practice evil. But, since God created man good, there is still good in the soul of man and even a longing to agree with God's laws. However, this desire is simply not strong enough to overcome the enslavement of sin, no matter how much good is in a person's mind. Man's "good" is no match for the power of sin and death, the nature of God's enemy.

God Regretted Making Man, Condemning Man under His Righteous Judgment

> The LORD saw that the wickedness of man was great in the earth, and that every intention of the thoughts of his heart was only evil continually. And the LORD regretted that he had made man on the earth, and it grieved him to his heart.
>
> — Genesis 6:5–6, ESV

> ...being filled with all unrighteousness, sexual immorality, wickedness, covetousness, maliciousness; full of envy, murder, strife, deceit, evil-mindedness; *they* are whisperers, backbiters, haters of God, violent, proud, boasters, inventors of evil things, disobedient to parents, undiscerning, untrustworthy, unloving, unforgiving, unmerciful; who, knowing the righteous judgment of God, that those who practice such things are deserving of death, not only do the same but also approve of those who practice them.
>
> — Romans 1:29–32

> But in accordance with your hardness and your impenitent heart you are treasuring up for yourself wrath in the day of wrath and revelation of the righteous judgment of God.
>
> — Romans 2:5

It seemed that the risky venture of creating man was a failure. How great must God's grief have been, seeing man — the desire of His heart — now filled with His enemy! What was in man was evil continually. God's heartache and disappointment was intense enough for Him to regret creating man. There is no record of God regretting creating Satan; yet, He regretted creating man. Why is this?

The stronger and deeper the love is, the more devastating the disappointment of losing the object of this love.

It seemed that all was lost. The man that God desired for His own pleasure and purpose was completely ruined and corrupted. Man, destined to be God's sons, became children of evil; instead of defeating His enemy, man joined himself with Satan and *became* God's enemy. God had no choice according to His righteousness but to judge and condemn man, His heart's love and desire. It seems the entire creation was witness to what appeared to be Satan's triumph over God, and that Satan was wiser than God and even qualified to replace God.

Calling on the Name of the Lord!

> And Adam knew his wife again, and she bore a son and named him Seth, "For God has appointed another seed for me instead of Abel, whom Cain killed." And as for Seth, to him also a son was born; and he named him Enosh. Then *men* began to call on the name of the LORD.
> – Genesis 4:25–26

Adam and Eve bore two sons: Cain and Abel. Cain murdered Abel out of jealousy and anger. Adam then conceived and bore another son, Seth. Seth had a son and called his name Enosh. The name "Enosh" means mortal, a word associated with sickness and disease. Seth realized early in this second generation of mankind that man is sick, frail, weak and mortal.

It is at this point, when men realized their fallen condition, that Scripture says men began to call upon the name of the Lord (Gen. 4:26). From then on until today, calling on the name of the Lord brings salvation to men.

> For there is no difference of Jew and Greek; for the same Lord of all *is* rich into all that call upon him. For every one whosoever, who shall call on the name of the Lord, shall be saved.
> – Romans 10:12–13, DBY

When any person realizes that he or she is fallen and in a poor, sick and dying state, this person has the choice to call upon the name of the Lord Jesus. In Romans 10:12–13, the word for "call" in the original Greek is the word *epikaleō,* which means, "an audible calling out to invoke the Lord Jesus." Human beings need to come to such desperation that they audibly call on the name of the Lord Jesus. He answers with the riches of His life, peace, joy, and more. Calling out to the Lord Jesus brings the Lord's riches into a person and saves this one from the fallen condition. His riches and salvation are for whosoever calls, without prejudice.

Practice: Calling on the Lord

So that you have the complete freedom to call out on the Lord, you will want to be in a place that only the Lord can hear you and no one else. You can be in your room, taking a walk in the park, or be in your car. Just start to call out to the Lord vocally. There is no standard way to do this other than the desire in you to call out and connect with the Lord Jesus.

"Lord Jesus," "Lord Jesus," "Jesus Lord," "Oh Lord," Oh Lord Jesus," "Jesus, Jesus, Lord Jesus," "I love you Lord Jesus, Oh my Lord Jesus…"

Try to call out softly. Try to call out loudly. Call out to Him in sincerity, with a loving heart, in desperation. Call out with a hunger for Him and a desire to be in fellowship with Him, to hear Him.

Do this for a few minutes — just calling out to the Lord Jesus. You may add prayers, but it is not necessary. Many times prayer can divert you to the things that you want to pray for. Calling on the Lord is solely to focus on connecting with the Lord Himself, to be filled with Him, and to have fellowship with Him. If you have never enjoyed the Lord by calling on His name like this before, then you may feel this to be peculiar. But if you persist and get passed your self-consciousness, then you will enter into the realm of Jesus consciousness.

As you learn to call on Him, you can practice calling on Him while you are driving, working, mowing, cooking, washing dishes, or doing laundry; there are so many opportunities throughout life where you can call out to the Lord Jesus and stay connected to Him.

10

GOD'S FULL AND WONDERFUL SALVATION

The unique way of salvation is by grace and through the faith of Jesus Christ. God's salvation is not so simple. It has to conform to His righteous requirements, and can only be accomplished by His life. This chapter will explore the key terms relating to God's complete salvation: grace, faith, redemption, justification, reconciliation, sanctification (both positional and dispositional), regeneration, feeding, renewing, transformation, conformation and glorification. The end result of this wonderful salvation is that mankind (male and female) will express God as His sons in full.

God's Full Salvation for Man Is by Grace Through Faith

> ...even when we were dead in trespasses, made us alive together with Christ (by grace you have been saved)...For by grace you have been saved through faith, and that not of yourselves; it is the gift of God, not of works, lest anyone should boast.
>
> – Ephesians 2:5, 8–9

These verses are clear and definitely state that mankind's (male and female) salvation is purely by grace through faith. In fact, just to make sure there is no misunderstanding, Paul included a contrast to illustrate that it is not even possible to work for salvation: how can man, being dead, work? If there were any effort on man's part at all, it would have opened the door for boasting.

This chapter will present how rich, high, and complete is God's salvation. The popular concept of salvation is understood to be going to heaven, rather than hell, after death. This kind of simplistic concept is not only common among Christians but in pagan religions as well. It's time to appreciate God's full salvation and bring fallen man from the absolute hopelessness of death (see Chapter 9) to something glorious far beyond imagination.

Even faith that brings believers into saving grace is a gift of God. There is nothing that man can do to receive this gift, other than be open and listen to the good news of Jesus Christ through which man receives faith.

Faith Enables Men to Receive the Invisible Things of Christ

Faith is a gift from God, which enables men to substantiate and receive the invisible things concerning Jesus Christ, and what He has accomplished.

> Simon Peter, bondman and apostle of Jesus Christ, to them that have received like precious faith with us through the righteousness of our God and Savior Jesus Christ.
>
> – 2 Peter 1:1, DBY

> Looking unto Jesus, the author and finisher of *our* faith.
>
> – Hebrews 12:2

These verses reveal faith was something the first believers received. It did not originate from them; rather, the author — or originator — was the Lord Jesus. This precious faith that believers received is the same faith that has been given to and received by believers throughout time, everywhere. No believer ever "worked-up" their own faith; neither was that even possible. Man only needs to receive and thank the Lord for this wonderful gift.

> Now faith is [the] substantiating of things hoped for, [the] conviction of things not seen.
>
> – Hebrews 11:1, DBY

Most people think that faith is something they can manipulate for their best interest. If they want something to come to pass, faith can make it happen. The harder one believes, the more likely the event could occur. They believe it is the power of faith that causes something a person wants to materialize.

However, this is contrary to the definition of faith according to the Bible. Real faith enables the receiver of this gift to realize or substantiate what is already there. Faith is the proof or conviction of things not seen. In other words, the items are already there, but it is faith that enables a person to realize it. Faith proves to people that it already exists.

For example, colors surround everyone. However, if a person is blind (or even colorblind), they will not be able to realize those colors. The same can be said of sound. If a person is deaf, music is simply not real to them. Likewise, God in Jesus Christ is very real: His death, resurrection and Lordship of all is true. But to the faithless, these items of truth are mere fairytales. Once faith is received, however, everything concerning Jesus Christ is substantiated, proving His reality.

Grace Is the Believer's Enjoyment of the Lord Jesus

As believers rejoice in Jesus, He works in them to fulfill His good pleasure. Grace came into existence with the Lord Jesus, and He affords real joy, pleasure, sweetness, rejoicing, and enjoyment to His believers

> For from his fullness we have all received, grace upon grace. For the law was given through Moses; grace and truth came [into being] through Jesus Christ.
>
> – John 1:16–17, ESV

The concept of grace in the New Testament is profound. It is much more than just a favor given or being kind to a person — being "gracious." Even the common definition among believers of "unmerited favor" does not truly unveil the meaning of this word. The grace that is of Jesus Christ didn't even come into being until Jesus came. Jesus brought the grace as defined by the New Testament. The Greek word for "grace" is *charis*, which means, "That which affords joy, rejoicing, pleasure, and enjoyment."

This kind of rejoicing and enjoyment simply didn't exist before the coming of Jesus Christ. And when a person receives Him, Jesus affords wave upon wave of joy and enjoyment, hence "grace upon grace." Grace is always fresh, a constant surging of enjoyment toward those who believe. Without Jesus, man (male and female) simply is not afforded real joy, rejoicing, pleasure and enjoyment.

While the law that was given by Moses was demanding, requiring, and condemning, grace came into being through Jesus Christ. While believers cannot fulfill the law and are under the curse of the law, Jesus Christ came to be their joy, rejoicing, and enjoyment. What a contrast! Why wouldn't everyone receive such a wonderful Jesus who originated grace for all men?

> Let us therefore come boldly to the throne of grace, that we may obtain mercy and find grace to help in time of need.
>
> – Hebrews 4:16

The throne of God to which believers come is not the throne of a judge, a commander, or even a king. Rather, the One on the throne, the God-man Jesus Christ, *is* grace affording believers joy, rejoicing and enjoyment. Interestingly, upon approaching this throne there is only one thing to find: grace. And that is exactly what is required for all the help every person needs.

What do all men pursue? In the end, it is just happiness. People pursue things like money, health, fame, relationships, drugs, and sex because they desire enjoyment. Since happiness is the end result of what men pursue, grace is exactly what they need no matter what situations they may end up in. A person's finances or health might be deteriorating; yet, in Christ they find themselves happy, full of joy, rejoicing, and finding enjoyment. If they are truly joyful, they have achieved their pursuit and are satisfied. This is the reason believers in the present experience of grace can stand firm, no matter what challenging situations arise. This is the Lord Jesus as grace in action.

> The Lord Jesus Christ be with your spirit. Grace be with you. Amen.
>
> – 2 Timothy 4:22

When a person receives the faith of Jesus Christ, Jesus — as the Spirit — joins to the believer's spirit. He resides in the core (or the seat) of their being, their spirit. Since He is with them, grace is also with them. No Jesus, no grace; with Jesus, with grace.

If grace is simply Jesus, then why use the word grace? Why say, "Saved by grace" and not just, "Saved by Jesus"?

The reason is because grace speaks of Jesus being the believer's present joy and reason for rejoicing and enjoyment. He is experiential, and His experiential salvation depends on the experiences of Christ as the believer's joy and enjoyment. The believer may be "saved," but if he or she is depressed, anxious or feels condemned, in that person's experience, salvation is far away. But as soon as they come to the throne of grace and find Jesus, He affords the believer joy, rejoicing and enjoyment. They are then practically and experientially saved from all troubling things.

Jesus Works in Believers to Both Save and Fulfill God's Will

> ...who has saved us and called us with a holy calling, not according to our works, but according to His own purpose and grace which was given to us in Christ Jesus before time began.
>
> – 2 Timothy 1:9

Here again, Paul clearly states that people are saved not according to their works, effort, or labor, but according to the Lord's purpose and grace. But the joy, enjoyment and pleasure that the Lord Jesus is to believers doesn't stop there. While they are enjoying Him, something else is transpiring: *salvation.*

Salvation, on one hand, is once for all. On the other hand, it is a life-long process. Unlike mere joy and rejoicing as an end in itself, grace is much more. The more believers enjoy Jesus, the more they are saved according to His purpose. The end result of grace is not just salvation that is good for the believer, but that they become a people that bring God pleasure, according to His eternal purpose.

> . . . through whom also we have access by faith into this grace in which we stand, and rejoice in hope of the glory of God. . . . For if by the one man's offense death reigned through the one, much more those who receive abundance of grace and of the gift of righteousness will reign in life through the One, Jesus Christ. . . . so that as sin reigned in death, even so grace might reign through righteousness to eternal life through Jesus Christ our Lord.
>
> – Romans 5:2, 17, 21

Faith is the only way to realize and take hold of grace, the source that will always afford joy, rejoicing, and enjoyment. Because of faith, believers simply cannot be removed from grace. It is in this grace believers remain and stand.

Faith makes the believers righteous before God, but it is the abundance of grace that causes their *reign* in life. Complete salvation in the Lord's eternal life is through the joy, rejoicing and enjoyment of the Lord Jesus Christ.

Therefore, enjoy Him!

> And He said to me, "My grace is sufficient for you, for My strength is made perfect in weakness." Therefore most gladly I will rather boast in my infirmities, that the power of Christ may rest upon me.
>
> – 2 Corinthians 12:9

> And Nehemiah continued, "Go and celebrate with a feast of rich foods and sweet drinks, and share gifts of food with people who have nothing prepared.

> This is a sacred day before our Lord. Don't be dejected and sad, for the joy of the LORD is your strength!"
>
> – Nehemiah 8:10, NLT

Paul was suffering in his current circumstance, and he prayed to the Lord to change it. The Lord's answer was, "My grace is sufficient for you." The Lord did not change Paul's circumstance; rather, He asked Paul to enjoy Him in it. The Lord — affording joy, pleasure, and enjoyment to Paul — was sufficient salvation for him. While Paul enjoyed God, the Lord's strength was manifested in his weakness. In the same way, when believers just enjoy Him, He can then work to save.

During Nehemiah's time, the people of God were dejected due to their hard situations. Nehemiah's charge was for them to eat and drink, and share their enjoyment with others. This joy in the Old Testament is the grace for us today. The joy of the Lord activates His strength to save. One can even say that outside of enjoying and being joyful in the Lord, salvation in daily experience does not work. To be saved daily, the believer must enjoy Him daily.

Redemption Based on Righteousness with the Blood of Jesus

> Christ has redeemed us from the curse of the law, having become a curse for us (for it is written, "Cursed is everyone who hangs on a tree").
>
> – Galatians 3:13

The words, "redeem" or "redemption" have two meanings: to pay a price to purchase something and to pay a ransom in order to secure a release. Man broke God's law by eating the forbidden fruit in the Garden of Eden and continued to break God's laws as embodied in the Ten Commandments throughout the ages. This unleashed God's judgment and brought the curse according to the law. God had to judge man according to the righteous requirements of His law. If, after man broke God's law he was not judged according to the law, then God would have also broken His own law by unrighteously forgiving man. Man's curse is fully based on the law, and redemption is a therefore a legal or judicial matter. The payment is based on the law.

Consider the following illustration: Say a man breaks the law by stealing from another person, and he is caught. The thief is then brought before a judge to determine guilt and punishment according to the law. If the thief happens to be the judge's son, that judge cannot arbitrarily forgive his son just because he loves him; if he did, he would be an unrighteous judge and the victim might not receive due restitution. The judge has to sentence his son according to the extent of the law, and that includes full payment back to his victim. This is the "curse of the law" for his crime. After the sentencing, if the son spent all his money and could not pay back his victim, he would continue under the "curse" until the debt is paid. The judge then, as his father and out of love, could pay the debt for his son. When the debt was fully paid, his son would no longer bear the curse of his crime.

This is what is meant by redemption based on righteousness. The demand for the price of death has to be paid according to righteousness. Yet, it was God's love to send His only begotten Son to pay the price of death on man's behalf.

> Not with the blood of goats and calves, but with His own blood He entered the Most Holy Place once for all, having obtained eternal redemption.
> – Hebrews 9:12

The judgment for breaking God's law is the curse of death. God's law would not have been satisfied unless man died. Man's sin was a capital offense. What an unbearable price and punishment! Goats and calves cannot die in man's stead to pay off God's judgment. That is like a thief owing someone a billion dollars, and trying to pay it off the debt with an apple.

Since the sentence was the death of man, a *sinless* man who wasn't under the curse of death had to die. Jesus Christ paid that price and the ransom to release man from this curse of death. Because Jesus is both God and man He can legally obtain eternal redemption. As a man, He has human blood to die for man's sins; as God, His blood has eternal value and is thus able to pay for the sins of all of mankind, throughout time and space.

> ...knowing that you were not redeemed with corruptible things, like silver or gold, from your aimless conduct received by tradition from your fathers, but with the precious blood of Christ, as of a lamb without blemish and without spot.
> – 1 Peter 1:18

All fallen men are living in a way that is vain or aimless, whether their manner of life is worldly (living for the riches and glories of this world), fleshly (desiring the shameful things of their passion) or even religious (practicing religious traditions from their forefathers). These lifestyles are worthless and empty.

Money, fame, possessions or religious rituals can never release man from vanity and emptiness; only the blood of Jesus Christ can do this. When a person receives and believes into Jesus Christ, his life becomes full and purposeful.

Forgiveness and Cleansing of Sins

> ...in whom we have redemption through His blood, the forgiveness of sins.
> – Colossians 1:14

> ...and without the shedding of blood there is no forgiveness of sins.
> – Hebrews 9:22, ESV

Since Christ paid the highest price by His death, it satisfied man's debt under God's judgment; therefore, sins are forgiven. According to the illustration above, when judgment that required paying back stolen money (plus any penalty according to the law) was paid, the thief was no longer guilty. Rather, he received a full pardon.

Man's debt to God according to His judgment was death; therefore, Jesus Christ needed to die in order to pay off man's debt under God's judgment. Now, the believer's past, present, and future sins are forgiven through simple faith in Jesus Christ.

> ...then He [God] adds, "Their sins and their lawless deeds I will remember no more."
>
> – Hebrews 10:17

God's memory is wonderful. When man sins, God cannot forget until the judgment is paid. However once it is paid, He cannot remember sin at all. To Him, it is like the believer has never sinned; they were never under judgment. After coming to faith in Christ, believers also need a memory like God's, in order to forget about their sins. Believers can stand with confidence and boldness before God, because in God's eyes, believers in Christ have never been sinners.

> But if we walk in the light as He is in the light, we have fellowship with one another, and the blood of Jesus Christ His Son cleanses us from all sin. ...If we confess our sins, He is faithful and just to forgive us our sins and to cleanse us from all unrighteousness.
>
> – 1 John 1:7, 9

The blood of Jesus is able to cleanse all people from even the *stain* of sin. If a person spilled grape juice on another person's shirt, they could genuinely be forgiven for the accident. However, there might still be a stain left from the juice as a reminder of the spill. What if the stain of sin remained to remind believers of their past sins? That would be terrible! The blood of Jesus is such that even the stain of sin is gone. There is no reminder of past, present or future failures. Believers simply receive His cleansing by confessing sin (admitting sin by repeating back to God what He is revealing to their conscience) for both forgiveness and cleansing. What a release to be freed from bearing the burden of a guilty conscience.

Justification – Righteous Before God

God approves believers based on His standard of righteousness. This is called "justification."

> . . . being justified freely by His grace through the redemption that is in Christ Jesus, whom God set forth as a propitiation by His blood, through faith, . . . to demonstrate at the present time His righteousness, that He might be just and the justifier of the one who has faith in Jesus.
>
> – Romans 3:24–26

To "justify" someone means to declare (or approve of) him or her righteous, or right. In this case, according to Romans 3:24–26, the "approver" or the "declarer" is God. In ancient biblical times, "propitiation" was the action of propitiating or appeasing a god, spirit, or person. In the case of Christ, the blood of Jesus appeased God's demand for judgment. Justification can happen for the believer because the blood of Jesus acts as propitiation. It has appeased God's demand of judgment. Since man's standard of righteousness is often quite low, it is easy for men and women to consider one another to be "righteous." But God's standard of righteousness is higher than the heavens. Therefore, it is amazing that God would declare man, through the faith of Christ, righteous! In God's valuation, believers are as righteous as He is. In fact, their righteousness is based on and is a manifestation of His righteousness. It is precisely because He is righteous that He is *required* to justify His children and declare that they are as righteous as He.

Say a judge fines a person $10,000 for a crime according to the law. After the entire amount of the fine is paid off including penalty and interest, if the judge comes back and asks for more money from the person, that judge would be considered unrighteous. Since the debt has been paid in full, the judge, according to righteousness, should then declare the person to be righteous; this person should owe nothing else.

Jesus Christ has paid off mankind's debt of sin in full through His death; therefore, God, according to His righteous judgment, is required to justify all those having the faith of Jesus; otherwise, He would be unrighteous.

> ...knowing that a man is not justified by the works of the law but by faith in Jesus Christ, even we have believed in Christ Jesus, that we might be justified by faith in Christ and not by the works of the law; for by the works of the law no flesh shall be justified.
>
> – Galatians 2:16

This justification that believers have received from God is not because of any effort to fulfill God's law. In fact, a person could try their utmost to follow God's laws and requirements, but they cannot be justified. So give up trying and just accept and enjoy what Jesus Christ has done! Trying to please God through endless effort to fulfill His laws will only guarantee being kept *under* the curse of the law, since one can never fulfill all His requirements. The only way to immediately fulfill all of God's demands is through the faith of Jesus Christ.

Reconciliation – Mutual Love and Respect

Once a person puts their faith in Christ, the requirement for their sin is satisfied and they become reconciled to God.

> For if when we were enemies we were reconciled to God through the death of His Son, much more, having been reconciled, we shall be saved by His life. And not only that, but we also rejoice in God through our Lord Jesus Christ, through whom we have now received the reconciliation.
>
> – Romans 5:10–11

Fallen men were not just sinners, but they became God's enemies. Due to the hostility between God and man, reconciliation was and still is needed. If a friend steals from another friend and gets caught, even if the person pays back everything, the likelihood is high that they will no longer be friends. Reconciliation is needed.

The death of Christ not only paid off man's debt to God, justifying those who believe before Him, but Jesus Christ also *reconciled* people to God. Those who believe are no longer enemies, but can carry on an intimate relationship as if the offense never happened. No wonder believers rejoice! In Christ, there is mutual love and respect between God and man.

Sanctification – Made Holy

Not only are believers justified and reconciled to God, they area also "sanctified" (or made holy). This means those in Christ are separated for God in their position.

> To the church [assembly] of God which is at Corinth, to those who are sanctified in Christ Jesus, called to be saints, with all who in every place call on the name of Jesus Christ our Lord, both theirs and ours.
>
> – 1 Corinthians 1:2

The moment a person believes and calls on the name of Jesus Christ the Lord, they are immediately sanctified and called "saints."

The words "sanctified" and "saints" are actually derived from the same Greek word *hagos,* which means "holy." Holy means something separated for God. Since faith brings people into Christ Jesus, believers immediately become holy — not because of their condition or behavior, but simply because of their new position in Christ.

> Woe to you, blind guides, who say, 'Whoever swears by the temple, it is nothing; but whoever swears by the gold of the temple, he is obliged to perform it.' Fools and blind! For which is greater, the gold or the temple that sanctifies the gold? ... 'Fools and blind! For which is greater, the gift or the altar that sanctifies the gift?
>
> – Matthew 23:16–17, 19

In the Old Testament, the gold or the animal to be offered to God became holy simply by changing its location or position from outside the temple to within the temple, or from wandering in the field to be on the altar. Even though the nature or characteristics of the gold or the animal didn't change, once the position was changed it was made holy.

This is the same with believers, who are now holy in their *position* in Christ. Even though their character is very much the same as before they believed, the fact that they have believed into Jesus Christ sanctifies them…and they are called *saints.*

The Organic Salvation by the Life of Christ

Jesus became the life-giving spirit indwelling and working in believers. This is what salvation is based on: the organic life of Christ.

> For if when we were enemies we were reconciled to God through the death of His Son, much more, having been reconciled, we shall be saved by His life.
>
> – Romans 5:10

This verse, Romans 5:10, lays out the believer's complete salvation in two parts: The first part is accomplished through His death, and the second is accomplished by His life.

Jesus' death of redemption fully accomplished forgiveness, cleansing, justification and reconciliation. This part is what is known as the "positional" or "judicial" side of salvation. However, there is an even more wonderful side of His salvation that is *within* the believer; this is known as the "dispositional" or "organic" side of salvation.

Faith in Jesus Christ brings His very divine eternal life into the believer's inner being. His life is now saving people organically.

Consider now, item by item, what the "saving in His life" means to the believer. This knowledge is wonderful, and the daily experiences are full of enjoyment.

Regeneration – The New Birth of the Divine Life

When a person believes into Jesus Christ, they receive the Spirit through faith.

> But as many as received Him, to them He gave the right to become children of God, to those who believe in [Gr. into] His name: who were born, not of blood, nor of the will of the flesh, nor of the will of man, but of God.
>
> – John 1:12–13

The immediate inner transaction that happens when someone first comes to faith in Jesus Christ is a new birth (or being born anew). Many refer to this as being "born again" or regeneration. This new birth is of God. This is the birth that brings in His life and nature, giving believers the right or authority to be children of God. There are no steps to climb to achieve this. All that is needed is for the person to receive Him, to believe into His name. A person's pet dog is a dog because it's born of a dog. It is absolutely impossible to be an offspring of anything other than what the animal is born of. Likewise, believers are sons of man because they are born of man, but at the same time are children of God because they are born of God.

> Jesus answered, "Most assuredly, I say to you, unless one is born of water and the Spirit, he cannot enter the kingdom of God. That which is born of the flesh is flesh, and that which is born of the Spirit is spirit. Do not marvel that I said to you, 'You must be born again [Gr. anew].'"
>
> – John 3:5–7

The only way for a person to enter into a particular kingdom is if that person has the life of that kingdom. For example, only plants are in the botanical kingdom; only animals can be in the animal kingdom. The only way to enter the human kingdom is to be born human. Following this line of thought, the only way to enter the kingdom of God is to be born of God – the Spirit.

"Water" in John 3:5 in context should refer to baptism, which was what John the Baptist did for the introduction of Jesus Christ. The water of baptism means the end and burial of the old creation, making it possible for a person to rise up in the new creation by being born of Spirit. The first birth was of the flesh; therefore, man is flesh. The second birth is of the Spirit. When the Spirit of God enters and joins with man's spirit, the innermost part of a person's being – their spirit – is then born of Spirit.

> Whoever believes that Jesus is the Christ is born of God, and everyone who loves Him who begot also loves him who is begotten of Him.
>
> – 1 John 5:1

What Does the New Birth Feel Like?

The only requirement to initiate this salvation of a new birth is belief that Jesus is the Christ, the Son of God, and that He resurrected from the dead.

How do people feel when they have this new birth? Experiences can vary from person to person. People may experience various levels of joy, peace, strength, and fulfillment. Sometimes this occurs immediately at the moment they pray and call on His name in faith to receive the Lord Jesus. Or this experience may come months later. In any event, sooner or later, it is inevitable that the new birth will be a powerful life-changing experience. One clear indication that new birth has occurred is the innate sense of love the new believer has for all other believers of the Lord Jesus Christ, regardless of socio-economic differences, skin color or ethnic diversity.

Feeding – Food for Growth

As newborn babes, believers need continual feeding to grow into salvation.

> ...newborn babes desire earnestly the pure mental milk of the word, that by it ye may grow up to salvation, if indeed ye have tasted that the Lord is good.
>
> – 1 Peter 2:2, DBY

Birth is simply the initiation of the new life in Christ. Every life at birth starts as a babe, and every babe needs to grow. This is the same for believers at their spiritual birth. Immediately, there is a deep desire for milk in order to grow. The salvation received is a growing salvation. The more a believer grows, the more they are saved in their daily experiences.

For example, even as a believer, a person may struggle with losing their temper. Or, they may experience anxiety or even bouts of depression. These are external signs that the believer needs the daily salvation from these symptoms of death. As believers ingest the pure milk of the Word, the new life in them grows and saves them from their temper and anxiety. This is the "much more" saving in His life Paul spoke of in Romans 5:10. The Lord is so good when believers taste His Word and grow in this way.

> ...and not holding firmly to the Head, from whom all the body, being supplied and knit together through the joints and ligaments, grows with God's growth.
>
> – Colossians 2:19, HNV

Religious practices, law, and various philosophies distracted the recipients of this letter to the Colossians; therefore, they were NOT holding firmly to Jesus Christ, the Head. Paul encouraged the Colossians to come back and hold fast to the Head from which the entire body of Christ is derived. As believers are in the supply of the body, they grow with God's growth.

According to this verse, spiritual growth is the very increase of God in man. As believers experience more and more of God, they grow up more and more. The believer's growth is not measured by a change in behavior or the mere increase of Biblical knowledge; it is from the increase of *God within the believers.*

Dispositional Sanctification

Dispositional sanctification is the process of being made holy. By partaking of God's holy and divine nature, the believer's entire being is being sanctified.

> Now may the God of peace Himself sanctify you completely; and may your whole spirit, soul, and body be preserved blameless at the coming of our Lord Jesus Christ.
>
> – 1 Thessalonians 5:23

Paul writes that sanctification — being made holy — is inward. It starts from the believer's spirit and soul and needs the God of peace Himself to grow in each believer day by day until the Lord's second coming. God Himself comes into the believer's spirit through the new birth, makes their spirit holy, and spreads His holiness to their souls and even to their bodies. Their entire being is made holy. In the entire universe only God is holy; therefore, only by God growing and increasing in believers can they be completely sanctified.

> ...by which have been given to us exceedingly great and precious promises, that through these you may be partakers of the divine nature, having escaped the corruption that is in the world through lust.
>
> – 2 Peter 1:4

How wonderful! Believers in Jesus Christ are partakers of the divine nature. The word "divine" literally refers to God. The divine nature is God's nature. As human beings with the human nature, believers can also partake of the divine nature. Believers are both human and divine. God's nature includes such items as unconditional love, perfect righteousness, unfathomable mercy, and genuine humility. As they partake, these items also become the believer's true nature.

It is this divine nature that makes believers holy. The more they partake of the divine nature, the more it affects their character since a person's character expresses his or her nature. This partaking of the divine nature has an effect on the person's character: dispositional sanctification. This means believers have escaped positionally into Christ through His death, so that they may partake of the divine life's nature. By this partaking, they also escape the corruption of their fallen nature.

> Do you not know that the unrighteous will not inherit the kingdom of God? Do not be deceived. Neither fornicators, nor idolaters, nor adulterers, nor homosexuals, nor sodomites, nor thieves, nor covetous, nor drunkards, nor revilers, nor extortioners will inherit the kingdom of God. And such were some of you. But you were washed, but you were sanctified, but you were justified in the name of the Lord Jesus and by the Spirit of our God.
>
> – 1 Corinthians 6:9–11

All fallen people have the sinful nature, and have committed at least one of these offenses. Some have lived out their fallen nature habitually and without restraint and are known to be such types of persons. Even some believers could have been known to exhibit one or more of these characteristics. That is why it is so important that one's nature and character is washed, sanctified, and justified by the Spirit.

Notice here that unlike judicial redemption (accomplished through the Lord's blood), this washing, sanctifying and justifying is through His Spirit. A person's disposition or character is within them, and only the Spirit of God indwelling a person can change. When believers are sanctified in this way, it doesn't necessarily mean they will never fail and fall into sin again. It does mean, however, they no longer express their fallen nature habitually to be then labeled as a certain type of sinner. This is the meaning of dispositional sanctification: God's nature is saving believers from inward corruption.

Renewing of the Mind

As the Spirit penetrates the believer's mind, their logic and reasoning begins to change to the mind of Christ.

> And do not be conformed to this world, but be transformed by the renewing of your mind, that you may prove what is that good and acceptable and perfect will of God.
>
> – Romans 12:2

People live and are guided by the way they think. What is important to them in their thinking is what they will pursue and how they will work things out. Therefore, the believer's mind needs renewing; otherwise, their thinking will be no different from the people of this age, and it will conform them to this world. However if the believer's thinking is changed through renewal, then their experiences, goals, and the way they live will follow. For example, if a person thinks God hates them and wants to punish them, their experiences in life will reflect that belief. Those life experiences would be drastically different if they thought that God loves them, wants the best for them, and counts them as righteous as Him. Or, if a person thinks money is the most important pursuit in life, they will live differently than if they thought that *God* should have the preeminence in their life. Changing one's thinking is central to the changing of one's character.

> Let nothing be done through selfish ambition or conceit, but in lowliness of mind let each esteem others better than himself. Let each of you look out not only for his own interests, but also for the interests of others. Let this mind be in you which was also in Christ Jesus.
>
> – Philippians 2:3–5

Reading His Word and receiving the knowledge of Jesus Christ renews the believer's mind and transforms it to His mind. The minds of immature believers will be focused on selfish ambitions, but as they open themselves up to read the Word concerning Jesus, they enter into fellowship with Him and their thinking begins to change — to be renewed. As a result of such a renewing of the mind, they spontaneously start to look out for the interests of others and to genuinely and unselfishly care for others; they do not consider themselves better than everyone else.

> ...and be renewed in the spirit of your mind.
>
> – Ephesians 4:23

The Word of God is also Spirit. It does not just pass on information, knowledge and logic for the mind, but it is also living and full of the Spirit. This potent Spirit works in the renewing of the mind. Logic is not the only thing that changes, but the Spirit in the believer's spirit penetrates and spreads throughout their whole inner being. That is why it is called the spirit of their mind. The more the believer's mind is renewed, the more he or she will be affected by the Spirit; the more the Spirit affects the believer's mind, the more he or she is renewed. For this reason when believers approach the Bible, they should try to understand its logic, and pray with their praying spirit to allow the Holy Spirit to guide them into the reality of all the things of Christ. This brings in the renewing of the mind.

Transformation

Through this life process of metamorphosis, believers are being changed from their old form to that of Christ.

> And do not be conformed to this world, but be transformed by the renewing of your mind, that you may prove what is that good and acceptable and perfect will of God.
>
> – Romans 12:2

The result of the renewing of the mind is transformation. The Greek word for transformation is the origin of the word "metamorphosis," meaning a profound change in form from one stage to the next in the history of an organism, as from a caterpillar to a butterfly.[17] Believers are also going through a transformation because the DNA of the life of Jesus Christ is in their very being. Transformation is part of the history of Christ's organic salvation of all believers. As they eat and drink of Him for growth and as their minds are renewed by the Spirit (and the knowledge of Him), a transformation takes place in their being.

The world conforms people to a certain way of thinking and living through external influences such as advertising and fashion. But believers are being transformed by an indwelling life according to the divine "DNA" from within.

> But we all, with unveiled face, beholding as in a mirror the glory of the Lord, are being transformed into the same image from glory to glory, just as by the Spirit of the Lord.
>
> – 2 Corinthians 3:18

---

17   http://www.dictionary.com/browse/metamorphoses

What are believers being transformed into? Paul says they are being transformed into the image of Jesus Christ, whom they are beholding. An "unveiled face" is a face that has turned from trying to keep God's law and now simply beholds the Lord. By beholding (and reflecting) Jesus, believers are continually being transformed to the Lord's image so that they transcend, love, forgive, endure, rest, and rejoice as He does. They become Him in life, nature, and expression, and He becomes them in their living, actions...and even their *reactions*. This is happening from glory to glory, and it is because of His indwelling, life-giving Spirit working in the believers.

Conformed and Glorified

The last step in the believer's salvation will happen when even their bodies will be transfigured to a glorious body to fully express God.

> For whom He foreknew, He also predestined to be conformed to the image of His Son, that He might be the firstborn among many brethren. Moreover whom He predestined, these He also called; whom He called, these He also justified; and whom He justified, these He also glorified.
>
> – Romans 8:29–30

This is the end result of transformation: believers are conformed to the image of God's Son in every way. Their spirit is joined to Him and becomes one Spirit. Their mind becomes the mind of Christ, their soul is fully in His image, and their bodies are glorified. Conformation and glorification is the end of God's full salvation. His organic salvation that began in the believers' spirit continues through the daily salvation of their soul, and will culminate at His return with the glorification of their entire being, including their physical bodies. What a wonderful salvation!

> ...who will transform our lowly body that it may be conformed to His glorious body, according to the working by which He is able even to subdue all things to Himself.
>
> – Philippians 3:21

Even though today Jesus Christ is in the believer and their inner character is being transformed, their physical body is still lowly in humiliation due to sin and death in the flesh. Because the believer's body is still flesh, it is susceptible to disease, aging, indwelling sin, and eventually death. No matter how much their disposition has become an image of Christ, their bodies remain the same until the day of glorification. On that day they will transfigure into a "butterfly" (metaphorically). In reality, and much more magnificently, they will have a body like Jesus' glorious body. That glorious body will discard the body of flesh, and not only be freed from sin and death, but be one filled with and expressing the glory of God. This is the final subduing of all things fallen, originating from Adam. This is salvation to the uttermost. How wonderful!

Practice! Enjoy the Lord through Singing

In addition to considering, praying and praising the Word, a simple and enjoyable way to enjoy the Lord is through singing. Sing hymns and songs from songbooks or from memory. Singing hymns and songs to the Lord will cause you to turn to the Lord and focus on Him. You will forget your anxieties and problems.

Better yet, make up your own songs by singing Scriptures using an existing tune or come up with your own tune. Get out of your comfort zone! It is not a matter of how good your voice is or how well your lyrics rhyme together, but it is making a joyful sound from a melody in your heart to the Lord.

Find a hymn online this week, and spend 10 minutes to sing to the Lord. Then spend another 15 minutes to sing a song to the Lord using a verse from the Bible that inspires you. Use a tune that you know or just make up your own tune. The key to this exercise is to forget about how well you can compose or how well you carry a tune, just focus on singing to the Lord and enjoying Him.

After you have enjoyed singing this new song to the Lord, then share it and sing it to someone else or at the next fellowship gathering. The Lord will be fresh in your experience of Him through your singing.

11

THE OIKONOMIA (ECONOMY) OF GOD

The Greek word for economy, *oikonomia*, was prominently used in the New Testament to describe a mystery relating to God's will, pleasure, and eternal purpose. Without a full understanding of this word and the concept of *oikonomia*, it would be very difficult to have a complete understanding what God is doing to fulfill His purpose. That is why the apostle Paul determined to bring light to this idea of *oikonomia*. All believers should not only participate in the *oikonomia* of grace, but they should take active responsibility for carrying out and furthering God's *oikonomia*.

Oikonomia and the Mystery of God's Eternal Purpose

Understanding *oikonomia* is critical to understanding the mystery of God's eternal purpose. The definition of this Greek word is "household management." *Oikonomia* is a word rich in meaning, and translators have used various English words for *oikonomia* in the New Testament, depending on context: administration, dispensation, plan, stewardship, and economy.

"Household management" in the first century described the proper administration needed to effectively grow a household. The following scenario uses the translated words (underlined) to describe *oikonomia:* a rich father who desired to build up his family would have an <u>administration</u> specifically to <u>dispense</u> food to multiple generations of his children scattered in his vast land, that they might be fed and grow to increase his household. The <u>steward</u> would be the one dispensing and responsible for carrying out this plan.

The anglicized word for *oikonomia* is "economy." Contemporary usage for this word is the production, distribution and consumption of goods. If any part of this chain is weak, the entire economy suffers. A growing economy equals a strong nation.

Oikonomia is composed of two words: *oiko* means "house," and *nomia*, derived from the Greek root word *nomos* which means "law"; therefore, *oikonomia* literally means "house-law."

Law *(nomos)* comes from the primary word *nemo* meaning, "To parcel out, especially food or grazing to animals." It seems counterintuitive that law, which is so strict and demanding, comes from a word meaning the parceling out of food. In God's view, His laws have an underlining purpose: to feed.

God's original intention in establishing law was not as something for His children to keep, but rather to give them food. Interestingly, the very first command from God was to eat: "of every tree of the garden you may freely eat" (Gen. 1:26).

Food was actually dispensed through the law since the entire law included the offerings and the eating of them. When a commandment was broken, in order to fulfill the law, an offering had to be made accompanied by the consumption of the offering. Righteousness according to the law was made possible by these offerings; when the offerings were made for sins and trespasses, a portion was to be eaten. In the New Testament, Jesus Christ is the real offering and believers do partake and eat of Him as the Lamb of God.

This is why Paul could say in Philippians 3:6 that concerning the righteousness which is in the law, he was blameless. However, Paul admitted in Romans 7 that he could not keep the law, but practiced evil. Then how could he say that he was blameless in the law?

This is because Paul also *made sacrifices* according to the law, in order to be *forgiven* according to the law. From the view of distributing food, the more the moral law was broken, the more offerings were needed — resulting in enjoyment from consuming the offerings.

This concept should be applied to believers in the New Testament. Every time there is conviction of sin or failure, believers should turn to Jesus Christ to enjoy Him as their redemption and their food for strengthening. This is why Paul could say in Romans 5:20, "where sin abounded, grace abounded much more." It seems clear that *oikonomia*, or *house-law*, has everything to do with the distribution of food for the household.

God's Economy Is How He Accomplishes His Will and Eternal Purpose

God makes known to His children His mysterious will, which is to head up all things in Christ. He accomplishes this through His economy.

> ...having made known to us the mystery of his will, according to his good pleasure which he purposed in himself into the <u>administration</u> *[oikonomia]* of the fullness of times; to head up all things in the Christ, the things in the heavens and the things upon the earth.
>
> —Ephesians 1:9–10a, DBY

God has a will — a purpose — according to His good pleasure. Human beings also set purposes and life goals that are according to *their* pleasure or to what is pleasing to them. God's ultimate purpose, however, is to head up all things in Christ. Everything in the entire universe will be summed up in Christ as the head. As seen in Chapter 7, this Christ in eternity is both God and man. God's purpose is that everything will have Jesus Christ as the Head. Believers will not be able to really grasp the depth and height of what this actually means until eternity.

While this won't happen in completeness until the future, God's economy *(oikonomia)* is needed during this span of time before eternity. Therefore, before time is filled up (or over with), God's economy is needed among men. It is God's economy that accomplishes what He desires, and it fulfills His purpose of heading up all things in Christ. Therefore, God's economy is God's way (method or plan) to accomplish His ultimate will.

These verses clearly show the prominence of God's economy *(oikonomia)* in relation to His will, purpose, and pleasure. Therefore, understanding God's economy is critical in realizing God's ultimate purpose. Believers who do not understand the concept of God's economy may easily become entangled with non-essential doctrines and subservient to religious regulations or hypes.

Next, let's prayerfully consider the following verses to come to a fuller grasp of God's economy.

Stewards Dispensing Grace—the Riches of Christ

Stewards in God's economy dispense grace (the riches of Christ for the believer's enjoyment) with a vision of the building of the body of Christ—God's household. An example of a steward in the New Testament is the apostle Paul. Paul received the *oikonomia* (stewardship, dispensation, administration) of the grace of God, so that he could then dispense this grace to the believers.

> . . . (if indeed ye have heard of the administration *[oikonomia]* of the grace of God which has been given to me towards [Greek: *into*] you, that by revelation the mystery has been made known to me, . . .
>
> – Ephesians 3:2–3, DBY

Paul wrote that God's economy had been given to him, and it was the economy of grace. He understood he was to be a steward in administering and dispensing this grace to people.

Grace is the spiritual food that believers need for sustenance and for spiritual growth. Grace was given to Paul so that he might be a "dispenser of grace" into men. God's entire economy is an economy of grace. Grace as the product, which arrived and was made available with Jesus Christ (John 1:17), is to be distributed to all that they may enjoy all the riches of Christ and grow by receiving grace. The entire chain of God's economy is grace, and its supply is unlimited because its eternal source is Jesus Christ.

All of humanity demands and seeks grace (pleasure and enjoyment). This is why stewards are needed to distribute grace to *all* men.

The Revelation Concerning the Mystery of Christ

The first item dispensed to the believers is revelation concerning the mystery of Christ—joint heirs, joint body and joint partakers. This is God's household.

> . . . that by revelation the mystery has been made known to me, . . . the mystery of the Christ, which in other generations has not been made known to the sons of men, as it has now been revealed to His holy apostles and prophets in the power of the Spirit, that they who are of the nations should be joint heirs, and a joint body, and joint partakers of His promise in Christ Jesus through the glad tidings.
>
> – Ephesians 3:3–6, DBY

God unveiled His mystery to Paul, and in turn Paul wanted to pass it on to other believers. Paul desired that others would understand God's will that has been kept in secret since the beginning of creation. This is also part of the stewardship of grace: to unveil the *result* of God's economy. God wants joint heirs, a joint body, and joint partakers. This is the joining of the Gentile nations with Israel to become one household, one family of God.

The first item Paul addresses in Ephesians 3:6 is that believers are "joint heirs" in this mystery, confirming that God as the Father is after a family. This family is destined to include many mature children (heirs). This concept is completely consistent with Paul's use of the word *oikonomia*. Recall that the original use of this word related to building up the household of the patriarch. Therefore, *God's* economy of grace culminates with the proliferation and maturity of His household, His offspring.

This mystery is also about a body that expresses Him and whose partakers enjoy Him. Note that the word "partakers" is also consistent with *oikonomia,* since those that share in this mystery are the beneficiaries of *oikonomia.* Today, it is through the glad tidings (or gospel) that grace is dispensed for partaking. For eternity, believers will continue to enter into and participate in this grace — the Tree of Life and the river of life (Rev. 22:1–2).

Dispensing the Unsearchable Riches of Christ for All Men

> …of which I am become minister according to the gift of the grace of God given to me, according to the working of His power. To me, less than the least of all saints, has this grace been given, to announce among the nations the glad tidings of the unsearchable riches of the Christ.
>
> – Ephesians 3:7–8, DBY

A minister is one who serves food. The food that Paul served was grace. Grace is the enjoyment of the unsearchable riches of Christ. The gospel (glad tidings, or the good news) is simply the unveiling of the unsearchable riches of Christ. The gospel is much more than believing in Jesus so as to not "go to hell" but instead "go to heaven."

Consider one item of the good news: the Lord's love. How unsearchably rich is His love! For eternity, believers will not be able to fathom its depth. The Scriptures describe Jesus' person, character, and function using many different symbolic images: He is the rock, shepherd, door, corner stone, top stone, morning star, first fruit, bridegroom, captain, bread of life…and much more. Each one of these items will take eternity to appreciate. His work on the cross, His resurrection, His ascension, and His enthronement to be both Lord and Christ are also unlimitedly rich. Believers can appreciate that the riches of Jesus Christ are inexhaustible, so too is the gospel (glad tidings). Jesus is the grace to be distributed and dispensed in God's economy.

God Desires All Men to See and Participate in His Economy

God desires that all men will see and participate in this economy or His dispensation; therefore, Paul was charged to enlighten all to see the *oikonomia* of the mystery.

> …and to enlighten all with the knowledge of what is the administration [oikonomia] of the mystery hidden throughout the ages in God, who has created all things.
>
> – Ephesians 3:9, DBY

As one who had received God's *oikonomia,* Paul was also to enlighten others to the understanding of this *oikonomia* of the mystery. It is interesting that God's *oikonomia* is a concept that needs enlightening, akin to the enlightening of the believers at the time of salvation. Clearly, it is essential that all believers see and understand God's economy as soon as they come to faith in Jesus Christ.

Believers who have been enlightened concerning God's economy, like Paul, will want all people to understand and participate in God's economy as well. However, unlike Paul's heavy burden for this, the amount of teaching and speaking among believers today concerning this knowledge of God's *oikonomia* is miniscule. Readers should ask themselves how many times they have heard of God's *oikonomia* in the last year. This is in spite of the fact that such knowledge is critical for believers to be able to stay on course — to live out the divine life and be equipped to serve God and men.

God's Purpose for the Assembly: To Glorify God and Shame His Enemies

God's eternal purpose of the built-up assembly is to bring glory to God and shame to His enemies.

> ...in order that now to the principalities and authorities in the heavenlies might be made known through the assembly the all-various wisdom of God, according to the eternal purpose, which he purposed in Christ Jesus our Lord.
> — Ephesians 3:10–11, DBY

The end result, or the outcome of God's economy is the building up of His household — the assembly — through which the all-various wisdom of God will be made known to all heavenly beings. This is especially true for Satan and all the angels that have followed His rebellion. As described in much more depth in Chapter 9, it was not possible for God to manifest *His* manifold wisdom without an adversary that was called the, "sum of all wisdom." The more complex the problem, the more wisdom is needed to solve the problem. The loftier the purposes and goals, the more wisdom will be displayed when the purpose is finally accomplished.

After the creation of man (male and female), Satan entered to fully corrupt man by injecting man with sin and death. This is the satanic life and nature. All of humanity became God's enemy and was condemned under the righteous judgment of God. Mankind that God loved and desired to be His own offspring was transmuted in the core of his DNA. It was in this dismal and seemingly hopeless state that God entered in to restore. God's recovery work through Jesus Christ didn't just rescue man back to the created state, but it went far beyond. In God's economy, man was born anew with the divine life and became a partaker of the divine nature. God gained His pleasure of having many sons — a family — and ultimately the household of God-man. This household, His assembly, is the culmination of His manifold and extensive wisdom at its pinnacle. This is the ultimate outcome of God's economy.

Christ in You the Hope of Glory

To Complete the Word of God Is to Dispense Food

The food dispensed is the completing of the Word of God; this is not simply announcing the objective Christ, but the Christ that needs to be consumed to become the *indwelling* Christ. This is the steward's struggle, but necessary for growing the members of God's family.

> Now, I rejoice in sufferings for you, and I fill up that which is lacking of the tribulations of Christ in my flesh, for His body, which is the assembly; of which I became minister, according to the dispensation *[oikonomia]* of God which is given me towards you to complete the word of God, the mystery which has been hidden from ages and from generations, but has now been made manifest to His saints; to whom God would make known what are the riches of the glory of this mystery among the nations, which is Christ in you the hope of glory: whom we announce, admonishing every man, and teaching every man, in all wisdom, to the end that we may present every man perfect [mature] in Christ. Whereunto also I toil [labor], combating [striving] according to His working, which works in me in power.
>
> – Colossians 1:24–29, DBY

Paul's words in 1 Colossians 1:24 may seem strange, to "rejoice in suffering," but some human experiences may be readily identified with this idea: a mother giving birth or raising a family, for example. Women suffer greatly giving birth, but they also rejoice in suffering knowing that their child is coming. A father also rejoices in his labor, which gives him the ability to provide for and raise his family.

Paul, too, rejoiced in the suffering related to God's economy (the raising up of God's household, the assembly). He rejoiced in his suffering for the believers. This suffering is not at all related to the sufferings of Jesus Christ for redemption, which is fully completed with no lack. However, what still lacks are stewards in God's economy, willing to suffer to fulfill their commission of God's *oikonomia*. Paul was such a minister according to God's *oikonomia* given to him for the believers.

His commission as a steward was to complete the Word of God by unveiling and making manifest God's mystery, "Christ in you, the hope of glory." His stewardship *(oikonomia)* was to dispense Christ in a way that would be consumed and ingested by believers becoming "Christ in [them]." As a faithful steward, Paul labored and toiled to take every opportunity to announce and teach "Christ in you, the hope of glory." Paul may have spoken on many topics and one can collect a number of subjects from his letters, but don't lose focus on what he considered to be the completion of the word of God and what he struggled to announce: "Christ in you, the hope of glory." If this point is missed or glossed over, then the heart of Paul is ripped out. A believer may think, "Okay, I've got it, Christ is in me. Now let's move on to study such and such." No! There is no moving on from this. In fact, all topics of the Scriptures should end or result with "Christ in you, the hope of glory." Paul continued to announce this. This was his struggle: how to announce "Christ in you, the hope of glory" in a way that will really stick and by it the believers would grow. His goal was that through his labor, each of God's children would be perfected and mature as God's household.

Teach to Lead People to God's Economy

This is why anything believers teach that does not directly lead to God's economy is a distraction, a deviation preventing believers from growing to maturity.

> . . . that you might enjoin [charge] some not to teach other doctrines, nor to turn their minds to fables and interminable [endless] genealogies, which bring questionings rather than God's dispensation [oikonomia], which is in faith.
>
> – 1 Timothy 1:3–4, DBY

Even during Paul the apostle's time, believers were distracted by many other teachings, doctrines, fables, genealogies and keeping of laws. The question believers should always ask in order to evaluate any "Christian" teaching is whether it produces God's economy. If it does, then it is healthy teaching. If it does not, then at best it is a distraction from God's plan. This is why understanding God's economy is of utmost importance. Without this understanding, believers will not have a reference point to discern various teachings and practices among believers today.

It is important to recognize that distracting teachings are not necessarily non-scriptural or heretical. Certain teachings could be related to discussing leadership, miraculous gifts, baptism, creationism, or holiness. None of these are bad topics, in and of themselves. However, if these teachings do not further God's economy by unveiling the riches for believers to partake of grace, for the growth of God's household, then they are not needed according to Paul's instruction to Timothy.

Apparently, there was a tendency in Ephesus to miss God's economy; therefore, by the time John wrote the letter to them in Revelation (Rev. 2:1), they had lost their first love for the Lord Jesus. Although they were upright to reject evil men, and were even scripturally knowledgeable enough to try and expose false apostles, they were about to lose their testimony as a shining lampstand because Jesus Christ was not their focus. If an assembly is no longer shining forth Jesus Christ, then it is no longer an assembly. How awful to be a gathering of Christians, and yet not be part of God's assembly for not shining forth Christ and lacking love for the Lord Jesus! How critical it is for an assembly to stay focused on Jesus Christ for the continuation of God's economy.

A Privilege and a Responsibility

This economy (stewardship) has been given to believers as both a privilege and a responsibility.

> ...according as he has received a gift, ministering it to one another, as good stewards [oikonomos] of the various grace of God.
>
> – 1 Peter 4:10, DBY

The apostles are not the only ones who have received the responsibility of God's economy; each and every believer has received this gift and is charged to minister to one another. As one in God's economy, believers are to minister the various grace of God to each other. This various grace is the unsearchable riches of Christ for believers to enjoy for their daily experiential salvation.

Unfortunately, it is almost universally accepted that the job of ministry has been assigned to the clergy class such as pastors, ministers, and priests. God's economy to fulfill God's will is tremendously hindered because of this erroneous concept. For God's economy to speed forward, an exponentially increasing number of faithful stewards are needed!

> For if I preach the gospel, I have nothing to boast of, for necessity is laid upon me; yes, woe is me if I do not preach the gospel! For if I do this willingly, I have a reward; but if against my will, I have been entrusted with a stewardship [oikonomia]. What is my reward then? That when I preach the gospel, I may present the gospel of Christ without charge.
>
> – 1 Corinthians 9:16–18

Paul's attitude is that of a person who has been entrusted with God's *oikonomia*; therefore, it was of necessity for him to dispense Christ to others. Basically he was saying that he didn't have a choice; he had to do this service. The more believers see and enter into God's economy, the more they will be compelled to be ministers of Jesus Christ and of His grace...and they will do this without charge. Paul's reward for being a steward is to be able to do this without charge, without anyone paying him or supporting him. How counterintuitive that his reward for the work of ministry is that no one has to give him money for his labor. How different this is from today's practice of hiring clergy to do the work of ministry. This shows that every believer that is just normally working and caring for their family should also be stewards and serve based on necessity, not being rewarded or getting paid to minister Christ.

> And the Lord said, "Who then is that faithful and wise steward [oikonomos], whom his master will make ruler over his household, to give them their portion of food in due season? "Blessed is that servant whom his master will find so doing when he comes. Truly, I say to you that he will make him ruler over all that he has. But if that servant says in his heart, 'My master is delaying his coming,' and begins to beat the male and female servants, and to eat and drink and be drunk, the master of that servant will come on a day when he is not looking for him, and at an hour when he is not aware, and will cut him in two and appoint him his portion with the unbelievers. . . . For everyone to whom much is given, from him much will be required; and to whom much has been committed, of him they will ask the more."
>
> – Luke 12:42–46, 48b, NKJV

Every believer has been called to further God's economy by being a steward. Luke's use of the word "steward" in this parable is consistent with its original meaning. This steward's goal was to take care of the household, and the function of such a person was to distribute and dispense food. However, Luke warns that believers should not live selfishly; they must care for the other family members in God's household. According to this parable, there is reward and punishment associated with diligence in carrying out the duties of dispensing food in the household of God.

One could argue whether this unfaithful steward in Luke 12:42–48 is eternally saved or not, but this doesn't change the fact that believers have a duty to provide food for the building up of the household. There is a requirement from the "master" to be a faithful steward, whether they provide a little or much. It seems that the more the Lord gives believers both physically and spiritually, the more responsibility they have to care for others in His household. Lord Jesus, may those You have entrusted as faithful stewards in Your economy embrace the responsibility of building up Your household!

The One God Working as Three (Trinity)

> Blessed be the God and Father of our Lord Jesus Christ, who has blessed us in Christ with every spiritual blessing in the heavenly places, even as he chose us in him before the foundation of the world, that we should be holy and blameless before him. He destined us in love to be his sons through Jesus Christ, according to the purpose of his will,
>
> – Ephesians 1:3–5, RSV

In the first chapter of Ephesians, the letter where Paul described God's *oikonomia* in vivid terms, the triune (three-one) God was clearly displayed and praised in three sections. This first section was a blessing to the Father. The Father has a will and a purpose, and His desire is to have many mature sons. As seen in a previous lesson, the Greek word for "son" is a compound word for both a son by birth and also a son with legal rights; this means a "son" of God has the maturity to fulfill the legal requirements to be an heir. It was the Father's pleasure and will from the beginning of eternity to have such sons. He didn't want just one only begotten Son, but many sons.

The number of offspring in a household measured the greatness of a father in biblical times. The Father God is the *real* Father, and He is full of life and riches that He desires to discharge, resulting in millions upon millions of mature sons who express His life and nature.

The Son Becoming the Head of All Things Realized through *Oikonomia*

> In him [Jesus Christ] we have redemption through his blood, the forgiveness of our trespasses, according to the riches of his grace that he lavished on us in all wisdom and insight. He did this when he revealed to us the secret of his will, according to his good pleasure that he set forth in Christ, toward the administration of the fullness of the times, to head up all things in Christ—the things in heaven and the things on earth.
>
> – Ephesians 1:7–10, NET

It is interesting to note that *oikonomia* is unveiled in this next section on the Son (Eph. 1:7–10). Jesus is the accomplisher by coming to man as grace. Through His death, He accomplished redemption so that believers would have complete forgiveness and cleansing of sins. Through His resurrection, He became the Spirit to dispense Himself into His people so that by His life all things are headed up in Him.

A Permanent Image Sealed into the Believers

The Spirit, through faith in Jesus Christ, becomes a permanent image sealed into the believer's being, giving believers a guarantee as sons in God's household of inheriting all that God is.

> In him you also, who have heard the word of truth, the gospel of your salvation, and have believed in him, were sealed with the promised Holy Spirit, which is the guarantee of our inheritance until we acquire possession of it, to the praise of his glory.
>
> — Ephesians 1:13–14, RSV

The riches of Christ were dispensed to believers in the hearing of the Word of the truth, which is the gospel. Believers should not think that the gospel is just for unbelievers; rather, the entire truth concerning the person and work of Jesus Christ — together with His eternal purpose and the way to fulfill His purpose through His *oikonomia* — is the good news. This gospel is for unbelievers as well as mature believers because this truth is so rich it cannot be exhausted. The more a person hears, the more they believe. The more they believe, the more the Spirit (through the believer's participation) leaves His permanent image on them.

When an item was sealed with a signet ring in ancient times, it left a permanent image of the seal on the item sealed. Not only so, but the ink or wax used for the seal was also transferred (or absorbed into) what was sealed, such as a piece of paper. In the same way, at the very moment of faith, believers are sealed and the Spirit is permanently transferred into the believer's being. The believer now bears His image.

The more truth heard and appreciatively received, the more this image of the Spirit grows and becomes more pronounced in the believer.

This seal of the Spirit is also the believer's guarantee that they will inherit all that God is in full. They are certain to become fully mature heirs of God. All that God is and has is theirs for eternity. What they are enjoying of God Himself today is just a pledge of an unimaginable amount to come. Understanding God's desire for heirs brings what has been discussed full circle — back to the Father's desire for sons. This is a beautiful portrait of the Trinity working together in God's *oikonomia* to fulfill His will, purpose, and pleasure from eternity to eternity through this period that man calls time.

God's *Oikonomia*: Love, Grace and Fellowship

God's economy for his eternal purpose was initiated by the Father's love, accomplished by the Son's grace, and made available for participation in the Spirit's fellowship

> The grace of the Lord Jesus Christ and the love of God and the fellowship of the Holy Spirit be with you all.
>
> — 2 Corinthians 13:14

God's *oikonomia* is summed up by Paul in 2 Corinthians 12:13, which echoes what has been previously discussed. Here Paul leads with the Lord's grace, because Jesus said that He is the way and no one comes to the Father but through Him. The Lord's grace is the believers' entrance into basking in the love of God. The more believers appreciate the death and resurrection of Christ, the more they comprehend the significance of God's forgiveness, leading them to realize and enjoy His love. This grace and love transpires instantly and continues perpetually in the fellowship of the Holy Spirit.

Fellowship means participation — partaking with and subsequently sharing with others. This fellowship is not just for reaching individual believers, but that every individual who participates also shares with others. If the love of God and the grace of Christ that believers receive do not reach others, the fellowship of the Holy Spirit is stifled. Just as the circle of fellowship within the triune God Himself grew to include believers, the practical circle of fellowship among believers also needs to grow. The fellowship of the Spirit is persistently seeking to expand, to include more partakers and dispensers of grace and love.

This is God's oikonomia.

God has already produced an unlimited supply of foodstuff; therefore, for believers to be in God's economy today is to identify, know, and enjoy the real food which is Christ's person and work. But it also includes distributing this food to others that they may also consume and enjoy this heavenly food. Believers should enlighten others concerning God's economy, so that they become the next generation of distributors (ministers). The result of this cycle is the building up of God's family, which is His will.

Practice: Teaching

Write down something new that you learned from this lesson:

Describe what you can practically apply in your life:

Think of a person, and what you want to teach that person from this lesson.

12

THE ASSEMBLY: GOD'S ETERNAL PURPOSE

Two Halves of the Entire Revelation of God

It is revelation from the Father when a person sees that Jesus is the Christ, the Son of the living God.

> He said to them, "But who do you say that I am?" Simon Peter answered and said, "You are the Christ, the Son of the living God." Jesus answered and said to him, "Blessed are you, Simon Bar-Jonah, for flesh and blood has not revealed *this* to you, but My Father who is in heaven."
>
> – Matthew 16:15–17

Jesus asked His disciples, "Who do you say that I am?" He asks all people today this same most important question. The answer determines whether one has eternal life or not. It is the belief that Jesus is the Son of God that gives a person eternal life. This is His person, who He is (John 20:31).

His title is the "Christ," which means He is anointed by God to fulfill God's purpose. The word "Christ" is derived from the Latin word *christus,* which in turn comes from the Greek *christos* meaning, "the anointed." The Hebrew equivalent of the word *christos* is *mashiach* meaning, "messiah" or "the anointed one." This refers to Jesus' work, His mission. Jesus is God in the flesh, and He was sent to fulfill God's purpose. To truly know who Jesus is, a revelation is needed from the Father. Men can hear about Jesus, but a veil covers their minds so they are blinded to know Him. When a person's heart is open and their spirit seeks truth, then the Father can reveal the reality of Jesus.

This alone is the initiation into eternal life, and this simple faith is how one continues in the eternal life. It is not anything for which a person can work. It takes a direct revelation from God; simply seeing who Jesus is transfers a person from death into life. This encapsulates the entire faith: Jesus is the Christ, the Son of the living God. All focus and attention is uniquely on Him.

Jesus Declares His Purpose of Building His Assembly

> And I also, I say unto you that you are Peter, and on this rock I will build my assembly, and hades' gates shall not prevail against it.
>
> – Matthew 16:18, DBY

Immediately following His revelation of who He is in Matthew 16:15–17, Jesus said, "And I say to you…" This indicates there is something more than what was just unveiled to Peter. Jesus adds to that revelation the second half — the unveiling of His goal: *He will build His assembly.*

This built-up assembly shall crush the gates of Hades (death), which is the power of Satan (Heb. 2:14). Satan and death will be crushed under the feet of the assembly (Rom. 16:20). Wherever Satan's kingdom is crushed and defeated, God's kingdom exists.

Knowing Jesus is only half of the revelation. Believers must consider the other half — the assembly. How important, mysterious, and deep within the Lord's heart must be His assembly, that He would add this to the Father's revelation! For certain, this assembly that the Lord said He would build is not the "church" as people know it today. The assembly cannot be the physical building with a cross, nor even a group of Christians practicing a form of rituals, regulations, politics, hierarchy, or hypocrisy so widely accepted as "church." This wonderful assembly that is deep in the Lord's heart needs to be unveiled. Believers need to know the assembly as the second half, just as they know Jesus. These two halves complete God's revelation.

Why Jesus Went through Death and Resurrection

It was for the building up of the assembly that Jesus died and resurrected.

> From that time Jesus began to show to His disciples that He must go to Jerusalem, and suffer many things from the elders and chief priests and scribes, and be killed, and be raised the third day. Then Peter took Him aside and began to rebuke Him, saying, "Far be it from You, Lord; this shall not happen to You!" But He turned and said to Peter, "Get behind Me, Satan! You are an offense to Me, for you are not mindful of the things of God, but the things of men."
>
> – Matthew 16:21

From the time Jesus unveiled His purpose to build up His assembly, He started preparing for His death and resurrection. That would be how he would build it up: through His death and resurrection. His death is to redeem men for the cleansing of their sins, and His resurrection is to enliven and fill men with the eternal life — His Spirit — that they become members of His assembly. That is Jesus' way of the building up His assembly.

Peter, who had just received the revelation from the Father concerning the identity of Jesus, was called Satan for objecting to what Jesus needed to do for the building up of His assembly. Even after receiving the revelation concerning Jesus, a believer can be an impediment to God's purpose. This should serve as a warning to believers today that they can likewise object and obstruct what Jesus Christ is doing in the building up of His assembly. Though they are believers, to the Lord they can be called Satan, adversaries to His plan and purpose (the definition of *Satan* is an adversary). Satan does his best to hinder the building up of the Lord's assembly, because he knows that it is the built-up assembly that will ultimately crush him. It is the crushing of the kingdom of death that brings in God's heavenly kingdom.

Descriptions of the Assembly (ekklesia)

There are many descriptions of God's assembly. These, showing the mingling and oneness between God and His people, portray that she is more extraordinary than what can be imagined.

The Household, the Family of God – The Father's Increase

> But if I delay, in order that you may know how one ought to conduct oneself in God's house[hold], which is the assembly of the living God, the pillar and base of the truth.
>
> *– 1 Timothy 3:15, DBY*

> Now, therefore, you are no longer strangers and foreigners, but fellow citizens with the saints and members of the household of God.
>
> *– Ephesians 2:19*

The word "house" in Ephesians 2:19 in the original Greek is *oikeios*. *Oikeios* does not refer to a physical structure. The word is more accurately translated, "household." *Oikeios* is the family of God. It is the Father with His many children. This is the Father's pleasure and will: that He has many sons. If a father only has one offspring, he would not be as significant a father as the father who has many offspring. God as the Father is great because He has millions of children. Not only has the Father God begotten them but He has also supplied them and cared for them that they might reach maturity. This is the glory of the Father God.

This household, this "family," is the assembly. The assembly that the Lord built comprises only of God's offspring. If a person is not born of God with His life and nature, they cannot be part of this "family" — the assembly. This is the unique and only way to enter God's household — by birth. This is the reason that believers are brothers and sisters to each other, because they all truly have the same Father, with the same eternal life and divine nature. It is for this assembly that God sent His only Begotten Son to the world that men might believe into Him and become part of God's family.

The Bride of Christ – The Son's Counterpart in Love

> And the LORD God said, "It is not good that man should be alone; I will make him a helper comparable to him." Out of the ground the LORD God formed every beast of the field and every bird of the air, and brought them to Adam to see what he would call them. And whatever Adam called each living creature, that was its name. So Adam gave names to all cattle, to the birds of the air, and to every beast of the field. But for Adam there was not found a helper comparable to him. And the LORD God caused a deep sleep to fall on Adam, and he slept; and He took one of his ribs, and closed up the flesh in its place. Then the rib which the LORD God had taken from man He made into a woman, and He brought her to the man. And Adam said: "This is now bone of my bones and

> flesh of my flesh. She shall be called Woman, because she was taken out of Man."
> Therefore a man shall leave his father and mother and be joined to his wife, and
> they shall become one flesh.
>
> — Genesis 2:18–24

When God created Adam, He said that it was not good that man should be alone. God wanted to make man a compatible mate. All creatures of the land and air were created and brought before Adam, so that Adam could "check out" each one to see if any were compatible to be his mate. He assigned a different name for each, such as: monkey, lion, eagle, and elephant. But he could not find one matching *him*.

So God put him to sleep and took out a part of his inner frame — his rib — and from this piece of man, God built another person. When Adam saw this person, he immediately recognized that she was out of him, part of him, and completely compatible with him. Therefore, he named her "woman" which is the feminine word for "man" in Hebrew. That means that man and woman are exactly the same species with the same life and nature. Even according to nature, mating can only be achieved among creatures of the same species.

According to Romans 5:14, the real Adam is Jesus Christ. So the story of Adam and Eve in Genesis is really about Jesus Christ. This metaphor portrays Jesus — who is the Son of God — looking for a compatible mate. He looked at everything created, from angels to every other kind of creature, and could find none compatible with Him. Then Jesus was put to sleep (death) and from His pierced side came blood and water (John 19:34). The blood signified man's redemption, and the water the Spirit for man's regeneration — life imparting. This was the process of creating His "compatible mate." This counterpart has the same life, nature, and expression as Jesus Christ.

> Husbands, love your own wives, even as the Christ also loved the assembly, and
> has delivered himself up for her.
>
> So ought men also to love their own wives as their own bodies: he that loves his
> own wife loves himself. For no one has ever hated his own flesh, but nourishes
> and cherishes it, even as also the Christ the assembly: for we are members of his
> body; we are of his flesh, and of his bones. Because of this a man shall leave his
> father and mother, and shall be united to his wife, and the two shall be one flesh.
> This mystery is great, but I speak as to Christ, and as to the assembly.
>
> — Ephesians 5:25, 28–32, DBY

The real husband and wife, the real "pairing up" in the universe, is Jesus Christ and His assembly. How great is this mystery! It describes His love that led to His death for the assembly whom He cherishes and nourishes as a man for his wife. The assembly is bone of His bone and flesh of His flesh. The assembly is just Christ's own body. This is the real love story of the universe. This is the real sacrificial love, willing to die for the person He loves. This portrayal of Jesus Christ and His assembly mirrors and gives the real meaning of the

Adam and Eve story in Genesis. How mysterious and highly valued is the assembly! It is the very compatible mate of Jesus Christ, the Son of the living God! The assembly and Jesus Christ are of the same species.

The great mystery is Jesus Christ as the husband and the assembly as the wife — one mystery consisting of two persons, joined as one. This supports the earlier statement that the entire revelation consists of knowing Jesus and knowing His assembly. What a profound and wonderful mystery!

The Body of Christ – The Spirit Tangibly Expressed

> There is one body and one Spirit — just as you were called to the one hope that belongs to your call
>
> – Ephesians 4:4, ESV

> For in one Spirit we were all baptized into one body — Jews or Greeks, slaves or free — and all were made to drink of one Spirit.
>
> – 1 Corinthians 12:13, ESV

The body of Christ is the embodiment of the Spirit of God. The body is the very expression and manifestation of the Spirit. The Father desires many sons to be His household, or family, as His increase. The Son desires a wife as His counterpart, and the Spirit desires a body for His expression. These aspects show the prominence, pleasure, and purpose of the assembly of believers in the heart of the Trinity.

The main significance of the body is that it is one. How terrible and frightful if any part of a person's body is severed. There is only one body of Christ since there is only one Spirit of God. No matter how many millions of believers are members, there is only one body, and no matter how diverse the members' backgrounds, they are still only one body. Each member is immersed into the one Spirit and drinks of the one Spirit. Therefore, the one Spirit is in each of the members and every member is immersed in the one Spirit. So how can believers not be one body? The Spirit is not divided; therefore, the body cannot be divided, and the members cannot be divided.

> ...and has put all things under His [Jesus Christ] feet, and gave Him to be head over all things to the assembly, which is His body, the fullness of Him who fills all in all.
>
> – Ephesians 1:22–23, DBY

After Jesus Christ resurrected and ascended, He received all authority in heaven and earth. All things are under His feet including God's enemy, Satan. Then as the Head of all things, He became the Head of the assembly, which is His body. This body is the fullness of God who fills all in all. The assembly is the fullness, the expression of the one who fills the entire universe. How awesome is that! It is hard to comprehend such an assembly with Christ as the Head, and she — the assembly — God's fullness! This assembly is what Jesus Christ was sent to build. What a mission! What an accomplishment!

The New Man—Purposed to Defeat and Shame God's Enemy

> For he himself is our peace, who has made us both one and has broken down in his flesh the dividing wall of hostility by abolishing the law of commandments expressed in ordinances, that he might create in himself one new man in place of the two, so making peace.
>
> – Ephesians 2:14, ESV

> The God of peace will soon crush Satan under your feet. The grace of our Lord Jesus Christ be with you.
>
> – Romans 16:20, ESV

When God created Adam, the first man (male and female), God said that man would have dominion over the whole earth and over all the creeping things. Previous chapters revealed this refers specifically to Satan, the serpent, the "king" of the "creeping things." God's intention was not that He would defeat His enemy Satan by Himself; He ordained man to be the one to defeat Satan. The first man, Adam, did not fulfill this commission; rather, the first man became a partner with Satan in rebellion against God.

The first man was created with the dust of the ground, but the new man is created in Christ. This new man is a corporate man consisting of two people – Jews and Gentiles – who have become one. Whatever hostility there was between people was eliminated through the death of Jesus Christ. When Jesus died, He abolished and terminated the various practices of worship and lifestyle (Eph. 2:15), the very things that kept people apart. If the death of Christ terminated the practices ordained by God because they kept His people – Jews and Gentiles – in animosity and separated, why would believers allow Christian practices (which can also be ordained by God) to divide each other? Therefore, abolishing all ritualistic practices brought His believers together into the one new man (Eph. 2:14). It is this new man that defeats God's enemy.

This supports what Jesus said in Matthew 16:18, that the built-up assembly would crush the gates of Hades. Again, the oneness of the believers is paramount in the defeat of Satan. It makes sense, then, that Satan's main tactic today is making sure believers are divided. It is the oneness of believers in Jesus Christ that fulfills God's eternal purpose and will cause the world to believe that Jesus is the Son of God sent by the Father. This oneness is what defeats God's enemy, Satan. No wonder prayer for oneness in John 17 was paramount in the heart of Jesus.

> ...in order that now to the principalities and authorities in the heavenlies might be made known through the assembly the all-various wisdom of God.
>
> – Ephesians 3:10, DBY

When Satan rebelled against God, he had no concept of the depth and height of God's wisdom. Satan could easily have thought that he was wiser than God. It is through the built up assembly that Satan, and the cohort of angels that were loyal to him, will finally know God's wisdom in His glory. Consider that the assembly is made up of human beings that were once corrupt and deadened by Satan. They were sinful enemies against God. It is out of this hopeless people that God came to redeem, to recover, to enliven, and build up into one — His family, wife, body, and the new man — to defeat Satan. What manifestation of wisdom! The more challenging the problem, the more wisdom is manifested when the problem is solved. Each believer was a big problem — a challenge — to God; yet, all have become living members in this wonderful assembly. What all-various wisdom of God!

The New Jerusalem – The Eternal Result of God Becoming One with Man

The final description of the mingling of God with man, showing the eternal result of God becoming man to make man the same as He is in life, nature, and expression (but not in the Godhead), is the New Jerusalem.

> The devil, who deceived them, was cast into the lake of fire and brimstone where the beast and the false prophet are. And they will be tormented day and night forever and ever.
>
> Then Death and Hades were cast into the lake of fire. This is the second death.
> — Revelation 20:10, 14

Just before the beginning of eternity, when time is about to expire, the Devil (Satan) will be fully defeated and his judgment executed. His place will be the lake of fire, and with him will follow death and Hades. All the negative things in this universe will go to the universal "garbage dump," and will not be a part of the new heaven and the new earth. Satan will no longer have a place with his weapon of death in the new heaven and earth.

> Now I saw a new heaven and a new earth, for the first heaven and the first earth had passed away. Also there was no more sea. Then I, John, saw the holy city, New Jerusalem, coming down out of heaven from God, prepared as a bride adorned for her husband. And I heard a loud voice from heaven saying, "Behold, the tabernacle of God is with men, and He will dwell with them, and they shall be His people. God Himself will be with them and be their God.
>
> Then one of the seven angels who had the seven bowls filled with the seven last plagues came to me and talked with me, saying, "Come, I will show you the bride, the Lamb's wife." And he carried me away in the Spirit to a great and high mountain, and showed me the great city, the holy Jerusalem, descending out of heaven from God, having the glory of God. Her light was like a most precious stone, like a jasper stone, clear as crystal.
> — Revelation 21:1–3, 9–11
>
> And He [God] who sat there was like a jasper and a sardius stone in appearance; and there was a rainbow around the throne, in appearance like an emerald.
> — Revelation 4:3

In eternity, the assembly is called the "New Jerusalem." The New Jerusalem, though a "city," is not a physical city at all. She is the bride, the Lamb's wife. The Lord Jesus is not marrying a physical city; rather, He is marrying His assembly for whom He died. This city, being the Lord's wife, is bone of His bone and flesh of His flesh. The two are one with the same life and nature. The New Jerusalem is the last and greatest symbol to describe the mysterious and profound union between God and man.

Jesus was called the tabernacle of God in John 1:14; here the entire city is the tabernacle of God. The tabernacle is the dwelling place of God. God first inhabited Jesus Christ at His incarnation. That habitation has expanded to include all of His people. This is the New Jerusalem. God found His eternal dwelling place within the assembly.

This city shines with the glory of God and her appearance is like a jasper stone (Rev. 21:11). Interestingly, God's appearance — on the throne — is also described as a jasper stone. This indicates the very nature and appearance of God permeates the city. The city and God are *one*.

> And he showed me a pure river of water of life, clear as crystal, proceeding from the throne of God and of the Lamb. In the middle of its street, and on either side of the river, was the tree of life, which bore twelve fruits, each tree yielding its fruit every month. The leaves of the tree were for the healing of the nations.
> – Revelation 22:1–2

The New Jerusalem is described in Scripture as a huge mountain (about 1,400 miles high). On top of this mountain is the throne of God and the Lamb. Flowing out of the throne is the River of Life that spirals all the way down the mountain until the base is encompassed. The Tree of Life, laden with fruit, also originates from the throne, grows like a vine from the middle of the river, and courses down along both sides of the banks. What a wonderful sight of life is this last descriptive sign of the assembly. This is the eternal kingdom of God!

The throne of God and the Lamb symbolize the Father and the Son within each other. For eternity, the Son is the Lamb, the Redeemer, with both divinity and humanity. The River of Life is the Spirit flowing out from God, becoming an integral part of the city. The Tree of Life, which is just God Himself, is the continual supply for the assembly, for eternity. The triune God (Father, Son and Spirit) is completely intertwined, mingled, and blended with His people — the assembly. There is absolutely no separation between the city and God.

Careful observation of the city reveals the Trinity, yet there is still a distinction. God is still the one on the throne, and He is still the Spirit flowing out with the Tree of Life to be the unique source of supply. Even though the assembly of His people is one with God in life, nature, and expression (and will be for eternity), God is still the one on the throne to be worshipped by all and the source for all in perpetuity.

All Believers Are Members of the Assembly

The New Birth

Faith in Jesus Christ is the unique qualification to be a member of the assembly; each member, loving one another and functioning in mutuality, builds up the assembly. This assembly is composed of God's children in every place — those who have called upon the name of the Lord.

> ...to the assembly of God which is in Corinth, to those sanctified in Christ Jesus, called saints, with all that in every place call on the name of our Lord Jesus Christ, both theirs and ours.
>
> – 1 Corinthians 1:2, DBY

God's assembly is made up of all believers in Christ Jesus. Anyone who has believed into Christ Jesus is sanctified or "set apart." Believers are no longer common, as is everyone else outside of Christ; this is what it means to be a saint. Unlike the Catholics' definition of a saint (as someone extraordinary), a saint is simply a person sanctified in Christ Jesus — which is every believer. "Every believer" includes all those who have called upon the name of the Lord Jesus in every place. Therefore, God's assembly is made up of people beyond Corinth — people everywhere and in every place.

> But as many as received Him, to them He gave the right to become children of God, to those who believe in His name: who were born, not of blood, nor of the will of the flesh, nor of the will of man, but of God.
>
> – John 1:12

The assembly consists of everyone in God's household, His sons. The assembly is an assembly of His children. It is clear from John 1:12 that the unique way to become a child of God is through faith, by believing in Jesus Christ and receiving Him. At the moment of faith, a person is reborn (born anew) and regenerated with the life of God. It is not something that man can will to do, or work for. A person cannot "buy" new birth. The only way to be a child of God, a member of His assembly, is by faith in Jesus Christ.

> For there is no distinction between Jew and Greek, for the same Lord over all is rich to all who call upon Him. For "whoever calls on the name of the LORD shall be saved."
>
> – Romans 10:12–13

Paul was clear in Romans 10:12–13: *everyone* who calls on the name of the Lord shall be saved. There is no distinction between persons. As long as one calls on His name, "Lord Jesus Christ" with a believing heart, they are saved. This very salvation makes the believer a member of His assembly. There are no classes to attend, no dues to pay, no behavior to modify, and no religious rituals to follow. It is the simple faith sounded out in a cry to the Lord Jesus Christ that brings people to salvation immediately.

A Practical Love for One Another

The new birth in Christ innately and spontaneously grants believers the desire and ability to love one another, thus fulfilling the Lord Jesus' new commandment. It is the divine life and the love of God that is the source of the believer's love for one another.

> We know that we have passed from death to life, because we love the brethren. He who does not love *his* brother abides in death. …But whoever has this world's goods, and sees his brother in need, and shuts up his heart from him, how does the love of God abide in him? My little children, let us not love in word or in tongue, but in deed and in truth.
>
> – 1 John 3:14, 17–18

> Beloved, let us love one another, for love is of God; and everyone who loves is born of God and knows God. He who does not love does not know God, for God is love.
>
> – 1 John 4:7–8

A person is spiritually dead before faith in Jesus Christ. The moment he or she receives Jesus Christ and the Spirit of Christ enters, the person passes from death to life. The proof a person is no longer in death, but in life, is their love for other believers. This verse doesn't say that the proof is giving to charity, become a law-abiding person, or stop a moral failure. 1 John 4:7–8 says the proof is reflected in the person's love for believers. This is the new life in Christ.

This love is not just in word, but also in deed. It is not just saying, "I love you, brother," but it is love in action. The Lord's love caused Him to sacrifice Himself and die for man. This same love causes a person to be willing to give up something for another. It is not practical if a person says he loves someone, but is not willing to provide physical help to that person when they are in need. The genuine assembly life is one where believers are manifesting the love of God and the life of Christ in them by practically helping and supporting other believers that are in need.

> We love because he first loved us. If anyone says, "I love God," and hates his brother, he is a liar; for he who does not love his brother whom he has seen cannot love God whom he has not seen. And this commandment we have from him: whoever loves God *must* also love his brother.
>
> – 1 John 4:19–21, ESV

The source of love for believers is God loving them first. If God's love is not fresh and present in the believer first, in their experience of Him, then their love for others will fall short. The more believers enjoy and appreciate God's love, the more there is the supply to love others. It is easy to love someone that is far away who cannot be seen. However, people that believers "see" regularly can be troublesome, needy, and harder to love. If God's love is not practically encompassing believers in their daily living in relation to loving those around them, then God might as well be a fantasy.

Fulfilling the New Commandment

The assembly fulfills the unique commandment of the New Covenant for people to love one another as the Lord Jesus has loved them.

> A new commandment I give to you, that you love one another: just as I have loved you, you also are to love one another.
>
> – John 13:34, ESV
>
> And this is his commandment, that we believe in the name of his Son Jesus Christ and love one another, just as he has commanded us.
>
> – 1 John 3:23, ESV

The genuine assembly fulfills the Lord Jesus' new commandment which is the commandment of the new covenant "that you love one another: just as I have loved you" (John 13:34 ESV). How did the Lord love? He loved by sacrificing Himself for man. He gave Himself up to die on the cross so that man may have eternal life. It is this same love that believers should have for one another. This command is only possible if Jesus actually lives in believers so that He can love within the believers; otherwise, loving one another as He loves is absolutely impossible.

> By this we know love, that he laid down his life for us, and we ought to lay down our lives for the brothers.
>
> – 1 John 3:16, ESV
>
> …who risked their necks for my life, to whom not only I give thanks but all the churches [assemblies] of the Gentiles give thanks as well.
>
> – Romans 16:4, ESV

The word for "life" in 1 John 3:16 is not referring to the physical life. It is the same word in the Greek for "soul" which is *psychē*. *Psychē* refers to the psychological being of man. The life of the soul is what the person treasures, that which is important to a person. The Lord Jesus laid down His entire life including His physical life for man. In the believers' case, it does not have to be to such an extreme. Yet, it is very practical for believers to lay down what they treasure in their soul to render help to another believer. For example, one may really treasure his time to watch a ball game. If that person is willing to give up that time to visit a brother or a sister in need, that is laying down his "life" as well. It may also be as simple as foregoing buying another pair of shoes or dress in order to give the money to a person in unfortunate circumstances, keeping silent when an argument is brewing, or apologizing to your spouse when there is an offense. Therefore, it is not a matter of sacrificing something in order to be individually more "spiritual." For example, some Christians consider that by denying things that they like to do would make them more pleasing to God as a sacrifice. But if there is no benefit to anyone else and Christ is not ministered due to the self-denial, then it is not the laying down of the soul life in caring for others for the building up of the assembly.

Every Member Functioning

The assembly is built up through the believers' growth as each one functions in the body of Christ.

> in whom the whole building, being fitted together, grows into a holy temple in the Lord, in whom you also are being built together for a dwelling place of God in the Spirit.
>
> – Ephesians 2:21-22

As previously shown, the assembly is the household or the family of God. Each believer is a member of this household. Notice the transition in metaphors, as Paul moves from describing a family to describing a temple. Just as the Father dwells in each of His children, God needs a living temple to dwell in. The assembly is a living temple with living members; therefore, the way this temple is built is through the growth of its members. Believers grow into the temple in the Lord.

And in order to grow, believers need to fit together into one. Drawing from this family metaphor, consider how family members can argue and be separated from one another. However, with a building, every piece of the material needs to fit together into one with other pieces of material. Otherwise, it is impossible to have a building. It is in this oneness of the believers that the entire building grows to reach maturity. Therefore, the building of the assembly means oneness with other believers, and believers together growing with more of God. The more believers increase their knowledge and experience of Jesus Christ, the more God's life and nature will increase in them (Col. 2:19), and the more they can be one in fellowship with all type of believers. This is the growth for the building up of God's temple.

> But speaking the truth in love, let us grow in every way into Him who is the head—Christ. From Him the whole body, fitted and knit together by every supporting ligament, promotes the growth of the body for building up itself in love by the proper working of each individual part.
>
> – Ephesians 4:15–16, HCSB

Paul tells believers that as they grow in every way into Jesus Christ by speaking the truth, the body is joined together. The one body grows and is built up by every individual member working and functioning. If each member does not carry out his or her duties, the body cannot be built up. Today, most believers learn passively from clergy. No matter how good and uplifting this person's teaching, as long as the members are not actively ministering and speaking Christ themselves, growth lacks, and the body is not built up. However, if there is a genuine "seeing" of God's eternal purpose being the assembly, there will be a rising up, not just to be a minister, but also to supply and motivate other believers to function and minister.

Satan's Tactic against God's Purpose: Cause Division

Immature believers are susceptible to Satan's strategy of dividing the body of Christ.

> God is faithful, by whom you were called into the fellowship of His Son, Jesus Christ our Lord. Now I plead with you, brethren, by the name of our Lord Jesus Christ, that you all speak the same thing, and that there be no divisions among you, but that you be perfectly joined together in the same mind and in the same

> judgment. For it has been declared to me concerning you, my brethren, by those of Chloe's household, that there are contentions among you. Now I say this, that each of you says, "I am of Paul," or "I am of Apollos," or "I am of Cephas," or "I am of Christ." Is Christ divided? Was Paul crucified for you? Or were you baptized in the name of Paul?
>
> – 1 Corinthians 1:9–13

All believers have been called into only one fellowship, which is that of Jesus Christ. Believers may mistakenly consider that the group they associate with is one fellowship, and every other group has its own separate fellowship. The truth is, all believers belong to only one fellowship. It is God that called, and Jesus Christ's work that brought all believers into His fellowship. Thus, the only way believers can all speak the same thing and have the same mind and judgment, is by staying in the unique faith concerning the person and work of Jesus Christ. This is the only thing that makes one a believer and brings a person into fellowship.

Speaking the same thing is definitely not related to having the same political views, or the same mind about education, child rearing, and careers. Focusing on these topics will divide. Despite having different views and opinions on such things, believers can be one and continue enjoying fellowship in Christ. This is the oneness that will cause the world to believe: people in diversity, yet one in fellowship, loving one another.

Since all believers are in the one body of Christ, there should be no divisions in Christ; nevertheless, it is common for believers to associate themselves with a sub-group within the body. When they have a preference for a particular minister or preacher of the Word, because of the help received, it is easy to say, "I am of so-and-so," to identify themselves according to the minister that they appreciate. But according to Paul, any labeling or naming of oneself other than a common believer or Christian who is a member in the one body, divides the body. The actual meaning of "denominating" is naming — being labeled by a name. "I am of Paul, I am of Apollos, I am a Lutheran, I am a Pentecostal, I am Baptist," and any other such designation divides the body of Christ. Even a spiritual name such as, "I am of Christ," as a way of excluding others, harms the body of Christ. The ones that say, "I am of Christ" may feel more spiritual and might possess a judgmental attitude toward those who say, "I am of Paul." They can separate and group themselves only with those who say, "I am of Christ." To say that, "I am of Christ" is certainly more spiritual and could be a reaction to those who say, "I am of Apollos," but when the "more spiritual" react to those "less spiritual," their reaction is also a cause of division.

Therefore, the genuinely more mature believers will not react or be distracted by those saying or doing things that are not entirely scriptural. They will continue to stay in the fellowship of Jesus Christ and bring all those around them into this fellowship no matter what position believers take because of immaturity. Since all believers are in the one body of Christ, all should refrain from denominating or labeling themselves or other believers. All believers are members of the same body and should be viewed and treated that way.

> And I, brethren, could not speak to you as to spiritual people but as to carnal, as to babes in Christ. . . . for you are still carnal. For where there are envy, strife, and divisions among you, are you not carnal and behaving like mere men? For when one says, "I am of Paul," and another, "I am of Apollos," are you not carnal? Who then is Paul, and who is Apollos, but ministers through whom you believed, as the Lord gave to each one?
>
> – 1 Corinthians 3:1, 3–5

Paul pointed out clearly that the Corinthian believers — who had formed a faction around various ministers — were babes in Christ. They were "carnal" or "of the flesh," just like people of the world. Immaturity in Christ causes believers to lift up various ministers and their teachings and practices, thus forming a faction around such persons or things. Even when ministers innocently preach the Word and bring people to Christ with pure intentions, factions are formed because of the immaturity of believers. It is incumbent to every believer to help each other to mature in Christ for the building up of the assembly, and for the ministers themselves to warn those under their influence of such a tendency as Paul did.

> And he has given [still giving] some apostles, and some prophets, and some evangelists, and some shepherds and teachers, for the perfecting [equipping] of the saints; with a view to the work of the ministry, with a view to the edifying [building up] of the body of Christ; until we all arrive at the unity of the faith and of the knowledge of the Son of God, at the full-grown man, at the measure of the stature of the fullness of the Christ; in order that we may be no longer babes, tossed and carried about by every wind of that teaching which is in the sleight of men, in unprincipled cunning with a view to systematized error.
>
> – Ephesians 4:11–14, DBY

> For I know this, that there will come in amongst you after my departure grievous wolves, not sparing the flock; and from among your own selves [elders] shall rise up men speaking perverted [turned aside] things to draw away the disciples after them.
>
> – Acts 20:29–30, DBY

Grammatically, the verb form for "given" in Ephesians 4:11 in Greek means that the Lord Jesus is *still actively giving* more gifted believers to be apostles, evangelists, shepherds, and teachers. These extra-gifted ones may have a greater or more fervent heart, a clearer understanding of the Scriptures, and a stronger will for God's purpose. As gifts to the body, their job is to equip *all* the believers under their influence, so that each and every follower of Jesus would rise up and do the work of ministry; then the body of Christ may be built up by all the members. When each and every believer rises up to serve others and function according to their capacity, the body can be built up. The *more* gifted members cannot build up the body directly; even the apostle Paul himself could not do it!

These members who are more gifted have a job: to equip and encourage the less gifted believers to do the work of building up. Today's system of clergy and laity, where a few believers do all the teaching and preaching but the majority stay passive year after year has not (and does not) equip believers to do what the clergies are doing; therefore, they cannot build up the body of Christ. What should happen is that after receiving the equipping from the "more" gifted ministers, all of these saints would go and preach the gospel, teach the truth, and meet in fellowship with all other believers themselves. This would directly build up the body of Christ.

It is clear from Ephesians 4:13 that for believers to arrive at oneness, the knowledge of the Son of God and faith are the nucleus — the destination; therefore, this has to be the focus of teaching for those that are mature and for the more gifted members to speak and to teach. But there are some "ministers" and "teachers" with an ulterior motive: they desire to build up their own group — their own following of believers. They teach something else — something different from the faith and the knowledge of the Son of God. They may emphasize some other scriptural points or biblical practices in order to turn believers aside from the main focus. This is usually evidenced in the elevation of various non-essential doctrines or practices to the same level as Jesus Christ. That means that a believer who does not practice their doctrine will be deemed inferior. With their cunning speech and trickery, using Scripture to their benefit by emphasizing a certain doctrine, personality, or practice, they carry off the babies in Christ into their group, their system of organization, and away from the building up of the one body of Christ. Believers should not underestimate the shrewdness needed to present Scripture in such a way that convinces immature believers that their way of practice or their special doctrine is worth forming a division around.

For example, only Paul spoke of women having their head covered in an assembly in just one chapter of an epistle; nevertheless, some Bible teachers highlight this in their teachings and form groups based on that emphasis. Tongue speaking is used the same way. Only Paul (and no other apostle in any other epistles) wrote concerning miraculous tongue speaking in two of his chapters. And in one it was spoken of with a caution. Yet, an entire denominational organization can be built around tongue speaking as its emphasis.

Let's take baptism as another example. Factions have formed over whether baptism has to be by water, or if it can be just by the Spirit. If water, more factions have formed over the debate over immersion or sprinkling. If immersion, even more factions have formed over whether the words spoken when a person is baptized should be "in the name of the Father, Son, and the Holy Spirit" or "in the name of Jesus Christ." Each of these doctrines can be used by Bible teachers (who quote Scripture) to deceive people into believing if a person is not in the group that teaches or practices that way, then their salvation may not be secure or completed. There are literally thousands of teachings that are blowing immature believers into various factions, each dividing themselves from other believers that are not like them.

Understanding the assembly (from the beginning of this chapter), Satan's tactic in dividing up the assembly is evident. God's purpose cannot be realized without oneness among believers. Whether the assembly is described as the household (temple) of God, the bride of Christ, the body of Christ, the new man, or the New Jerusalem, the oneness of the believers within the oneness of the triune God is paramount. While Satan is doing his best to divide, believers need to do their best to grow and hold on to the oneness of the Spirit until arriving at the built-up assembly according to the ultimate result of Christ's work. Again, this is why understanding John 17 is critical for understanding God's purpose.

No Separation Based on Racial, Cultural, Political, Socio-Economic Differences

> ...and have put on the *new man* who is renewed in knowledge according to the image of Him who created him, where there is neither Greek nor Jew, circumcised nor uncircumcised, barbarian, Scythian, slave *nor* free, but Christ *is* all and in all.
> – Colossians 3:10–11

> For you are all sons of God through faith in Christ Jesus. For as many of you as were baptized into Christ have put on Christ. There is neither Jew nor Greek, there is neither slave nor free, there is neither male nor female; for you are all one in Christ Jesus.
> – Galatians 3:26–28

Believers of Jesus Christ have a new identity. Their identity is a new creation in Christ. When people are first born, according to their natural characteristics, they are divided by all the various differences listed above. But once believers are born anew in their second birth, their first identity is terminated and buried with Jesus Christ. Their new identity is Christ, "Christ is all and in all." In the assembly, those that are Jews should no longer consider themselves Jews; neither should the Chinese, white people, or people of colors identify themselves as such. All believers should no longer view themselves or other believers according to their natural first birth, but according to their new second birth: Sons of God in Jesus Christ.

It is natural and easy to be segregated and separated based on various differences. It is very difficult and even impossible without the new birth and life in Christ for people that are diametrically opposed to each other to become one. Worldly people have this ideal that diverse people can be one as memorialized by John Lennon's song "Imagine." But it is abundantly clear that the more the world talks oneness, the more divided and segregated it becomes. But in the genuine assembly, divisions based on preferences of the old creation in the natural life cannot exist. In Christ, though believers are diverse and different, the acceptance of each other in fellowship is one.

Christianity today has many churches that are segregated by various doctrines, practices, politics, racial, or socio-economic demarcations. Although not scriptural, some claim that it is necessary to care for various Christians within an environment in which they are comfortable. According to this reasoning, if Christians are not able to gather in a place they feel at ease in, then they may not gather at all with other Christians for hearing the Scriptures and fellowship. Whether this logic is acceptable to the Lord is for Him to decide; He is the judge — though the Apostle Paul considers this kind of grouping to be a sign of being a baby in Christ (1 Cor. 3:1–4). Believers who are more mature and see the oneness of the body will receive and treat believers that are in various churches and Christian groups as equal members in the body of Christ, and they should be greeted and accepted without discrimination or judgment. The greeting of believers extends to wherever they are, no matter what denominational church or Christian group they attend.

Some believers, due to their understanding of the Scriptures, have condemned denominational churches and groups. They group themselves as a unit for the oneness of the Body of Christ, against the system of denominations. However, if they don't proactively greet and extend themselves to all the believers in the various "divided" groups, then they too become segregated in their correct teaching. Their strong denunciation of institutional churches isolates them, segregates them, and makes them even more divisive. This is like those that have become divisive by saying that they are of Christ (1 Cor. 1:12). A group can fall into the same trap of divisiveness declaring it is the group of the one body.

Deceitful Teachings Damage the Assembly

Teachings that uplift something other than Christ or distract believers from Christ, damage the assembly. These deceitful teachings from Christian workers are aimed at carrying believers away from the simplicity of life in the body of Christ into a system of error.

> For I am jealous for you with godly jealousy. For I have betrothed you to one husband, that I may present you as a chaste virgin to Christ. But I fear, lest somehow, as the serpent deceived Eve by his craftiness, so your minds may be corrupted from the simplicity that is in Christ. For if he who comes preaches another Jesus whom we have not preached, or if you receive a different spirit which you have not received, or a different gospel which you have not accepted--you may well put up with it!
>
> For such are false apostles, deceitful workers, transforming themselves into apostles of Christ. And no wonder! For Satan himself transforms himself into an angel of light. Therefore it is no great thing if his ministers also transform themselves into ministers of righteousness, whose end will be according to their works.
>
> – 2 Corinthians 11:2–4, 13–15

It is evident from Paul's writing that Satan is very deceptive and cunning. He is not easily recognizable and his corrupting teachings cannot be easily discerned. The assembly is betrothed to only one husband: Jesus Christ. He, as the Bridegroom, deserves the bride's complete attention, adoration, and focus. That is simplicity. It is just Jesus Christ, His person, and His work. Believers need to be aware that Satan's tactic is to corrupt this simplicity by adding on other items in addition to Jesus Christ. Take note that the attack starts in the mind, through appealing and seemingly Scriptural teachings…but the goal is always to add something else to Jesus Christ.

These deceitful teachers corrupt believer's thoughts, side-tracking them by using many different appealing and eloquent methods — even pulling quotes from the Bible. Though their teachings may be law-centered, and culturally and politically relevant, the end result is the same: the believer loses heart and love towards Jesus Christ and misses out on the enjoyment of the riches of Christ. Doubt creeps in to the effectiveness of the work of Christ, and the believer begins to trust in human effort rather than in the work of the Spirit, which inevitably causes divisions.

Many times these "deceitful workers" may even have good intentions. They may be perfectly fine Christians without any conscious intent of misleading believers. It could be ignorance; they might be completely unaware Satan is using their teachings to mislead people. When Jesus called Peter "Satan," Peter was only voicing his concern that Jesus not go to suffer and die on the cross. His intentions were good, but it was adverse to the Lord's purpose; therefore, Jesus called him Satan. Similarly, Christian teachers may possess a good heart and intentions, but if they distract believers from Christ to something else, even if Scriptural, they are doing the work of Satan.

More Teachings that Sever Believers from the Enjoyment of Christ

Philosophy, traditions, forms of living and worship, ordinances, being judged as not worthy, and asceticism — all these sever believers from the enjoyment of Christ and harm the body.

> See to it that no one takes you captive by philosophy and empty deceit, according to human tradition, according to the elemental spirits of the world, and not according to Christ. For in him the whole fullness of deity dwells bodily, and you have been filled in him, who is the head of all rule and authority.
> – Colossians 2:8–10, ESV

The enemy's goal is to take believers captive and enslave them by suppressive teachings that are not according to Jesus Christ. Through the ages men have held to various philosophies concerning life and living. They have their logic and reasoning as to what human life is about, and that logic and philosophy governs how they live. The Chinese have their own philosophies, Moslems hold to their own traditions, and western culture has its own unique logic and ways of living. However, the assembly is *according to Christ alone*, and it liberates people from the enslaving spirits of the world. The assembly's focus is only related to being filled in Christ, who is the fullness of all that God is, and the Head of all rule and authority. Believers need to reject these various teachings in the assembly, since they are deceitful and not beneficial for building up the one body.

> Let no man therefore judge you in meat, or in drink, or in respect of a feast day or a new moon or a sabbath day: which are a shadow of the things to come; but the body is Christ's.
> – Colossians 2:16–17, ASV

When teachings other than those that further God's economy (see Chapter 11) are preached to believers, obstacles to the oneness of believers are generated. In Colossians 2:16–17, Paul addresses teachings relating to keeping dietary laws, or observing certain days and festivals of the Old Testament, that were being taught among believers. Judgments were being passed on to Christians, according to the Jewish laws of the Old Testament. Those influenced by these teachings of Jewish ceremonial laws were judging the mostly Gentile believers who didn't abide by these laws.

These Old Testament ceremonial laws were all shadows being cast by the coming One. This is not unlike the sun shining and casting a shadow on the ground. The shadow is not real. The person or object that casts the shadow is real. Jesus Christ is the person that came; so in the assembly, believers have the body, which is Jesus Christ, and not the shadow. In the assembly there is only reality, and no shadows; therefore, there should be no judgment of one another according to the shadows of the Old Testament. By implication, this should apply to all practices in the New Testament. For example, the practice of partaking of the bread and the cup is a symbol or "shadow" of eating and drinking Jesus, which is the reality. Therefore, no judgment or division should occur over how to practice such a symbol.

> Let no man rob you of your prize by a voluntary humility and worshipping of the angels, dwelling in the things which he hath seen, vainly puffed up by his fleshly mind, and not holding fast the Head, from whom all the body, being supplied and knit together through the joints and bands, increasing with the increase of God. If ye died with Christ from the rudiments of the world, why, as though living in the world, do ye subject yourselves to ordinances, Handle not, nor taste, nor touch (all which things are to perish with the using), after the precepts and doctrines of men? Which things have indeed a show of wisdom in will-worship, and humility, and severity to the body; but are not of any value against the indulgence of the flesh.
>
> – Colossians 2:18–19, 20–23, ASV

Then Paul addressed teachings influenced by Greek philosophies that say that man is too vile to worship God directly; it is the proud person who thinks they can approach God and have direct fellowship with Him. This philosophy says one needs to humbly approach angels instead (Col. 2:18), and let the angels be the mediator with God.

This kind of thought, however, leads to angel worship. Today even among many Christians, people adore and uplift angels who are just their servants (Heb. 1:14) and lose sight of Christ, who is their prize. The goal of these type of distracting teachings is to cause believers to let go of Christ as the unique Head, and instead to trust in and adore angels. When believers do not hold on to Christ, there is no growth or increase of God, and therefore, no knitting together for the building up of the assembly.

Finally, there is the teaching of asceticism. This doctrine teaches that since man's body is lustful, it needs to be restricted and punished severely. Almost every religion of the world has this element and practice. According to man's wisdom (and most Christians will readily agree), since man is lustful by nature, it would be wise to develop a strong will to stay away from temptations and relentlessly control the urges of the body. However, according to Paul, this type of practice has no value against the flesh. Rather, it is a distraction from what Christ has already done for all believers. All believers have already died with Christ and resurrected with Him. A strong will is needed in order to stay focused on Christ, to enjoy Him, and to minister Him, rather than a focus on dealing with the negatives of the flesh.

These destructive teachings and concepts listed in Colossians 2 subtly appeal to the religious mind; they sound spiritual and full of humility. It is hard to resist such teachings, especially when they relate to practices that are in the Bible. It is difficult not to adore angels!

And knowing that the body is by nature lustful, it is easy to accept asceticism. But Paul forcefully pointed out that these teachings distract believers from Jesus and cause divisions in the body of Christ. Therefore, great discernment is needed when listening to Christian teachers, to identify whether their teachings are profitable for bringing believers into oneness to enjoy Christ, or whether they will sidetrack them from Christ — causing destruction to the oneness of the body.

Practice: Speaking and Reading Hymns

One of the easiest ways to participate and function in a gathering of believers is the practice of speaking songs and hymns to one another. In most Christian gatherings when hymns are sung, typically one song after another is sung with very little break in between each. According the following verses, the early believers practiced speaking songs and hymns in addition to singing them.

> And do not be drunk with wine, in which is dissipation; but be filled with the Spirit, speaking to one another in psalms and hymns and spiritual songs, singing and making melody in your heart to the Lord.
>
> – Ephesians 5:18–19

In verse 18 above, Paul charged the believers to be filled in Spirit. Although being drunk with wine is a waste, Paul still used it to compare and contrast being filled in Spirit. The similarity may lie in the fact that both bring a sense of freedom from self- consciousness and a release from burdens, as well as joy and pleasure. Being drunk is a complete waste and harmful, whereas being filled with the Spirit accomplishes God's will (Eph. 5:17).

Paul, in these verses, told Christians how to be filled in the Spirit. The first way is by "speaking to one another in Psalms and hymns and spiritual songs." This came even before singing and making a melody to the Lord. Even though the speaking of songs and hymns was clearly instructed by Paul, this is rarely practiced among believers. Typically, in the gathering of Christians where hymns are sung, they are sung successively without a break between songs; Hymns are sung looking down at a hymn book, looking toward the front, or looking up to heaven. They are not sung to one another, and even more rare: there is no speaking to one another using the lyrics of the songs. This speaking to one another means that there is communication directed at one another — I speak to you and you speak to me using the lyrics of the songs.

The better hymns and songs are those containing truth of the Word and experiences from the composers. When there is no designated speaker in a gathering, many times Christians don't know what to speak to one another. The songs and hymns provide the words necessary to easily start speaking to one another the things of Christ.

Let's practice using Amazing Grace:

Amazing Grace how sweet the sound
That saved a wretch like me
I once was lost, but now I'm found
Was blind, but now I see.

There is no standard or correct way to do this other than according to your initiative and the Lord moving in you.

Person 1: "I want to say something about grace, God's grace, the grace of the Lord Jesus Christ. It is amazing and sweet. The Lord's grace is absolutely amazing, and I can't have enough of it."

Person 2: "Why is it amazing?"

Person 3: "It is amazing because grace was able to save a wretch like me. I was really in a wretched condition. I was so wretched that I thought God gave up on me, but one day, Jesus came to touch me and saved me."

Person 2: "That reminds me of a verse in John 1:18 that the law was given by Moses, but grace came through Jesus Christ — the contrast is between law and grace. With law there is a demand on people, and with that demand, since we can't fulfill it, is condemnation. But with Jesus Christ came grace.

Person 1: "Do you guys know that grace in the Greek literally means pleasure, joy, rejoicing and enjoyment? So that means it is the joy, the enjoyment of the Lord Jesus that saves us."

Person 3: "I can definitely testify that I got saved through enjoying Jesus. It wasn't my trying to keep the law that saved me. In fact, in my wretched condition it was impossible to keep God's law. I didn't want to have anything to do with it, but then I found pleasure in the Lord Jesus. He is so enjoyable. He is joy and rejoicing to me. He gives me more pleasure than alcohol and worldly entertainments. He saved me."

Person 2: "Now I see. I was blinded to Jesus, but now I see Jesus."

This is just a simple example, but this kind of speaking before or after singing will make the singing come alive. The singing will have more meaning and a greater appreciation of the Lord Jesus. Again, there is no correct way to do this! Just start practicing speaking songs and hymns. The only caution is not to speak too long. By each speaking only a few seconds or a minute, much can be conveyed one to another.

13

(SECTION A)
THE PRACTICAL ASSEMBLY LIFE

After seeing such a wonderful and mysterious vision concerning the universal assembly, most Christians may think that it is a complicated matter to build up such an awesome assembly. That is not true. Actually, the building up of this glorious assembly is practical, simple, here, and now right in the homes of believers. The difficulty is not in the practical assembly; the challenge is in stripping off nearly 1500 years of tradition in order to gather in the simplicity of an assembly. Every believer intuitively knows how to meet organically, but what may take years is "unlearning" of the religious traditions that have conditioned people (both Christians and non-Christians) to behave a certain way in "church."

So, believers need to unlearn the various liturgies, organizations, programs, and formats of church when it comes to God's assembly. Start from the simplest and most basic: a relationship with people within the relationship with Jesus Christ. Now, continue on in that.

The Assembly Is Practical and Enjoyable...Now

The local assembly is found in homes. Unlike all other religions with temples and designated worship centers, the assembly started and continues meeting today in homes, house by house, from house to house.

> So continuing daily with one accord in the temple, and breaking bread from house to house, they ate their food with gladness and simplicity of heart, praising God and having favor with all the people. And the Lord added to the church [assembly] daily those who were being saved.
>
> – Acts 2:46–47

At the day of Pentecost, Peter preached the gospel and 3,000 people received salvation. Immediately they started assembling from house after house, in every home. Up until that time (and even today), every major religion had their temple, holy places, or a dedicated building for worship. God's assembly, however, was absolutely new and outside of religion.

The call was to assemble in every house. Instead of leaving normal life with family and friends to go to perform a "worship" service, God wants to embed Himself within His people in the midst of their human living. He wants to be in the middle of their most intimate, comfortable, relational, and transparent settings. Jesus is calling out people to assemble right there in each of their homes.

The Jewish temple had a large open court area, which became the place for public gatherings. Because this open space was where people already congregated, the early apostles used this venue for their public preaching and teaching. However, God didn't intend believers in the New Testament to go back to the rituals and priesthood of the Old Testament.

Interestingly, in AD 70, God allowed the temple to be completely destroyed so that it was not even *possible* to worship God in the way of the old covenant — the way of ritual in a dedicated place.

> But Saul ravaged [laid waste] the assembly, entering into the houses one after another, and dragging off both men and women delivered them up to prison.
>
> – Acts 8:3, DBY

Before the apostle Paul became a believer in Jesus Christ, he was called Saul. Saul was a persecutor of the assembly. He was zealous for the Jewish religion, and in His ignorance, he persecuted and tried to destroy God's assembly. Remember, the assembly was the very desire of God. Although Saul was blinded from knowing God's assembly, Satan certainly knew and made use of Saul with his zeal and ignorance in an attempt to destroy the assembly — God's purpose.

So how did Saul ravage or lay waste the assembly? He went from house to house. He didn't go to the temple where the apostles were publically and openly preaching and teaching. He didn't go to any other buildings. He went to the homes of the believers, from house after house where the assembly was, dragging believers off to prison. Wouldn't it have been more efficient for Saul to simply arrest everyone listening to the preaching at the temple? Weren't believers already gathered in large numbers for him to arrest there? Yes, but according to the New Testament revelation, that would not have been the way to devastate God's assembly — because the assembly was located in homes.

This shows convincingly the practicality of the assembly of Christ — His body — that the assembly was and is uniquely located in the homes of those gathering in the name of Jesus Christ. The revelation of the Scripture concerning God's assembly is awesome and amazing: the family of God, the bride of Christ, and the body of Christ. Yet, the *outworking* and the *building* of such an assembly occurred right in every believer's house — their dwelling place.

Just as the Jewish religion is completely intertwined with the temple as the focal point of gathering and worship, Christians (since the fourth century) started doing the same as all the other religions. They identified themselves according to the physical building with which they were associated.

Today, a common question is, "Where do you go to church?" Both Christians and non-Christians understand that to mean, "What building do you go to for worship?" Worshipping is identified with organizations that have a church *building*.

Churches, whether intended or not, have become a divider of believers in the one body of Christ. However, the Lord's desire is to recover believers back to the one assembly — that is, gathering in simplicity in all the homes. This is where the assembly is located — not in any building or public place — but in homes where the believers live and are gathered into the name of the Lord Jesus Christ. The intention of this book is not to convince Christian to stop attending churches; rather, to start building an assembly in their homes for fellowship with believers regardless whether they attend different churches or not at all.

Salute [Greet] Prisca and Aquila, my fellow-workmen in Christ Jesus....and the assembly at their house. Salute [greet] Epaenetus, my beloved, who is *the* first-fruits of Asia for Christ.

– Romans 16:3, 5, DBY

Salute [Greet] the brethren in Laodicea, and Nymphas, and the assembly which is in his house.

– Colossians 4:15, DBY

...and to the sister Apphia and to Archippus our fellow-soldier, and to the assembly which *is* in your house.

– Philemon 1:2, DBY

The assemblies of Asia salute [greet] you. Aquila and Priscilla, with the assembly in their house, salute [greet] you much in *the* Lord.

– 1 Corinthians 16:19, DBY

Gaius, my host and [the host] of the whole church [assembly], greets you. Erastus, the treasurer of the city, greets you, and Quartus, a brother.

– Romans 16:23

The Lord is building the mysterious, universal assembly that transcends time and space. It includes all of God's people throughout time, no matter where they are located. But every time the practical assembly is mentioned, which is how and where believers can practically enter into participation and fellowship, it is located in the homes. From the above verses, it is clear this gathering of thousands of believers in homes did not occur only in Jerusalem. After Saul, (the "assembly-devastator") was converted, he became known as Paul — a Jesus-believer and an "assembly-builder." Paul then went from city to city bringing the good news of Jesus Christ, and those that believed were called out to assemble in homes. One can search the Scriptures and will not find the assembly located anywhere else but in homes.

Whether the assembly in a certain locality has thousands of believers meeting in many different homes (such as in Jerusalem), or just a few as when the gospel first went out in Philippi, the *one* assembly in a locality is practically located in either hundreds of houses or in just one home.

This is the reason why it is critical that believers are willing to open their homes to be a place of assembly. If there is not even one home that is willing to host the assembly in a locality, then the assembly would be homeless. If there are one hundred homes in a locality willing to host the assembly, what a testimony of the Lord's one body there will be in that locality. All the verses relating to the assembly in a specific home seems to indicate that the home became a regular meeting place of the assembly. Due to this, those particular homes became known as the assembly in their house.

All Believers in Each Locality Is the "Assembly"

All genuine believers of Christ are members of the one assembly in their respective locality, town, or city.

> And Saul was consenting to his [Stephen] being killed. And on that day there arose a great persecution against the assembly which was in Jerusalem, and all were scattered into the countries of Judaea and Samaria except the apostles. . . But Saul ravaged the assembly, entering into the houses one after another, and dragging off both men and women delivered them up to prison.
>
> – Acts 8:1, 3, DBY

It is clear that in accordance with the eternal life of God and the divine nature of the Trinity, the believers are one — in one unique assembly. Any division among believers is against the very life and nature of God; therefore, this is also true practically. In God's eyes no matter how many homes there are with believers gathered into the Lord's name, there is only one assembly. Just as the universal assembly does not have a proper name, neither do the various assemblies in different localities. It is simply the assembly in any particular locality (town or city) where there are believers.

For certain, by Chapter 8 of Acts, there were at least 8,000 believers; however, it was still called the assembly (singular) that was at Jerusalem. To persecute this one assembly, Saul went from house to house.

> What you see write in a book, and send to the seven assemblies: to Ephesus, and to Smyrna, and to Pergamos, and to Thyatira, and to Sardis, and to Philadelphia, and to Laodicea.
>
> – Revelation 1:11, DBY

Jesus told John in Revelation to write down in a letter what he was seeing and send it to the seven assemblies. Then he listed the seven cities the letter was to be sent to — seven assemblies, seven cities. When compared with Ephesians 1:1, Scripture clearly shows the assembly consisted of all the believers (saints) in the city.

In the Lord's view, all the believers in any particular town or city are part of the one assembly in that locality. It was assumed in those days that all the believers in a locality were in fellowship with one another. So when a letter from an apostle reached a city, it was understood that all the believers in that city would have access to it. A believer or a group of believers not connected to a network in their locality could miss the letter and would not have heard what the Spirit was speaking to the assembly.

Conversely, the first recipients of a letter were responsible to pass the letter on to ones connected to them. Therefore, it was clear there should be a natural and organic network of fellowship among believers so that when a letter was sent to a city, all the believers in the assembly would hear the Spirit speaking, no matter which house they normally gathered.

Each and Every Member Functions for the Building Up of the Body

Everyone in the assembly needs to function as an individual member, because each one has a gift for the body.

> Now concerning spiritual *gifts,* brethren, I do not want you to be ignorant: You know that you were Gentiles, carried away to these dumb [mute] idols, however you were led. Therefore I make known to you that no one speaking by the Spirit of God calls Jesus accursed, and no one can say that Jesus is Lord except by the Holy Spirit. There are diversities of gifts, but the same Spirit. There are differences of ministries, but the same Lord. And there are diversities of activities, but it is the same God who works all in all. But the manifestation of the Spirit is given to each one for the profit of *all:* for to one is given the word of wisdom through the Spirit, to another the word of knowledge through the same Spirit, to another faith by the same Spirit, to another gifts of healings by the same Spirit, to another the working of miracles, to another prophecy, to another discerning of spirits, to another different kinds of tongues, to *another* the interpretation of tongues. But one and the same Spirit works all these things, distributing to each one individually as He wills. For as the body is one and has many members, but all the members of that one body, being many, are one body, so also *is* Christ. For by one Spirit we were all baptized into one body — whether Jews or Greeks, whether slaves or free — and have all been made to drink into one Spirit. For in fact the body is not one member but many. . . . But now indeed *there are* many members, yet one body. And the eye cannot say to the hand, "I have no need of you"; nor again the head to the feet, "I have no need of you." No, much rather, those members of the body which seem to be weaker are necessary.
>
> – 1 Corinthians 12:1–14, 20–22

Paul declared in 1 Corinthians 12 that every single believer, as a member in the body, had a function just like each part of a person's physical body has a specific function. Not only does each believer have a function, but also his or her function is necessary and indispensable. Everyone is needed. This is a description of every normal assembly. How different in churches where most believers are passive listeners, and most of the "functions" of the body are done by appointed personnel? It does not matter much whether any of the lay people are there or not. Other than a loss of monetary gifts they may bring, the "worship" service does not miss a beat if any of the lay people are not present.

It is absolutely clear that each individual member has at least one gift from the Spirit to use in the one body. These gifts given are innate in every believer. The body of Christ cannot be built when the majority of the believers are dormant and not exercising their gifts. The major reason for this deficiency is because believers are trained by tradition to go to church, rather than assembling according to the New Testament ordained way in homes. When the assembly is in a home (house to house), with no clergy, where everyone is accepted equally as a brother and sister in Christ, and where there is an open forum without a set program and format, believers will be in an environment where their gifts will develop and manifest naturally according to the gifts given to each one.

The Bible teaches there is diversity with each member performing a distinct function. Unfortunately, churches are grouped according to what the leadership and church system decides is acceptable or not for their church. Therefore, each individual church's membership is by and large uniform, since the practices and doctrines for each church are set. If a person does not conform to that particular church's views, then they do not belong. This is not the oneness of the body; it is organizational uniformity. On the contrary, the real assembly — the body of Christ — is diverse. Each member is needed, yet absolutely one because the one Spirit is in each of them, and the one Lord who is the Head of the body is there.

Take notice how this chapter begins: the Gentiles are being carried away to dumb idols, but the believers are speaking in the Spirit of God. Their speech is focused on lifting up Jesus Christ as Lord. The idols are dumb (or mute); they have no life or tongue to speak, whereas the Spirit — symbolized by a flaming tongue (Acts 2) — is *full* of "speaking." Speaking Jesus Christ as Lord is the believers' manifestation that they are not worshipping idols, but the living and speaking God. This is why just about all the gifts and ministries given to believers listed in this chapter of Corinthians are related to the ability to speak. Idol worshippers are silent in their worship, but believers in their assembly, speak by the Spirit for the building up of the body.

> For as we have many members in one body, but all the members do not have the same function, so we, being many, are one body in Christ, and individually members of one another. Having then gifts differing according to the grace that is given to us, let us use them: if prophecy, let us prophesy in proportion to our faith; or ministry, let us use it in our ministering; he who teaches, in teaching; he who exhorts, in exhortation; he who gives, with liberality; he who leads, with diligence; he who shows mercy, with cheerfulness.
>
> – Romans 12:4–8

Although all believers are one body, each believer is still an individual, a distinct person in the body. Each individual has their own function that is different from all other members in the body. It is certain that not one member can be replaced by another member in his or her function. That is why every believer is needed to function to their full capacity.

Romans 12:4–8 include a list of gifts that is somewhat different from the list in 1 Corinthians 12 (read Romans 12 for the entire list). Since each believer has received the grace of Christ, each one has a gift as well. This gift is not based on any theological training or Bible school degree. It is based on the grace received of the Lord. The more believers enjoy the riches of Christ as grace — their gift in the body — their function in the body will increase.

Only in the assembly in homes, house by house, can there be an environment where every member can function without the regulations of any organized system. Today's churches can be a place to either build up or tear down the body of Christ. Positively, churches today are more akin to a school for teaching the Bible or a synagogue where people can go, knowing that people of faith are located there. But negatively, churches can be dividers of the body, separating believers based on the system of doctrines and practices of respective churches. There will be more discussion on this topic later. But certainly it is not an environment where every believer is free to function according to the gift given to them for the building up of the body...especially when any teaching and practice contrary to the system of teaching and practices of that church will be rejected.

> . . . from whom the whole body, joined and held together by every joint with which it is equipped, when each part is working properly, makes the body grow so that it builds itself up in love.
>
> – Ephesians 4:16, ESV

This is how the body of Christ is built up practically, with every member and every part working properly. If every part of the human body did not properly work, it would be a major medical issue. Even insignificant parts of the body, if not working properly, can be a huge annoyance and handicap! Compare that to Christianity today, where the majority of believers are dormant. How can there be the practical building up of the Lord's body? But when every part is working, then there is the building up of itself. Every assembly in the home can build up itself when the believers exercise their function. The environment is one of love, manifested when believers function together to build the assembly in their homes. There will be increase and growth, just as when the assembly started in Acts from house to house.

A Description of Assembly in the Homes

What does a home assembly look like, where each member functions and contributes for the practical building up of the body? Paul gives insight to this in 1 Corinthians 14:26:

> What then, brothers? When you come together, each one has a hymn, a lesson, a revelation, a tongue, or an interpretation. Let all things be done for building up.
>
> – 1 Corinthians 14:26

Chapter 14 of 1 Corinthians is the only portion in the New Testament that describes the practical functioning of each member gathered in an assembly. (In the last chapter of this book, on "Service," this will be explored in detail). Other portions in the Acts describe a gathering for preaching or teaching by the apostles, but those gatherings are not called the "assembly," which specifically is what the Lord is building according to God's eternal purpose. Chapter 12 of 1 Corinthians teaches that each member of the body has a function, and Chapter 14 clarifies how the functioning and building up of each member together is actually practiced.

In the Old Testament when all of Israel came together in Jerusalem for their feasts, a couple of them seven days long, everyone heading to worship God at the temple had to bring the top 10 percent of their crops and their herd (Deut. 14:22–27). Everyone brought their portion from the good land that God had given them; this was their tithe. For example, if a family grew wheat, they brought the top 10 percent of their wheat. If they had a herd of cattle, they needed to bring the top 10 percent from the herd. It was a sin for any Israelite to go to a feast empty-handed with nothing to present (Ex. 23:15). What they brought for worship to God were the items shared among all the Israelites for feasting. In essence, it was a giant "pot luck" feast. The tithes and sacrifices became a feast for both God and man.

1 Corinthians 14 can be described as the *application* of the Old Testament feasts in the New Testament. Specifically, in verse 26, the Bible says each one has something to bring for sharing in the assembly. "Each one has" means that every single believer (male and female) coming to the assembly is likened to a person coming to a feast — a spiritual feast — bringing the top enjoyment of Christ ready as an offering for both God and man to feast on and enjoy. This feast of the assembly is not prepared by a couple of professionals; rather, each and every one of the believers has a responsibility and a privilege to contribute and share what they have gained of Christ. This is the food for feasting in the assembly. Not everyone has to share large portions, since it is according to the capacity of each of the members; therefore, even five words (1 Cor. 14:19) is a good contribution if that is a person's portion.

Churches today are typically centered on the speaking of one person. The attendees, for the most part, are passive listeners of a message. Churches can be a good school for Christians to learn doctrines and be inspired by the message, but they are not the assembly as described in the New Testament. The speaking in the churches today at best may be likened to the apostles' preaching at the temple or the synagogues or even one of the schools where the apostle Paul taught (Acts 19:9). However, they are not an assembly where all the believers bring their portions of Christ to share, no matter how big or small. All the proper teachers in the various churches need to equip and encourage the attendees listening to them to go home, build up the assembly, and practice the functioning of every member. If they do that, then they are facilitating the building up the assembly.

This kind of assembly is even different from "home fellowship" or cell groups sponsored by a church, because typically those home groups are structured to follow the agenda of the church under its auspices; the gathering runs according to the direction of that church's organization with assigned leadership. In such a case, there is not the complete freedom for any believer to speak what the Lord has shown them, and where the Spirit has the liberty to move from believer to believer and reveal what is in the Lord's heart. A genuine home assembly that is not merely an extension of a church organization has the elements of this entire chapter, which we will cover in Chapter 18.

Elements of Practice in an Assembly

In an assembly, there are elements of praying, singing, speaking, and reading, but absolutely no instructions on how to do any of these or for how long.

> What is the *conclusion* then? I will pray with the spirit, and I will also pray with the understanding. I will sing with the spirit, and I will also sing with the understanding. Otherwise, if you bless with the spirit, how will he who occupies the place of the uninformed say "Amen" at your giving of thanks, since he does not understand what you say?
>
> – 1 Corinthians 14:15–16

> ...speaking to one another in psalms and hymns and spiritual songs, singing and making melody in your heart to the Lord.
>
> – Ephesians 5:19

> Until I come, devote yourself to the public reading of Scripture, to exhortation, to teaching.
>
> – 1 Timothy 4:13, ESV

The Bible does not provide any schedule, program, or liturgy for Christian gatherings. What it does indicate (in the verses above) are various elements that are present, but it does not say how to do each or for how long. For example, it does say that there is praying and singing in the assembly, but it is left completely open whether prayer is to be loud and excited or somber, lengthy or short, or how many people are to pray. There is no indication whether singing is to be in the form of solos, duets, or congregational, and no details are given regarding tempos of music or instrumental accompaniments. Since there are no such details of "how to," believers should be open to and encourage the Spirit's moving within each one, including the spontaneity from individual initiatives when gathered together. Believers need to be vigilant to prevent formality of liturgy where the Spirit is stifled, and individual initiatives are not allowed.

A Genuine Local Assembly Reflects the Universal Assembly

Every genuine local assembly is a miniature in the nature and expression of the universal assembly, with the person and work of Christ as the assembly's unique foundation.

> Simon Peter answered and said, "You are the Christ, the Son of the living God… And I also say to you that you are Peter, and on this rock I will build My church [assembly], and the gates of Hades shall not prevail against it."
>
> – Matthew 16:16, 18

> According to the grace of God which was given to me, as a wise master builder I have laid the foundation, and another builds on it. But let each one take heed how he builds on it. For no other foundation can anyone lay than that which is laid, which is Jesus Christ.
>
> – 1 Corinthians 3:10–11

It is clear Matthew 16 refers to the universal assembly throughout time and space. The universal assembly is built upon the rock – Jesus, the Christ and the Son of the living God. Peter literally means "a stone." Jesus changed Simon's name to Peter, a stone for the building. All the believers are just like Peter, living stones for God's building (1 Pet. 2:5). The only qualification to be a "stone" for the assembly that the Lord is building up is having the faith of Jesus Christ.

When Paul wrote to the local assembly in Corinth, he said that he had laid the unique foundation of God's building in that locality, which is Jesus Christ. "The foundation" in 1 Corinthians 3:10–11 is the same as "the rock" in Matthew 16. The rock is the solid foundation for the building. Thus, any local assembly gathered in homes *must* have the unique foundation of Jesus Christ. If a home gathering and its fellowship are not based solely on Jesus Christ, then it cannot be considered an assembly.

Let's say that a home gathering has Jesus Christ *plus baptism by immersion* as its foundation for gathering. Then that gathering will reject or make uncomfortable a believer who practices sprinkling of water for baptism. If so, then that gathering cannot be considered as an assembly (according to these verses). As long as the foundation is Jesus Christ, then any believer, no matter the variance of practices or doctrines, will be received equally as a stone for the building of that assembly. The foundation is not Jesus Christ *plus* something else, or someone else. It is uniquely Jesus Christ and Him alone.

An Assembly Is Part of the Christ with Many Members

> For as the body is one and has many members, but all the members of that one body, being many, are one body, so also is Christ. For by one Spirit we were all baptized into one body — whether Jews or Greeks, whether slaves or free — and have all been made to drink into one Spirit.
> – 1 Corinthians 12:12–13

The metaphor of the body in 1 Corinthians 12:12 is referring to Christ. Christ has many members. Most people understand this to read, "For as the body is one and has many members…so also is the assembly." No, Paul specifically says, "…so also is *Christ*" (emphasis added). The Christ is no longer just Jesus, but the Christ now includes all the believers as members that have been baptized into the one universal body. This includes all kinds of people throughout time and space. The entire body was baptized all at once into one body and all the members were given to drink one Spirit; this includes all those who do not yet believe. Certainly this is the universal Christ, which includes Jesus as the Head, and all the believers as members of the body.

> …that there should be no schism [faction] in the body, but that the members should have the same care for one another. And if one member suffers, all the members suffer with it; or if one member is honored, all the members rejoice with it. Now you are the body of Christ, and members individually.
> – 1 Corinthians 12:25–27

Later in the chapter Paul told the Corinthians there is no schism (faction or division) in the body. Certain divisions or schisms had surfaced among them in their local assembly. The body life is so practical that its people have the same care for one another and share in the same joy and suffering. This kind of mutual caring and sharing would not be applicable in the universal sense (for example, it would not be practical to care for and share in the suffering of those being martyred in Rome a couple of centuries back). So in this very practical and applicable situation of the assembly in the homes, Paul told believers that they are the body of Christ, *now*. Most Christians understand that the assembly in Corinth was only a part of the body of Christ, since the body of Christ is universal. But no, Paul calls that little local assembly the body of Christ.

In the practical assembly here and now, believers need to have the vision and bear the responsibility of being the body of Christ with many members. How awesome that a local assembly meeting in a home is the fully functional body of Christ with nothing lacking! Sometimes Christians speak of caring for believers thousands of miles away because they are in the body; yet, they neglect or divide from those close to them in their own city. According to Paul, the body of Christ is those believers right around them in their locality. The first responsibility for believers is to guard against division from those closest to them and have the same care for the believers right around them in their local assembly.

Those who do not see the local assembly as the body of Christ and treat it as only a sub-part of the body may understand the assembly to function like this: "The eyes of the body are in Los Angeles and the mouth is in New York, so we here in Zurich need so-and-so in order to see, also so-and-so in order to hear what the Lord is saying, since we are not the eyes or the mouth." Those with such a view will always look to the outside for help and consider themselves inadequate in their own assembly. They will also try to unify the assemblies into a federation since they consider themselves deficient, being a "part" and not the "whole." In attempting to federate, they will organize and systematize all the local assemblies, and in doing so they will damage and even divide the body of Christ from others not in their federation.

A federation exists when a special union is formed among some of the local assemblies. Those that are in this union feel more loyalty with each other than those assemblies outside. Those not in this union would need to fulfill certain requirements to become part of this federation; this may be by accepting the same leadership structure or adopting the same doctrines and practices. Basically, it becomes a subset of the body of Christ. Any subset in the body of Christ is by definition divisive.

An Assembly Receives *All* Believers

> For you are all sons of God through faith in Christ Jesus. . . .There is neither Jew nor Greek, there is neither slave nor free, there is neither male nor female; for you are all one in Christ Jesus.
>
> – Galatians 3:26, 28

The Bible says, "there is no partiality with God" (Rom. 2:11). That means He treats everyone the same regardless of nationality, ethnicity, socioeconomic status, political view, or gender. His only regard is whether a person has believed into Christ. Anyone in Jesus Christ is a son of God regardless of differences and variances. Everyone in Jesus Christ is one. Though there is distinction based on where each person comes from (by birth or culture), those differences should not be dividers. Rather, there is now absolute oneness without any possibility of separation in Christ. This is the universal assembly where all the believers receive one another, even though distinct due to their various backgrounds.

> Receive one who is weak in the faith, *but* not to disputes over doubtful things. For one believes he may eat all things, but he who is weak eats *only* vegetables. Let not him who eats despise him who does not eat, and let not him who does not eat judge him who eats; for God has received him. Who are you to judge another's servant?. . . One person esteems *one* day above another; another esteems every

> day alike. Let each be fully convinced in his own mind. He who observes the day, observes it to the Lord; and he who does not observe the day, to the Lord he does not observe it. . . .
>
> — Romans 14:1–4a, 5–6

It is one thing to have a theoretical oneness with all believers one day in the future, but for believers who are very different to share a meal together in a home assembly today is quite another. Paul used the example of eating and observing certain days in Romans 14:1–6, because in his day, the difference between Jews and Gentiles was distinctive and divisive. It can be so divisive that even the apostle Peter got carried away at one point and separated himself from eating with Gentile believers (Gal. 2:11–13). Observing certain days can also be divisive; the Jews were to keep the Sabbath day special, while the Greeks made no distinction of days.

Paul charged believers in Romans 14:1–6 to receive each other no matter the differences because God received them in Christ regardless of their habits, convictions, or practices. God's desire is that the very practical local assembly here and now reflects the universal eternal assembly.

Diet and days may have been the biggest contentious practices in Paul's day, but today Christians divide over a host of various practices: method of baptism, how to have communion, leadership format, music genre, women's roles, or liturgical style, etc. Additionally, Christians divide over doctrinal differences: predestination versus free will, the manifestation of the Spirit, or the time of tribulation, creation versus evolution, etc. This is not to mention ethical, socio-economic, political affiliation, or differences based on race or gender. No matter the dissimilarity, God has received each believer who lives to the Lord according to their conviction; therefore, there should be an equal receiving of all believers in an assembly. Any despising and rejecting which causes stumbling goes against the very nature and expression of God's assembly. Therefore, a Christian group that despises or rejects a believer cannot be considered an assembly; at most, it can be a defined as a Christian church, organization, or school, but not the one body of Christ.

> But why do you judge your brother? Or why do you show contempt for your brother? For we shall all stand before the judgment seat of Christ. For it is written: "*As* I live, says the LORD, every knee shall bow to Me, and every tongue shall confess to God." So then each of us shall give account of himself to God. Therefore let us not judge one another anymore, but rather resolve this, not to put a stumbling block or a cause to fall in *our* brother's way.
>
> — Romans 14:10–13

When judgment is passed on certain believers, condemning them because of their convictions and practices, it becomes a stumbling block to them. Another stumbling block occurs when believers think anyone who participates in certain practices different from their own is a weaker believer. Some are so strong with their own conviction that they will purposely promote or practice their conviction in front of other believers, even when they know that these believers have a contrary view. This causes believers to stumble. Let's consider again the issue of eating. When a person knows that a certain believer does not eat meat for religious reasons and might be offended or stumble when offered meat, if the one with the freedom to eat meat does so right in front of his brother (or even pushes his freedom of eating meat on him), this becomes a stumbling block.

Because of this, any practice or non-essential doctrine should be handled carefully, so that what is good for one is not pushed on others.

This matter of receiving believers into fellowship and not causing them to stumble is so critical that Paul brought up the matter of Christ's judgment seat. This is where all believers will give an account one day. How followers of Jesus judge their brothers and sisters in Christ will affect their own verdict before Christ at the time of judgment. This is a serious matter, yet many Christian groups are built and organized around certain practices and non-essential doctrines that automatically judge those who believe differently. Some groups claim that they receive all believers, but their acceptance comes with an intention: whomever they receive will eventually be converted and adopt *their* practices. That is not receiving; that is proselytizing.

In a genuine assembly, there should be complete freedom for diversity in practices where each believer is equally accepted with equal opportunity to share and contribute their portion of Christ. All believers with a heart for God's purpose who seek the building up of the assembly, which is the Lord's body, need to take this chapter of Romans into serious consideration.

> …for the kingdom of God is not eating and drinking, but righteousness and peace and joy in the Holy Spirit. For he who serves Christ in these things *is* acceptable to God and approved by men. Therefore let us pursue the things *which make* for peace and the things by which one may edify [build up] another.
>
> – Romans 14:17–19

Paul brought the believers back to the central point — the essential point: the kingdom of God is righteousness, peace, and joy in the Holy Spirit. In essence Paul said, "Don't get hung up with any of the non-essentials and practices, because they are not the focal point. Instead of being concerned by all the various practices that can become a point of contention between believers, let's stay focused on the kingdom of God."

The kingdom of God does not include various practices: diet, days, how to baptize, form of leadership, and on and on. The kingdom of God, which is the assembly here and now, is righteousness, peace and joy in the Holy Spirit. If believers become distracted by the various practices, either by rejecting believers or offending them through the strong promotion of certain doctrines or practices, the kingdom of God is missed. If there is no kingdom of God with all that the Holy Spirit encompasses, then there is no assembly.

The goal for each believer should be the kingdom of God. If a particular doctrine or practice helps one to arrive at the Holy Spirit, then it is good for that person. What is good for one person, however, does not mean it is good for all. For example, one may pray in a tongue and really receive the joy of the Spirit, but that does not mean that *everyone* has to pray in a tongue in order to have the same joy. There is no need to insist on or oppose praying in tongues. If a believer who does not pray in a tongue is not joyful because *someone else* is praying in tongues, then the one not joyful is not in the kingdom because the joy of the Spirit is not present. All believers should be able to share their experiences with each other, whether it is relating to tongue speaking, baptism, prayer, or help from a certain minister, but without intending to dispute or judge others. The ultimate destination for all believers' sharing should be the same: righteousness, peace, and joy in the Holy Spirit.

> Now may the God of patience and comfort grant you to be like-minded toward one another, according to Christ Jesus, that you may with one mind [one accord] and one mouth glorify the God and Father of our Lord Jesus Christ. Therefore receive one another, just as Christ also received us, to the glory of God.
>
> – Romans 15:5–7

Some Christian groups teach that in order to glorify God in one accord, believers need to practice the same things, have the same leadership, or hold to the same doctrinal understanding. This kind of unification between believers, however, is not what Paul was teaching here; rather, those who try to force unification actually end up being more divisive. The "one accord" to glorify God is not from everyone doing the same things, but receiving each other though practices are different. Receiving other believers in the one fellowship spontaneously results in the "one accord" and the "one mouth." It is in this mutual receiving absent of judgment that God the Father is glorified — expressed in His wonderful attributes. Conversely, judging, rejecting, and promoting a pet doctrine or practice will cause believers to stumble and make Satan proud, since his devices are working among believers to hinder the building up of the assembly.

An Assembly Is Part of the One Fellowship

A local assembly is part of the one common and universal fellowship between all believers.

> That which was from the beginning, which we have heard, which we have seen with our eyes, which we have looked upon, and our hands have handled, concerning the Word of life — the life was manifested, and we have seen, and bear witness, and declare to you that eternal life which was with the Father and was manifested to us — that which we have seen and heard we declare to you, that you also may have fellowship with us; and truly our fellowship is with the Father and with His Son Jesus Christ. And these things we write to you that your joy may be full.
>
> – 1 John 1:1–4

The unique message declared by the apostles is Jesus Christ. It is this singular message that brought (and continues to bring) believers into the fellowship. This fellowship is not just with those that brought the message but also with the Father and the Son, Jesus Christ.

Fellowship in the original Greek is the word *koinōnia,* which means, "Sharing something that is in common." The meaning could include distribution and joint participation of both physical and spiritual things. The root word of *koinōnia* comes from the idea of joining together. Since believers are now in both the Father and the Son, they jointly participate in all that is in the Father and Son. What all the believers "have in common" is Jesus Christ; therefore, there should be a sharing of all good things among the believers, both physical and spiritual.

This is the result of receiving the gospel: each and every believer enters into this fellowship that is in the Father and the Son. Once a person believes, experientially, he or she feels connected to every other believer in Christ. Initially, there is no thought of, "What kind of Christian am I?" Or, "What Christian group do I belong to?" because the eternal life received is one within all believers. There is a feeling of connection and belonging with every believer throughout time and space. It is not until corrupt thoughts enter the believer's mind that Christians begin to consider segregation among believers. The fullness of joy is not in division, but in the one fellowship with all believers in the Father and the Son.

> God is faithful, by whom you were called into the fellowship of His Son, Jesus Christ our Lord.
>
> – 1 Corinthians 1:9

Writing to the divided believers in Corinth, Paul reminded them of the one fellowship that they had been called into by God — the fellowship of Jesus Christ. How can there be divisions in the body if there is only one fellowship? It is important to note that fellowship in the Bible is never in plural; it is always singular. There is no concept of fellowships (plural) because in the entire universe, there is only one fellowship of Jesus Christ.

It is common for Christians to ask, "What fellowship do you belong to?" That very question leads to a concept contrary to the truth, that there are different fellowships to which believers can belong. No! All believers are in the one and the same fellowship. If a Christian group has their own fellowship that means they have specific requirements for a person to be part of their fellowship. In such a case, they may be the fellowship of Chinese Christians, the fellowship of those baptized by immersion, or the fellowship of the tongue speakers — but they would not be the unique and inclusive fellowship of Jesus Christ.

A group of Christians is sectarian if their "fellowship" is smaller than the fellowship of Jesus Christ. That means they are selective with whom they fellowship. The only thing that needs to be common among believers in order to have equal standing in the fellowship is Jesus Christ. Believers can be different politically, ethnically, or doctrinally; the only common item that must be shared is Jesus Christ. That is the very meaning of fellowship.

> Finally, brethren, rejoice, be made complete, be comforted, be like-minded, live in peace; and the God of love and peace will be with you. Greet one another with a holy kiss. . . . The grace of the Lord Jesus Christ, and the love of God, and the fellowship of the Holy Spirit, be with you all.
>
> – 2 Corinthians 13:11–12, 14, NASB

Paul wrote his first letter to the Corinthians when they were struggling with divisions among themselves. He hoped to remind them of their calling by God into the one fellowship of Jesus Christ (1 Cor. 1:9). Now at the end of his last letter to them he emphasizes that the fellowship is of the Holy Spirit. In this fellowship is the sharing and participation of the love of God and the grace of Jesus Christ. This is the same fellowship that is within the Trinity in eternity, and this is the unique fellowship into which God has called every believer. Just as there is no separation, segregation, or division within the triune God (it is not within the nature of the Trinity), believers participating in this fellowship cannot have divisions. A believer in the fellowship of the Holy Spirit will always draw other believers into fellowship, because that is the nature of God.

This is the same and only fellowship that is practical among the local assembly in Corinth. This is Paul's final word: believers in Corinth will rejoice in this one fellowship. It is what will make them complete, comforted, peaceful, loving, and like-minded with one another. This is the beautiful and wonderful condition of an assembly of believers in the fellowship of the Holy Spirit. This should be the normal experience of believers in a genuine assembly because an assembly is defined by having the fellowship of the Holy Spirit. There may be gatherings and groupings of Christians, but an assembly exists according to the revelation of the Scriptures, and it depends on the fellowship of the Holy Spirit. The more fellowship, the more assembly; the less fellowship the less assembly; if a group denies fellowship with any other believers, then no assembly.

The One Fellowship Extends to All Assemblies and Believers

> It pleased those from Macedonia and Achaia to make a certain contribution [fellowship] for the poor among the saints who are in Jerusalem. It pleased them indeed, and they are their debtors. For if the Gentiles have been partakers of their spiritual things, their duty is also to minister to them in material things.
> – Romans 15:26–27

Macedonia and Achaia are part of today's Greece. The believers there were Gentiles; yet, they were contributing to the poor Jewish believers in Jerusalem. What a testimony of oneness in the one fellowship! Jews and Gentiles, especially back in those days, were notorious for the deep enmity and separation between them. But in the one fellowship of the triune God, the Gentile believers extended their fellowship (which is the same Greek word as "contribution" in Romans 15:26) to Jews in their region as well as to Jewish saints in completely different regions. This is the practicality of fellowship. It is not just spiritual fellowship, but it reaches down to material riches that believers are not just willing, but happy to share. The Gentile believers were happy to minister material things to their fellow Jewish believers. What a testimony to the world of the oneness of believers — surely part of the fulfillment of the Lord's prayer in John 17.

Fellowship is not just local, among the believers' own group of people. It reaches out to believers in another region whom they may have never met or seen. Fellowship always reaches out and expands, and is not withdrawn or limited.

In the name of protecting their "fellowship" from outside corrupting influences, some groups of believers have become sectarian by discouraging or even forbidding believers in their group from fellowshipping with believers outside of the group. God is well able to protect His own fellowship. He certainly does not need man to be His protector.

> Salute the brethren in Laodicea, and Nymphas, and the assembly which [is] in his house. And when the letter has been read among you, cause that it be read also in the assembly of Laodiceans, and that ye also read that from Laodicea.
> – Colossians 4:15–16, DBY

Here is Paul's direct encouragement for the two assemblies, Colossae and Laodicea, to have fellowship together. Paul sent one letter to the saints in Colossae and another letter to the believers in Laodicea. Instead of carbon copying both and sending two letters to both places, he asked the Colossian believers to travel to Laodicea, greet the saints there, and read the letter to the assembly meeting in Nymphas' house. After that, they were to bring the letter written to the Laodiceans back and read it in Colossae. This shows the blending traffic of fellowship between believers and assemblies in two different localities. Each assembly could claim that they were indeed the body of Christ with no lack (1 Cor. 12:27); yet, if a local assembly became isolated and withdrawn within themselves, surely they would miss the Lord's word given to another locality.

As in this case, the Lord can communicate a word to one locality but intend it for all believers everywhere. If fellowship with a locality does not exist, the Lord's speaking with His riches and revelation would be missed. How critical it is for believers to extend themselves outside their conveniences and comfort zone. Whatever believers have received from the Lord is common to all believers, and there must be a sharing and receiving of fellowship in order to realize all that the Lord is doing. Every assembly needs to seek out other assemblies, even outside their own area, for fellowship. The more fellowship, the richer and stronger is that assembly.

A Command to Go Greet

It is essential to expand the sphere of fellowship to practically include all believers in other homes; therefore, Paul commanded the believers to go greet (Rom. 16).

> Greet Prisca and Aquila, my fellow workers in Christ Jesus, who risked their necks for my life, to whom not only I give thanks but all the churches [assemblies] of the Gentiles give thanks as well. Greet also the church [assembly] in their house. Greet my beloved Epaenetus, who was the first convert to Christ in Asia. Greet Mary, who has worked hard for you.
>
> Greet Apelles, who is approved in Christ. Greet those who belong to the family of Aristobulus. Greet my kinsman Herodion. Greet those in the Lord who belong to the family of Narcissus. Greet Asyncritus, Phlegon, Hermes, Patrobas, Hermas, and the brothers who are with them. Greet Philologus, Julia, Nereus and his sister, and Olympas, and all the saints who are with them. Greet one another with a holy kiss. All the churches [assemblies] of Christ greet you.
> – Romans 16:3–6, 10–11, 14–16, ESV

It may seem like this last chapter of Romans is not very significant, since almost the entire chapter consists of salutations and greetings to a long list of a variety of people. However, it is actually the most practical and insightful chapter relating to the assembly in the book of Romans. This chapter shows not just the one fellowship, but how to increase this fellowship of Christ in the body. Out of all the letters that Paul wrote, there must have been a reason he spent twenty-three verses — a whole chapter — on greetings, while all of his other letters only spent two or three verses on greetings.

While many believers never think about studying this chapter, if they practiced what Paul commanded those in Rome to practice, the attitude of believers toward one another would be revolutionized; it would bring about the manifested oneness of the body that the Lord prayed for in John 17.

First, let's consider the background. When Paul wrote this letter to the Romans, he had not been to Rome, nor was there record of any other apostles going there. Since he had not visited Rome, it is logical to assume that he did not know all the believers there; yet, he still listed a number he knew by name in Romans 16. Some of them he had met during his missionary journeys (such as Aquila and Priscilla while they were in Corinth). It can be assumed that some of the other names mentioned are names Paul heard from others, such as the two groups of believers he mentioned in Romans 16:14–15. History confirms that within the territory under the administration of the Roman Empire, unrestricted and relatively safe travel throughout the empire existed, thus expanding commerce rapidly. Citizens and freemen of the empire took advantage of this and were able to travel and relocate freely within this territory. Many residing in Rome traveled outside of Rome to Greece or Israel. Rome (being the capital) also attracted people from other regions, who relocated there. This is clearly affirmed by the backgrounds of the twenty-three people listed in the Romans 16, plus the five groups of people Paul mentioned…*even though he had never been to the assembly in Rome!*

Although Paul personally brought some of the believers in Rome to faith in Christ, and at least a couple became his fellow workers such as Prisca (Priscilla) and Aquila. It is also reasonable that many were brought to faith by other apostles and preachers that were active during Paul's time. Certainly some could have come to Christ in Judea. Perhaps when they went to Jerusalem for the feasts they heard the gospel through the ministry of the twelve apostles, or through Philip in Samaria, or from one of the many scattered believers who went throughout the territories preaching the gospel (Acts 11:19).

Here in Rome, they had become a collection of believers meeting in different homes who had come to faith in Christ through various preachers; they were as diverse as the population of Rome. There were well-to-do believers with large households, as well as slaves, Jews, Greeks, Roman citizens, and freemen from throughout the empire. In such a situation, it certainly would have been easy for the Christian community to segregate and separate themselves from each other. Even an assembly such as Corinth, which was raised up by the apostle Paul, experienced division. One can imagine the believers in Rome would have had even more of a propensity for division because of the diversity in practices and doctrines resulting from their various cultural backgrounds, social status, and preference of ministers who brought them to faith in Christ.

The epistle to the Romans may be considered Paul's systematic theology, covering the entirety of the gospel of God with the revealed mystery (16:25). After expounding on God's complete salvation, from man's condemnation to man's glorification (chapters 1 to 8), Paul continues in chapter 12 to unveil the mystery of the one body of Christ with many members. Each individual member is a gift that needs to function in the one body; since there were such a variety of people with an assortment of cultural and religious backgrounds, there would naturally have been a tendency to segregate and judge one another among the various groups. Because of this, Romans 14 was needed. Paul presented a strong case along with a warning that the believers needed to receive one another. Though all were believers and had been received in one body by Christ, it was natural for them to settle in their comfort zone and group together with others that were similar to them.

Considering this generation of believers — with groups segregated by non-essential doctrines, practices, preference of ministers, politics and ethnicity, among other things — the situation in Rome may be considered a microcosm of today's Christian environment. No wonder Paul declared in Romans 15 that the believers would glorify God if they received one another. Though diverse in practices, they would be in one accord and with one mouth. Due to a thorough mixture of people and backgrounds, both cultural and spiritual, Rome was the ideal environment to show the oneness of believers, according to John 17, through the gifts of the eternal life, the truth, and the Lord's glory.

"Receiving" in Romans 14 may be considered passive, in the sense that if believers come to a gathering or to a home assembly, the one hosting with all the saints needs to receive them for fellowship without passing judgment. But in Chapter 16, Paul charged the believers in Rome to go and greet other believers. Greeting in this sense is proactive. Paul commanded believers to go and greet the various people he listed.

The word "greet" is not just saying "hi" when walking past someone. The word for "greet" in the Greek means: to embrace, to be joined, a union, to visit or joyfully welcome a person (Strong's and Thayer's). It was customary that greetings took place by entering into a house and the occupant welcoming that person to stay for a while (Matt 10:12; Acts 21:7). Greetings include intimate dialogues with another person (Luke 1:40-55; Acts 21:19). Additionally, the verb form for "greet" here is aorist middle deponent imperative, which means Paul was commanding whoever received his letter to take continual action to go and greet those listed. Because believers today are to obey the Scriptures just as the first century, they should take similar action to go and greet brothers and sisters in other homes and groups. They should continue to do this regardless of whether they have done so in the past.

The first ones to greet were Priscilla and Aquila, and the assembly that was in their house. Priscilla and Aquila were under Paul's tutelage and worked closely with him in Ephesus before moving back to Rome; therefore, Paul should have had confidence that they had the same understanding and heart for God's purpose concerning the body as he. Although there were other home groups in Rome, it may have been because of Paul's assurance that they would be practicing according to his vision of the body of Christ that Paul only acknowledged the assembly in Priscilla and Aquila's home. Since the saints who gathered in their house were the assembly, Paul directed any who received his letter to go and greet them first. As the assembly, they had the reality of the one body and were the pattern of building on Jesus Christ as the unique foundation; also, every believer was functioning to their capacity and receiving all believers into the one fellowship. With the believers in Rome greeting them first, Paul could be assured anyone who went to greet them would be received into fellowship. By experiencing the assembly as a pattern, more and more believers would also learn the proper standing and functioning of an assembly.

At the same time, as the first recipients of Paul's letter, Priscilla, Aquila, and the assembly in their house had the foremost responsibility of proactively going and greeting everyone on Paul's list. They were not to wait for the believers in Rome to come to their house to greet them, but they were to venture out and greet other believers in Rome. They were to go and embrace into fellowship the believers in the other households and groups. Through this greeting of one another, all the believers in Rome would blend into one, and the assembly would spread from house to house. It would no longer be only in Priscilla and Aquila's house because the nature and expression of the universal assembly grew and spread from house to house just like in the earlier days with the assembly in Jerusalem. When Aquila and Priscilla were in Ephesus, they were instrumental in bringing Apollos into a clearer understanding of Jesus Christ (Acts 18); in Rome, they helped believers see and practice the assembly life, the one body of Christ, without any divisions among believers.

As the number of believers in Rome who read Paul's letter increased, the greetings and thus the fellowship among the saints grew exponentially. What a beautiful sight and testimony to the oneness of believers as they go from house to house greeting each other! Paul ended this section instructing readers to greet one another with a holy kiss. This kind of greeting expressed pure love and intimate fellowship among the believers. None would be isolated in their own home group, seeing the same believers year after year, but instead would be part of a growing network of homes in one fellowship with much traffic and support between them, because they were indeed one assembly. Today, most believers are segregated and isolated in their church or in their home. If believers accept Paul's directive to seek out other believers and greet them, the Lord will have a way to build up the assembly, His body.

Although there are so many churches and Christian groups today, believers can still heed Paul's command to go and greet fellow believers in other groups. In God's eyes all of His children are in one family, in the one body of Christ. As such, believers should not acknowledge any division, no matter what church or denomination may be segregating Christians. Greetings to a believer meeting in the Catholic church should be the same fervent greeting given to a believer in the Baptist Church, a Pentecostal Church, a non-denominational church, or even a believer not attending any church. For the purpose of mutual greetings among believers, no recognition should be given to which church a person belongs (since churches are artificially organized by men). No matter which church one belongs to or if a believer is completely outside the institutional church, each needs to proactively greet and receive other believers. What if believers with an emphasis on Pentecostal experiences greeted those that disparage tongue-speaking? What would happen if those with a preference for reformed theology greeted those that preach salvation is a choice? Believers would automatically become one in the reality of the body of Christ, and non-essential doctrines and pet practices would fade in priority and cease being an issue between believers. The intimate fellowship in Jesus Christ alone will cause the assembly to bloom from house to house. This will take place outside of and in spite of almost 2000 years of separation within institutional Christianity.

> I appeal to you, brothers, to watch out for those who cause divisions and create obstacles contrary to the doctrine that you have been taught; avoid them. For such persons do not serve our Lord Christ, but their own appetites, and by smooth talk and flattery they deceive the hearts of the naive.
>
> – Romans 16:17–18, ESV

As the believers were to go about visiting and greeting all the believers in the one body in Rome, Paul warned they would run into some who would not receive or give such greetings, believers who had decided to stand apart from the common fellowship of the body of Christ. There were Christian teachers who taught things contrary to the apostle's teaching of Jesus Christ and His one body with an intention of causing division — a standing apart — between those under their teachings and the rest of the believers. While the greetings among all believers were going on, these teachers deceived the hearts of the naïve in order to corral them into their own separate group. If this were today, they might say their group is different because they have the "real baptism," and other believers are not baptized in such a way. Another might say they have a special and higher revelation, so their group is not like the other believers because *they* receive their teachings from minister so-and-so.

Paul appealed to the believers to watch out for such teachers and avoid them. This should not be extended to the naïve or simple believers who are deceived by those teachers' smooth-talk; it is not their fault they were misled into a sectarian group. Those who teach differently with the goal of recruiting their own followers are not serving the Lord; they are serving their own appetite for either material gain or power to control those that they have corralled into their sect. This is a serious matter, which can only be exposed through the indiscriminate greetings among believers. If greetings do not occur between groups of believers, these self-serving teachers and their groups can stay hidden. But once greetings transpire from house to house, those standing apart will be exposed; teachers and leaders of these stand-apart groups should be noted and avoided.

This division in Romans 16:17–18 is much more serious than the "division" identified in 1 Corinthians 1:10 — the division among those in the assembly in Corinth. That division was like a schism, a rift within a family. Family quarrels are never good, and sometimes result in devastating rifts; however, family members still acknowledge they are in the same family, despite the rift. They just need to grow out of such childish arguments. But the "division" in Romans 16 is a standing apart. It is like saying, "I am not part of that family. We are our *own* family." This type of division is intentional separation, and those promoting such separations need to be marked and avoided.

Those serving the Lord Jesus Christ for His purpose will teach those under their leadership to follow Paul's command to go, visit, and greet all the various believers, even though they are not in their church or assembly. Those that serve their own appetite to build their own sect do their best to isolate those under their leadership; they do not want their members to be open in greeting and receiving others, or be intimate with believers who are not part of their group.

> The God of peace will soon crush Satan under your feet. The grace of our Lord Jesus Christ be with you.
>
> – Romans 16:20, ESV

This chapter may seem insignificant, but Paul intentionally included this verse at the end of such a chapter on greetings. Satan will be crushed under the feet of all the mutually greeting ones that are brought into oneness in fellowship. This verse is similar to Matthew 16:18 where the Lord Jesus said that He will build His assembly and the gates of hell shall not prevail against it. In Matthew, Jesus was giving the promise, or a prophecy; here, however, Paul and the early believers are living out the *reality* of the practical building up that will crush Satan. When believers are in oneness in the one fellowship, built on the one foundation Jesus Christ, with all the members functioning and active, Satan is crushed. It is the oneness of believers that defeats the enemy and satisfies the Lord's desire in His prayer in John 17.

Practice: Greeting Believers

Consider one or two other believers that you may know who are not part of the group of Christians with whom you are normally in fellowship. Pray for them and for an opportunity to "greet" them. Contact them to arrange a time to meet and greet. Preferably you can visit their house, but it could be over a meal, coffee, or on a walk at the park. Tell them that you are touched by the Lord to have some fellowship with them and get to know them better. When you meet them, in addition to the normal chit-chat of getting to know each other better, you can also give your testimony and/or ask for theirs; ask them for prayer or if they have any requests for prayer. Share a portion of the Word and/or ask if they have read anything inspiring in the Bible recently. In a short time, you will wonder why you didn't do this earlier and will want to greet other believers more often.

Write down a few names that the Spirit is placing in your heart for you to contact and set up a meet and greet time. Pray for them — before and while you are reaching out to them.

Name 1: _____

Name 2: _____

Name 3: _____

13

(SECTION B)
THE PRACTICAL ASSEMBLY

The first section of this chapter showed from Scripture how the local ekklesia practiced. Whether there were tens of thousands of believers in a city or a few believers in a town, the assembly was practical and enjoyed in the homes, and the fellowship was just one. In Section B of this chapter, other important practical matters relating to the assembly will be considered. These items include the nature of the "two or three" gathering into the Lord's name, who the assembly should exclude, and the difference between a ministry and an assembly.

Two or Three Gathered in the Lord's Name

> "If your brother sins against you, go, show him his fault between you and him alone. If he listens to you, you have gained back your brother. But if he doesn't listen, take one or two more with you, that at the mouth of two or three witnesses every word may be established. If he refuses to listen to them, tell it to the assembly. If he refuses to hear the assembly also, let him be to you as a Gentile or a tax collector. Most certainly I tell you, whatever things you bind on earth will have been bound in heaven, and whatever things you release on earth will have been released in heaven. Again, assuredly I tell you, that if two of you will agree on earth concerning anything that they will ask, it will be done for them by my Father who is in heaven. For where two or three are gathered together in my name, there I am in the midst of them."
>
> – Matthew 18:15–20 WEB

Matthew 18:20 is a wonderful oft-quoted verse—that when two or three gathered together anywhere and at any time, and when their activities focus on Jesus Christ and into this sphere of His name, He is in their midst. Believers need to take advantage of this promise. Most of the time Christians only consider the things of Christ, fellowship, or prayer when in church. If they are not in church or at an "official" Christian event, then there is not much thought of the practice of fellowship to be in Christ. Experientially, the Lord is not in their midst. If believers want the Lord's presence with all of His riches and blessings, then they need to find every opportunity to gather into the Lord's name. Only then is the Lord brought everywhere that they are located, all the time.

Nevertheless, these "twos or threes" by themselves are not the assembly. In context, based on verses 16 and 17, the "twos or threes" must bring unresolved matters to the assembly. The assembly has the final say concerning the matter. If the offending brother hears the assembly, then he continues in the fellowship of the assembly; but if he does not hear the assembly concerning his sin, then he is to be treated as an unbeliever. As an unbeliever, it does not mean he is cut off from care and love, since believers should love, cherish, and nourish every weak and unbelieving person. This is quite different from churches today, where being excluded does not seem like a punishment at all. The proper assembly in the home, according to the divine revelation, must have been so enjoyable that being excluded from assembling is a devastating loss for the unrepentant brother.

Whether in one home or many homes, in any given locality there is only one assembly; yet, there should be many "twos or threes" gathering into the Lord's name throughout the day: in restaurants, schools, parks, malls, homes, cars…everywhere. All these "twos or threes" are part of the one assembly. They have the vision and realization that they are all in the one assembly—one fellowship. These "twos or threes" also gather with other "twos or threes" from house to house according to 1 Corinthians 14 as the one assembly. In such a situation, though there is diverse fellowship and multitudes of activity, there is still one body. In such oneness of the body, the "twos or threes" have the authority to bind and loose in their prayers. The Father listens to the prayers of all the "twos or threes" that are in full harmony in the one assembly.

Whatever these "twos or threes" bind or loose on earth shall be bound and loosed in heaven. This shows the effectiveness of their prayers. God is waiting for such prayers in oneness with His will for the building up of His kingdom. God will not act on His own. He needs the prayer of believers in harmony before He will act. This shows the need for believers to be one in order to move God's hand to answer prayers.

Just as Peter was given the keys of the kingdom of the heavens to bind and to loose, all of these "twos and threes" can also bind and loose for the sake of the building up of God's kingdom, His assembly. To "bind" is to bind Satan and all of his forces that they would be out of commission, and become of no effect. In Matthew 12:22–29, the Lord Jesus healed a blind and a dumb man due to demon possession so that the man saw and spoke. He explained that the man was a vessel captured in the house of a "strong man." In order to take away vessels from the strong man's house (to heal this person), He must bind the strong man.

Today many people are spiritually blinded from seeing who Jesus Christ is and they are spiritually dumb so that they cannot speak Jesus Christ and minister Him. In the spiritual realm, if a person sees Christ then he or she needs to speak Christ. Those that cannot see or speak Christ are captured in Satan's house, his kingdom. Therefore, binding prayers are needed to bind Satan and all his evil forces so that the blind and dumb people in his house can be released and healed of their sight and speech; they need to see Jesus and speak Him.

These "twos and threes" also have the authority to "loose." In Acts 2:24 Paul states that God—in raising up Jesus from the dead—has loosed the pangs of death. To "loose" in prayer is for people to be loosed from the hold of death. People should not be in death, but rather, they should be loosed from death and released into eternal life. So binding is for the enemy and the loosing is for people. Both are so that people can be transferred from Satan's kingdom to God's kingdom. This kind of prayer is not according to self-interest, but according to God's will for the building up of the assembly—and it is the kind of prayer desperately needed today.

Ministers Wrongly Competing with the Assembly

All the ministers with their ministries should be for the building of the one assembly, but instead many ministers may be building their own ministry in detriment to the assembly.

> For as we have many members in one body, but all the members do not have the same function, so we, being many, are one body in Christ, and individually members of one another. Having then gifts differing according to the grace that is given to us, let us use them: if prophecy, let us prophesy in proportion to our faith; or ministry, let us use it in our ministering; he who teaches, in teaching; he who exhorts, in exhortation; he who gives, with liberality; he who leads, with diligence; he who shows mercy, with cheerfulness.
>
> – Romans 12:4–8
>
> There are diversities of gifts, but the same Spirit. There are differences of ministries, but the same Lord. And there are diversities of activities, but it is the same God who works all in all. But the manifestation of the Spirit is given to each one for the profit of all:
>
> – 1 Corinthians 12:4–7

In both of these chapters relating to the many members in the one body, Paul includes two lists showing that every individual member in the body has at least one gift for the benefit of the entire body. The lists contain a variety of gifts ranging from the very practical to the supernatural. The practical gifts given include those that every believer can possess, ranging from such things as giving to those in need and hospitality (Rom. 12:13), to some supernatural gifts such as healing and working miracles. Just as in the physical body where each organ has a specific function, the members of the body of Christ also have specific functions to serve the one body. All of these gifts, ministries, and activities are from the Spirit, the Lord, and God; therefore, believers should recognize and accept that while there are such diverse ministries, they are all for the body.

It is unfortunate when believers do not accept all the gifts and ministries that the Trinity has given to the members of the body. Some may refuse to accept that miraculous healings can still happen today and denigrate those that have witnessed and experienced such things. At the same time, others may reject a word of wisdom, warning believers not to be distracted or naively follow the "hype" surrounding many claims of miracles. Some may consider a ministry that cares for recovering addicts as a waste of resources, while others may consider any resources given to a ministry outreaching to business people unscriptural (since the Bible charges believers to give to the poor). According to Paul, however, believers should realize that the mind and the ways of the Lord are above man's limited and biased views. It is by receiving all the gifts and ministries that believers can be balanced and gain the benefit from all the gifts, ministries, and activities that have been bestowed upon the body of Christ.

Among all the believers, some have developed their gifts quicker and have the capability to initiate a ministry as a stronger believer. By exercising their gifts to preach the Word, teach the Bible, or do works of faith, they will draw a following of people into their ministry. It is critical to recognize that most of the various churches and Christian groups today are really a grouping based on someone's ministry, such as of a pastor or preacher. They are gathered to hear the teachings and inspirations from a particular gifted believer. Other Christian groups are ministries based on reaching the poor, people in prison, a particular ethnic community, or college students.

The entire Lutheran denomination, for example, is based on the ministry of Martin Luther, and there are many other regional and global organized churches that are based on (or a continuation of) a gifted minister. On one hand there is no doubt that many of these gifted ministers have provided tremendous benefits to believers, but on the other hand, if only the ministry itself is being built while the assembly is being neglected, the body is thus splintered and most believers are not functioning members in an assembly. They are rather just audiences or supporters of a particular ministry. There is to be a clear distinction between building up a ministry and the building up of an assembly as described in the Bible.

There is absolutely no doubt from these two portions of Scripture that the various and diverse ministries and activities are for the one body. Any ministry that focuses on the growth of the ministry but stand apart from the assembly become sectarian like Paul warned the believers.

Cancer occurs when a particular type of cell continues to increase, even when not needed, to invade and damage the physical body. Similarly, many problems among believers are due to ministries competing for followers and resources in the body of Christ. The gifted ministers or the followers of these gifted ministers who do such things will have a couple of characteristics. First, they will do their best to grow their followers and "hold' them, rather than release them to build the assembly in their homes. Second, they will speak negatively against other ministries in competition to gain more followers to grow and spread their own ministry.

For example let's say a particular gifted believer has a burden to reach out to college students. To carry out his mission, he develops a method of open-air gospel music and preaching to bring people to faith in Christ. It would be appropriate if this person, becoming successful in this way, to have a following and train others to do what he does in order to reach more college students for Christ. His ministry would be profitable for the body when those who become believers through his ministry then entered into the one fellowship of the assembly from house to house, receiving and greeting all the other non-college students in their community. But what if this gifted brother started to speak negatively against another minister on campus whose method of reaching unbelievers is through one-on-one Bible studies? What if he started to belittle a prison ministry as being a waste of time? What if, when the number of people who follow him increases, he builds a church to group them together so that they do not know how to receive and fellowship with non-college students? Then this gifted brother's ministry is no longer for the body but is for growing his own ministry "church." His ministry may well grow and prosper, but by corralling those helped through his ministry into his church, the blending and the one fellowship of the assembly is neglected.

All believers need to rise up to minister, to exercise their gifts in the body. Everyone needs to serve and be a co-worker with the Lord. Some that are more gifted and capable in their service will draw a following of believers after them. It is natural to admire and follow ministers who have been used by God, whether that minister is prominent or lesser known. On one hand, it is proper for a worker of the Lord to acquire co-workers from those that they have helped, as Paul did with his younger co-workers Timothy, Titus, Silas and others. Every useful minister of the Lord should have some helpers to expand the reach of his ministry. On the other hand, it is dangerous for a minister to gain a following to the point where they form a group or even a sect that competes with the assembly of the Lord, even the Lord Himself. Therefore, all ministers both great and small need to have a mind-set of humility, and be ready to serve others and give up their own following of believers for the sake of the assembly.

John the Baptist, Competing with Jesus

> After this Jesus and his disciples went into the Judean countryside, and he remained there with them and was baptizing. John also was baptizing at Aenon near Salim, because water was plentiful there, and people were coming and being baptized. ...And they came to John and said to him, "Rabbi, he who was with you across the Jordan, to whom you bore witness — look, he is baptizing, and all are going to him." ...He must increase, but I must decrease.
>
> – John 3:22–23, 26, 30

> Then the disciples of John came to him, saying, "Why do we and the Pharisees fast, but your disciples do not fast?"
>
> – Matthew 9:14, ESV

John the Baptist was clearly used by God to proclaim Jesus at His coming. John can be considered the first gospel preacher. He was the first to lead people to Jesus Christ and declare Him as the Son of God, the one who takes away the sins of the world. Since Jesus came and started His ministry (including baptism), John's work of introducing Jesus was completed; it was no longer needed. John should have just pointed people to Jesus, sent all of his own disciples to Him, and joined himself to Jesus' ministry. Instead John continued baptizing people just "because water is plentiful there." Even though John was clear concerning the preeminence of Jesus, it seems that his own disciples were not. They viewed Jesus as a competitor to their rabbi, John. Their concern was that people were going to Jesus to be baptized instead of to John.

When John started his ministry he harshly condemned the Pharisees (Matt. 3:7). It is hard to imagine that within two years, John's disciples linked arms together with the Pharisees in challenging Jesus — condemning Him for eating and drinking with sinners instead of fasting. John's disciples kept the religious laws, but missed the person that John was so clear in proclaiming. John himself knew that Jesus' followers must increase and his followers must decrease, but he still held on to his ministry and his followers; thus, he unwittingly became a competitor to Jesus.

Any believer who is being helped by a particular minister should be cautious that they do not become a group or a sect formed around their minister in a way that separates them from the assembly, the body of Christ. Ministers also need to be vigilant and know when their ministry's usefulness is over, and not become a source of distraction from the Lord. John's ministry reveals that even the person introducing the Lord to others can become a distraction and compete with the Lord. Therefore, it is critical to function with the full conviction that all the ministers' labor is to ultimately build up the assembly, and not to build up their own ministries.

A Ministry Is Different from a Local Assembly

> And it happened, while Apollos was at Corinth, that Paul, having passed through the upper regions, came to Ephesus. And finding some disciples
>
> And he went into the synagogue and spoke boldly for three months, reasoning and persuading concerning the things of the kingdom of God. But when some were hardened and did not believe, but spoke evil of the Way before the multitude, he departed from them and withdrew the disciples, reasoning daily in the school of Tyrannus.
>
> – Acts 19:1, 8–9
>
> But I will tarry in Ephesus until Pentecost.
>
> The churches [assemblies] of Asia greet you. Aquila and Priscilla greet you heartily in the Lord, with the church [assembly] that is in their house.
>
> – 1 Corinthians 16:8, 19

When Paul went to Ephesus, as was his custom, he first preached in the synagogues, since those were congregational places of people who already worshipped God and read the Scriptures of the Old Testament. He started there. It was an efficient way to reach a large number of people with the message of Jesus Christ. When those in the synagogue didn't believe, Paul secured a place in a school to daily continue his teaching. That school was the place where he established his ministry of teaching, preaching, and reasoning daily with anyone willing to enter into dialogue with him.

It is critical to note here that while the school was the place where he daily "worked out" his ministry, the actual assembly in Ephesus was in Aquila and Priscilla's house. Paul didn't call the place where he was doing his ministry "the assembly," because that was the place of his ministry; the local assembly was in someone's home. Paul's actions confirm a ministry is not the assembly, but all the ministries are *for* the assembly. Another minister, such as Apollos, may well set up another school for his ministry, but that will not be the assembly either. No matter how many ministers set up schools to teach and preach, they are all for the one assembly that is gathering from house to house. The assembly is one, though ministries are many.

Ministers Are for the Assembly

All ministers are for the assembly, and an assembly can receive services from multiple independent ministers.

> For when one says, "I am of Paul," and another, "I am of Apollos," are you not carnal? Who then is Paul, and who is Apollos, but ministers through whom you believed, as the Lord gave to each one? I planted, Apollos watered, but God gave the increase. So then neither he who plants is anything, nor he who waters, but God who gives the increase.
>
> Therefore let no one boast in men. For all things are yours: whether Paul or Apollos or Cephas, or the world or life or death, or things present or things to come — all are yours.
>
> — 1 Corinthians 3:4–7, 21–22

The apostle Paul chastised the Corinthian believers for being spiritual babes and acting like fallen men when they quarreled over who was a better minister and they started taking sides. Paul went on to say that the ministers — workers of the Lord — are just servants. They are nothing, and not worthy to cause a faction. They should be focusing on God and Jesus Christ, the unique foundation (3:11).

Ministers (workers) are servants to serve the assembly of the Lord. Although one minister may plant and another may water, the assemblies do not belong to any of the workers… they belong to the Lord. There should be no competition between ministers since their goal should be that God will give the growth to the assembly and God will receive all the glory. Although Paul initiated the assembly in Corinth through his preaching of Jesus Christ, he recognized and allowed for other ministers — such as Apollos and Cephas (Peter) — to help and participate in the assembly that he started. A genuine assembly can receive the ministry of various independent ministers. This is very different from a church that is founded by a particular ministry, since that church would not allow for independent ministers who might teach things that may be contrary to their ministry.

Today, most denominations have their own seminary and only those graduated from their own seminary can be a pastor/minister in that particular Christian organization. This is further proof that organized Christian groups have a different nature from the assembly that the Lord is building.

Due to the nature of an assembly's diverse ministries and activities, there are opportunities for harmful teachings and unscrupulous teachers that may distract believers from Christ. This is why Paul, in his epistles, pointed out the ministers that were diverting believers away from Christ. He himself did not demand subjection from the assemblies that he raised up; rather he wooed them back to accept him as a minister by reminding them of the sacrifices that he had made on their behalf (1 Cor. 10–11).

Ministers wanting to protect the believers under their care and to avoid the confusion that various ministers could cause, will use this consideration as a good reason to keep out non-approved ministers from the group that they are leading. But this solution will cause worse damage to the body of Christ than the problem that they are trying to solve. Today, just about all Christians are segregated; various ministries attempt to "protect their flock," and the genuine assembly expressing the one body of Christ is almost invisible. If the apostle Paul didn't stop other ministries from coming into an assembly that he originated, and he had to appeal to an assembly to receive him again, ministers today should not think they know better than Paul by excluding other ministries or ministers.

As in Colossians, Philippians, Galatians and his other writings, Paul did his best to dispute with those who taught contrary to the New Testament revelation; yet, he did not ask the assembly to remove those teaching wrongly. Teaching something that may be harmful to the assembly is not sufficient ground to remove such teachers. It is only when they draw away believers to form a separate group independent of the one fellowship of the assembly, or when they do not teach that Jesus Christ is come in the flesh, that they need to be marked out and avoided. That is why Paul emphasized the need for listeners to discern what they were hearing in 1 Corinthians 14. If all believers read the Bible and know the Spirit for themselves as they should, then there will be proper discernment to know whether a speaking or teaching is healthy to receive or harmful and necessary to reject. When everyone has the freedom to speak and teach (though at times it may be conflicting and confusing), over time believers in the assembly will grow and will know the Lord and the truth according to the New Testament. This is the building up of an assembly without man's external control and manipulation.

Mutual Support among Ministers for the Building Up of the One Body

Ministries, though independent from each other, should cooperate with and provide mutual support for the building up of the one body.

> Now concerning our brother Apollos, I strongly urged him to come to you with the brethren, but he was quite unwilling to come at this time; however, he will come when he has a convenient time.
> — 1 Corinthians 16:12

> Do your best to speed Zenas the lawyer and Apollos on their way; see that they lack nothing.
> — Titus 3:13

Paul strongly urged Apollos to travel to Corinth and visit the saints there, but Apollos had the freedom to make an independent decision not to go. It was Paul's disciples, Priscilla and Aquila, who helped Apollos to understand the New Testament revelation more fully; therefore, Paul should have seniority over Apollos, with a higher and clearer vision of the New Testament revelation. In the New Testament, there is no hierarchy in the body where one can tell another independent minister what to do. A gifted believer who has started a ministry cannot exercise any authority and demand a minister in another ministry to do anything. Paul could urge, but it was still up to Apollos whether to comply. For example, if a minister starts a prison ministry, he cannot demand someone else in, say, a college student ministry, to do anything.

Although Apollos did not comply with Paul's request, Paul still viewed him as a co-laborer, working together for the building up of the one body (1 Cor. 3:6–9). There can be multiple independent ministries, but ultimately they should all work together for the building up of the assembly. This being the case, Paul asked Titus, who was a junior partner in Paul's ministry, to make sure that Apollos was taken care of and that he lacked nothing in his travels. Even though Apollos didn't do what Paul strongly urged him to do, Paul nevertheless cared for him and supported him in his ministry. What a beautiful coordination of working together between independent ministers! There was no competition or backbiting, but only full support. This would be like a minister who has a ministry to preach the gospel through contemporary music giving his support and resources to someone with a teaching ministry; they would not be merely building up their own church, but rather the one body of Christ.

> And count the patience of our Lord as salvation, just as our beloved brother Paul also wrote to you according to the wisdom given him, as he does in all his letters when he speaks in them of these matters. There are some things in them that are hard to understand, which the ignorant and unstable twist to their own destruction, as they do the other Scriptures.
>
> – 2 Peter 3:15–16

Peter in his epistle recommends and supports Paul's writings. Peter was one that Paul openly condemned. He exposed Peter's hypocrisy when, in unfaithfulness to the truth, Peter withdrew from eating with the Gentile believers because Jewish believers were coming from James in Jerusalem. Though it must have been very embarrassing to be publically reprimanded by Paul, Peter remained faithful in supporting Paul and his ministry. Peter even recommended that Paul's writings were at the same level as the Scriptures.

It was Peter who had a ministry to the Jews, and yet he recommended and supported Paul whose ministry was toward the Gentiles. What one accord and coordination between these independent ministers! This can only happen because of the understanding and realization that they were not building up their own ministry, but the body of Christ. It is difficult to recommend a minister if he or she is only concerned about building up their own ministry. In fact, if the ministry were to cause believers to stand apart in division with other believers, then that particular minister should not be recommended but should be marked out as a problem in the body. Believers should be warned of his or her selfish work. However, if those ministers are building the one body by encouraging all those under their ministry to fellowship with all other believers, no matter how diverse and different, their ministry should be supported.

Leadership within a Ministry versus Leadership within an Assembly

> So those who conducted Paul brought him to Athens; and receiving a command for Silas and Timothy to come to him with all speed, they departed.
>
> – Acts 17:15

> For this reason I have sent Timothy to you, who is my beloved and faithful son in the Lord, who will remind you of my ways in Christ, as I teach everywhere in every church [assembly].
>
> – 1 Corinthians 4:17

When a gifted believer starts a ministry, that person becomes the natural leader and authority in that ministry. If successful in helping others, whether through their preaching or teaching activities, this minister will naturally gain a following. Out of this group of followers and supporters, some will want to join in to help grow and spread this ministry. Any believers who join in to support this gifted minister who started that ministry should consider the founding minister as the authority of that ministry. As the leader of that ministry, the founding minister can ask those subordinated to him what to do. Paul was the one, for example, who commanded his subordinate ministers to come here or go there in contrast to Apollos.

A ministry is similar to doing a work with a goal, a direction, and a method. If a person is going to join an existing ministry and be part of that ministry, it only makes sense that those joining that ministry would take the leadership of the founding minister. Let's say someone is going to build a suspension bridge. It would be silly if a person joins in and gives their unsolicited advice and takes resources to build a boat or a platoon bridge instead. If a person believes they have a better idea to travel across the water by building a boat, they should start their own work (ministry) to build a boat! They should not try to take over and disrupt the team that already established the goal of building a suspension bridge.

Paul has a direction, a message, and a method to achieve his goal of preaching to the Gentiles to build up the one body of Christ. Disciples like Timothy, Silas, and Titus had received help from Paul and wanted to be part of Paul's ministry; therefore, Paul had the natural authority and leadership to command them for the sake of carrying out his ministry. Apollos, on the other hand, didn't consider himself as part of Paul's ministry; thus, he could operate independently. Yet Paul and Apollos embraced the same ultimate goal of building up the one assembly of Christ.

> The elders who are among you I exhort…Shepherd the flock of God which is among you, serving as overseers, not by compulsion but willingly, not for dishonest gain but eagerly; nor as being lords over those entrusted to you, but being examples to the flock.
>
> Likewise you younger people, submit yourselves to your elders. Yes, all of you be submissive to one another, and be clothed with humility, for "God resists the proud, but gives grace to the humble."
>
> – 1 Peter 5:1a–3, 5

In individual ministries there are authority figures, but in an assembly there are no such persons. No one can be the "lord" no matter his or her spiritual maturity. Each member in the Lord's body is directly connected and answers only to the Lord Jesus as the Head. In any family, there are those that are relatively more mature and older, who may be considered "elders." But elders are not in any way part of a hierarchy, able to tell other members what to do or where to go; rather, they are shepherds (pastors) or feeders. Because they are older, they have the knowledge of the Word to feed other believers; as overseers, they are to alert the other believers concerning anything harmful in the assembly.

As such older ones, they should be examples of or a pattern to the other believers. Too many Christian leaders have the testimony of, "Do what I say, but not what I do." Leadership in the sense of being an example means that the "leaders" are living a life that is a pattern in speech, in conduct, in love, in faith, and in purity (1 Tim. 4:12). If their lives are such a pattern, then believers should follow and learn.

The elders should not be motivated by any gains for themselves. In the Greek, "dishonest gains" is actually one word, *anagkastós*. When read in English as two words, one can interpret it to mean that there can be "honest" gains. But read as one word, *anagkastós* compares "gains" with "eagerness." That means that any believer having the maturity to feed others will do it eagerly, and any motivation because of "gain" is dishonest or filthy.

Some may point out that 1 Peter 5:5a says that believers *should* submit to such elders. They may ask, "Doesn't that show the authority of the elders over the other believers?" The problem with that interpretation is that it neglects the next phrase in the same verse that says, "...be submissive to one another." By this phrase, the idea of hierarchy—that one has authority over another—is completely eliminated. If coercion and force is not used, then submission is completely voluntary, not compulsory. Since elders are not lords, then they do not have the authority to use force or threats to compel anyone to do their will. Believers may or may not submit, based on their conscience and understanding. At the same time, elders should also submit to younger believers, if the Lord is speaking and leading through them regardless of their age.

This affirms unequivocally that the assembly is the family—the household—of God. The Lord Jesus is the only one with absolute authority, and He is the chief feeder of all the saints. Therefore, as brothers and sisters in the same family, everyone is equal in status but some may be relatively ahead of others in life experiences and knowledge. These are then the older brothers and sisters to help the chief shepherd in feeding here on earth. What a beautiful assembly is the household of God.

Paul's ministry practiced pointing out the elders in an assembly at some point, but when he wrote many of his letters he addressed the *entire* assembly and didn't single out the elders. He recognized that elders themselves could be corrupted and become a problem to the believers. Because of this, when Paul spoke to the elders in Ephesus (Acts 20:28–30), he warned them that even among themselves there would be ones who would rise up to speak perverse things to draw believers away. By the time John wrote his letters to a number of local assemblies that Paul raised up, such as Ephesus in Revelation 2, he completely ignored any type of leadership or elders in the assembly, but rather said that anyone in the assembly could hear the Spirit speaking. Thus anyone who heard the Spirit speak could rise up to overcome the degradation among the assemblies at the time. Believers should not wait for anyone to lead them; the Spirit is leading and speaking, and they should simply follow Him. Following the Spirit is what creates a leader.

The assembly desperately needs mature believers — those eager to feed others, to be examples to others, and even to know how to submit to younger believers. Simultaneously, believers need to be warned that if they place their trust in any one person (man or woman) who are leaders, pastors or shepherds, but not directly and actively study the Scriptures and listen to the Spirit for themselves, one day they will find themselves misled and/or disappointed.

Therefore, in order for the assembly to be built up, every believer needs to rise up and be actively seeking the Lord and functioning according to the gifts that the Spirit has given to each one.

Ready to Serve and Be Nothing

> But Jesus called them to [Himself] and said, "You know that the rulers of the Gentiles lord it over them, and those who are great exercise authority over them. Yet it shall not be so among you; but whoever desires to become great among you, let him be your servant."
>
> – Matthew 20:25–26

> ...with all humility and gentleness, with patience, bearing with one another in love, eager to maintain the unity of the Spirit in the bond of peace.
>
> – Ephesians 4:2–3, ESV

Once a minister (whether carrying out a ministry or being a shepherd) in an assembly is successful in their service to the Lord, it becomes easy to become prideful and to desire to guard the fruit of one's labor. The more successful a Christian's work, the more temptation for pride. When pride enters, disputes with others become inevitable. Certain expectations arise, for respect and privilege. Additionally, in the attempt to guard, protect, and maintain the fruit of their labor, ministers might exercise authority to retain certain control over those receiving their ministry with seemingly good intentions. This can be in the form of warning them to not listen to certain other ministers or associate with certain types of Christians that "believe and practice such and such."

However, this attempt to "protect" can develop into segregation, and at worst, a systematic division among believers. The end result is that their following of believers (or churches) increases to the detriment of the assembly. Pride, thus, becomes a seed of division from other believers. All ministers, great or small, have to remember to stay in Christ, the servant.

"Minister" literally means "a servant." Therefore, in the assembly, the great among the believers is their servant; the greater the minister, the greater the servant. A servant, especially during biblical times, did not even have the right to be offended by those he or she was serving. It is one's pride that gives rise to being offended — when others disrespect, ignore, or contradict them. Offense leads to contention, which then leads to divisions.

The life of Christ with genuine humility is the antidote for the natural, built-in pride every person is born with. All ministers need to abide in the life of the new birth, the life of a servant. When offense occurs because of pride, there immediately needs to be a retreat into the indwelling Christ. It is in this humility — gentleness with patience — that believers, especially successful ministers, can bear with one another in love so that the oneness of the Spirit is maintained and grows. The glory that the Lord Jesus received was the result of His being a servant. This glory of the Lord Jesus is now given to the believers so that they can also live in the same pattern as the Lord Jesus: one that results in glory through service. It is through serving in this pattern that believers are kept one.

Types of Believers an Assembly Should Not Receive

Those Who Divide Should Be Marked and Avoided

> Now I urge you, brethren, note those who cause divisions and offenses, contrary to the doctrine which you learned, and avoid them. For those who are such do not serve our Lord Jesus Christ, but their own belly, and by smooth words and flattering speech deceive the hearts of the simple.
>
> — Romans 16:17–18

> But avoid foolish disputes, genealogies, contentions, and strivings about the law; for they are unprofitable and useless. Reject a divisive man after the first and second admonition.
>
> — Titus 3:9–10

A person causing a division in the body through differing teachings to divert believers away from the focus of Jesus Christ's person and work needs to be avoided and even rejected.

"Division" in Romans 16:17 in Greek, *dicostasia*, is a strong word meaning, "to stand apart." Those under the influence of this person's teaching will stand apart from simply being believers in the common fellowship of the one body of Christ. They will consider themselves different or special from other believers. These divisive teachers are not motivated to build up the oneness of the body; rather, they purposely want to cause a separation among believers. They may want to have their own group of followers, or they may simply want to be contentious to show that they are right and superior and others are wrong and inferior. Either way, through their speech and actions, they oblige believers to have to choose to be in one group or another — to be on one side or another.

All believers should be on the same side, in the one assembly, because there is only one Jesus Christ, one Spirit of God, one fellowship, and one body of Christ. Therefore, any such divisive teachers (after two admonitions to point out their damaging and divisive actions) that do not stop their destructive ways should be rejected from the fellowship of the assembly.

Believers Who Do Not Teach that Jesus Christ Is God in the Flesh

> For many deceivers have gone out into the world, those who do not confess the coming of Jesus Christ in the flesh. Such a one is the deceiver and the antichrist.

> Everyone who goes on ahead and does not abide in the teaching of Christ, does not have God. Whoever abides in the teaching has both the Father and the Son. If anyone comes to you and does not bring this teaching, do not receive him into your house or give him any greeting, for whoever greets him takes part in his wicked works.
>
> – 2 John 1:7, 9–11 ESV

It can be assumed that the deceivers John spoke of in 2 John 1 considered themselves Christians. They were not unbelievers, since by definition unbelievers *do not* believe that Jesus is God come in the flesh. And, 1 Corinthians 14 says there are *unbelievers* in the assembly — meaning they should not be avoided (1 Corinthians 5:10); therefore, these deceivers must have been people who passed themselves off as Christian teachers. Because they probably used the Bible to teach, they had the ability to deceive. However, they did not teach that Jesus Christ is God becoming flesh (man).

This is the fundamental faith concerning the person of Jesus Christ — He is both one hundred percent God, and one hundred percent man. He is the complete God and a genuine man. Anyone identified as a Christian and teaching that Jesus Christ is either not eternally God or not eternally man is against the person of Jesus Christ, and thus is anti-Christ. Such a teacher should not be received.

One Living Habitually in Sin

Believers that habitually and openly practice sin and immorality which love can no longer cover should not be received into the assembly.

> Above all, keep loving one another earnestly, since love covers a multitude of sins.
>
> – 1 Peter 4:8, ESV

> Let no corrupting talk come out of your mouths, but only such as is good for building up, as fits the occasion, that it may give grace to those who hear.
>
> – Ephesians 4:29, ESV

Because of the closeness of fellowship in the assembly life between believers, there will be opportunities to know each other's faults and even sins. There will be times when believers will hear of and even witness a failure or a sinful fall of another believer. In all such occasions, the Scriptures instruct believers to cover their brother or sister with love, and not to spread in gossip the weaknesses of other believers. In some situations, believers may have to share what has been learned with another believer, to pray for and support the believer with a certain weakness. In any case, it is not to spread that news, and it should be contained and covered so that believers in the assembly will not know of each other's faults, weaknesses, failures and sins. They should not spread the information to others, since it could corrupt and damage the assembly.

> It is universally reported *that there is* fornication among you, and such fornication as *is* not even among the nations, so that one should have his father's wife. And you are puffed up, and you have not rather mourned, in order that he that has done this deed might be taken away out of the midst of you.
>
> Your boasting *is* not good. Do you not know that a little leaven leavens the whole lump? Purge out the old leaven, that you may be a new lump, according as you are unleavened. For also our passover, Christ, has been sacrificed.
>
> I have written to you in the epistle not to mix with fornicators; not altogether with the fornicators of this world, or with the avaricious [covetous] and rapacious [extortioner], or idolaters, since *then* you should go out of the world. But now I have written to you, if any one called brother be fornicator, or avaricious [covetous], or idolater, or abusive, or a drunkard, or rapacious [extortioner], not to mix with him; with such a one not even to eat. For what have I *to do* with judging those outside also? you, do not you judge them that are within? But those without God judges. Remove the wicked person from amongst yourselves.
>
> – 1 Corinthians 5:1–2, 6–7, 9–13, DBY

When a believer's failures become habitual and universally known, no longer an occasional sin that can be covered by love, the assembly should not tolerate and accept this believer as if everything is okay. The assembly in Corinth even boasted of having such a sinful brother in their midst. The apostle Paul likens this openly sinful brother to "leaven" that will corrupt the entire assembly, because other believers who witness such "leaven" would have the encouragement of giving in to the temptation of sin, thinking that it is acceptable. Therefore, this brother should not be welcomed into the assembly, or participate in the assembly's meals. This does not mean that some caring believers cannot visit this brother and help him to repent of his sin, but it does mean that he should be excluded from the gathering together of the assembly. This exclusion includes all those believers that are known to be people that live in the manifestation of their sinful nature in various ways as listed in verse 11 above.

This exclusion, however, should not include unbelievers or those new in the faith, since they don't know better. The unbelievers or new believers living in sin should still be welcomed; otherwise they will not receive the Word of faith and encouragement in the assembly for them to come to Christ and grow in the faith. Functioning in this way reveals the heart of the Lord. On one hand, He reaches out to all people in order that they may be saved from their sinful conditions; on the other, He protects the assembly from corruption.

One Who Is a Busybody, Not Working

> But we command you, brethren, in the name of our Lord Jesus Christ, that you withdraw from every brother who walks disorderly and not according to the

> tradition which he received from us. For you yourselves know how you ought to follow us, for we were not disorderly among you; nor did we eat anyone's bread free of charge, but worked with labor and toil night and day, that we might not be a burden to any of you, not because we do not have authority, but to make ourselves an example of how you should follow us. For even when we were with you, we commanded you this: If anyone will not work, neither shall he eat.
>
> . . . And if anyone does not obey our word in this epistle, note that person and do not keep company with him, that he may be ashamed. Yet do not count him as an enemy, but admonish him as a brother.
>
> – 2 Thessalonians 3:6–10, 14–15

What an example the apostle Paul gave to believers! Though he labored in preaching the gospel, and he had the right to receive financial support from those he was helping spiritually, he purposely worked to support himself materially to not burden any of the believers under his care. This is why he asserted so strongly that every believer should work to support himself without being a burden on others, limiting leisure time that could lead to becoming a "busybody" who bothers others. It can be assumed that Paul was referring to people with able bodies who could work to support themselves.

Although believers who are not willing to work should be put to shame, they should still be cared for in love that perhaps they may repent and walk orderly.

A Testimony of This Working

What has been described concerning the practical ekklesia (assembly) in this chapter is being enjoyed today. Currently, there is a growing network of independent home assemblies in the San Francisco Bay, Northern California area. It seems that every month or two new home gatherings are starting up or existing ones that used to be isolated are now enjoying the fellowship with an extended group of like-minded believers. In these various homes, unbelievers are coming to faith in Jesus Christ, and dormant believers are being revived to seek the Lord. Believers are growing and functioning normally, and they are manifesting the various gifts of the Spirit and grace.

The believers in this network of home assemblies are made up of people from a wide range of ethnic backgrounds, education, socioeconomic status, Christian upbringings, and even a number of former career pastors and ministers from various institutional churches. But the fellowship is one, and the blending among the believers is increasing with a sharpening focus solely on Jesus Christ. There is a sense that the Lord is moving, and from month to month, there are testimonies of something fresh and dynamic taking place among the home assemblies.

This expanding fellowship in oneness among believers and homes started with greeting. A few believers, on a regular basis, began to go and greet other home assemblies that were discovered. Then a few times a year a weekend "vacation fellowship" would take place where everyone was invited — not to hear a dedicated speaker — but to greet, fellowship, and enjoy the Lord Jesus together in an informal environment. Another few times a year, a similar gathering took place, just for a day. As word of the enjoyment of these events goes out, additional believers discover anew the joy of the one fellowship of Jesus Christ in His one body.

This building up is growing and increasing because there is the freedom for believers to exercise their ministry and have an operation without the constraint of human organization and hierarchy. Some are led to visitations, some are led to evangelizing on the streets, while others are led to do the same on college campuses. Some are led to care for the homeless and those fighting addictions, some are led to write and teach, and some are led to songs and worship. But each are focused on the building of the one body in the homes from house to house. There is a witness and a testimony that the Lord is recovering the practical outworking of Romans 12, 14, 16, and 1 Corinthians 12 and 14. There is an expectation that the Lord is doing this around the globe among believers seeking to be in one fellowship for the building up of the body of Christ.

Practice: Binding and Loosing Prayers

Find one or two other believers that are like-minded in the pursuit of the kingdom, the building up of the Lord's one body. Consider meeting by phone, Skype or in person to pray binding and loosing prayers. Commit at least 15 minutes for such prayer this week and if possible once a week or every two weeks. Consider together situations Satan needs to be bound so that someone can be released from enslavement, or into resurrection life. Pray as specifically as possible in order to witness the answers from God in heaven. For example, a prayer for the Lord to save someone is too general; it is hard to know the timing of when the Lord can answer such a prayer. However, praying for someone to be available and open to meet up this week, or that there will be an opening to speak the Word to a specific person during a meet up this week will cause the Lord to answer specifically within a definite time frame.

I will ask _____ to pray with me this week.

These are the items that I want to pray for with binding and loosing authority:

#1 _____

#2 _____

#3 _____

14

(SECTION A)
THE OLD COVENANT AND
THE NEW COVENANT

The matter of the Law is a source of challenge and confusion to many Christians. Some try to fulfill the Law and fall under its condemnation when they continually fail. Others maintain they no longer live under the Law, but that can be confusing. Do they mean that they can steal from others and drive as fast as they want?

Which part of the Law are Christians still under and which part are they not? And if all Christians are still under *some* form of law, then what is the difference between the old covenant and the new covenant? And if Christians have eternal life no matter what they do, and are not under the Law, then by what standard will they be judged by God? Hopefully, this chapter will give clarity and answers to these questions.

What Is a Covenant?

In the Bible, the Law is central in the relationship between God and people, and also between human beings in society. This relationship between people and God is defined by an old covenant and a new covenant.

A "covenant" is an agreement made with an oath. God made such a covenant with Israel when He gave the Ten Commandments to Moses on Mount Sinai. That covenant was called an "old covenant" by Paul in 2 Corinthians 3:14, and the "first covenant" in a few verses in Hebrews (Heb. 8:7; 9:1, 15). The Ten Commandments are embodied in the old covenant. Basically, that first covenant was a bilateral agreement where there were binding conditions for both man (male and female) and God: if men fulfilled the Law of God as stated in the covenant, then God would bless them; if men broke the Law, curses would come on them. That first covenant didn't work out for man since man kept breaking the Law and was continually under the curse. Because of God's love for man, He first promised and then established a new covenant which is unidirectional, and unconditional: God declared that He alone would do the amazing things for man without man doing anything to earn those things. This chapter will mainly expound on these two covenants.

These two covenants govern the relationship between God and man. This means how God treats people and judges them, and how man is to approach God and thus have relationship with his Creator. By understanding these two covenants, a person can be released from the bondage of the Law into a life of freedom and joy in Jesus Christ. When believers are not clear about which covenant they are living under today, they will experience condemnation, confusion, disappointment, and ultimately spiritual death amidst moments of joy and victory in Christ. A believer will vacillate between the two until one day he or she finds clarity and understands the difference between the old covenant and the new covenant in their relationship with God.

The Law and Morality

A major portion of the Ten Commandments is related to morality. It governs human interaction within a society. Moral laws relate to justice and judgment, and are often translated as "ordinances" in the Bible. These laws are based on God's holy nature. Their purpose is to promote and safeguard the welfare of human society. When Jesus came, He uplifted the moral law that governed human interactions.

This moral law is embodied in the Ten Commandments with numerous statutes and ordinances. Think of the Ten Commandments as the frame; all auxiliary laws, statutes, and ordinances flesh out this frame. Though only the "frame" is considered — the Ten Commandments — a large portion of the Law provides the basis of morality for a civil society. If the first four commandments concerning God and Sabbath are dismissed as "religious," the following six then form the foundation of a safe and healthy society, secular or otherwise. The fifth commandment says to "honor your father and your mother" (Deut. 5:16), and number seven commands God's people not to commit adultery (Deut. 5:18). Interestingly, both of these are the core of building up and protecting a healthy family unit. It is well accepted that the breakdown of families is a key reason for a variety of societal woes, and vice versa — strong family units are foundational for a healthy society.

The rest of the Ten Commandments include the following: do not murder, do not steal, do not bear false witness and do not covet. These four, with their supplemental statutes and laws, are to control the actions stemming from evil desires. If these acts or deeds can be controlled and prevented, then men can live together safely and harmoniously, and grow a society together for everyone's benefit. Regardless of whether a person is religious, fears God or not, these laws are meant to protect human beings from each other. Therefore, man, (including all Christians), will always be under such laws for an orderly society. Today's secular governments around the globe have set up laws to govern society that are similar to the moral laws in the Old Testament. Therefore, everyone should be subject to the moral laws as described in the Bible if their goal is a safe and just society. Breaking these laws will bring negative consequences, and in many cases the law-breaker will face legal prosecution, whether a Christian or not.

The famous and possibly greatest moralist and philosopher of China is Confucius. He lived about 1000 years after the giving of the Ten Commandments. One of the main focuses of his teachings was the importance of a strong family unit. His encompassing "golden rule" of morality toward each other in a civil society was: "What you do not wish for yourself, do not do to others." Interestingly Jesus presented a similar idea when He summarized the moral part of the Ten Commandments: love your neighbor as yourself. The difference is that Confucius taught from a negative point of view — not doing something *bad* to others. But Jesus' view was positive — *doing* something good to others.

The old covenant Law with its supplemental ordinances was mainly to control and prevent man from doing harmful things: man was not to murder or commit adultery, steal or bear false witness. A righteous person was one who did not commit these negative actions. But when Jesus came, He uplifted these moral laws to a divine level of sacrificial love with pure intentions of the heart. If anyone thought that it was even possible to fulfill the old Law, then the uplifted Law from Jesus was completely impossible to fulfill. There is no one before Jesus that would have dreamed of this standard of morality. If man could live anywhere close to Jesus' standard, human society would not only be safe, but it would also be a loving, caring, generous, joyful, and peaceful society, like nothing man has ever known.

Here are a few examples of the "uplifted" Law:

- The old Law said, "An eye for an eye." This meant if someone blinded another in the eye, the injured person could blind him back as compensation. The new Law, however, requires the person to whom evil is done to turn the other cheek, walk the extra mile, and give if they are asked (Matt. 5:38–42).
- The old Law required people to love their neighbor and hate their enemy. The new Law requires people to love their enemies, and bless those who curse them (Matt. 5:44).
- The old Law said, "Do not murder." The new Law says not to be angry with someone without a cause (Matt. 5:21, 22).
- The old said, "Do not commit adultery." The new says to not even to look with lust at another person (Matt. 5:27, 28).
- The old says nothing about being anxious. The new says, "Do not be anxious" (Matt. 6:25).
- The old said to not bear false witness. The new says to speak grace to the hearer for building up (Eph. 4:29).

Certainly if men can treat each other in love and handle relationships such as described by Jesus' moral laws, then surely that would be a model society! Therefore, whether a Christian or not, everyone should consider the morality according to Jesus and everyone should do their best to follow Jesus' moral laws.

It was impossible for men to keep the old law, but even more so the new. But that doesn't mean that people shouldn't try. Just as people should do their best not to break the Law and end up in jail, they should also do their best to care for their fellow human beings. The old Law mainly tries to control man's action, but the new Law goes deeper to change man's heart and soul. For example, it is one thing to not murder someone (which requires an action), but it is a whole different level of obligation to love an enemy — a matter of the heart. While men should do their best to keep the highest standard of the moral Law as described by both the Old and New Testaments, anyone who honestly tries will welcome the good news of the new covenant. What is impossible to man is possible with the life of God.

Ceremonial Laws

> Having abolished in the flesh the enmity, [even] the law of commandments [contained] in ordinances; that he might create in himself of the two one new man, [so] making peace;
>
> – Ephesians 2:15 ASV

According to this verse and a similar one in Colossians 2:14, there is an entire body of law that was abolished when Jesus died on the cross. This body of law is what separates Jews from Gentiles. It is because of this body of law that Jews cannot co-mingle and eat with Gentiles, and that their living habits keep Gentiles at a distance. By abolishing this body of law, Jews and Gentiles can become one in the new man, and there can be peace between peoples. This body of law is called "ceremonial laws."

Jesus Christ (the reality) fulfilled the Old Testament ceremonial laws (the shadow). In addition to moral laws in the old covenant, there are also statutes and ordinances relating to performing certain ceremonies, as well as regulations on daily living such as: animal sacrifices and offerings, the priesthood and its duties, keeping the Sabbath, dietary restrictions, and the annual feasts. This category of law in the Old Testament was a type, or a shadow, of the coming Christ; Jesus Christ is the reality of this entire category of law.

Jesus Christ is the *real* offering to God; therefore, animal sacrifices are no longer needed. He is the *real* high priest and temple, so the high priest with the Levitical priesthood performing its duties is not needed. Jesus Christ is the *real* rest; therefore, the regulation regarding the Sabbath is gone. This is true for all the ceremonial laws not related to morality. In previous chapters, the topic of Jesus Christ as the reality and fulfillment of the Old Testament types and shadows has been covered more fully.

Believers in the New Testament have the liberty to either continue with these laws, or not. Some may choose to observe the Sabbath, or continue with the Old Testament diet (which many people consider to be healthier than a diet containing "non-clean" food). Regardless of whether a Christian practices these regulations or not, no one should judge another over them. As long as believers continue to receive and fellowship with one another regardless of differences in living regulations, then they are non-issues.

Therefore, whether Old Testament or New, all people should attempt to keep these moral laws to the best of their abilities, Christian or not. Keeping them will improve society, and breaking them can cause negative personal and societal consequences. Some Christians may choose one set of morals to live by when in the society of believers and another standard while they are within the secular society. However, the New Testament does not support this. There is certainly something special within a community of believers, since there is responsiveness and reciprocation when the virtues of the highest morality are displayed. This highest morality is encapsulated in the Lord's new commandment: "Love one another as I have loved you." At the same time, it should be the same divine love with which believers love and honor (consider precious) all people (1 Pet. 2:17). Certainly it would take the same divine love to love one's enemies, and there is no separation given as to whether the "enemy" spoken of by Matthew is a Christian or a non-Christian. (The author doesn't agree that the believer should love ignorantly, in a way that could possibly bring harm to himself and to his loved ones).

Ceremonial laws and regulations on living habits are completely voluntary depending on each person's preferences, local customs, and rules. For certain, whether a person observes these laws and regulations should not be a factor in the relationship with God. As far as God is concerned (in the New Testament), they are no longer needed.

The rest of this chapter will focus on the huge gulf of differences between relationships with God based on the old covenant versus those based on the new covenant. The difference is night and day, death and life, blessing or cursing. It is part of the good news that all men should hear.

The Old Covenant – The Law

> Then the LORD said to Moses, "Write these words, for according to the tenor of these words I have made a covenant with you and with Israel." . . . And He wrote on the tablets the words of the covenant, the Ten Commandments.
> – Exodus 34:27, 28b

These verses clearly reveal the Ten Commandments were a covenant. This is a critical point to understand in order to follow the rest of the chapter. The old covenant was tied to the Ten Commandments with all of its statutes and ordinances. Here is a review of the Ten Commandments:

1. You shall have no other gods before Me.
2. You shall not make idols.
3. You shall not take the name of the LORD your God in vain.
4. Remember the Sabbath day, to keep it holy.
5. Honor your father and your mother.
6. You shall not murder.
7. You shall not commit adultery.
8. You shall not steal.
9. You shall not bear false witness against your neighbor.
10. You shall not covet.

These Ten Commandments are not the entire Law of the Old Testament, but rather they form the basis for a host of supplemental rules and ordinances relating to topics such as: marriage and family, times and seasons, diet, business practices, judicial procedures, property rights, criminal laws and restitutions, the priesthood and the Levites, tithing, the temple and sanctuary, sacrifices, and offerings. It is based on these laws that God made a covenant with Israel.

The Old Covenant Is Conditional

There is blessing to those who obey the Law and cursing for those who break it.

> You have seen what I did to the Egyptians, and how I bore you on eagles' wings and brought you to Myself. Now therefore, if you will indeed obey My voice and keep My covenant, then you shall be a special treasure to Me above all people; for all the earth is Mine.
>
> Then all the people answered together and said, "All that the LORD has spoken we will do." So Moses brought back the words of the people to the LORD.
>
> *– Exodus 19:4–5, 8*
>
> Cursed *is* the one who does not confirm *all* the words of this law by observing them. And all the people shall say, 'Amen!'
>
> *– Deuteronomy 27:26*
>
> Now it shall come to pass, if you diligently obey the voice of the LORD your God, to observe carefully all His commandments which I command you today, that the LORD your God will set you high above all nations of the earth.
>
> But it shall come to pass, if you do not obey the voice of the LORD your God, to observe carefully all His commandments and His statutes which I command you today, that all these curses will come upon you and overtake you.
>
> *– Deuteronomy 28:1, 15, KJV*

The Israelites were slaves in Egypt for more than 200 years serving Pharaoh. Then God came to deliver them by sending various plagues to Egypt. His goal of delivering the Israelites was to bring them to Himself. After God carried them out on "eagles' wings," He made a covenant with them by the giving of the Ten Commandments. The agreement was conditional: "If you obey…then I will bless"; "If you do not obey…curses will come upon you." From a contract law perspective, this was considered a bilateral (or a conditional) agreement. God would do His part of blessing man or bringing curses to man depending on whether man obeys or disobeys His laws.

The worst part was that the grading or judging was not based on a curve — or where sixty percent is a passing D grade. Judgment, according to this agreement, is based on man's agreement to keep all of the laws. This means one hundred percent obedience to the Law, or the person has failed. If a person breaks just one of God's laws, they have broken them all (James 2:10). This may not seem fair now, but when this agreement was originally presented, Israel absurdly signed on and agreed to this conditional agreement. Israel didn't negotiate; it confidently said "yes," "amen," and "we will do it."

Israel was so weak that she needed God to bring her out from slavery on eagles' wings, and yet proudly said she (the Israelites) could do whatever God commanded. Man's blindness, or pride, makes him think that he can obey everything that God commands. Ironically, when

Moses came back from the mountain to give Israel the Ten Commandments, Israel was already breaking them: As Moses descended the mount, God's people were worshipping a calf made of gold. Throughout the Old Testament, Israel was cursed and under judgment again and again for disobeying God's law.

Works of the Law

It takes a lot of effort and energy to comply with the law; therefore, it is called "the works of the law."

> . . . yet we know that a person is not justified by works of the law . . . because by works of the law no one will be justified.
>
> – Galatians 2:16, ESV

> For by works of the law no human being will be justified in his sight, since through the law comes knowledge of sin.
>
> – Romans 3:20, ESV

According to Paul, fulfilling God's Law depends on man's effort and work. It does not come naturally. God's Law and man's fallen nature are not compatible; therefore, it takes a lot of effort to work at keeping God's Law. The problem is that no matter how much men do their utmost to work at keeping God's Law, they will fail on at least one point. For certain, everyone fails with the tenth commandment, "Do not covet." It is impossible for fallen people not to yearn for what others have! Just that one area of failure brings in the entire curse. So as long as man is working on keeping God's Law, he is under a curse, and he cannot be justified.

Recall that "justified" means to be completely righteous before God. Since human beings cannot continue keeping all of the Law, therefore, none can be justified and none can be counted righteous.

"Works of the law" also means that to be counted righteous depends on merit; it is a merit reward system. If one can work hard enough to keep God's Law, then he can gain enough merit for God to reward him with justification or salvation. Many people may think that they deserve merit from God just for making an effort to try harder, even if they can't keep the whole Law. But, according to these verses in Galatians and Romans, no matter how hard people try, they can never be justified.

Ephesians 2:9 states if works can save men, then they would be able to boast that they have "earned" salvation. The religious law keepers in Paul's day (who in their own estimation had been doing a relatively good job in keeping the Law) had become judgmental about others whom they deemed to have failed in keeping the Law. Over time, a law keeper will either become disappointed, discouraged, and give up on God, or they become proud and judgmental of people around them who are not up to their religious standards.

The Dreadful Results of Law Keepers

One of the main results of keeping the Law is being cursed.

> For all who rely on works of the law are under a curse; for it is written, "Cursed be everyone who does not abide by all things written in the Book of the Law, and do them."
>
> – Galatians 3:10, ESV

> "Cursed be anyone who does not confirm the words of this law by doing them." And all the people shall say, "Amen."
>
> – Deuteronomy 27:26, ESV

For the sake of society, man has to continuously work at keeping the moral laws, but because he can't keep all of them, he falls under the curse. This is a Catch 22, a "damned if you do and damned if you don't" scenario. If a person does not care about God's blessing or cursing, then they will only use their effort to be a good citizen in society. However, once a person tries to live under the old covenant, they will want to please God and will desire to keep God's Law, in order to please Him and receive His blessings. This category of people living under the old covenant will always come up short and will continually fall under condemnation. How terrible to live in such a way, constantly having to work at keeping God's Law, but always falling short and coming under condemnation. What a dreadful religious life to live! The law keeping life is a cursed life.

Indwelling Sin Is Revived and Results in Death

> What then shall we say? That the law is sin? By no means! Yet if it had not been for the law, I would not have known sin. For I would not have known what it is to covet if the law had not said, "You shall not covet." But sin, seizing an opportunity through the commandment, produced in me all kinds of covetousness. For apart from the law, sin lies dead. I was once alive apart from the law, but when the commandment came, sin came alive and I died. The very commandment that promised life proved to be death to me. For sin, seizing an opportunity through the commandment, deceived me and through it killed me.
>
> – Romans 7:7–11, ESV

Typically, people think that the Law is supposed to control and eradicate sin. It is ironic that Paul would teach that the Law *revived* sin, or made sin alive. Previously, Paul was physically alive, going about his merry way doing whatever he wanted, and he could have even had some spiritual admiration of God. Then he became aware of the Law and wanted to please God. At that moment, sin "came alive" and death in the sense of incapacitation, condemnation, and defeatism came in. Paul died to any hope of a relationship with God. It is not the Law's fault that "death" occurred for Paul; it was sin taking advantage of the Law that brought death to him. Sin deceived him, causing Paul to think he should use his best effort to keep the Law — the works of the Law. Once he tried, due to sin, he found out he couldn't fulfill the Law; therefore, his condition *after* becoming aware of the Law was worse than his initial state *before* Law. The very Law meant for life (if man could keep it) turned out to be for death because of sin.

Using Paul's struggle with coveting as an example: Paul didn't know that coveting was against God. So he lived his life coveting this and that, thinking that it was normal. It didn't strike him that anything was wrong with coveting.

But one day, Paul learned that in order to please God, he needed to abide by God's commandments. He learned that one of the commandments is "do not covet." Because he had become religious and wanted to please God by being a good law keeper, he wanted to stop coveting. Once that decision was made, sin awakened. It came alive and overwhelmed his desire to stop coveting. Paul's coveting became more pronounced. Now that he was aware of this sin, he could not stop himself from all kinds of coveting. This continuing defeat was killing him in the form of condemnation and despair, spiritually. Therefore, whatever desire and hope that he might have for a relationship with God was completely killed off.

Worse yet, the Lord had uplifted the standard of the commandments to a whole other level that included loving one's enemies. There are now even more (and a higher standard of) laws for a religious Christian wanting to please God by way of the old covenant to be killed. If Paul was killed by trying to fulfill the laws of the Old Testament then Christians who want to please God by fulfilling the laws, which would include those in the New Testament, will be killed ten times faster than Paul.

Minister of Death or Life

> ...who also made us sufficient as ministers of the new covenant, not of the letter but of the Spirit; for the letter kills, but the Spirit gives life.
>
> – 2 Corinthians 3:6

Believers should ask themselves what kind of ministers they are. What are they ministering — the new covenant, the Spirit which gives life, or the old covenant which is the letter of the Law that kills? The letter of the Law referenced in 2 Corinthians 3:6 refers to the old covenant (2 Cor. 3:14) which relates to the works of the Law. If one's ministry is merely to tell people God's Law, teaching them that they need to try to keep God's Law in order to reap God's blessings, that ministry will lead people to spiritual death. The letter of the Law ministered in such a way kills.

When believers read the Bible, "the letter," they also need to be mindful how they are approaching the Bible. Is it just the letter of Law to them, or will they turn their hearts to the Lord (2 Cor. 3:16) and receive the life-giving and life-transforming Spirit? Whenever they come to the Bible, believers need to look to Jesus in order to turn their hearts to Him. This is the way to be transferred out of the old covenant and into the new.

The Positive Purposes of the Old Covenant

What was God's purpose in giving the Law and making such a covenant with man? Was God a hater who wanted to punish man and make man miserable? Why would He propose such an agreement? Didn't He have the forethought that man would fail at keeping His Law?

Yes, God knew, but He didn't force man to sign such an agreement. A more relevant question may be: why was man foolish enough to sign up and agree to such a covenant with God? This question is still relevant today; there is something innate in man that actually thinks he will be able to fulfill the Law, if he works hard enough at it.

Let's consider for a moment, from the Scriptures, God's purposes for giving the Law. First, it's important to understand the context leading up to this covenant (the commandments given). God called Abraham and his wife Sarah out of today's Iraq into the "good land," today's Israel. There in the good land Abraham gave birth to Isaac and Isaac gave birth to Jacob. Jacob bore twelve sons before God changed Jacob's name to "Israel."

Jacob and his twelve sons became Israel, which included twelve "tribes." Israel brought his entire family to Egypt because of a famine. It turned out that one of his sons — Joseph, whom his jealous brothers sold as a slave years earlier — became what would be equivalent to a prime minister of Egypt. Because of his position, Joseph was able to give his family (seventy people) a portion of land in Egypt and take care of them during the famine. Israel (the twelve tribes) remained in Egypt for more than 200 years.

Initially, (because of Joseph) Israel was treated well. However, when Joseph passed away and as Israel's population grew, they lost favor with the Egyptians, eventually becoming slaves to that nation. By the time God called Moses to bring Israel out of Egypt, there were close to two million Israelites. After spending multiple generations in Egypt the Israelites understood Egyptian culture and its gods. But they had no knowledge of the God of Abraham, Isaac and Jacob (their patriarchs). It was for this reason Moses said to God, "When I come to the children of Israel and say to them, 'The God of your fathers has sent me to you,' and they say to me, 'What is His name?' what shall I say to them?" (Ex. 3:13)

Israel didn't even know the name of its God, the true God, the nation was so far removed from the knowledge Him.

God, through Moses, rescued Israel from Egypt and its tyranny. He carried Israel out of Egypt on "eagle's wings," but the nation had absolutely no idea who God was. They did not know what He was like, or what His purposes were. It was within this context, after Israel had just crossed the Red Sea, which God met Moses on Mount Sinai and gave Israel His covenant, the Ten Commandments.

God's Testimony of Who He Is

God had positive purposes in giving the old covenant. First, the Law testified to who God is.

And he gave to Moses, when he had finished speaking with him on Mount Sinai, the two tablets of the testimony, tablets of stone, written with the finger of God.
— Exodus 31:18, ESV

The law of the LORD is perfect, reviving the soul; the testimony of the LORD is sure, making wise the simple.
— Psalm 19:7, ESV

To man, the old covenant was the ten foundational commandments on how to behave; but to God, it was His testimony. The Law to man was a demand — a standard for man to live up to. But to God, the Law is actually a testimony of Himself. Without His testimony, man has little or no concept of who God is, what He is like, or what His character is like. After giving His testimony, man finally had a very good description of God. Stories of the Greek gods, for example, include testimonies that the gods are perhaps powerful, but also lustful, ambitious, angry, or deceitful. Who is the *real* God, the true God, and what is He like? Mankind needed Him to reveal this. That is the meaning of the Law being God's testimony.

Therefore, this is the detailed testimony that God gave concerning Himself. One may say that this is His formal introduction to man. Before His testimony, man could only guess what kind of character God possessed; but after His testimony, there was no doubt concerning His character. People can make their own judgment after such a testimony whether they will admire and adore such a God, or belittle Him without respect. God's testimony is sealed in stone, by a covenant, written down for generations of humankind to know God's nature and character. He certainly gave a testimony that people can prove true or not from generation to generation.

Additionally, God would not give a law that He could not fulfill Himself. What if God steals or He covets? Then He will have to sentence Himself to death for breaking the Law. That cannot be; therefore, whatever laws God gives He is certain to fulfill eternally. He will not even break one of them…ever. Otherwise, God would not be righteous, and He would not be qualified to judge.

The Law then is a description of God's nature, not His actions. A person's nature cannot change, but actions can. Eventually, the higher Law in the New Testament commands people to love their enemies. That is also a description of God's nature. Matthew, in Chapter 5, who spoke concerning the various uplifted laws, ended his gospel with the command to "Be perfect as your heavenly Father is perfect" (Matt. 5:48). Matthew was speaking of the Father's perfect nature. "Being perfect" is not an "act" for God. It is who He is — His innate, eternal attribute.

God's eternal plan was to have an unbreakable union or marriage with man for eternity. In the Old Testament, Israel represented the man with whom God joined Himself. This is why God called Israel His "wife" and His "bride" (Isa. 54:5–6; Jer. 62:5).

The next section shall review how the first three commandments are specifically likened to a marriage vow. The fourth through the tenth commandments can be considered part of His testimony to woo Israel to marriage by displaying what a good "husband" He will be. God was trying to impress His bride by giving His testimony so that she would be drawn to Him, marry Him, and depend on Him as her husband.

4. **Sabbath** – God is a person who is at rest. He has done everything and prepared everything. He is not fighting, and He is not working. He is at rest for eternity, a peaceful God.
5. **Honor father and mother** – God is a family man. He cares for family. As the Father, surely He loves all of His children. Even within the Trinity, there is a "family"

relationship between the Father and the Son: mutual honor. This honor flows to all the members of His household — His sons, for eternity.

6. **Do not murder** – God treasures life. He is the author of life, and He loves life. His anger is controlled and limited. Additionally, He does everything righteously.

7. **Do not commit adultery** – God is faithful. Once He has joined Himself with someone, He will never break His bond with that person. No matter if His chosen one strays, He will continue to be faithful to her for eternity.

8. **Do not steal** – God is self-sufficient. In fact, He is the only one in the universe that is. He does not steal because all things belong to Him.

9. **Do not bear false witness** – God is truthful. God cannot lie. Whatever He says is the reality, the truth. Man can bank on it.

10. **Do not covet** – God is fully satisfied not just in Himself but also in the eternal purpose of His household (the bride, the body — the assembly). He does not covet anything outside of Himself.

What an amazing testimony of God, of His person, and His character! After such a testimony, man now knows who God is and what He is like. There is no other god in the history of various religions that has given such a testimony. This testimony inspires adoration, admiration, love, and worship from men (male and female). This should inspire man to say, "I do," to be joined to this wonderful God as their husband.

The Covenant: A Mutual Marriage Vow between God and Israel

> Then I passed by you and saw you, and you were indeed at the age for love. So I spread the edge of My garment over you and covered your nakedness. I pledged Myself to you, entered into a covenant with you, and you became Mine. This is the declaration of the Lord GOD.
>
> I will judge you the way adulteresses and those who shed blood are judged. Then I will bring about your bloodshed in wrath and jealousy.
> – Ezekiel 16:8, 38, HCSB
>
> Indeed, your husband is your Maker — His name is Yahweh of Hosts — and the Holy One of Israel is your Redeemer; He is called the God of all the earth. For the LORD has called you, like a wife deserted and wounded in spirit, a wife of one's youth when she is rejected," says your God.
> – Isaiah 54:5–6, HCSB

According to the context of Ezekiel 16, the covenant that God made with Israel on Mount Sinai was actually a marriage covenant. God proposed to Israel, and Israel said "I do": God and Israel were "married." They entered into a union together. Later the prophets wrote often concerning God as the husband and Israel as the wife, or God as the bridegroom and Israel the bride (Isa. 62:5). The covenant, then, was a marriage pledge from God to Israel where He declared who He is, what He is like, how much He loves her, and how He will take care of her. Israel didn't have anything to worry about for her entire life, except to enjoy all His riches. Then in return, God asked her whether she would make the same pledge and to match Him in every way and be His wife. Israel said, "YES, Amen, we will do it."

Understanding that the Ten Commandments were actually a marriage vow, the first three commandments, then, fit right into place as well as the others that were already described above:

1. **Do not have other gods besides me** – This is the first of a marriage pledge. God will not commit adultery, meaning God will never forsake the one with whom He has joined Himself and go to another. He is now asking His bride not to have another "man." He is the one, the unique one to His wife, and she will have only Him and be with Him alone. He is her only lover and husband.

2. **Do not make images of other gods for God is jealous** – God is a jealous husband. He doesn't want to compete with anyone else. He wants His wife to love only Him and not remember any of her past lovers or any other "men." It would be a fair request for a faithful husband to ask his wife to remove pictures of other men that might tempt her. God, in a sense, is asking His bride to remove "pictures" – anything that would remind her of another lover that would pull her away from her one husband, God. God promised to love His wife faithfully, and He expects the same from His bride.

3. **Do not take God's name in vain** – In western culture, the wife takes on the family name of the husband and marries in to the husband's family. Similarly, Israel took on God's name, which means Israel is married to God; thus, everything God is and possesses – all His riches – belong to her. The bride also has God's same name. To take God's name in vain meant that Israel, though having God's name, was treating His name as nothing. She did not take advantage of the riches and power of His name, but acted as if she was poor, weak, and miserable. Let's say Bill Gate's wife, Melinda Gates, went around begging for food dressed in rags. She is the wife of the richest man in the world and bears his name, but wouldn't be acting like it! What vanity, and how that would shame not just her, but her husband, Mr. Gates. Israel as God's bride, bearing His name, should live and behave as one who possesses God. All God is and has is hers.

God made a marriage vow to Israel and asked her to make the same vow back, and she agreed. This became the old covenant – a marriage covenant between God and man, represented by Israel.

Alas, Israel as the wife didn't keep her marriage vow. She started taking on many lovers (gods), so many that God referred to her as a prostitute. In His jealous rage, He allowed these "lovers" to take advantage of her, beat her, strip her, and take everything away from her (Ezek. 16). Every time she repented, God as her wonderful and faithful husband, came and took her back to bring her back to health and to make her the beautiful wife again (Isa. 54). This is the love story between God and man (Israel). In the Old Testament prophetic books, this theme of Israel as the unfaithful wife — including God allowing judgment to befall her, His faithfulness to not forsake her, and ultimately His grace in taking her back as His only wife — is clearly portrayed throughout many of its chapters.

God "Breathes Himself Out" through the Word

God "breathes Himself out" through the Word, that man might receive life.

> ...every Writing is God-breathed, and profitable for teaching, for conviction, for setting aright, for instruction that is in righteousness.
>
> – 2 Timothy 3:16, YLT

> It is the Spirit who gives life; the flesh profits nothing. The words that I speak to you are spirit, and they are life.
>
> – John 6:63, NKJV

The giving of God's Law is His speaking that is recorded in the Scripture. His speaking is simply His "breathing out." Paul refers to this as the Law being "God-breathed." It is impossible to speak without breathing out. When God spoke the Law, it was full of His breathing out. His breath is life to man. God "breathes out" so that man can "breath in" and receive God's breath: His life. Jesus said that His Word — His speaking, is Spirit and life. Man receives breath and life from God's speaking (in the Scriptures).

God's intention in speaking forth the Law is so that man can receive His breath through His speaking and become alive with Him. The real profit in Scripture for teaching, conviction, and instruction is that the breath of God is ministered into the hearer (reader). Without receiving God's breath through His Word, Scripture is then just black and white letters like any other book that can teach and instruct. But what is *profitable* occurs when man receives God's breath that brings life in its teaching and instruction in righteousness. Whenever believers come to read the Bible to hear God's speaking, they should not forget to breathe in God's Spirit, through faith and prayer.

Negative Purposes of the Old Covenant

> The old covenant also had negative purposes, such as exposing man's sinful nature.
>
> ...for by the law is the knowledge of sin.
>
> – Romans 3:20

> Moreover the law entered that the offense might abound...
>
> – Romans 5:20

> I would not have known sin except through the law...For apart from the law sin was dead.
>
> – Romans 7:7b–8

When Adam and Eve ate of the forbidden tree, they didn't just disobey God, but they ingested sin into their being. This sin is actually the satanic life and nature that came into man. It can be said that it affected Adam's DNA and mutated his genetics, making all subsequent generations sinners by nature. Though men had sin and commit sin, they didn't know that the evil things they were doing was sin. They might have thought that it was just part of human nature to steal and to murder (just don't get caught doing it), and that it was normal to covet and crave things and persons around them that didn't belong to them. They didn't have any knowledge of their sin.

Therefore, God gave the Law that men would come to the knowledge of sin. When the Law came, men realized that there was a standard to fulfill. Once they realized this and tried to live by this standard of the Law, they realized what sin was and that it was in them. In fact, sin became alive in them to make sure that they could not fulfill the requirements of the Law. Many people have a common misperception that the Law was given to *control* sin but according to the verse above, the Law actually *caused* sin to abound.

There is nothing wrong with the Law; it is holy and righteous, and it did what God intended it to do. The Law uncovered sin in man, so that man recognized that he is a hopeless sinner that cannot live up to the standard of God's Law.

> For the mind-set of the flesh is hostile to God because it does not submit itself to God's law, for it is unable to do so. Those who are in the flesh cannot please God.
> – Romans 8:7–8, HCSB

The flesh refers to fallen man and the mind-set of fallen man without the life of God. Man in his flesh is hostile to His Creator. Fallen man is an enemy of God, and therefore, not able to submit to God's Law. Even when there is a desire in man to want to submit to God's Law, fallen man is unable to do so. It is not possible for fallen man to please God — to fulfill God's Law.

Without the Law, men may actually think that they are quite good, that they can live in a way that is pleasing to a higher power. They can think highly of themselves–how they are good and charitable to people. The Law's job, however, is to expose what is really in people so that men will no longer deceive themselves. Through God's Law, they will hopefully come to their senses and realize their true condition so that they can turn to Jesus Christ for salvation.

A Guardian to Keep Men Safe

> Now before faith came, we were held captive under the Law, imprisoned until the coming faith would be revealed. So then, the Law was our guardian until Christ came, in order that we might be justified by faith. But now that faith has come, we are no longer under a guardian,
> – Galatians 3:23–25, ESV

One can imagine the danger of living in a lawless society — a society with no law, no law enforcement, and where anything goes. It would be a fearful place and men would end up killing each other openly. Therefore, the Law was given to guard man, to keep man safe. Many countries today are like one big prison where there are surveillance cameras everywhere to make sure people do not break the law; it is intended to keep their citizens safe.

God's desire is not for man to stay under the Law, in its prison. God's purpose is to use the Law as a guardian, a pedagogue, to safe guard and guide man to the faith of Jesus Christ. Before coming to faith, man is like a little child that needs to be under a guardian who will make sure that the child does not do anything foolish and harmful. The pedagogue's goal is to lead man to Jesus Christ. The guardian's job is done once man comes to faith in Jesus Christ. Men that try their best to be justified according to Law, if they are honest with themselves, will admit that they are a failure at keeping God's Law. When they arrive at this point of hopelessness before God according to the Law, then they will come to the faith of Jesus Christ in order to be justified before God. At that point, the law has done its job, and is no longer needed.

Freed from the Law and Joined to Jesus Christ

> Or do you not know, brethren (for I speak to those who know the Law), that the law has dominion over a man as long as he lives? For the woman who has a husband is bound by the law to her husband as long as he lives. But if the husband dies, she is released from the law of her husband. So then if, while her husband lives, she marries another man, she will be called an adulteress; but if her husband dies, she is free from that law, so that she is no adulteress, though she has married another man. Therefore, my brethren, you also have become dead to the law through the body of Christ, that you may be married to another — to Him who was raised from the dead, that we should bear fruit to God.
>
> – Romans 7:1–4

In eternity, God's desire is to be joined to man, to be one with man — to *marry* man. He will be the husband, the male; man (male and female) will be the wife, the female. In the Bible, the exemplary role of the husband is to be the provider, protector, the giver of riches, and source of love to the wife. The wife's exemplary role is to be the receiver, enjoyer, a lover, and the fruit-bearer to the husband. When God declared His nature and character through the Law, He testified that He is qualified to be the husband, that He is the "male" in the universe. The Law is actually a detailed description of what a true husband is like. The Law then is not the requirement for the wife (the female) but for the husband (the male).

Mankind was created by God to be the universal female as the counterpart to be joined to God as the universal male. This was the significance of God being the Tree of Life — that man might ingest Him, be joined to Him, be one with Him, and that He would become the source of life within man. Instead, Satan tricked man into declaring his independence from God, to be god in and by himself. Just as Satan wanted to replace God, he deceived man to take the same position as he to replace God. And just as Satan wanted to be the "man" in the universe, man took Satan's side to also become the "man" in the universe. Therefore, man (male and female) left the position of the female by eating of the tree of knowledge of good and evil and became the male.

Fallen man (which the Bible calls the "flesh" and the "old man") took the position of the male, and the man originally created by God to be the female became trapped inside the fallen man — married and joined to him. Since fallen man took the position of the male, then the law of the male (God) is applied to him. Every "man" in the universe has to live up to the law of the male in the universe. Both Satan and fallen man have to live up to the Law of God.

Basically, God says, "This is what the male — the husband of the universe — is like; this is who He is and His character." Then the fallen man — the imposter who has joined himself to Satan — says to God, "I am now the male of the universe. I don't need you." Then God says, "Okay, if you are the male, the husband, then you need to live and act like one. Let me give you my testimony. This is the Law for you to keep to prove that you are the male of the universe." Therefore, the Law is for the husband to keep, to show that he is the male.

Satan was the first one to be exposed that he is not qualified to be the male because he broke God's Law: Satan coveted God's position, which was the source of his rebellion. Then he gave a false witness and lied to Eve in order to give her a wrong impression of God to deceive her. Then, acting out as sin in man, he committed the first murder by killing Abel (John 8:44). The fallen man, with sin in the flesh, has the same nature as the devil: therefore, as the "male," fallen man is under the "law of the husband." Of course the fallen man (the flesh) not being able keep the law of the husband (God), is also exposed as not being qualified to be the husband — the male of the universe. As long as the fallen man is alive, then the original created man (the female) is also bound to her first husband since she is joined to him, the fallen man. Since her first husband is under the Law and the curse for breaking the Law, she is also under Law and shares the same curse.

According to Romans 7:1–4, the only way for her to be freed is if her first husband dies. If he dies, then she can marry another husband. The good news is that when Christ died on the cross, the flesh (the fallen man — the old man) was crucified with Him (Rom. 6:6; Gal. 2:20). The old man (the husband) died with Christ. This death released the wife, the original created man, to be joined to a new husband — the resurrected Jesus Christ. Now, man as the female has a new husband, and this new husband has proven Himself by fulfilling all of God's Law. He is therefore qualified to be the real husband to man, to take care of all of man's needs. Now man, joined to Christ, can take pleasure in being the "wife," — the enjoyer, the receiver, and the lover to Christ, and bear fruit to God.

By joining with the resurrected Christ, united with Him and with His life and nature, she bears the fruit of the Spirit: love, joy, peace, long suffering, kindness, goodness, faithfulness, gentleness, and self-control. This is the spontaneous character and expression of the "wife" who is joined with and receives the rich supply from her "husband," Jesus Christ.

It is critical to understand that the old covenant does not refer to the Old Testament; it is a *condition* for a relationship with God. The old covenant exposes the sin of the fallen man. Therefore, even though Christians are no longer in the Old Testament period, they can continue to live according to the principle of the old covenant. A Christian living under the Old covenant will read the New Testament and find even more laws to be under and be condemned by. But believers living in the new covenant, however, can read the Old Testament and find only Jesus Christ — the husband — for their enjoyment.

14

(SECTION B)
THE NEW COVENANT

Four Blessings of the New Covenant

In Section A of this chapter, the old covenant relating to its nature, the reasons why it was given, and the results of the old covenant was discussed. In Section B of this chapter, the focus is on the new covenant. Everyone who understands the good news of the new covenant will rejoice and would be considered extremely foolish not to accept the new covenant from God with thanksgiving. The new covenant is unconditionally fulfilled without man's self-efforts. There are four blessings to the new covenant. Below are two portions: one from the Old Testament and a repeat in the New Testament.

> Behold, the days are coming, says the LORD, when I will make a new covenant with the house of Israel and with the house of Judah — not according to the covenant that I made with their fathers in the day that I took them by the hand to lead them out of the land of Egypt, My covenant which they broke, though I was a husband to them, says the LORD. But this is the covenant that I will make with the house of Israel after those days, says the LORD: I will put My law in their minds, and write it on their hearts; and I will be their God, and they shall be My people. No more shall every man teach his neighbor, and every man his brother, saying, 'Know the LORD,' for they all shall know Me, from the least of them to the greatest of them, says the LORD. For I will forgive their iniquity, and their sin I will remember no more.
>
> – Jeremiah 31:31–34

> For this is the covenant that I will make with the house of Israel after those days, declares the Lord: I will put my laws into their minds, and write them on their hearts, and I will be their God, and they shall be my people. And they shall not teach, each one his neighbor and each one his brother, saying, 'Know the Lord,' for they shall all know me, from the least of them to the greatest. For I will be merciful toward their iniquities, and I will remember their sins no more."
>
> – Hebrews 8:10–12, ESV

It is remarkable that the new covenant is spelled out clearly in just two verses in Jeremiah when the old covenant law took about ten chapters to describe. This shows the simplicity of the new covenant. It is direct, to the point, and Jehovah God will unilaterally accomplish everything in the new covenant. In the old covenant, Jehovah God kept His side of the bilateral agreement, but Israel, representing mankind, didn't (and couldn't). They failed over and over again, but that was part of God's design. One of the reasons for God to give the Law, as we have seen in the previous chapter, was to expose man's sinful nature; therefore, they were destined to fail. Meanwhile, God's plan has always been the new covenant. God simply declared what He will do in clear terms in three sentences. There is no condition for man to fulfill before God. The prominent parts of the new covenant indicate God being life to man, man receiving God as life, being joined to God in perfect union, and spontaneously living according to God's nature. God will accomplish what He covenanted to do for man, because the new covenant was actually in God's heart and His eternal purpose before creating man in the very beginning.

This was God's desire from the very beginning by providing the Tree of Life to man. If man would have eaten the Tree of Life instead of partaking of sin, then man would have received God's life and nature and have become one with God. Man would express God and have dominion over God's enemy, Satan. Man would not need the last part of the new covenant relating to the forgiveness of sins. If man had not partaken of the tree of the knowledge of good and evil, then man would not have had sin that needed forgiving. Therefore, the positive aspect of the old covenant, as described earlier, affirms God's eternal purpose from the beginning—expressing Himself and being joined to man. God gave the negative aspect of the old covenant as a temporary solution to guard man and to expose sin, so that man would welcome the new covenant and fulfill what God yearned for from the very beginning. Thus, the old covenant would never have been needed if man ate from the Tree of Life from the start. Now that the new covenant is available, the old covenant is obsolete and ready to vanish away completely (Heb. 8:13). The new covenant was God's purpose from the very beginning, even before time.

1. The Imparting of the Law of Life into believers

> I will put my Spirit within you, and cause you to walk in my statutes, and you shall keep my ordinances, and do them.
>
> —Ezekiel 36:27, HNV

> Therefore you shall be perfect, just as your Father in heaven is perfect.
>
> — Matthew 5:48, HNV

The first thing God provided in His new covenant was to put His Law in His people's minds and hearts (Jer. 31:33; see also Heb. 8:10). The Law in the old covenant was on a tablet outside of man, but the Law in the new covenant became an integral part of man and his character.

The heart signifies the nature, character, and personality of man's very being. The word "write" indicates inscribing something. The Law inscribed in man's heart means that the Law of God is now part of man's nature, just as it is part of God's nature and character. Previously, man had a fallen nature, so he needed to work at following God's Law that was foreign to him. He had to work at it with much effort, because the Law was alien to him. This is similar to a monkey trying to act like a man! As hard as a monkey tries, it will eventually fail, because it is still a monkey. In the new covenant, man does not even have to try to follow God's Law because the nature of God with its Law is now man's nature.

How does this happen? The new covenant is the Spirit of God that comes into and becomes an integral part of man. The Spirit of God is no longer outside of man, but within man — joined and mingled in perfect union with man. This one verse in the Old Testament is a prophecy of the believers' reality in the New Testament. This fact of the Spirit of God coming into man is the vital difference between the old and the new.

Notice that it is the Spirit that causes man to walk according to His Law. It is no longer man's effort working to keep God's Law; rather, the Spirit of God with His life and nature is what causes man to live God's Law. With the Spirit within man, God gave a promise: "You shall" keep my Law (Ezek. 36:27). The word "shall" means that keeping God's Law is inevitable. Due to the Spirit of God in man, man shall keep and do God's laws. Sooner or later, man shall, without a doubt, without a choice, predictably, express the very life and nature of God.

This is similar to the Lord Jesus saying, "You shall be perfect as your heavenly Father is perfect." After telling the disciples about the uplifted Law that is humanly impossible and laughable to even attempt to fulfill, He gave a promise that they shall be perfect or complete as their heavenly Father. Why? Because they are born of God, and God is their Father. Like father, like son. God's characteristics will be in the sons. This is like an earthly father telling his newly born son, "You shall grow up and be like me — able to run, play ball, talk, and work with me." Even though the baby is completely helpless at that point, the father knows that because the baby is born of him and possesses his life, one day the baby will grow up to be a man like him. This is the essence of the new covenant, God's Spirit coming into man.

> Therefore, no condemnation now exists for those in Christ Jesus, because the Spirit's Law of life in Christ Jesus has set you free from the law of sin and of death. What the law could not do since it was limited by the flesh, God did. He condemned sin in the flesh by sending His own Son in flesh like ours under sin's domain, and as a sin offering, in order that the Law's requirement would be accomplished in us who do not walk according to the flesh but according to the Spirit.
>
> – Romans 8:1–4, HCSB

The entrance of the Spirit into man brings the Law of the divine life within man. This is the Spirit's Law of life. Every life has a law. This law is not outside of the life; rather, the life is the law. An apple's "life" will bear apples. It will never bear oranges or bananas. That is the law of the apple's life. It is completely dependable and predictable. The life-law of a dog will cause this dog to run, bark, wag its tail, and grow hair like a dog. When human beings produce an offspring, it is absolutely predictable that — based on the law of life — the child will grow with human characteristics. No prayer is needed — "Lord, please make sure that my baby is human!" That would be a ridiculous prayer.

The Spirit of God with His life also is a law. This law is not the same as the Ten Commandments outside of man requiring man to act and behave like God. Rather, when the Spirit enters man and joins man with God's life and nature, the law of the divine eternal life enters as well. This is the Law that frees believers from the law of sin and death and fulfills God's requirement in every believer. It is no longer man's effort to fulfill the requirements of God's Law, but the Spirit's Law is their law of life. What freedom from condemnation when a person realizes it is God's Law of life that shall inevitably fulfill the highest requirements of God's character in each and every believer!

What the external Law could not do since man's flesh is sinful, God terminated on the cross. He then entered into man with His Spirit, and by His Law of life causes His character to be fully expressed in man; thus, God and man together fulfill God's external Law.

This is why the new covenant is not conditional. How wonderful is this new covenant! God *will* do it and He is doing it. Man's part is simply to enjoy God as life and to allow God's life to grow and mature. (Please read the four chapters on *Life* to understand man's part in cooperating to let God's life grow in the believers).

Believers should no longer place attention and emphasis on keeping God's external Law, but focus on the Spirit — the relationship of God within them as the eternal divine life.

> ...who also made us sufficient as ministers of the new covenant, not of the letter but of the Spirit; for the letter kills, but the Spirit gives life.
>
> – 2 Corinthians 3:6, NKJV

Here, the ministry of the Spirit is uniquely associated with the new covenant and clearly disassociated with the letter of the Law in the old covenant. The new covenant is all about the minister imparting and dispensing the Spirit that gives the eternal divine life, whereas the old covenant, with its letter of the law, kills. What a contrast!

Believers today have been made sufficient (or competent) ministers of the new covenant; they are able to minister the Spirit. If they minister the Spirit to people, then they bring people into the new covenant. If they minister the letter of the law, however, they bring death (condemnation, paralysis, division, and other spiritual weaknesses). It is one or the other. Therefore, believers need to be clear concerning the new covenant with the Spirit of life and leave behind the old covenant with its letter of law.

2. He Is Our God and We Are His people

> But you are a chosen race, a royal priesthood, a holy nation, a people for His possession, so that you may proclaim the praises of the One who called you out of darkness into His marvelous light.
>
> – 1 Peter 2:9, HCSB

To be God's people is much more than just a group of human beings that He has acquired. The Greek word for "people" in Hebrews 8:10 and 1 Peter 23:9 is *laos*, which means, "A people, tribe, nation, all those who are of the same stock and language" (Thayer's Greek Lexicon). The word "stock" means "the descendants of one individual" which is a group having unity of descent (Merriam-Webster). So When God says, "They shall be My people," it is very significant indeed.

In the new covenant, believers are not just a mass of human beings belonging to God as the Creator; their ancestry is *God.* They descended from God. They are the same "kind" as God. They are no different intrinsically in their life and nature. They are His people, His relatives, and they communicate with each other using the same language.

When God said, "they shall be my people," this did not have the same meaning as the owner of some puppies saying, "these are my puppies." Rather, it would be like Jacob in the Old Testament looking at Israel today and saying, "These are my people", since they are his offspring. See the difference? A human and a puppy are two different kinds with different languages; however, Israel's ancestry is actually from Jacob.

How can believers be God's people and also from His lineage? The reason is God's Spirit is in them. Since believers are born of God, and are now inextricably joined to Him with His life and nature, they are God's people.

Yet, God is still their God. God is still the distinct One to be uniquely worshipped and adored for eternity. The uplifting of human beings to become God's people in the way of birth does not diminish in any way God's status, glory and uniqueness; rather His people can express Him and proclaim His praise at the highest level above all of creation. This proclamation is not just in words but also as His people. The very life and nature of God is multiplied, and His glory is magnified. Therefore, being God's people is wonderful for His believers and glorious to God.

3. Knowing God

> Nevertheless you have an anointing from the Holy One, and you all know. I have not written to you that you do not *know* the truth, but that you do *know* it, and that no lie is of the truth. ...Now as for you, the anointing that you received from him resides in you, and you have no need for anyone to teach you. But as his anointing teaches you about all things, it is true and is not a lie. Just as it has taught you, you reside in him.
>
> – 1 John 2:20–21, 27, NET

The third blessing of the new covenant reveals no one has to teach God's people to know God; all shall know Him from the least to the greatest. There are two different Greek words for the word "know" in Hebrews 8:11 and 1 John 2:20–21. The first "know" is from the Greek word, *ginosko,* and the second "know" is from the Greek word, *oida (or verb form, eido).* According to Vine's New Testament Expository Dictionary, *ginosko* frequently suggests inception or "progress" in knowledge," while *oida* suggests "fullness" of knowledge. According to J.N. Darby, ginosko signifies objective knowledge — what a man has learned or acquired. Oida conveys the thought of what is inward — the inward consciousness in the mind or intuitive knowledge not immediately derived from what is external. Based on these definitions, the third blessing says that believers in the new covenant do not need man to teach them an external, objective knowledge of God, because each and every one has an inward, intuitive knowing of God in fullness.

Knowing God in the way of *oida* for believers is the same way that Jesus knows *(oida)* the Father. In John 8:55 Jesus said to the Jews concerning God: You do not know *(ginosko)* Him, but I know *(oida)* Him. The unbelieving Jews didn't even have an inception of knowing God externally, but Jesus, as the Son, knows God in full, inwardly and intuitively. It is very significant that believers know *(oida)* God in the new covenant the same way as Jesus knows *(oida)* God, the Father. How is this possible? It is only because of the first blessing of the new covenant, that the Spirit of God is residing in the believers and became part of their inward being. The Spirit of God is in them, similar to the Spirit being in Jesus; therefore, they can intuitively and inwardly know God in full just as Jesus did while on earth.

First John 2:20 supports this same thought. God, the Holy One, anoints believers. This anointing is the Spirit (Acts 10:38), and because of this anointing, all believers know *(oida)* the truth. They do not need men to teach them because the anointing Spirit teaches all things related to the truth. This teaching causes them to reside or remain in Jesus Christ. This does not mean believers do not need any external teachers to instruct them from the Bible concerning the truth. It does mean that if they pay attention to the anointing within them, the Spirit will witness in them, and they will intuitively know what is and is not truth as they listen to Bible teachers. It is the Spirit in them that discerns what is healthy, of the truth to accept, and what to reject and avoid.

The goal of the Anointing's teaching is for believers to remain and reside in Jesus Christ. The anointing Spirit is not for teaching believers which car to buy, which class to take, or what career to choose, but to always live in Jesus Christ — to remain in Him. As believers live through the day, the anointing is constantly moving, and this moving is a witness that they are in Him. The anointing Spirit's work is always to bring believers back to Jesus Christ when they are experientially distracted. This is the third blessing of the new covenant: that believers know *(oida)* God as the truth, making them unmovable as they reside in Jesus Christ.

4. Sins Are Forgiven and No Longer Remembered

> Therefore, let it be known to you, brothers, that through this one forgiveness of sins is proclaimed to you, and by this one everyone who believes is justified from everything from which the Law of Moses could not justify you.
> – Acts 13:38–39, NET

The last blessing God extended with the new covenant is, "I will forgive their iniquity, and their sin I will remember no more." This is of course wonderful news for all humankind, for all are sinners. This forgiveness is accomplished only through Jesus Christ. Faith in Jesus Christ is the unique action necessary for justification, or to be made righteous in God's sight. God has an amazing memory. On one hand, God can never forget man's sins no matter how hard men try to please God by the works of the Law. On the other hand, once a person believes into Jesus Christ, God forgets all of man's sin. To God, it is as if man never sinned. When Satan tries to accuse a believer before God, God will say to Satan, in effect, "What are you talking about? I don't have any record of this person's sins. This one is sinless and righteous in my judgment."

To most believers, this is the first and most important blessing: being forgiven by God. But to God, it is the least important! This is the last item of the new covenant. God's eternal purpose was not to forgive man's sins. God's eternal purpose was to be joined with man in eternal union. Sin came in to the picture in Genesis 3 and put a stop to God's plan; therefore, God had to clean up sin in man before continuing with His eternal plan. After man was cleansed from sin through the cross of Jesus Christ, God continued His plan of coming into man and becoming one with man. The first three blessings of the new covenant were part of God's eternal plan; the last item relating to sin was a temporary setback that God had to solve and which He did. Therefore, Christians should not fill their thoughts with the issue of sin and forgiveness of sin. Once forgiven, they need to give their attention to enjoying God in Jesus Christ with the working of the Spirit's Law of life. Believers are of the same tribe and language as God and know God inwardly and intuitively in full.

The Effective Date and the Executor of the New Testament

The new covenant (New Testament) took effect with the death of Jesus Christ.

> Likewise He also took the cup after supper, saying, "This cup is the new covenant in My blood, which is shed for you."
>
> – Luke 22:20

> For where there [is] a testament, there must also of necessity be the death of the testator. For a testament is in force after men are dead, since it has no power at all while the testator lives.
>
> – Hebrews 9:16–17

The Greek word for "covenant" and "testament" is actually the same word: *diathēkē*. *Diathēkē* is "a promise or an agreement made with an oath." The testament is a person's will, that is, what that person will distribute to others in the event of his death. A testament is fully enforced or effective at the time of death. All the items in a testament before the death of the testator are promises, but once the testator dies they are no longer promises, but a bequest. The items rightfully belong to the recipient (or the inheritor) declared in the will or testament. For example, a father may write in his will or testament that he will give his house to his son. Before the father dies, it is only a promise. Legally, the father can change his mind and change his will to give the house to someone else. But if the will says that the house is to be given to the son, and the father dies, the will can no longer be changed. In fact, as soon as he dies, ownership of the house transfers to the son; it is his inheritance. It is a done deal and nothing can change it.

The new covenant became effective at the death of Christ. God, who made the covenant, shed His blood with the death of Jesus Christ (Acts 20:28). Jesus declared that the cup, representing the shedding of His blood, is the cup of the new covenant. Jesus' death made the new covenant effective, or "in force." Before his death, only God's promise of one day having a new covenant with His people persisted. That promise was fulfilled and executed when Jesus died on the cross. No longer a promise from God, the new covenant was an enforceable and effective will or testament.

The writer of Hebrews says that a testament has no power when the testator still lives. Since the testator died — Jesus Christ — the New Testament is fully in force with all authority. What is written is no longer a list of promises, but a bequest for all believers — their inheritance.

This is very significant. Whatever God promised is now a bequest. It is rightfully the believers. Most believers still read the Bible as God's promises. They may pray, "Lord, remember your promise in your Word," or "I claim what you have promised to me." However, Paul in 2 Corinthians 1:20 said that *all* the promises of God in Christ are YES and AMEN. They are no longer promises, but bequests for believers to receive and enjoy freely for themselves. The new covenant with its four blessings actually includes all of God's promises. All other promises made by God may be considered sub-points of the four, just as all the statutes and ordinances in the Old Testament are considered to be sub-points of the Ten Commandments. Understanding that the New Testament is in force through Christ's death, and that what has been spoken as a promise now rightfully belongs to the believers, should instill in believers the boldness to freely take hold of their inheritance. It is rightfully theirs.

Jesus Is the Executor (Guarantor) of the New Covenant

Today in resurrection, Jesus is the executor (or guarantor) of the new covenant.

> But now He has obtained a more excellent ministry, inasmuch as He is also Mediator of a better covenant, which was established on better promises.
>
> — Hebrews 8:6

> How much more shall the blood of Christ, who through the eternal Spirit offered Himself without spot to God, cleanse your conscience from dead works to serve the living God? And for this reason He is the Mediator of the new covenant, by means of death, for the redemption of the transgressions under the first covenant, that those who are called may receive the promise of the eternal inheritance.
>
> — Hebrews 9:14–15

Compared to the Levitical priesthood in the Old Testament and the animal sacrifices that could never take away the sins of the people, Jesus Christ has obtained through His death and resurrection a *better* ministry. The Old Testament priests were operating under the old covenant, but Jesus Christ is guaranteeing that God's people will receive all the items in the new covenant. In these verses the Greek word for "mediator" according to Vine's Expository Dictionary means, "one who acts as a guarantee." Jesus, being the Mediator of the new covenant means that He guarantees that the terms of the new covenant (testament) will be fulfilled to the beneficiary. In modern day, the person who guarantees that the beneficiary receives all the items of the inheritance or bequests is called an executor.

The better ministry of the Lord Jesus Christ is as the guarantor or the executor of the new covenant. Since His resurrection and ascension, Jesus' ministry is to make sure that believers receive all that is rightfully theirs according to the new covenant, which is fully in force due to the death of the Testator. The four blessings of the new covenant are no longer promises, but bequests that have been accomplished and are just waiting for the beneficiaries (believers) to partake of them and inherit them as their own. There is nothing more for the beneficiaries to do other than to claim what is rightfully theirs and enjoy their inheritance.

On one hand the Lord Jesus is praying in the heavens that the believers will realize what is theirs; on the other hand, He is working out every item of the new covenant from within the believers. Therefore, in every way and from every angle, Jesus is working to make certain that every item of the new covenant is made real and enjoyed by the believers.

Receive All that God Has Accomplished by Faith

This only I want to learn from you: Did you receive the Spirit by the works of the law, or by the hearing of faith?

Therefore He who supplies the Spirit to you and works miracles among you, [does He do it] by the works of the law, or by the hearing of faith?

But that no one is justified by the law in the sight of God [is] evident, for "the just shall live by faith."

...that the blessing of Abraham might come upon the Gentiles in Christ Jesus, that we might receive the promise of the Spirit through faith.
— Galatians 3:2, 5, 11, 14

Now that the new covenant is in effect, everything that God promised is now a bequest. There is a guarantor (executor) of the "will," to make sure that the beneficiaries receive what is rightfully theirs. What next? The only thing left to do is simply have the faith to receive what already belongs to all mankind just for the taking. There is no payment or condition; the believer needs only to take and enjoy. This is faith. Faith is realizing what is already there: receiving, accepting, taking, and enjoying it.

This would be like a father who died and left $10 billion in the bank as an inheritance for his lost son. The lost son was living on the street like a beggar. The executor of the father's estate goes out to look for the son, to give the son the good news that he is the beneficiary of the $10 billion bequest. He also gives the son a checkbook. But the son does not believe what has been told to him and continues to live on the streets. Though the money is rightfully his and sitting in the bank in his name, because of his unbelief, it does not benefit him at all. Maybe one day, he will be so hungry and desperate that he will muster up enough faith to write a check for ten dollars. Lo and behold, it cashes. The next time, he might venture out to write a check for $100. Eventually through experience, his faith increases where he writes a million-dollar check.

This is what Christ has done for all of humankind. It is only the believers that benefit, because they have the faith to claim what is theirs: forgiveness and resurrection power. They have even ascended to have all-things under their feet. It is as if believers have blank checks, and they should just write what they want the "I AM" to be to them. This is faith to receive all the bequests of the new covenant. This is not just for initial salvation but also for every step of journey with Christ, for every environment and difficulty that believers encounter, and with the expectation of fulfilling God's calling. It is all there for the taking, by faith. Believers started by faith and will continue to live by faith. Praise the Lord for the new covenant!

Salvation: Irrevocable, Eternal, and Secure

> ...who has saved us and called us with a holy calling, not according to our works, but according to His own purpose and grace which was given to us in Christ Jesus before time began.
>
> – 2 Timothy 1:9

> And I give them eternal life, and they shall never perish; neither shall anyone snatch them out of My hand.
>
> – John 10:28

> For the gifts and the calling of God are irrevocable.
>
> – Romans 11:29

Since salvation in the new covenant is a unilateral gift from God, and all that is needed to receive salvation is faith (also a gift from God), many believers have the assurance that salvation is secure: Once a person has believed and received Jesus Christ as their Savior, no matter if they go through periods of moral failures and even a rejection of God, their salvation is eternal. The above verses are commonly used to support this point of view. First, it is God who does the calling, and this calling is for His purpose. Since it was not dependent on man's doing to begin with, then no matter if a believer temporarily falls away, God is faithful to His own purpose and grace to finish what He has begun.

At the time of faith, Jesus Christ came into the believer to join with him and give him eternal life. The eternal life is not in the future, but at the very moment of faith in Jesus. Because this life is in the believers, they shall never perish. There is no condition given to keep eternal life. Once a person has it, that life is now part of him or her, and no matter what they do, or how much they try to run away from the Lord, the eternal life is now fused with them and cannot be un-fused. It is like eating food. Once food is eaten and digestion starts, the elements of the food become part of the body. It is impossible to separate the food digested from the body. Jesus Christ is the *real* food, and once eaten through faith, He is one spirit with the believer, and the two can never be divided. There is nowhere to run, and it is impossible to undo.

Faith is a gift. Eternal life is a gift. Every item of the new covenant is a gift. Once God has called a person to participate in these gifts, His gifts and calling are irrevocable. He gave and He called, and neither is reversible, even by God. What a wonderful assurance! Salvation does not depend on man to be accomplished, and it does not depend on man to be kept. God truly did it all, and there is nothing for man to boast about in relation to salvation (as if man deserved even one iota of it). All the glory and praise goes to God, the Lord Jesus Christ.

People will then say, "What is the point of man having a will to choose? Don't people have to do something to receive salvation?" The answer is absolutely YES. Men need to choose to hear the good news. They need to decide to hear the news of what Jesus has done for them. They are already judged and condemned for eternal death. However, they need to hear the gospel of Jesus Christ, and it is in the hearing that they receive the gift of faith. If they are not even willing to read or listen to this wonderful news of salvation, then they do not have a chance to be rescued (saved). The next section will show that the *will* to choose for a believer is just as important.

Coming Judgment: Motivation to Enjoy and Dispense

Though the believers' salvation is secured, Scripture also reveals believers will still be judged at the Lord's second coming. Sometimes these portions of Scripture are interpreted to mean that believers can lose their salvation if they are unfaithful.

Because these verses seem to conflict, certain camps among believers argue and divide over the matter. One side believes strongly that once saved by grace, always saved (let's call this the "grace" side). This other side says, "What about those that have fallen away from the Lord and are living in sin? How can they be saved?" (Let's call this the "work" side).

Those on the "grace" side will counter that Christians living in sin were never saved in the first place. Those on the "work" side teach that believers can lose their salvation if they are not faithful. The "grace" side will accuse the "work" side for making salvation a matter of works and not of grace — believers always have to work for their salvation, nullifying the grace of God. The "work" side may accuse the "grace" side of having a "cheap grace," that they only want salvation without the obedience to follow the Lord's commands.

This section will attempt to harmonize both sets of verses so that both are accepted without contradiction, thereby, providing the comfort of security to believers and yet still motivating them to grow and be faithful during the course of their Christian life.

Believers Shall Still Be Judged at Jesus' Coming

> Why do you pass judgment on your brother? Or you, why do you despise your brother? For we will all stand before the judgment seat of God.
> — Romans 14:10, ESV

> For we must all appear before the judgment seat of Christ, so that each one may receive what is due for what he has done in the body, whether good or evil.
> — 2 Corinthians 5:10, ESV

Paul clearly teaches in Romans and 2 Corinthians that believers will have to stand before Christ for judgment. Believers will be judged by what they have done when they were alive on earth in their physical bodies; have they done good or evil? They will be judged based on whether they have practiced oneness with all believers by a non-judgmental receiving of all those that have the faith of Jesus Christ which the Lord has received. Wait, didn't this chapter concerning the new covenant just make a strong case for the unconditional and unilateral work of God — that believers cannot work for their salvation and have eternal security? Now, Paul says there is judgment based on how believers have lived and acted... isn't this *conditional?* This seems to be a complete contradiction to the new covenant.

There seems to be more bad news for the "grace" side:

> ...work out your own salvation with fear and trembling.
>
> – Philippians 2:12

This is one of the more perplexing verses in the Bible, which seems to contradict the idea of God doing the work for man's salvation by grace. Here Paul says clearly that believers need to "work out" their own salvation. "Fear and trembling" sure sounds like there is an unknown element at the time of judgment, and whether one passes the judgment or not is not assured. Those on the "grace" side will cite the next verse that it is God who is working in the believers (Phil. 2:13); therefore, there is no need to worry since God will do it in them. This is a good argument from a one-sided point of view, but from an unbiased reader, that simply does not explain away verse 12, which says believers need to work out salvation in fear and trembling. This is just one verse out of a body of Scripture verses that the "work" side can cite from their point of view; salvation can be lost if the believer does not continue faithfully as a Christian.

The Standard of Judgment for New Covenant Believers

In the old covenant it is clear that the standard for judgment is whether the Law is kept. True, in the new covenant everything is done by God and the initiation and continuation for man to be saved is only grace through faith. Then on what basis or standard will God judge believers? To fully dive into this topic would take multiple chapters; instead, let's consider the key points with direction for further studies, if so desired.

> I planted, Apollos watered, but God gave the growth. . . . For we are God's fellow workers. You are God's [cultivated] field, God's building.
>
> For no one can lay a foundation other than that which is laid, which is Jesus Christ. Now if anyone builds on the foundation with gold, silver, precious stones, wood, hay, straw — each one's work will become manifest, for the Day will disclose it, because it will be revealed by fire, and the fire will test what sort of work each one has done. If the work that anyone has built on the foundation survives, he will receive a reward. If anyone's work is burned up, he will suffer loss, though he himself will be saved, but only as through fire.
>
> – 1 Corinthians 3:6, 9, 11–15, ESV

This is a key portion of Scripture to show first that there is a standard of judgment based on the believers' work. Second, it also made clear that believers are still saved even if they do suffer at the time of judgment; therefore, these verses show the harmonizing of both the "grace" and "work" sides, and that they do not actually contradict each other.

A plant is a beautiful picture of growth and building and is an appropriate analogy to help explain the above. A seed is planted into the earth and is regularly watered. The life in the seed makes use of the soil and the water to produce a plant. The content of a plant is 100 percent made up of water plus the minerals of the soil. The plant grows by photosynthesis: the sun causes the water in the plant to exchange for poisonous carbon dioxide (CO_2). In the process, oxygen is released and carbohydrates (sugar, or energy) and cellulose are generated for the growth and building up of the plant. The life (DNA) of the seed will spontaneously determine what the plant (an apple, orange, or rose, for example) will be when grown.

The Bible says that the seed for planting is Jesus Christ as the Word of God (1 Pet. 1:23), the watering is the Spirit (John 7:39), and the sun for growth is the Father (Rev. 21:23). When a believer is full of the Spirit (water), then everything poisonous of Satan (CO2) is utilized as an ingredient to generate energy (sugar). This causes growth (cellulose) and even a release of the Spirit (oxygen) to enliven others. The plant itself is the joining and mingling in the most profound way between earth (humanity) and water (the Spirit). The "DNA" of the seed, Jesus Christ, determines that the maturity of the plant will have the same exact image as He. This is how a "plant" (believer) grows to become God's building, fulfilling His eternal purpose.

Every believer (one who is regenerated with the seed) is the field that God is cultivating. So in that sense, every believer should be growing and building on the foundation of Jesus Christ. They all need to produce something from growth for God's building during the time that they are on earth. The day of judgment will be the final testing by fire to see what each believer has produced for the building up of the body. If the material is gold, silver, and precious stones, then fire will only improve on its glory; and the believer will receive a positive reward. But if the material is wood, hay, or straw, then certainly they will be burned up, and the believer shall suffer some form of loss. The believer shall still be saved, but through fire. Their salvation is assured, but the journey at that time is through fire rather than through faith.

Gold, silver, and precious stones representing materials that can go through the fire of God's judgment are only what is directly related to the triune God. Wood, hay, and straw (that cannot go through God's judgment) are related to humanity only, without the elements of the Trinity. Believers should care for the growing "seed of life" within them, which will only produce the indestructible material for God's building. If a believer neglects to grow and dispense life for building, then he or she is left with his original elements of wood, hay, or straw. Such a believer will suffer loss. Any suffering of loss at the day of judgment is not good news. After this suffering of loss, the person is still saved, but through the judging fire instead of being saved through faith in Jesus Christ. Although the end result is still salvation, the journey that this person will go through at that time will not be pleasant, since it is through fire.

This is a warning to believers, that though they have received the divine seed at regeneration, they are to continue to grow and produce Christ for the building up of the one body with all believers. This also shows that the standard of judgment for believers is whether they are producing precious materials for the building up of the assembly. (Refer back to the chapters on *Life* to understand how to grow.)

> For land that has drunk the rain that often falls on it, and produces a crop useful to those for whose sake it is cultivated, receives a blessing from God. But if it bears thorns and thistles, it is worthless and near to being cursed, and its end is to be burned.
>
> – Hebrews 6:7–8, ESV

In the context of these verses, the "land" is clearly referring to genuine believers that have "tasted the heavenly gifts" and "shared in the Holy Spirit" (Heb. 6:4). The land (believers) that has received God's blessing of grace should be producing food for building up, but instead the writer of Hebrews says it produces thorns and thistles. At judgment, these believers are near to being cursed. Though not actually cursed (since they are saved), they will still suffer a sort of "fire" or "burning." The standard shown for judgment here is related to producing something that can feed others for building up.

> And the Lord said, "Who then is the faithful and wise steward, whom his master will set over his household, to give them their portion of food at the proper time? Blessed is that servant whom his master when he comes will find so doing. Truly, I say to you, he will set him over all his possessions. But if that servant says to himself, 'My master is delayed in coming,' and begins to beat the menservants and the maidservants, and to eat and drink and get drunk, the master of that servant will come on a day when he does not expect him and at an hour he does not know, and will punish him, and put him with the unfaithful. And that servant who knew his master's will, but did not make ready or act according to his will, shall receive a severe beating.
>
> – Luke 12:42–47, RSV

In this parable, Luke describes a faithful and wise steward. This steward's master honored him for dispensing and serving food to the master's household in due season. Referring back to Chapter 11 on *oikonomia*, this was a faithful steward in God's economy: he provided food regularly to grow God's household. The unfaithful servant should not be considered an unbeliever, since he considers the Lord "my master" who will come back. He even knew his master's will. Certainly an unbeliever would not consider the Lord as his master and would not know His will. Instead of feeding the household, however, the unfaithful steward mistreated his fellow servants; therefore, his portion at the Lord's coming back is punishment, even a severe beating.

In the three scriptural portions above, the standard of judgment for believers seems clear: it is based on the divine seed that they have received growing to maturity, and the feeding through service or ministry to God's people. This standard is very different from law keeping according to the old covenant; rather, it relates to life receiving and life dispensing in the new covenant. The Lord has done everything. His anger and judgment is then toward those who do not continue to receive by faith all that He has accomplished and to serve God in love as food to the needy in the world.

The goal of the last part of this chapter is to wake up and motivate believers. Although the new covenant is unilateral and unconditionally fulfilled by God, this does not mean that believers receive a "free pass" no matter what they do after they are regenerated with the eternal divine life. It is precisely because God has done everything that His anger and judgment extends toward those who do not take advantage of it and enjoy all that He has already accomplished.

The parable in Matthew 22 describes a king who prepared a great feast. Everything was prepared, and people were invited to the feast at no charge. His anger was toward those who didn't come to take freely all that He had prepared for them to enjoy. Certainly this parable can be interpreted toward unbelievers, but it sets the same principle even toward believers. The Lord is still calling His believers to dine with Him as seen in Revelation 3:20. God is after believers who will continue to receive by faith all that He has accomplished and is now rightfully theirs as bequests. It is this continual receiving of His riches that causes believers to build up the one body of Christ and grow to maturity. Believers will be judged by how much they have matured through the receiving and enjoying of His riches.

Simultaneously, the receiving of His riches is integrated with and dependent on the believers dispensing of His riches as stewards to others around them. God is a sharing and giving God; therefore, those that are truly growing in Him must also share and give to others. This dispensing of His riches is what will cause His assembly to be built up (the one body expressed practically) and fulfill His eternal purpose. Therefore, the believers' judgment is also based on their faithfulness to be a dispenser of the unsearchable riches of Jesus Christ. In the new covenant God has done everything; believers now have the privilege and responsibility to enjoy and dispense what they have received, to take in and give out. This is completely different from the standard for judgment in the old covenant.

When the Lord Jesus returns to judge and to bring in His kingdom, His kingdom will last a thousand years before the ending of time and the beginning of eternity (Rev. 20). At the Lord's return, the resurrection of all believers will occur, and, together with those that are still alive, they will be judged before Him. Some Bible teachers have suggested that it is during the millennial (1000 years) kingdom that the faithful believers will "rule and reign" with Christ, while the unfaithful believers will use this time to grow to maturity, as described by phrases in the verses above: "saved through fire," "near a curse," and "receive punishment." This is an additional topic that this book is not focused on.

For now, calling attention to these verses raises the possibility that believers (though saved) should not be passive and lethargic concerning the coming judgment; rather believers need to wake up and rise up to be well-pleasing to the Lord by being full participants in the new covenant, growing to spiritual maturity, and contributing to fulfill the Lord's desire for the oneness of all His believers as prayed for in John 17.

Practice: Teaching

Write down something new that you learned from this lesson:

Describe what you can practically apply in your life:

Think of a person, and what you want to teach that person from this lesson.

Part 3

ONE IN HIS GLORY, HIS MINISTRY

(Chapters 15–18)

> "And the glory which You gave Me I have given them, that they may be one just as We are one:
>
> —John 17:22

As the Son of God in the Godhead, Jesus did not need to receive glory. He possessed glory from eternity to eternity. John 1:14 says that after Jesus became man, the disciples "beheld His glory, the glory as of the only begotten of the Father." Jesus in His divinity, as the Son of God, did not need to receive glory from God the Father.

When Jesus Christ became a man, He laid aside His glory of divinity and became a lowly man, even a slave. He served God and man unto death — the death of the cross. He resurrected on the third day, and in His ascension, He was crowned with glory and honor (Heb. 2:9). It was this glory that was given to the believers that they might be one even as the Father and the Son are one (John 17:22).

For the believers to receive this glory from the Lord Jesus Christ means that He, as the first man to receive this glory, will lead the believers on the same pathway to glory. Since He has already pioneered the way, He comes into His believers with this glory and leads them (Heb. 2:9–10). When believers follow Him on the same pathway, the result is glory. That is why He said to His disciples that if they wanted to follow him, they must pick up their own cross to follow Him (Matt 16:24). Certainly the believers' cross is not to die for redemption. The Lord Jesus was the only one that was qualified to die for the redemption of all creatures. He died once for all. The cross of the believers is to follow Him in the service to God and man. Just as He served God and man by the ministry of life for the building up of the assembly, believers need to and can do the same. Unlike Jesus, however, who went first through the entire process of the cross before receiving glory, believers already possess His glory. It is this glory that empowers believers to bear the cross and serve. Whoever would bear this cross to be a servant can be one with all other believers. If not, it is inevitable, at a certain point, this person cannot be one with other Christians.

"Bearing the cross" is not suffering just for suffering's sake. It is not asceticism. It is not silently accepting mistreatment. It is service to God and man. The night Jesus prayed His last prayer in John 17 was the night He washed His disciples' feet (including Judas' feet — the one who betrayed Him). Washing feet was a normal occurrence in those days, and it was done by the lowliest of slaves. Jesus did this for His disciples and asked them to do the same to one another (John 13:14).

Washing each other's feet according to Jesus was a symbol of love for one another. Serving and caring for another shows the person's love. Jesus, knowing Judas would soon betray Him, still washed his feet. How hard it is for the person who was offended and disrespected to love the very person who made such an offense. How hard it is to serve that person. Naturally, it is actually impossible, but the Lord did that and more. This is the glory that He gave His believers. It is this glory that strengthens and empowers believers to follow and serve as He did.

What does God want and how can He be served? God desires all men to be saved and come to the full knowledge of the truth. The ministers are the ones who serve Christ to men so that they will be filled with the Holy Spirit and thereby become a living offering to God to satisfy God (Rom. 15:16). Ultimately God will have His eternal purpose fulfilled through the building up of His assembly, the men offered to Him (Eph. 3:10–11). Man's needs actually mirror God's needs. Yes, man (male and female) has various needs relating to poverty, health, and relationships, but his ultimate need is salvation — the eternal divine life of God for His eternal purpose. Therefore, serving God and man is really performing and working toward the same objective. When Christ is ministered for man's salvation, and the teaching of Jesus Christ is taught for growth with the purpose of building up the assembly, then both God and man are satisfied. The servants or workers have done their job.

Glory in Bearing Much Fruit

> But Jesus answered them, saying, "The hour has come that the Son of Man should be glorified. Most assuredly, I say to you, unless a grain of wheat falls into the ground and dies, it remains alone; but if it dies, it produces much grain. He who loves his life will lose it, and he who hates his life in this world will keep it for eternal life. If anyone serves Me, let him follow Me; and where I am, there My servant will be also. If anyone serves Me, him My Father will honor."
>
> – John 12:23–26

The best thing for a physical seed is burial — "death" by being covered in dirt. If a seed does not "die", then it remains alone. However, if it dies, it will resurrect, not by itself, but with many other seeds just like it. The glory of the seed, then, is its fruit. All the beautiful and tasty fruit that appears is just the duplication of the seed that was planted. Before a seed is planted, it typically does not appear beautiful. It is just a seed. But after its death and resurrection, fullness of beauty manifests: a tree laden with fruit.

In the same way, the Lord's suffering and death was not just for redemption but imparting life. His ultimate service was not simply dying for man's sins, but to give man life. His purpose was to reproduce many others just like Himself as brothers. Those produced through His death and resurrection would be His duplicates, bearing His image and likeness (Rom 8:29). This is not only redemption for the forgiveness of sins but also regeneration for an assembly of believers as God's family, the body of Christ. This is for the building up of the assembly, which was God's eternal purpose in the beginning. This built up assembly is to the praise of His glory (Eph. 1:12; 3:21).

Now this glory is given to believers, which means they are to follow the Lord in the same path to glory. When believers are told to serve and follow the Lord in John 12:25–26, they must also not love this life of the world, or have the glory of this world, but be willing to serve as Jesus did and produce much fruit. In John 15, the Lord told His believers exactly this. He told them that they are all branches in the vine, and each branch needs to produce and bear fruit. It is through this fruit that the Father is glorified (John 15:8) as the caretaker and source of the vine. This glory produced through bearing fruit brings in the fullness of joy (15:11), and it is the manifestation of love for one another (15:12).

Although believers cannot suffer for redemption, but like Jesus, believers can suffer with Him for the bearing of remaining fruit, which is for the building up of His body. The apostle Paul in Colossians 1:24 said that he rejoiced in his suffering and that he was filling up that which was lacking in the afflictions of Christ for His body, the assembly. From a human point of view, there is only one similar kind of affliction which involves rejoicing while in anguish, and that is childbirth. Jesus used this exact metaphor for rejoicing in suffering in John 16:21–22. Women undergo much affliction and suffering to bring a child in to the world, but all is worth it once the baby is born. This is the "rejoicing in suffering," the suffering of "death" that believers should participate in, and through it to share in the same glory of producing much fruit.

Ministering Christ to others so that Jesus Christ might be reproduced and grow in people is the highest service to both God and man. This is to bear and produce remaining fruit resulting in full maturity in Christ (Col. 1:28–29). This glorious service requires the attitude of a humble servant. It is not just a matter of preaching or motivating people at an "altar call" to come forward to receive Jesus Christ. It is a continuing service like that of a nursing mother, cherishing people in a very practical way, serving them for the sake of the dispensing of the grace of Jesus Christ to them. People that are served practically by those in this pathway to glory will become open to receive Jesus as their Lord and Savior, and as a result, grow in Christ.

When this attitude and view of glory takes hold of believers, they will treat everyone around them, whether believers or non-believers, in the way of Jesus Christ: not as a lord, but as a servant. This is the loving and esteeming of others. It means being willing to be wronged by others and taking the status of a slave that has no ground to be offended. It involves feeding and caring for others. A person in this place of glory will not cause friction with other believers; rather, this person is one with all believers as a servant.

The Need to Be Faithful

> Let a man so consider us, as servants of Christ and stewards of the mysteries of God. Moreover, it is required in stewards that one be found faithful.
> — 1 Corinthians 4:1–2

In this part of the book, the matter of being a minister in the Lord's ministry will be considered. The most popular Greek word for "minister" is diakonos, which means, "a servant," or "one who executes the command of another." The other Greek word used is hypēretēs, which literally means, "the under-rower," or the subordinate who is doing the rowing of a boat. Thus, a minister works for both God and man in service. Just as Jesus was a servant to both God and man, so should all believers.

Faithfulness is one of the basic requirements of a servant. The word "faithful" in 1 Corinthians 4:1–2 means to be reliable, dependable, or trustworthy. It is not the amount of service one has undertaken that counts, but that no matter how little one has undertaken, service is carried out faithfully. A person can be faithful in a few things and still receive a reward from the Lord (Matt. 25:21). In this part of service and ministry, this needs to be kept in mind and before the Lord. In just about all the service items described in which a believer can participate, they are not burdensome or hard to do. The requirement is whatever action one decides to take, he or she should practice faithfully; otherwise, the result will be minimal or disappointing.

For example, if there is a leading from the Lord to pray for a few people, then pray — if not everyday — at least once a week. If not for an hour, then try to pray at least a couple of minutes. The same can be said concerning visitation. If one can't take time out to visit every week, then how about visiting once a month? The point of faithfulness here is consistency in service. Then the Lord will have a way to work and produce results within your service.

Being a Minister in Four Stages

This part on service or ministry is divided into four stages of service:

The First Stage

The first stage is accomplished through a begetting father, as Paul said about himself in 1 Corinthians 4:15: "...I have begotten you through the gospel." Through the gospel, Paul ministered the eternal life to people, and they became born anew. That was his service as a father: to beget life.

The Second Stage

The second stage is accomplished with Paul and his co-workers. In 1 Thessalonians 2:8 Paul said that he and the disciples were as nursing mothers. The function of a nursing mother is to cherish and nourish new and young believers that they may grow. Paul didn't just bring forth new birth through his gospel, but he wanted to help the new believers grow through ministry: acting as nursing mothers, caring for young believers over a period of time.

The Third Stage

In the third stage, Paul functioned as a father again, exhorting and encouraging the growing believers. This is the stage of discipling believers toward serving and working as the apostles, learning to do what the apostles are doing. In this function, the believers are being called and encouraged to work and serve alongside those that are discipling.

The Final Stage

The final stage is the work of building up the assembly. The first three stages lead to this final stage, which is the building up of the one body of Christ. Paul said in 1 Corinthians 3:10 that he was the "master builder," building up the temple of God, which is the house of God — the body of Christ, the assembly. As the master builder, he encouraged all the believers to build up the local assembly with him. All believers should be co-workers and co-builders with Paul to build up the assembly.

15

MINISTRY: SPEAKING TO PROPAGATE CHRIST

Believers Have a Unique Service

Many people, including unbelievers and sinners, do a variety of good works for humanity. Believers should also remember to serve the poor and do what they can toward improving society; but the highest and best service that believers can provide to humanity that no one else can provide, not even the angels, is to minister Christ to people — that they may receive faith and have eternal life by being begotten of God. Believers are the only ones on earth today that have such a privilege and responsibility to minister Christ to all people around them. This is the propagation of Christ: believers begetting more believers, to be sons of God.

Just as life is defined by the ability to reproduce itself, God, having the divine and eternal life and being the *real* life, also reproduces. It is God's desire and pleasure to have many children, many sons of God. It is through this proliferation of His life that He is expressed, and His enemy is defeated and put to shame. God's salvation for men is much more than whether or not a person is going to heaven after they die. God's salvation is to give man the very heavenly, divine, eternal life — moment by moment — that they might live and enjoy Him as children of God *today*.

It is an utterly amazing mystery that the way for the eternal life of God to be transferred to men is only through faith. And people cannot work up this faith; this faith is a gift of God that is transmitted as people hear the wonderful things concerning Jesus Christ. The greatest gift in the entire universe is free, and there is nothing anyone can "do" to deserve it. There is power in speaking of Jesus Christ being both God and man and speaking of the work of His crucifixion and resurrection. This kind of speaking brings faith and thus salvation to the hearer.

Every believer, the instant they receive Jesus Christ as their Savior, has the privilege and the responsibility to spread the good news of Christ to others around them that they may come to salvation. There is no training needed, no methods to learn; they are only to speak the Christ they have heard and received. The spreading of Christ to others is called "fruit bearing." Every believer is called to do this service.

As believers present the person and work of Christ to others, the God of glory will have a way to appear and call more people to Himself. The believer's job is not to have all the answers for skeptics or to convince people concerning Christ; they are simply to present and watch God's Spirit work in the hearers. Therefore, believers should always maintain a cordial relationship with friends and relatives, with the hope that they will have opportunities to speak Christ to them again and again.

The Propagation of the Life of Christ

God's purpose is the propagation of the life of Christ in order to beget many children. The definition and natural function of life is the cycle of metabolism and reproduction. Life is expressed and dominates through propagation.

> Then God said, "Let Us make man in Our image, according to Our likeness; let them have dominion over the fish of the sea, over the birds of the air, and over the cattle, over all the earth and over every creeping thing that creeps on the earth." So God created man in His *own* image; in the image of God He created him; male and female He created them. Then God blessed them, and God said to them, "Be fruitful and multiply; fill the earth and subdue it; have dominion over the fish of the sea, over the birds of the air, and over every living thing that moves on the earth."
>
> – Genesis 1:26–28

The first outstanding point revealed in Genesis 1:26–28 is that man (male and female) was created in God's image and likeness. God wanted to be expressed and manifested through man. Since man is in God's image and likeness, when people see man, they see God. That is the meaning of "expression." Man *expresses* God.

The second outstanding point is that man will have dominion and subdue the earth. There was something on the earth that needed subduing, and man was appointed to do this work and have dominion. Finally, God made clear how both of these intentions were to be carried out by man; man should be fruitful and multiply and fill the earth. In God's purpose, being fruitful and the multiplication of human life were critical to fulfilling His desires.

God is rich in every facet of His character. If there were only one man on the earth bearing His image and likeness, how small and insignificant would His expression on the earth be! By being fruitful, man multiplied himself to millions and billions. How rich is the expression of God!

If the evil aspect of man (because of the fall into sin) did not occur, then the various characteristics of love, care, honor, creativity, faithfulness, diligence, righteousness, and goodness in man expressing the attributes of God could be seen. When this man is spread throughout the earth due to generation upon generation of fruitfulness, then God is expressed in every corner of the earth.

God's intention in creating man (male and female) was that man would have dominion "…over all the earth" (Gen. 1:26). This phrase should already include *everything* that is on the earth, but God added, "and over every creeping thing." These "creeping things" must be something special in addition to all the creatures on earth.

This is a special category of creatures called out by God. In Genesis 3:14, God cursed the serpent to creep on his belly on the earth. Then in Revelation 12:9, John writes that the serpent is Satan — the devil — and he, along with his angels, were cast to the earth. This indicates Satan (the snake) is the leader of all the creeping things, including the demons and angels that followed him. God's intention is that man will be the one to defeat and have dominion over Satan, the "creeping thing." God didn't want to deal with Satan directly; that is the reason Satan is not afraid of God. This is revealed in Satan's freedom to approach God and challenge Him in the book of Job. Man was appointed by God to subdue and defeat Satan.

Again, dominion occurs through God's command to be "fruitful and multiply." As human beings, God's command for man to obtain dominion over all the earth is surely being fulfilled through the multiplication of human life on every continent on earth. Most importantly, God's desire is that man will ultimately defeat and subdue Satan through the multiplication of life.

> You did not choose Me, but I chose you and appointed you that you should go and bear fruit, and that your fruit should remain, that whatever you ask the Father in My name, He may give you.
>
> – John 15:16

In Genesis, created man became the old creation as a result of man's fall into sin. Man now expresses evil because of the fall, instead of expressing God. Instead of subduing and dominating Satan, man became allied with Satan and an enemy of God. Therefore, the Lord Jesus terminated the old and brought in a new creation in Himself (2 Cor. 5:17). This new creation started with the Lord Jesus Himself, and He brought forth much fruit (John 12:24). Now, based on His resurrection life, God is charging His believers as branches of the vine to go and bear remaining fruit.

This echoes what was spoken in Genesis when God told man to be fruitful and multiply. It is through fruit-bearing — the multiplication of the eternal life of Jesus Christ within humankind — that men are born anew: *a new creation.* Thankfully, the early believers took the Lord's charge and spread the Word, bearing fruit. Many generations and millions of believers on earth later, this new generation continues to bear remaining fruit.

Through fruit bearing and the multiplication of the divine life in man, the new creation (the new man — the body of Christ, the assembly) is realized. This is what the first man in Genesis failed to do: express God and subdue Satan. This corporate new man with Jesus Christ as the Head and all the believers as His body fulfills God's original intention with man. Through the body of Christ, God is fully expressed (Eph. 1:22–23) and Satan is destroyed (Luke 10:19; Rom. 16:20).

> And they sang a new song, saying: "You are worthy to take the scroll, and to open its seals; for You were slain, and have redeemed us to God by Your blood out of every tribe and tongue and people and nation, and have made us kings and priests to our God; and we shall reign on the earth."
>
> – Revelation 5:9–10

The many fruits born in every tribe, tongue, people, and nation become the kings and priests of God. This brings in God's kingdom to express His life and to reign on the earth for eternity. Here in Revelation, the conclusion of the Bible, God's eternal divine life has spread and multiplied into people of every tribe, tongue, and nation. Fruit- bearing through believers has reached every part of the earth. All those reached who have received God's life are made kings and priests to God. This mirrors the idea of God's purpose: dominion and expression. The "kings" are for dominion over enemies, and "priests" express God. Satan is subdued, and God is expressed. No wonder there is fullness of praise to the Lord Jesus Christ who has accomplished this!

The God–Man Life of Christ Spread to All Men

> For God so loved the world, that He gave His only-begotten Son, that whosoever believes into Him may not perish, but have eternal life. For God has not sent His Son into the world that He may judge the world, but that the world may be saved through Him.
>
>   – John 3:16–17

The common misconception about God is that He is a judge coming to condemn man. That is the opposite from the truth. The truth is that God loved man and sacrificed His most precious and dearest only-begotten Son for mankind. He didn't come to condemn man; man was already lost and condemned. God came to save man through Jesus Christ who died for all of God's beloved mankind.

Due to sin, man was already judged and marked for death. Jesus Christ came and saved man first by dying for man to save man from God's judgment of death and then to give man the eternal divine life through His resurrection. This is the propagation of life, the multiplication of life, from one man to millions of men.

> I [Jesus] have come that they may have life, and that they may have it more abundantly.
>
>   – John 10:10

Certainly the life spoken of in John 10:10 cannot be physical life since humankind was physically well and alive without the coming of Jesus Christ. The life John spoke of must be very special, and one only Jesus Christ can give. Some have interpreted this to mean a life of material blessing — that Jesus Christ came to give mankind a bigger house, a better car, and more money to spend. The problem with this interpretation is that Jesus Himself and all His disciples, as well as all the early apostles, did not gain material riches.

The abundant life Jesus came to give man is the eternal divine life of God, which is incomparably better than any material riches. This is consistent with the rest of the New Testament. Jesus Christ came through incarnation, crucifixion, and resurrection so that man may have God's eternal and divine life. His goal was not just to save man from condemnation, but also to provide man eternal life in abundance. This eternal life is not just in the future, something men need to wait for until after their death; this life is now. Jesus came that every believer may know, experience, grow, and reproduce fruit of this life now.

> ...who [God] desires all men to be saved and to come to the knowledge of the truth.
>
>   – 1 Timothy 2:4

Paul unveils God's heart for man in 1 Timothy 2:4 — His loving, caring, and merciful heart for every man (male and female). God does not have any ill will or hurtful thoughts toward man...any man. God desires all men to be saved and not to perish; therefore, He needs His believers to reach all men, so that all men may know the truth and come to salvation. Based on this verse, believers do not need to decide to whom God has chosen to preach the gospel, or to whom to teach the truth, since God has no such preference. He desires all men to be saved.

The Increase and Duplication of Christ

> But as many as received him [Jesus Christ], to them gave he *the* right to be children of God, to those that believe into his name; who were born, not of blood, nor of the will of the flesh, nor of the will of man, but of God.
>
> — John 1:12–13, DBY

What does it mean to be saved, to have the eternal divine life? It is to be born of God. How can man be born of God? Men are born of God by receiving Jesus Christ and believing into His name. To receive the Lord Jesus is to believe into His name. The immediate result is that the person is born of God — that is, they receive God's life. Since believers have God's life, they have the birthright to be children of God. There is no other condition to be a child of God other than to receive Him — to believe into the name of Jesus. It is this simple faith in Jesus that gives all His believers the new birth in Christ. Jesus Christ is the good news that must reach all men.

> ...having predestined us to adoption as sons by Jesus Christ to Himself, according to the good of His will.
>
> — Ephesians 1:5

"Adoption" does not accurately translate the Greek word *huiothesia* used by Paul in Ephesians 1:5. *Huiothesia* is a compound word made up of "son" — an offspring by birth — and "appoint" which means, "to set in place."

The normal understanding of "adoption" is merely a legal procedure without the birth of a genuine offspring, whereas the Greek word clearly defines believers as sons by birth with God's life. However, believers also have a place in maturity — a legal standing — to be God's appointed sons. This is the Father's will. How great and wonderful is Father God, who has begotten millions upon millions of sons, who have matured for the universe to glorify the Father in His many sons.

> For whom He [God] foreknew, He also predestined to be conformed to the image of His Son, that He might be the firstborn among many brethren.
>
> — Romans 8:29

God's children are the many brothers of Jesus Christ. The destiny of all God's children is that they will be conformed to have the exact image of God's firstborn son, Jesus Christ. Those who follow Jesus are His exact reproduction; they may not look like or act like it now, but one day, all believers will bear the same image as Jesus Christ, their eldest Brother.

Jesus Christ as the "firstborn" refers to both His divinity and humanity. The "only begotten Son" refers to His divinity alone and His position within the Trinity. Men, upon receiving the divine life, become brothers of the firstborn Son of God with both humanity and divinity.

The Faith to Receive Life Is Transfused through Speaking Christ

> But that no one is justified by the law in the sight of God is evident, for "the just shall live [alive] by faith."
>
> ...that the blessing of Abraham might come upon the Gentiles in Christ Jesus, that we might receive the promise of the Spirit through faith.
>
> For you are all sons of God through faith in Christ Jesus.
>
> – Galatians 3:11, 14, 26

Anyone would gladly pay any price to receive something so precious and unspeakably costly as the life of God and to become a son of God. If the price is not material riches, then at least man should pay by being a good person and obeying God's laws. While inconceivable to man, God's desire is to give His life to man at no charge and with no precondition. In fact, it is His good pleasure to give His eternal life to man freely. The conduit and means of receiving the eternal divine life is simply *faith*. This is mysterious, yet true! It is uniquely the simple faith in Jesus Christ that makes a person righteous and alive through the Spirit; they are born anew as sons of God. There are no other conditions or requirements other than faith in Jesus Christ. This can never happen by attempting to fulfill God's law. Even while sinners, the faith in Jesus Christ transferred believers from being condemned to being the righteous, living sons of God.

Hearing the Word: Christ

Faith with regenerating power comes through hearing the Word, which is Jesus Christ.

> For by grace you have been saved through faith, and that not of yourselves; it is the gift of God.
>
> – Ephesians 2:8

Even the faith needed to believe into Jesus Christ is not something a person can create. Faith is not of the person; rather, it is a gift of God. A person can't even take credit and boast that it was their ability to believe. Faith is a gift that comes to people from God. This is just amazing!

People may think, "Okay, I don't have to pay for God's life, but surely I need to pay for faith." Or, they may think, "Well, faith is the hard part because I just can't believe all this stuff about Jesus Christ and eternal life." There is more good news for people! There is no need to try to believe or work up faith on their own...they can just let it happen!

> So faith comes from hearing, and hearing through the word of Christ.
>
> – Romans 10:17, ESV

Ministry: Speaking to Propagate Christ | 295

This gift of faith is transmitted from God through hearing, and it is the Word of Christ that the person hears that gives them faith. As a person hears things of Christ, something in them stirs, and they start to appreciate the Christ that they are hearing. On the one hand, there may be protests within them, making them believe they are hearing a fairy tale that cannot possibly be true. On the other hand, that person is being drawn and attracted; it is the beginning of faith percolating in the deepest part of their being. At a certain point in their hearing, they will react by receiving and calling on the name of the Lord Jesus whether it is the very first time or after many times. In any case, faith is getting through. After that, faith takes root, and not believing is no longer an option.

For believers who are speaking the good news of Jesus Christ, there must be confidence that God is working whenever Jesus Christ is preached: Who He is and what He has accomplished. If believers have this confidence, they don't need to be anxious about whether they are preaching properly or with the correct "technique." They can trust the working of the Spirit and the hearing of faith. They don't need to argue or try to convince the person. Their responsibility is to present Jesus Christ as best they can and allow the hearing of faith to work in the listener.

> This only I want to learn from you: Did you receive the Spirit by the works of the law, or by the hearing of faith? Are you so foolish? Having begun in the Spirit, are you now being made perfect by the flesh?
>
> Therefore He who supplies the Spirit to you and works miracles among you, does He do it by the works of the law, or by the hearing of faith?
>
> – Galatians 3:2–3, 5

These questions from Paul were rhetorical. The answer for whether the Galatians received the Spirit by works of the law or by faith was obvious: it was the hearing of faith. It is also the hearing of faith that daily supplied the Spirit for the Galatians.

Believers begin by the hearing of faith, and continue the Christian journey also by the hearing of faith. A person's own works or effort does not give them the new birth, nor does it provide the continuous supply of the Spirit. Many believers mistakenly think (under deception of even Bible teachers) that after becoming a Christian, they then need to keep God's laws. If they do not, God will withhold His blessings from them, and they will lose God's favor. This was the case with the Galatians. They drifted back to keeping the law under the influence of some Jewish Christian teachers. Paul was fighting for them to come back to faith. Believers started their journey in faith and should continue in the same faith.

> Truly, truly, I say to you, whoever hears my word and believes him who sent me has eternal life. He does not come into judgment, but has passed from death to life. Truly, truly, I say to you, an hour is coming, and is now here, when the dead will hear the voice of the Son of God, and those who hear will live.
>
> – John 5:24–25, ESV

It may be the first time a person has heard the Word of Christ, or it may be the hundredth time, but at a certain point, faith is generated in the person through their hearing. They

296 | ONE: Unfolding God's Eternal Purpose from House to House

appreciated the Word that was heard and started to believe in Jesus Christ. At that point, they cannot help but believe, and they were born anew and now live.

It is interesting to note that hearing takes the least effort, when compared to eating, drinking, or even breathing. There is not even a muscle relating to hearing. Even with breathing, a little effort is needed! But hearing is so easy and effortless that even "the dead" can hear His voice and live. This is the greatest miracle of the gospel: dead men receive life and live.

> ...having been born again, not of corruptible seed but incorruptible, through the word of God which lives and abides forever.
>
> — 1 Peter 1:23

As people hear the Word of Christ, His Word comes into their being and they are born again, or born anew. Even though fallen man was condemned to death, God did everything to save man. The only thing man needs to do is stop and hear the good news of God's salvation — Jesus Christ. They don't even need to agree or try to believe. Even in their skepticism, they just need to hear, consider the Word, and let it sink in to do its work of generating faith in them. It is effortless and simply amazing!

Speaking the person and work of Christ transmits faith and life into others. An example of Jesus speaking to unveil Himself may be found in John 8:28–30, where Jesus spoke of Himself as the "Son of Man" and the "I AM," — the name of God.

> Jesus therefore said to them, When you shall have lifted up the Son of man, then you shall know that I AM, and that I do nothing of myself, but as the Father has taught me I speak these things. And he that has sent me is with me; he has not left me alone, because I do always the things that are pleasing to him. As he spoke these things many believed on him.
>
> — John 8:28–30, DBY

In the Old Testament, God's name was unveiled as "I Am" meaning "self-existing" and "ever-existing." Here in John 8:28–30, Jesus also spoke of His crucifixion. As He spoke these things concerning Himself, who He is and what He is to do, faith was transmitted and many believed.

The First Gospel Message

The first gospel message, declared by Peter, concerned Jesus Christ:

> "Men of Israel, hear these words: Jesus of Nazareth. ..., — Him, being delivered by the determined purpose and foreknowledge of God, you have taken by lawless hands, have crucified, and put to death; whom God raised up, having loosed the pains of death, because it was not possible that He should be held by it.
>
> "... he, foreseeing this, spoke concerning the resurrection of the Christ, that His soul was not left in Hades, nor did His flesh see corruption. This Jesus God has raised up, of which we are all witnesses. Therefore being exalted to the right hand of God, and having received from the Father the promise of the Holy Spirit, He poured out this which you now see and hear."

> "Therefore let all the house of Israel know assuredly that God has made this Jesus, whom you crucified, both Lord and Christ." Now when they heard this, they were cut to the heart, and said to Peter and the rest of the apostles, "Men and brethren, what shall we do?" Then Peter said to them, "Repent, and let every one of you be baptized in the name of Jesus Christ for the remission of sins; and you shall receive the gift of the Holy Spirit."
>
> – Acts 2:22–24, 31–33, 36–38

This is the first gospel message after the Lord's death and resurrection. It is full of description concerning Jesus (both God and man), His work of crucifixion, resurrection, and ascension, and how as a man He is also made both Lord and Christ. The speaking of this complete gospel message caused men to believe, repent and be immersed into Jesus Christ.

Those who asked Peter "what shall we do?" must have received faith already as they were hearing the gospel of Jesus Christ. They started to see with the eyes of faith that the One that they have crucified is now the Lord and Christ in resurrection. Their question was initiated by the faith that was being infused into the deepest part of their being through the hearing concerning Jesus Christ.

Answering, Peter said to them "repent." Repent or repentance means a change of mind or purpose (Vine's Expository Dictionary). At one time, those without faith were thinking that Jesus was nothing, their purposes were not of God, and they were shutting out the Spirit. Now they need to repent: to treasure Jesus Christ, to be for God's purpose, and to receive the Holy Spirit. Repentance is not to turn from evil to good, but to turn from idols to God, from death to life, and from sin to grace.

Although repentance is a gift from God (Acts 5:31; 11:18), it also needs cooperation from those receiving faith. Repentance includes making a reversal or change in the actions or directions in one's life based on a change in thinking. The first action they took was baptism, which was a distinct change in direction for them at the time. Each believer needs an initial repentance as in Acts 2, but repentance should continue throughout the Christian life whenever one is distracted away from God (Rev 2:5). The stronger the repentance or the more drastic steps that are taken to change direction, the deeper the faith in experiencing more love, joy, peace and power of the Holy Spirit.

The Apostle Paul's Gospel

> For we do not preach ourselves, but Christ Jesus the Lord, and ourselves your bondservants for Jesus' sake. For it is the God who commanded light to shine out of darkness, who has shone in our hearts to give the light of the knowledge of the glory of God in the face of Jesus Christ.
>
> – 2 Corinthians 4:5–6

> Moreover, brethren, I declare unto you the gospel which I preached unto you, which also ye have received, and wherein ye stand; By which also ye are saved, if ye keep in memory what I preached unto you, unless ye have believed in vain.

> For I delivered unto you first of all that which I also received, how that Christ died for our sins according to the scriptures; And that he was buried, and that he rose again the third day according to the scriptures.
>
> ~ 1 Corinthians 15:1–4

Paul preached Christ Jesus the Lord. As Christ Jesus the Lord was presented, God did the work of shining in the darkened heart of the hearer. This light was the very seeing of Jesus Christ in the gospel. As Paul preached the simplicity of His person, crucifixion and resurrection, the hearer received faith and was saved.

Speaking to Minister Christ

Every believer has the privilege and responsibility to bear fruit for God's purpose, through speaking, to minister Christ and continue His ministry.

> Jesus said to them again, "Peace be with you. As the Father has sent me, even so I am sending you." And when he had said this, he breathed on them and said to them, "Receive the Holy Spirit. If you forgive the sins of any, they are forgiven them; if you withhold forgiveness from any, it is withheld."
>
> – John 20:21–23

This is a clear message in John 20:21–23 from Jesus Christ that believers are to continue His mission. Just as He was sent by the Father with the Spirit to accomplish God's eternal purpose, Jesus is sending those who believe in Him in the same way, with the Spirit. Not only do believers have the life of the Spirit, but they also have the authority of the Christ that is on the throne. He is sending believers with the life and power of the Holy Spirit; when they speak Christ as faith into people, and people believe and receive Jesus as the Savior, their sins are forgiven. Not bringing the good news of Jesus Christ to others, or if people do not receive the words of Christ, results in people remaining in their sins. What an awesome privilege and responsibility that the Lord has given all His believers! This mission is not just for a few elite Christians or trained professionals; rather, everyone who has received the Spirit through faith has the God-given and innate capability to fulfill this directive from the Lord.

> ...because of the hope which is laid up for you in heaven, of which you heard before in the word of the truth of the gospel, which has come to you, as *it has* also in all the world, and is bringing forth fruit, as *it is* also among you since the day you heard and knew the grace of God in truth.
>
> – Colossians 1:5–6

Paul's use of the phrase, "bringing forth fruit" in Colossians 5:6 clearly refers to the people who have heard "the word of the truth of the gospel." When a person hears this word and receives faith, they know the grace of God in truth. Such a person is a fruit of the gospel. In every generation, and in every place, a harvest of such fruit is needed. Therefore, it is the believer's privilege and responsibility to spread and speak the word of the truth of the gospel.

> And the things that thou hast heard of me among many witnesses, the same commit thou to faithful men, who shall be able to teach others also.
>
> – 2 Timothy 2:2

Here five generations of passing on the Word of the truth can be seen. It was through the speaking of faithful men that people heard the truth and became believers. Now it is this generation's responsibility to find more faithful men to pass on what has been learned and enjoyed of Jesus Christ, so that more faithful men will in turn teach others. Each one should have the clear realization that this is not the end or the terminal point; rather, believers are channels. If the believer does not become a channel to pass on to others what they are hearing and learning of Christ, they will become a "dead sea," devoid of life.

Each Believer Is a Branch in the Vine to Bear Fruit

> I am the true vine, and My Father is the vinedresser. Every branch in Me that does not bear fruit He takes away; and every branch that bears fruit He prunes, that it may bear more fruit.
>
> I am the vine, you are the branches. He who abides in Me, and I in him, bears much fruit; for without Me you can do nothing.
>
> – John 15:1–2, 5

A vine is basically all of the branches combined together. Without branches, the plant is just a stump and not a vine. The believers are the "branches" making up the entire vine: Christ. Jesus Christ as the vine is being cultivated by the Father to bear much fruit for His glory. This is the Father's goal: to have a fruitful vine. The duty of each branch of this vine is to bear fruit. If a branch does not bear fruit, it is devoid of the supply and enjoyment of the vine. It is a blessing when a branch bears fruit and a loss when it does not. The believer has the responsibility and privilege to supply other people with Christ, so that they too may be borne as fruit — His increase — for the Father's enjoyment and pleasure.

Fruit bearing also brings joy to the Lord, resulting in the believer's fullness of joy:

> These things I have spoken to you, that My joy may remain in you, and that your joy may be full.
>
> – John 15:11

Bearing fruit — bringing people to know and enjoy Jesus Christ — is the Lord's joy, and it is the believer's *fullness* of joy. Luke 15:7 states there is more "joy in heaven" over one sinner coming to Christ than ninety-nine "righteous" persons. It is one of the greatest joys and causes for rejoicing that mere men and women could be instrumental in bringing someone to salvation and growth in the Lord. It is a real loss if a believer has not experienced this fullness of joy. Once a believer experiences the joy of ministering Christ to people, it can be "addicting." They will continually desire the fullness of joy resulting from the joy of the Lord in bringing men to salvation.

> By this My Father is glorified, that you bear much fruit; so you will be My disciples.
>
> – John 15:8

The Father is glorified because of the expression of His rich life through reproduction.

As the cultivator and even the source of the entire vine, the Father is truly glorified as the "much fruit" is borne. What a shame if a cultivator tended to a vine but there was no fruit! The Father is expressed and glorified through His many sons as the fruit. A disciple, as defined by the Lord, is one who bears much fruit. Christians shouldn't be just His believers, but even more, His disciples.

Therefore, believers should take action to go and speak Christ to fulfill their commission!

> You did not choose Me, but I chose you and appointed you that you should go and bear fruit, and *that* your fruit should remain, that whatever you ask the Father in My name, He may give you.
>
> – John 15:16

What a privilege that believers are chosen and appointed to go and do His will of bearing remaining fruit, that people would be regenerated and continue to receive the supply of His life!

Beautifully, the word for "remain" in John 15:16, *menō,* is the same Greek word for "abide"; therefore, the fruit borne by the branches should be just like another branch that abides and also bears fruit. This echoes 2 Timothy 2:2, where Paul instructs believers to pass on the truth to faithful men who would teach others also. So when believers ask the Father for "whatever" in relation to doing the Lord's will of bearing remaining fruit, He may give to them.

Go and Spread the Good News Now

> Go therefore and make disciples of all the nations, baptizing them in the name of the Father and of the Son and of the Holy Spirit, teaching them to observe all things that I have commanded you; and lo, I am with you always, [even] to the end of the age." Amen.
>
> – Matthew 28:19–20

Immediately after the Lord promised He would always be with His people, He charged the disciples to go and make more disciples by baptizing and teaching them. No matter the obstacles in carrying out this charge, believers are assured that the Lord is with them through it all. In fact, it is in carrying out this charge, that believers experience His presence the strongest.

The meaning of "go" does not indicate believers are to journey somewhere other than where they already are to fulfill this charge. In the original Greek, "go" is the word *poreuō,* which means, "to pursue the journey on which one has entered" or "to continue on one's journey." Thus, when Jesus told the disciples to "go," he meant discipling was to start immediately as the believer went on their way. So whether believers are "going" at work, at home, or through their daily living, they can fulfill this charge of making disciples. Disciples don't have to go to a foreign land to be a missionary; discipling starts now, regardless of location, concurrent with the believer's daily life.

> After these things the Lord appointed seventy others also, and sent them two by two before His face into every city and place where He Himself was about to go. Then He said to them, "The harvest truly [is] great, but the laborers [are] few; therefore pray the Lord of the harvest to send out laborers into His harvest. Go your way; behold, I send you out as lambs among wolves."
>
> – Luke 10:1–3
>
> Do you not say, 'There are still four months and then comes the harvest'? Behold, I say to you, lift up your eyes and look at the fields, for they are already white for harvest!
>
> – John 4:35

The harvest refers to the gathering of fruit. All the people of this earth should be harvested for the Lord. God desires all men to be saved. How great is this harvest! As believers look at all the people around them, they should not assume certain people are not open or ready for receiving faith. With the Lord's eyes, it will be revealed that in fact they *are* ready to harvest. If the believer's goal is not to "convert" or convince but simply to speak Christ, and if they believe that the Word of Christ heard will work in the unbelievers, then they will indeed recognize people are ready to hear. It is important to pray for the more laborers, because there are too few when compared to such a great harvest.

Friends and Relatives Are Chosen

It is important for believers to start speaking to those closest to them both in relationship and in proximity.

> And the following day they entered Caesarea. Now Cornelius was waiting for them, and had called together his relatives and close friends.
>
> While Peter was still speaking these words, the Holy Spirit fell upon all those who heard the word.
>
> – Acts 10:24, 44

There is no need to wonder who is "chosen." The believer should consider at least all their relatives and close friends as chosen and speak Christ to them as if they are. Here, Cornelius invited all his relatives and close friends to hear the Word of Christ. As they were hearing, faith was activated, and the Holy Spirit fell upon all of them who heard the Word. The believer's responsibility is to pray for and speak Christ to relatives and friends. There is no need to argue or try to convince. The Spirit's job is to work in them to generate faith so that they can receive the Lord Jesus Christ and be saved.

Believers Should Start from Wherever They Are

> But you shall receive power when the Holy Spirit has come upon you; and you shall be witnesses to Me in Jerusalem, and in all Judea and Samaria, and to the end of the earth.
>
> – Acts 1:8

The place and time to start speaking Christ is here and now. Where were the disciples in Acts 1:8? They were in Jerusalem; they started right where they were and then extended themselves to Judea, Samaria, and to the ends of the earth. Many times believers grow discouraged from listening to Satan's lies, thinking that they need to go somewhere else to preach the gospel as a missionary. It is truly commendable to travel to a foreign land to be a missionary, but without going to a foreign territory, each believer has the great responsibility of speaking Christ in the place where they are currently and to those closest to them.

Everyone is qualified, starting from the youngest and the newest in Christ. It is important that believers guard themselves against letting past or present failures hinder them, or worry about saying something wrong. Instead, they should be bold and say, "Come and see."

Nothing Can Disqualify a Believer from Speaking Christ

> The woman then left her water pot, went her way into the city, and said to the men, "Come, see a Man who told me all things that I ever did. Could this be the Christ?" Then they went out of the city and came to Him.
>
> And many more believed because of His own word.
>
> — John 4:28–30, 41

The woman in John 4 had five husbands, but at this point she was simply living with another man; she would be considered a person living in sin. In spite of her current sinful situation, after receiving faith, she went and told others in her town about Jesus. Through her speaking she influenced many to come to Jesus, and eventually many became believers. Believers who have not yet overcome all their sins are still qualified to tell others about Jesus. Many times, the liar — Satan — convinces believers that because they are still struggling with sins and failures, they are not qualified to speak Christ. They may think, "How can I speak about Jesus being my Savior if I am still a failure myself, struggling with sin?"

Accepting the lie that a person needs to be a "good" Christian before they can preach the gospel, has kept many believers silent concerning Christ. In actuality, that in itself is a testimony — that those believers still struggling with sins can still have the joy of the Lord in speaking for the Lord! This does not mean believers should not grow and be transformed to His image; but how they grow and when they will be transformed is not in their timing and by their work, but altogether the Lord's. The believer's work is to speak Christ right where they are, just the way they are. The Lord can prune and cut away the unwanted parts, as people bear fruit. According to John 15, the Father does His pruning work to shape His children as they are bearing remaining fruit, and not before.

It is important to note that it was a woman and not a man, a sinner not a pious person, which was the first record in the gospels of a believer bringing the good news of Jesus Christ to people; this woman brought people to Jesus. This established the principle that *anyone* can bring people to the Lord through the gospel no matter who they are or their condition.

> Immediately he [Saul] preached the Christ in the synagogues, that He is the Son of God. Then all who heard were amazed, and said, "Is this not he who destroyed

> those who called on this name in Jerusalem, and has come here for that purpose, so that he might bring them bound to the chief priests?"
>
> — Acts 9:20–21

Saul, who was also called Paul (Acts 13:9), started preaching Christ's person immediately after receiving faith. That was why the people were amazed; just a couple of days prior he was persecuting Jesus, and now he was preaching Jesus. Saul was the one dragging Christians to prison and consented to the stoning of another believer. However, no matter how negative a person's past, as soon as they believe, they are qualified to start speaking Christ.

God Can Still Use Inaccurate Preaching of the Gospel

> Philip found Nathanael and said to him, "We have found Him of whom Moses in the law, and also the prophets, wrote — Jesus of Nazareth, the son of Joseph." And Nathanael said to him, "Can anything good come out of Nazareth?" Philip said to him, "Come and see."
>
> — John 1:45–46

The information Philip told Nathanael concerning Christ was not absolutely correct. Jesus was of Bethlehem and not Nazareth, and He was strictly not the son of Joseph. He was the Son of God of Mary. Nevertheless, Nathanael came to Jesus and became a believer. Therefore, do not be concerned with the accuracy of speaking. Many believers are silent concerning Christ, worried that they may not know enough or that they will say the wrong thing about Christ. The Lord can use any believer's speaking, even in its infancy and inaccuracy. What can be said for sure with one hundred percent accuracy is, "I have found Him" and "come and see."

Be Patient...It Is God's Timing

God called Abraham by appearing to him multiple times, but it took years before Abraham responded to God's calling. Thus, believers should not expect quick results either.

The gospel is a matter of attracting, not trying to convince or condemn. Believers should not argue and offend, so that it is easy to speak to people again at another time.

> And he said, "Brethren and fathers, listen: The God of glory appeared to our father Abraham when he was in Mesopotamia, before he dwelt in Haran,
>
> — Acts 7:2

> The people who sat in darkness have seen a great light, and upon those who sat in the region and shadow of death Light has dawned."
>
> — Matthew 4:16

The first record of the God of glory appearing to Abraham was in Mesopotamia. Abraham did not obey and follow God's calling there (Acts 7:2-7). It seems that it was Abraham's father not Abraham himself that took the first step to leave Mesopotamia and went to Haran. God then came and appeared to Abraham again to call him in Haran

(Gen. 11:31 – 12:4). It was at this point after many years since God's first appearance that Abraham followed God's calling. This shows that even Abraham, the "father of faith," did not follow God the first time he was called.

This can be the case with many unbelieving friends and relatives. It may take many years and multiple times of the God of glory appearing to them through the speaking Christ before faith is accepted and they believe to become a follower of Jesus. Jesus Christ is the great light that is attracting people in darkness. The believers' job is to shine out Christ in their living and in their speaking of Christ. It is up to the Lord's timing when and where those who are being prayed for and hearing Jesus will be attracted and come to Him. Therefore, be patient and be bold, but don't be "preachy," and don't argue to offend. As long as people are willing to hear Christ, they then have a chance to receive faith and become a believer of Jesus Christ.

Practice: Speaking Christ to Others

Every day this week make a decision to speak to someone – anyone – about Jesus Christ. Speak about anything concerning who He is and what He has done, even if it is for 1–2 minutes. You are not preaching, and you are not trying to convert, you just want to open your month to start saying something about how good Jesus is. Speak to your pet if there is absolutely no one available to speak to, because this practice is just to get your tongue loose in order to say something about Jesus.

You can even say something like this: "Hi (anyone)! I told God this week that I will do my best to say something about Jesus to one person. I just need a minute of your time (then proceed to say whatever is in your heart about Jesus).

You don't need a formulated message. You are simply letting the Spirit have a way to flow out of you, and the Spirit can flow even if you are saying things that are not exactly correct. You can always give your testimony of how you came to know Jesus. Certainly no one can argue with your testimony!

16

CHERISHING:
AN OPENING FOR THE WORD

Bearing Remaining Fruit

Every believer has been called to bear remaining fruit, which will in turn bear the next generation of fruit. To bear such remaining fruit means that after a person is born anew three matters are needed: Cherishing, nourishing, and exhorting or discipling.

> By this My Father is glorified, that you bear much fruit; so you will be My disciples.
>
> You did not choose Me, but I chose you and appointed you that you should go and bear fruit, and that your fruit should remain, that whatever you ask the Father in My name, He may give you.
>
> — John 15:8, 16

In the last chapter it was established that "bearing fruit" is the responsibility of every believer. This means ministering Christ to people, that more people would become sons of God, or if they are already believers, that they receive spiritual nourishment to grow to maturity through the faith of Jesus Christ. To glorify the Father and be designated as disciples by the Lord, believers must be fruit bearers.

Most Christians neglect this point. They think that if they practice being a Christian on their own and are active members in a local church, they are glorifying the Father and are a follower of the Lord. This is not so!

It is critical that every believer take up the call to bear fruit. God chose each person and appointed him or her with His authority to go and bear fruit — remaining fruit. The word for "remain" in the Greek is the same word for "abide," which is that a believer who abides in the Lord bears fruit. So, *remaining* fruit is *abiding* fruit that also *bears* fruit.

Every believer's responsibility is not just to lead others to the Lord to be regenerated, but also to lead people to the Lord who will continue for the rest of their lives in the Lord and will also bear remaining fruits. *This is life.* Life begets generation after generation; this is how life multiplies.

A preacher speaking the gospel to hundreds or even thousands of people at a time is good, but this is not what is emphasized here. Fruit bearing is related to a personal and relational caring and feeding of a person until they are established in the faith, can fend for themselves spiritually, and are able to do the service of fruit bearing as well. Even those that come to know the Lord through a preacher at an event or on TV need spiritual parenting from one or more believers until they reach maturity. Just like physical families, a set of parents gives birth and cares for a few children for many years until those children reach adulthood and beyond. It is a tremendous matter for each believer to have a similar view of fruit bearing in order to bring up spiritual children. The Lord preached to thousands, but He personally took care of twelve disciples including a few women for a period of three and a half years. Just as the human race has populated the entire earth through the multiplication of families, if every believer will simply grow their own spiritual family of Christ, there will be millions and millions of living and active believers on the earth.

If a believer would be open to take a look and consider, in every Christian gathering there are individuals that could use personal care and shepherding. There are individuals at various times that could use fellowship and prayer in a personal connection; yet, just being in a group does not automatically provide such care. They could be in a group and go through the "service" and the motion, and yet feel isolated and not receive the personal care needed. If those with a serving heart take notice, the Lord will lead them to such individuals to provide cherishing and nourishing. The opportunity to serve is everywhere if the heart is seeking and there is a willingness to take action.

> ...and so also were James and John, sons of Zebedee, who were partners with Simon. Jesus said to Simon, "Don't be afraid. From now on you will be catching people alive." When they had brought their boats to land, they left everything, and followed him.
>
> – Luke 5:10–11, WBT

When the Lord called Simon (Peter) to follow Him, the mission He gave Simon was that from then on, for the rest of his life on earth, he would be "catching people alive." Peter was to be like a fisherman for the Lord, catching men as fish. Unlike every fish (when caught fish die), people that are "caught" by the Lord come alive. They were actually dead *before* they were caught. No wonder Simon and the other fisherman with him left everything to follow the Lord. How much more glorious such a service and mission to catch men alive rather than fish! All believers are called with the same purpose.

Today with millions of believers, how many have followed the Lord's call to catch people alive? The majority of believers have been going to church for years; yet, they do not serve the Lord in the way of fruit bearing. They consider that to be the clergy's job, and that is why they are paid. They are the "professional shepherds." Believers need to wake up and hear the Lord's call to rise up to serve the Lord Jesus and the people around them.

> And the things that you have heard from me among [through] many witnesses, commit these to faithful men who will be able to teach others also.
>
> – 2 Timothy 2:2

In 2 Timothy 2:2, Paul describes the multiple generations of fruit bearing (passing on truth) that should occur from one generation to the next. Every believer who has heard the truth and received eternal life has a duty: to commit what he or she has received to faithful men, who will in turn teach others also. What would happen if Paul and the other disciples didn't find faithful men to commit what they had received? It would not have passed on to believers today. When every believer is not dormant, but is activated in this way, the spread of the gospel and the growth of believers will increase at an exponential rate, which is the pattern for every life form.

Cherishing: Tender Love and Care with the Intention to Nourish

To cherish is to "warm up" others in the humanity of Christ with tender love and care with the intention to nourish. A cherished person is comfortable, peaceful, happy and open; a person that is "warmed up" is ready to hear the truth of the gospel.

> But we were gentle among you, just as a nursing mother cherishes her own children. So, affectionately longing for you, we were well pleased to impart to you not only the gospel of God, but also our own lives [souls], because you had become dear to us.
>
> – 1 Thessalonians 2:7–8

Although a nursing mother's goal is to feed for life and the baby's growth, most of her time, energy, and attention are in fact focused on cherishing the baby. Paul and his co-workers were like such a mother, cherishing the new believers that they might remain and grow. Actually, cherishing others starts as soon as the believer recognizes they have been called to bear fruit as a nursing mother. Cherishing means fostering with tender care. Those that are cherished are happy, comfortable, and open to receiving nourishment. I remember that when my kids were babies, many times I had to act as if the food in the spoon was an airplane ready to fly into their mouth just to get them to eat. This "play" was actually my way of cherishing them to open their mouth to receive nourishment.

Being gentle means being mild and loving, even towards people who are difficult, stubborn, and hard to deal with. Many unbelievers are obstinate and argumentative when it comes to the gospel. Even when trying to help young and new believers to grow in the Lord, it is often difficult to feed and teach those young and new believers the truth until they grow to the point where they can eat and drink the Lord on their own. Just as a good mother would never get angry and reject her child for becoming dirty or making mistakes, believers who are nursing mothers (for the sake of fruit bearing) also should forgive and love the spiritual babes, including unbelievers when their words and actions are offensive or disappointing. If believers are to bear fruit, they need the gentleness of the Lord to continue cherishing those around them so that one day, they will become open to receive the gospel. They also need to cherish the younger and newer believers so that they will continue to feed on the Lord and grow. As long as believers want to minister Christ to bear remaining fruit, cherishing will continue. Since the matter of cherishing is so essential for fruit bearing, it will be the main focus of this chapter.

Nourishing: Feeding Others Christ through the Spirit and the Word

In addition to cherishing others, believers need to feed people Christ through the Spirit and the Word that they may partake of the divine life and nature.

> Husbands, love your own wives, even as the Christ also loved the assembly, and has delivered himself up for it, . . . For no one has ever hated his own flesh, but nourishes and cherishes it, even as also the Christ the assembly.
>
> – Ephesians 5:25, 29

The Lord is nourishing and cherishing His assembly — His believers — like a man takes care of his own body or as a husband lovingly cares for his wife. His "cherishing" is His loving care even to the point of sacrificing Himself for His wife, and His "nourishing" is His sanctifying work by the washing of water in the Word. As presented in previous chapters, this water represents the Spirit. As believers are filled with the Spirit, they are washed from within. A person's physical appearance reflects healthy nourishment (or the lack of it). To nourish someone spiritually, then, is to supply the Spirit in the Word to others. If an unbeliever takes in such a nourishing Spirit, that person is born anew with the Spirit. If believers receive the ministry of such nourishment in the Spirit, they will grow and become transformed into a glorious bride.

> So when they had eaten breakfast, Jesus said to Simon Peter, "Simon, son of Jonah, do you love Me more than these?" He said to Him, "Yes, Lord; You know that I love You." He said to him, "Feed My lambs." He said to him again a second time, "Simon, son of Jonah, do you love Me?" He said to Him, "Yes, Lord; You know that I love You." He said to him, "Tend My sheep." He said to him the third time, "Simon, son of Jonah, do you love Me?" Peter was grieved because He said to him the third time, "Do you love Me?" And he said to Him, "Lord, You know all things; You know that I love You." Jesus said to him, "Feed My sheep."
>
> – John 21:15–17

When Jesus first encountered Simon Peter, He called Simon Peter to catch people alive. Now in His last physical encounter with Simon Peter, Jesus asked him to feed and to care for His sheep — the people that were brought to the Lord and reborn in the divine life. First Simon Peter was to "catch" and bring people to the Lord; then, he was to feed them for growth. The way to love the Lord is to nourish and feed the Lord's people. Every believer who loves the Lord has the same request from the Lord: to bear remaining fruit by shepherding and feeding — cherishing, nourishing and exhorting.

Lambs may be considered new and young believers. Sheep are older (more mature) believers. Both the young and the more mature believers need nourishment; everyone who loves the Lord, even a newer believer, is qualified to nourish both the young and the mature.

Exhorting: The Father's Right and Responsibility

As a father that begets, there is the right and responsibility to exhort — to strongly encourage and admonish.

> Not as chiding do I write these things to you, but as my beloved children I admonish you. For if you should have ten thousand instructors in Christ, yet not

> many fathers; for in Christ Jesus I have begotten you through the glad tidings. I entreat you therefore, be my imitators.
>
> – 1 Corinthians 4:14–16

A father is one who begets, or gives birth. Spiritually, a father gives life to another through the gospel of Jesus Christ. Paul was not only a begetting father — he was also the nursing mother. He cherished the believers that he had begotten (as shown in the verses above). Since he gave birth, nursed and cherished the believers with gentleness, he was qualified to admonish, warn, and ask the believers to imitate him. Today, as during Paul's time, there are many instructors that can pass on Scripture or spiritual knowledge and tell people what to do, but what is needed are more begetting fathers able to bring forth children of God through the gospel, and to care for them until maturity.

> For you remember, brethren, our labor and toil; for laboring night and day, that we might not be a burden to any of you, we preached to you the gospel of God. You *are* witnesses, and God *also*, how devoutly and justly and blamelessly we behaved ourselves among you who believe; as you know how we exhorted, and comforted, and charged every one of you, as a father *does* his own children.
>
> – 1 Thessalonians 2:9–11

Paul didn't receive an appointment from an organization; he wasn't given a title of a "minister," "pastor," or "elder." It was completely out of love and life that he cared for the new believers in Christ. He didn't receive a salary to do this as a job. He worked night and day to support himself, in order to preach the gospel and shepherd the believers without being a burden to them. Just as when parents have a child physically, their life-style and behavior change for the sake of the child; likewise, when one takes up a burden to care for others in Christ, it affects their behavior, as it did Paul's. Being such a father, Paul exhorted and comforted the new and young believers as his own children.

To exhort someone does not mean telling them to do something that the believer himself is not doing; rather, to exhort is to ask someone being shepherded to do what the one shepherding him is doing. In the Greek, to "exhort" is the word *parakaleō* that means, "To call someone to come along side," or to participate in the same work or the same journey. A father's job in this sense is to encourage and ask those he is cherishing and nourishing to come alongside him to do the same work of begetting, and shepherding others in Christ for the building up of His body.

The Essential and Continuing Factor: Cherishing

Cherishing is the first essential and continuing factor to bear remaining fruit. Christ cherished mankind by coming down from His glory to serve man, and ultimately die for man — His ultimate service.

> But Jesus called them to Himself and said, "You know that the rulers of the Gentiles lord it over them, and those who are great exercise authority over them. Yet it shall not be so among you; but whoever desires to become great among

> you, let him be your servant. And whoever desires to be first among you, let him be your slave—just as the Son of Man did not come to be served, but to serve, and to give His life a ransom for many."
>
> — Matthew 20:25–28

A person who is cherishing is serving, and the one being cherished is being served. Think of a mother cherishing her baby: Her life centers on serving the baby. She will do whatever her child beckons. The rulers of the world expect others to serve them. Such rulers will never cherish their subjects. In the body of Christ, the more believers are able to serve others, the greater and more mature they are. This is completely opposite to both the secular and the religious world. If people desire to bear remaining fruit as the Lord desires, then they need such a serving heart of the Lord.

> Blessed are those servants whom the master, when he comes, will find watching. Assuredly, I say to you that he will gird himself and have them sit down to eat, and will come and serve them.
>
> — Luke 12:37

Isn't it amazing that the Lord Jesus in the coming kingdom will continue to serve His children? He came as a man to serve men through His death on the cross, to rid humanity of sin. He continues to serve His people by supplying them with all His riches in their spirit, and this will continue on into His kingdom.

Physically, a mother will continue to cherish her children and care for them with a serving heart even when her children are full grown and mature. So, too, in the future, will Jesus continue to serve the faithful believers at His table, that they might enjoy Him in His coming kingdom. What a cherishing Lord! The point here is that believers need to have such a serving heart as the Lord, one that never stops and never rests but continues into the kingdom.

> Who, being in the form of God, did not consider it robbery to be equal with God, but made Himself of no reputation, taking the form of a bondservant, *and* coming in the likeness of men. And being found in appearance as a man, He humbled Himself and became obedient to the *point of* death, even the death of the cross.
>
> — Philippians 2:6–8

Philippians 2:6–8 reveals the principle of cherishing: laying aside one's glory and honor and becoming a humble servant for the sake of caring for the needs of others. The Lord went from the highest position to the lowest, so that He could cherish and serve others, even those of the lowest status among people. How much have believers been cherished by the Lord! They were truly warmed up when they recognized His death on the cross solved all their problems of sin, death, Satan, and even self. Through this cherishing, believers open up to receive His nourishing.

Eating and Drinking with Sinners

The Lord practically cherished, and warmed up people around him, especially sinners, by eating and drinking with them.

> The Son of Man has come eating and drinking, and you say, 'Look, a glutton and a winebibber, a friend of tax collectors and sinners!'
>
> – Luke 7:34

> And the Pharisees and scribes complained, saying, "This Man receives sinners and eats with them."
>
> – Luke 15:2

> But when they saw it, they all complained, saying, "He [Jesus] has gone to be a guest with a man who is a sinner."
>
> – Luke 19:7

The Lord uses the best way to a man's heart: through his stomach. A good meal with people is the easiest and quickest way to make them happy. They feel cared for, open, and accepted. A good meal can also erase a lot of suspicion and bad feelings. Believers should learn from the Lord: Cherishing others for fruit bearing requires making opportunities to have meals with them. Note also that it was the religious people that condemned the Lord for having such meals with sinners. Religion is cold, strict, and impersonal, in contrast to the Lord who is warm, approachable, relaxed, personable, non-judgmental, and accepting.

Did Not Judge or Condemn Sinners

> Jesus said to her, "Go, call your husband, and come here." The woman answered and said, "I have no husband." Jesus said to her, "You have well said, 'I have no husband,' "for you have had five husbands, and the one whom you now have is not your husband; in that you spoke truly."
>
> – John 4:16–18

In this conversation, Jesus was full of gentleness and love for an adulterous woman. He could have called her a liar for saying that she did not have a husband, but he didn't. Even when he exposed her real shameful situation, there was not a tone or hint of condemnation. He accepted her, though she was immoral and lived a loose lifestyle for years. What cherishing! What is the rest of story? After this conversation, the woman received the Lord Jesus as the Living Water and was satisfied. Afterward, she told everyone in town to come and meet Jesus. He didn't ask her to leave her shameful relationship of living with a man outside of matrimony or to patch up her failed relationships. He just gave her "Living Water" to drink without any condition. This was the Lord's cherishing so that she could receive the nourishing.

> Then the scribes and Pharisees brought to Him a woman caught in adultery. And when they had set her in the midst, they said to Him, "Teacher, this woman

> was caught in adultery, in the very act. Now Moses, in the law, commanded us that such should be stoned. But what do You say?" This they said, testing Him, that they might have *something* of which to accuse Him. But Jesus stooped down and wrote on the ground with *His* finger, as though He did not hear. So when they continued asking Him, He raised Himself up and said to them, "He who is without sin among you, let him throw a stone at her first." And again He stooped down and wrote on the ground. Then those who heard *it*, being convicted by *their* conscience, went out one by one, beginning with the oldest even to the last. And Jesus was left alone, and the woman standing in the midst. When Jesus had raised Himself up and saw no one but the woman, He said to her, "Woman, where are those accusers of yours? Has no one condemned you?" She said, "No one, Lord." And Jesus said to her, "Neither do I condemn you; go and sin no more."
>
> – John 8:3–11

Religious people use fear and condemnation to manipulate those that are afraid of God's judgment. This is pretty much a universal tactic of all religions, successfully operating this way for centuries. But this is not the Lord Jesus' way. His way is to forgive and save sinful people from certain death. How cherishing! If believers are to spread the Lord Jesus to friends, relatives, and others, then they need to both enjoy and express the Lord's forgiveness to others. For bearing remaining fruit, believers should care for people without condemnation or judgment. People should feel comfortable and accepted when in a believer's presence. Then they will have a way to present Christ as the nourishment for regeneration and growth.

Forgave All Sin and Debts

> Then Peter came to Him and said, "Lord, how often shall my brother sin against me, and I forgive him? Up to seven times?" Jesus said to him, "I do not say to you, up to seven times, but up to seventy times seven. Therefore the kingdom of heaven is like a certain king who wanted to settle accounts with his servants. And when he had begun to settle accounts, one was brought to him who owed him ten thousand talents. But as he was not able to pay, his master commanded that he be sold, with his wife and children and all that he had, and that payment be made. The servant therefore fell down before him, saying, 'Master, have patience with me, and I will pay you all.' Then the master of that servant was moved with compassion, released him, and forgave him the debt. But that servant went out and found one of his fellow servants who owed him a hundred denarii; and he laid hands on him and took *him* by the throat, saying, 'Pay me what you owe!' So his fellow servant fell down at his feet and begged him, saying, 'Have patience with me, and I will pay you all.' And he would not, but went and threw him into prison till he should pay the debt. So when his fellow servants saw what had been done, they were very grieved, and came and told their master all that had been

> done. Then his master, after he had called him, said to him, 'You wicked servant! I forgave you all that debt because you begged me. Should you not also have had compassion on your fellow servant, just as I had pity on you?' And his master was angry, and delivered him to the torturers until he should pay all that was due to him. So My heavenly Father also will do to you if each of you, from his heart, does not forgive his brother his trespasses."
>
> – Matthew 18:21–35

Sometimes it is easier to forgive unbelievers than to forgive fellow Christians. The case above is a story about forgiving a fellow believer. Christians can be much more demanding and unforgiving toward their own brothers and sisters in Christ, because they think that they should know better. But those who care for fellow believers and help them to grow in the faith, must take this story to heart and have compassion to forgive the little things, in comparison, for what they have personally done that needs forgiveness. In caring for younger believers over a long period of time, it is inevitable that these less mature believers will do or say something that will offend the one doing the shepherding. At such a time, the shepherding one may want to give up on caring for them. However, if the goal is to bear remaining fruit, the shepherding one cannot give up. Therefore, it is important to take the Lord at His Word and forgive 490 times. It is pretty certain that cherishing occurs when forgiving a person that many times; the forgiving believer will be able to nourish the other person and help him to grow to maturity.

Received and Blessed Little Children

> Then they brought little children to Him, that He might touch them; but the disciples rebuked those who brought *them*. But when Jesus saw *it*, He was greatly displeased and said to them, "Let the little children come to Me, and do not forbid them; for of such is the kingdom of God. Assuredly, I say to you, whoever does not receive the kingdom of God as a little child will by no means enter it." And He took them up in His arms, laid *His* hands on them, and blessed them.
>
> – Mark 10:13–16

Jesus specifically cherished children. Who brought the little children? It must have been their parents who wanted Jesus to touch their sons or daughters. Because Jesus cared for and cherished the little children, He cherished the entire family — including the parents. As shown in previous chapters, God's salvation is for the entire family. He wants to see family-by-family come to salvation. Therefore, if believers are to cherish and lead a family to the Lord and to grow in the Lord, it is vital that they also cherish the *children* of the family, just as the Lord did. Sometime believers erroneously consider children to be a distraction when they try to minister the Lord to unbelievers or new believers. On the contrary, Jesus cherished them and in turn cherished the entire family.

A Good Listener to the Ignorant

> Now behold, two of them were traveling that same day to a village called Emmaus, which was seven miles from Jerusalem. And they talked together of all these things which had happened. So it was, while they conversed and reasoned, that Jesus Himself drew near and went with them. But their eyes were restrained, so that they did not know Him. And He said to them, "What kind of conversation is this that you have with one another as you walk and are sad?" Then the one whose name was Cleopas answered and said to Him, "Are You the only stranger in Jerusalem, and have You not known the things which happened there in these days?" And He said to them, "What things?" So they said to Him, "The things concerning Jesus of Nazareth, who was a Prophet mighty in deed and word before God and all the people, and how the chief priests and our rulers delivered Him to be condemned to death, and crucified Him. But we were hoping that it was He who was going to redeem Israel. Indeed, besides all this, today is the third day since these things happened. Yes, and certain women of our company, who arrived at the tomb early, astonished us. When they did not find His body, they came saying that they had also seen a vision of angels who said He was alive. And certain of those who were with us went to the tomb and found it just as the women had said; but Him they did not see." Then He said to them, "O foolish ones, and slow of heart to believe in all that the prophets have spoken! Ought not the Christ to have suffered these things and to enter into His glory?" And beginning at Moses and all the Prophets, He expounded to them in all the Scriptures the things concerning Himself. Then they drew near to the village where they were going, and He indicated that He would have gone farther. But they constrained Him, saying, "Abide with us, for it is toward evening, and the day is far spent." And He went in to stay with them. Now it came to pass, as He sat at the table with them, that He took bread, blessed and broke it, and gave it to them. Then their eyes were opened and they knew Him; and He vanished from their sight. And they said to one another, "Did not our heart burn within us while He talked with us on the road, and while He opened the Scriptures to us?"
>
> – Luke 24:13–32

Two disciples in Luke 24 heard about Jesus' resurrection and didn't believe; dejected, sad, and disappointed, they left Jerusalem where Jesus was crucified. On their way to Emmaus, Jesus, in resurrection, came alongside them, and started a conversation — but they did not recognize to whom they were speaking, for "their eyes were restrained." Jesus asked questions, and let them speak out what was troubling them. It is almost comical that they were telling Jesus about Himself — and even got it wrong (Jesus was not only a prophet but the Son of God)! Yet, Jesus didn't rebuke, belittle, or judge them.

After Jesus listened to these two men patiently for a long while, He began to speak from the Scriptures concerning Himself. Eventually, when they broke bread together for a meal, they recognized it was Jesus, and they believed. Here, the Lord modeled a great example of cherishing for nourishing. It is very cherishing for a troubled person to be able to speak and pour out what is bothering them to someone willing to listen without passing judgment. To warm up and open others' hearts, believers need to learn to listen more and speak less (note: in the above portion of Scriptures, seven verses were of the Lord listening, but only three were of the Lord speaking). People's hearts are often opened when they speak freely. If believers ask the right questions and listen to others without correcting or judging them, they are qualified and able to nourish them by unveiling Christ in the Scriptures and lead them to partake of Jesus Christ as food.

Condemning the Hypocrisy of the Religious

Jesus exposed and condemned the hypocrisy of the religious, but cared for those beaten up by religion.

> Then Jesus spoke to the multitudes and to His disciples, saying: "The scribes and the Pharisees sit in Moses' seat.
>
> For they bind heavy burdens, hard to bear, and lay *them* on men's shoulders; but they *themselves* will not move them with one of their fingers. But all their works they do to be seen by men. . . . But woe to you, scribes and Pharisees, hypocrites! For you shut up the kingdom of heaven against men; for you neither go in yourselves, nor do you allow those who are entering to go in. Woe to you, scribes and Pharisees, hypocrites! For you cleanse the outside of the cup and dish, but inside they are full of extortion and self-indulgence. Blind Pharisee, first cleanse the inside of the cup and dish, that the outside of them may be clean also. Woe to you, scribes and Pharisees, hypocrites! For you are like whitewashed tombs which indeed appear beautiful outwardly, but inside are full of dead men's bones and all uncleanness. Even so you also outwardly appear righteous to men, but inside you are full of hypocrisy and lawlessness.
>
> — Matthew 23:1–2, 4–28

The Lord was harsh, exposing and condemning the leaders of religion — and this religion was even Scripture-based. A religion teaches people how to behave and live in a way that would please God, but without God, and without the enjoyment and the presence of God. In fact, religions become an impediment and a roadblock to God. They are very deceptive because on one hand they talk about God, and they try to keep God's laws to please God, but in actuality they drive people away from God through their demands and hypocrisies. In order to expose this deception and make a clear distinction between Himself and religion, Jesus condemned and denounced it openly. He wanted to make the hypocrisy of religion clear — that it is just for outward show, full of death, and that He has nothing to do with it. This condemnation of religion is a cherishing to those that are turned off, disappointed, and repulsed by it. Many who have been damaged by religion (equating it to God) will recognize through the Lord's condemnation of it that the Lord Jesus is *different*...and allow themselves to be cherished by Him.

> Then Jesus answered and said: "A certain *man* went down from Jerusalem to Jericho, and fell among thieves, who stripped him of his clothing, wounded *him*, and departed, leaving *him* half dead. Now by chance a certain priest came down that road. And when he saw him, he passed by on the other side. Likewise a Levite, when he arrived at the place, came and looked, and passed by on the other side. But a certain Samaritan, as he journeyed, came where he was. And when he saw him, he had compassion. So he went to *him* and bandaged his wounds, pouring on oil and wine; and he set him on his own animal, brought him to an inn, and took care of him.
>
> – Luke 10:30–34

In response to a challenge by a religious law keeper, Jesus told this story of a man beaten up by thieves. The "thieves" refer to the religious law keepers that regularly expose, condemn, beat up, and leave half dead those that cannot keep their religious laws. This is why the priest and Levite (both referring to prominent religious personalities) did not stop to help him. The Samaritan, however, belonging to a people *despised* by the religion of that time, refers to Jesus who was despised and rejected by religion. He was the one that came to take care of this wounded half-dead man. The man who was beaten up by religion received care from and was saved by Jesus.

Thus, believers need to cherish those who are dejected and wounded by religion so that they will become cherished and thus receive the Lord Jesus — or turn back to Jesus — who is life and diametrically opposite to religion.

The Practical Experience of the Crucified and Resurrected Christ

Cherishing and nourishing others is the real and practical experience of the crucified and resurrected Christ. The Lord's own death and resurrection was for fruit bearing.

> But Jesus answered them saying, "The hour is come that the Son of man should be glorified. Verily, verily, I say unto you, Except the grain of wheat falling into the ground dies, it abides alone; but if it dies, it bears much fruit. He that loves his [soul] life shall lose it, and he that hates his life in this world shall keep it to life eternal.
>
> – John 12:23–25, DBY

Most serious Christians are familiar with the teaching that they need to deny themselves and hate the life of this world in order to be holy and please God. Many then interpret this to mean they should not derive any pleasure from things of the world or things that bring worldly enjoyment. This becomes a big religious requirement that they put on themselves and fellow believers. Many believers, not able to keep this requirement, become discouraged; thus, spiritually deadened. However, this is not what the context of these verses is saying.

In John 12:23–25 and in later verses, Scripture teaches death produces much fruit — *life*. The purpose and outcome of Jesus' death is life for many others — *fruit*. Jesus was not denying Himself just so He wouldn't indulge in the things of this world; rather, His full attention was focused on the resulting "fruit," and it was for this "fruit bearing" He died.

Likewise, when believers take action for the sake of caring and bearing others, they are denying themselves. A mother does not go through changes in lifestyle and much suffering just because she should, with no outcome. No, she automatically does so for a new birth — for the joy and rejoicing of a new life — the fruit of her womb.

Sent to Speak the Word and Follow Christ for the Increase

The Word concerning "bearing the cross" and "denying the soul-life" was related to being sent to speak the Word and following Christ for the increase (building up) of the assembly.

> And as you go, preach, saying, 'The kingdom of heaven is at hand.'
>
> And he who does not take his cross and follow after Me is not worthy of Me. He who finds his [soul] life will lose it, and he who loses his [soul] life for My sake will find it.
>
> — Matthew 10:7, 38–39

In the context of telling His disciples to go preach the gospel, Jesus spoke of taking the cross to follow Him. For believers to follow Him by losing their soul-life and taking up the cross, does not mean suffering for suffering's sake; it is to heed Jesus' call to go and share the good news and enjoyment of Jesus Christ to others around them. When believers experience the joy and rejoicing that comes with bringing people to salvation, they gladly consider whatever time, energy, and missed pleasure of the world well worth the sacrifice. They get to see someone come to salvation or grow in Christ.

Contrary to Jesus' *physical* death, the Lord is not asking His believers to lose their *physical* life since "life" in this verse does not refer to the physical life. It refers to the believer's soul, or *psychological* life. To be worthy of the Lord is to go and bear fruit, even at the cost of losing the temporary pleasure of the soul life.

> And I also, I say unto thee that you are Peter, and on this rock I will build my assembly, and hades' gates shall not prevail against it.
>
> From that time Jesus began to show to his disciples that he must go away to Jerusalem, and suffer many things from the elders and chief priests and scribes, and be killed, and the third day be raised.
>
> Then Jesus said to his disciples, If any one desires to come after me, let him deny himself and take up his cross and follow me. For whosoever shall desire to save his [soul] life shall lose it; but whosoever shall lose his [soul] life for my sake shall find it.
>
> — Matthew 16:18, 21, 24–25, DBY

Jesus unveiled His purpose in these verses in Matthew 16 of building His assembly — His body — and the way that He would do it: by going to His death followed by His resurrection. After this, He told those that follow Him to build His body as He — by taking up the cross, denying self, and losing their soul-life. Again, this is not the same as the philosophy of asceticism — treating oneself harshly in order to control baser desires. It is also not the same

as some erroneous thought that to deny oneself is to do the things that the person doesn't
want to, and not do the things that they like to do, as an end in itself. Many Christian leaders
even use verses like these to teach those under their leadership to deny themselves with
any criticisms and continue to support their leadership even if those in leadership do some
things that are wrong. This type of "denying" does not build up the body, but damages it.
The next set of verses will discuss practically what is means to "deny yourself."

> He said to him the third time, "Simon, son of Jonah, do you love Me?" Peter
> was grieved because He said to him the third time, "Do you love Me?" And
> he said to Him, "Lord, You know all things; You know that I love You." Jesus
> said to him, "Feed My sheep. Most assuredly, I say to you, when you were
> younger, you girded yourself and walked where you wished; but when you
> are old, you will stretch out your hands, and another will gird you and carry
> *you* where you do not wish." This He spoke, signifying by what death he
> would glorify God. And when He had spoken this, He said to him, "Follow
> Me."
>
> – John 21:17–19

The Lord asked Peter three times whether Peter loved Him. Each time after Peter
answered in the affirmative, the Lord responded by commanding him to feed and to care
for His sheep and lambs. These lambs and sheep referred to the Lord's people from young
to old. For Peter to *show* his love for the Lord, he was charged with feeding and shepherding
God's people.

The Lord explained that this feeding and shepherding of His people means others
would lead Peter to do things that he would not want to do. Caring for others by feeding
and shepherding may often require the believer to go somewhere or do something that at
times may not be convenient. It would not be the wish of the shepherding one, but for the
sake of those being shepherded, he or she will do what is required. Maturity is manifested
when a believer is led by the needs of those that they are feeding and shepherding. This is
the practical denying of oneself in order to care and feed the Lord's people, to follow Jesus
to build up His assembly, His body. This is the kind of "death" that glorifies God because it
issues in much fruit.

Again, consider a new mother. Before she has her baby, she can stay out late and party
if she wants. Once she conceives, however, the child controls her life. In that sense, concern
for the child's well-being will lead her, even when it goes against her wishes. Likewise, when
believers take up the care for others' spiritual well-being, the need to feed and shepherd
them will direct how the caring ones live.

Bearing the Cross for the Ministry of Life
The apostle Paul experienced the crucified Christ in caring for those that he was bearing.

> For we who live are always delivered to death for Jesus' sake, that the life of
> Jesus also may be manifested in our mortal flesh. So then death is working in us,

> but life in you. And since we have the same spirit of faith, according to what is written, "I believed and therefore I spoke," we also believe and therefore speak.
>
> – 2 Corinthians 4:11–13

In the apostle Paul's case, it was his activities in spreading the gospel and ministering Christ to people that resulted in much persecution and suffering. This was his experience of denying himself and taking up his cross, "...delivered to death for Jesus' sake." But the kind of suffering spoken of in 2 Corinthians 4:11 was not an end in itself; there was a positive outcome. The result was that the resurrection life of Jesus worked in those to whom he ministered. While he went through "death," those watching and listening to him were receiving life. Though he was suffering, his spirit of faith was active and strong. Continuing to speak and minister Christ was Paul's demonstration of inwardly seeing the positive things that the Lord was doing beyond his death experiences. He was not murmuring and complaining about his suffering; rather, in his speaking out of his spirit of faith of the glorified Jesus, life was imparted.

> Now, I rejoice in sufferings for you, and I fill up that which is behind of the tribulations of Christ in my flesh, for his body, which is the assembly; . . . Christ in you the hope of glory: whom we announce, admonishing every man, and teaching every man, in all wisdom, to the end that we may present every man perfect [mature] in Christ. Whereunto also I toil, combating according to his working, which works in me in power.
>
> – Colossians 1:24, 27b–29, DBY

How could Paul rejoice in his sufferings unless he was looking at the outcome of his labor, and not at the sufferings? Paul had the same heart and motivation as Jesus to build up the body — the assembly. Just as Jesus suffered and went to the cross for the building up His body, Paul did the same. Paul participated in the Lord's tribulation for the dispensing of the riches of Christ through the ministering of the Word, in order that believers would see and live according to the reality of Christ in them, the hope of glory.

This is both for the cherishing and the nourishing of the believers under his care that they would grow to maturity and be perfected in Christ. Today, believers also can partake of the afflictions of Christ for the sake of cherishing and nourishing others for the building up of the body. The correct understanding of suffering for believers, therefore, is related to the labor of building up of His body.

Denying the Self In Order to Save Some

Paul cherished others by being flexible so that diverse people would receive him, for the sake of gaining them for Christ.

> ...and to the Jews I became as a Jew, that I might win Jews; to those *who are* under the law, as under the law, that I might win those who are under the law; to those *who are* without law, as without law (not being without law toward God, but under law toward Christ), that I might win those *who are* without law; to the

> weak I became as weak, that I might win the weak. I have become all things to all *men*, that I might by all means save some. Now this I do for the gospel's sake, that I may be partaker of it with *you*.
>
> — 1 Corinthians 9:20–23

A practical example of someone denying themselves for the purpose of fruit bearing is found in 1 Corinthians 9:20. Paul was a Jew who grew up under strict Jewish customs. Yet, he denied himself from His comfort zone, his culture, and his natural inclination and biases in order to fit in with the people around him that he was burdened to gain for Christ. If a minister of Christ expects others to be like him and compatible with him, it would be almost impossible for such a minister to bring people to and nurture people for Christ. Consider Jesus Christ: He came and fit into every person's environment and culture around the world. No matter a person's ethnicity or socioeconomic situation, nobody has to change first before receiving and believing into Christ. Jesus stepped out of His heavenly environment to fit into man's lowly and earthly surroundings.

The more believers are willing to deny themselves, leave their own comfort zone, and be genuinely comfortable with people from their diverse backgrounds, the more the Lord can use them to minister to others. This teaching of "deny yourself" according to Scriptures can be practiced only in the context of doing the work of ministry to others.

A Portrait of a Cherishing Person

What is it like to live in the humanity of Christ and express His divine attributes?

> Love is patient, love is kind. Love does not envy, is not boastful, is not conceited, does not act improperly, is not selfish, is not provoked, and does not keep a record of wrongs. Love finds no joy in unrighteousness but rejoices in the truth. It bears all things, believes all things, hopes all things, endures all things.
>
> — 1 Corinthians 13:4–7, HCSB

This chapter on love is embedded in the chapters relating to ministering in the body (Chapter 12) and the building up of His assembly (Chapter 14). It is in this context that love is defined, because it is only in this real love that believers can minister Christ and build up others. Without experiencing Christ and having this love expressed through His children, it is impossible to care for others for the building up of His body.

The closest example of this kind of love is, again, between a mother and child. That is why if believers are to serve the Lord and be fruit bearers, everyone needs to be such spiritual mothers and fathers caring for both non-believers — that they will come to Christ — and for the newer, younger, or weaker believers — that they may grow and become such ministers themselves. This is what it means to, "love one another just as I [Jesus] have loved you" (John 13:34). Unlike today's popular usage of the word "love," the biblical usage is much deeper with the implication of sacrificing something for the person being loved.

Therefore, loving "sinners" by caring for their salvation, and loving other believers by caring for their growth, touches the core of one's character and motivation. This kind of love, truly, is the death to the selfish life and requires the denial of natural, selfish inclinations. Every believer should express this kind of love, not just a few select clergymen.

Practice: Cherishing!

Spend time cherishing others for the sake of nourishing them with Christ.

Try going out of your comfort zone and out of your way to do something for someone else. Reach out to cherish someone close to you (or around you) by considering one or two of the examples of Christ and how you can follow His pattern to do the same to cherish another person.

List a few names of people close to you that need cherishing:

After each name, write down what you may want to do to cherish that person in the coming days or weeks:

Person #1:_____

Prayer: _____

What can I do: _____

Person #2:_____

Prayer: _____

What can I do: _____

17

NOURISHING AND MAKING DISCIPLES IN HOMES

Before starting this chapter, there needs to be a clear understanding that a minister, servant, or worker of the Lord Jesus is not a "special" believer belonging to a "special group." According to New Testament revelation, *every* believer should be a minister, servant, or worker. Every believer should serve the Lord according to their God-given capabilities. Some ministers may be much more capable then others, or might have a much bigger impact on many more people. But every believer needs to understand that he or she is a minister, even if they can only impact one person.

Societies are built when each family does its part to raise its children well. This is the same for God's assembly — the divine society is raised family by family in the spiritual sense. The goal of these chapters is not to motivate some to become really big ministers, in the sense of having an impact on thousands of people, but to inspire every believer to do their little part according to their capacity. What is presented in these chapters is something that every believer can do. It does not require any special gift or talent, only faith that the Lord is doing the work and diligence to start caring for just one other person's spiritual well-being.

Nourish: To Unveil the Person and Work of Jesus Christ

I planted, Apollos watered, but God gave the increase. So then neither he who plants is anything, nor he who waters, but God who gives the increase.

For we are God's fellow workers; you are God's field, *you* are God's building. According to the grace of God which was given to me, as a wise master builder I have laid the foundation, and another builds on it. But let each one take heed how he builds on it. For no other foundation can anyone lay than that which is laid, which is Jesus Christ.

– 1 Corinthians 3:6–7, 9–11

Paul and Apollos are good examples of effective servants, ministers, of the Lord. They planted and watered. Paul first went to Corinth, to plant the seed of life. Apollos followed, and watered. Paul then wrote letters to the Corinthians to water them even more by pointing them back to Jesus Christ, in the midst of the various problems the Corinthians were facing. No matter what difficulties the Corinthian believers were facing, Paul unveiled and applied Jesus Christ for their focus and experience. It is the Word transmitting Jesus Christ that is the seed of life, and it is the Spirit of Jesus Christ that is the water of life. Scripture by itself is not the seed of life; if Jesus Christ is taken out of the message, and if the Spirit of Jesus Christ is not ministered in teachings, then the listener is not being watered. It is the planting and watering from ministers that allows God to grow believers.

As shown in previous chapters, receiving Christ as the Word comes through understanding and logic, and the receiving of the Spirit as water comes through faith. This is what it means to "nourish" someone. The cherishing of people as discussed in the previous chapter is for this nourishing. Without this nourishing, the best a minister can be is a good humanitarian worker or a good friend to provide comfort. However, caring for people's physical and psychological needs (cherishing) should lead to satisfying people's deepest and eternal needs, which is Jesus Christ — their true spiritual need. Therefore, cherishing is for nourishing.

Ultimately, nourishing is for God's building. The Corinthians weren't just a "field" — a farm — for growing. "Growing" is God's act of "building." God is building the assembly through the growing of the believers. God's building (the assembly) is not physical. It is the spiritual building made up of Christ growing in men. The more Christ grows in many men (male and female), the more God's spiritual house is built, His building. All ministers — servants and workers of the Lord — are for this one building. All their work of service is for God's eternal purpose of having this building, God's household, the bride of Christ, and the body of Christ. There should be as many ministers as there are believers who work together with the same ultimate goal: fulfilling God's eternal purpose of having an assembly.

Since the foundation laid by Paul is Jesus Christ, all those coming after him to build need to take heed to build with the precious materials which are produced by the seed of life and the water of the Spirit. Understanding the chapters on truth and life will help believers know what teachings are healthy to use for planting and watering. There is, therefore, no need to develop this matter further here. As long as there is an understanding of what is nourishing — the unveiling of the person and work of Jesus Christ — and that is what believers are ministering, nourishing will happen. Those being supplied will grow, and the assembly will be built up.

Leading and Discipling Believers towards Growth and Maturity

The believer is to function as a begetting father by feeding others, acting as a father to his own "children" that they may walk worthily of God. One who feeds also has the authority to lead and disciple others.

> ...but have been gentle in the midst of you, as a nurse [nursing mother] would cherish her own children. Thus, yearning over you, we had found our delight in having imparted to you not only the glad tidings of God, but our own lives also, because you had become beloved of us. For you remember, brethren, our labour and toil: working night and day, not to be chargeable to any one of you, we have preached to you the glad tidings of God. You are witnesses, and God, how piously and righteously and blamelessly we have conducted ourselves with you that believe: as you know how, as a father his own children, we used to exhort

> each one of you, and comfort and testify, that you should walk worthy of God, who calls you to his own kingdom and glory.
>
> – 1 Thessalonians 2:7–12

In order to raise a family properly, a father needs to cherish and nourish his child. But there is also the need to guide and disciple in order for the child to become a useful person. If a person only grows physically, but does not know how to work and get anything done, then that person cannot contribute to the growth of the family in the long run. Therefore, in addition to giving birth and nourishing for growth, there is the need for training so that a person can work and contribute to the family and society.

Likewise, a proper minister (servant) of the Lord will do the work of a "father" in their ministry. They will learn to cherish, nourish, and disciple the believers under their care so that those believers will, in turn, serve the Lord to accomplish God's purpose.

Since Paul cherished and nourished the Thessalonian believers as a nursing mother, he had the standing and stature to exhort them as a father. The word for "exhort" in the Greek, once again, is *parakaleō,* which means, "To call for someone to come alongside." Paul wanted those to whom he had brought to the Lord and ministered Christ, to be ones that would then come alongside him to do what he was doing with the same goal and purpose. This is what it means to make disciples, and thus gain more co-laborers to spread the kingdom of God.

The analogy Paul used in this section is clearly of a father and mother rearing their children. Consider how, as a mother, the ministers were "nursing" new believers as babies. As those new believers grew, the ministers (as fathers) called these young believers to come alongside them to do what they were also doing. This is what it means to "exhort" as a father. It is common for fathers when doing a project, whether remodeling, fixing a car, or gardening to call their kids over to work alongside them and to help them. Doing so teaches children how to do things, finish projects, and to help complete parents' various goals.

In ancient societies, this was a common way for fathers to train their children. When a father worked in a specific trade, his sons were expected to learn and continue in that trade. The "trade" of every believer is to minister Christ, and the goal is to build up the assembly. This was Paul's ministry and goal; therefore, he exhorted those that he was caring for to also serve the Lord as he did.

Comfort Follows Exhortation

Anyone who starts to serve the Lord will experience some form of suffering, rejection, or disappointment. That is why comfort follows exhortation. Paul comforted those whom he was exhorting. If the minister does not have the ability to comfort those he is discipling, those new believers will not last in their service; they will become discouraged and give up. That is why comforting is such a critical part of being a father who exhorts. A father that only knows how to exhort, but not comfort, will incite resentment with his children. It is the same spiritually. Those exhorting others to serve also need to provide comfort when needed.

The goal for believers is that, through the ministers' cherishing, nourishing, and exhorting with comforting, they will walk worthy of God's calling. There is only one chapter in the New Testament that explains what it means to be worthy of being called by God: Ephesians 4. In Ephesians 4 Paul says that to walk worthy of God's calling means keeping the oneness for the building up of the body of Christ through the functioning of every member of the body.

Fathers – Worthy of Being Imitated

There is a need in the body for more fathers, not more instructors; a begetting father is worthy to be imitated.

> I do not write these things to shame you, but as my beloved children I warn you. For though you might have ten thousand instructors in Christ, yet *you do* not *have* many fathers; for in Christ Jesus I have begotten you through the gospel. Therefore I urge you, imitate me.
>
> – 1 Corinthians 4:14–16

The difference between an instructor and a father is that an instructor can only teach; a father can teach and also beget. A father's relationship with those he teaches is a *life* relationship, whereas, an instructor can only transfer knowledge. A father also has innate love and patience not associated with an instructor. Paul said that there are "ten thousand instructors in Christ," but not many fathers. In this hour, there is a desperate need for more servants of the Lord who are also fathers, with the ability to impart life to others. Because of his relationship with the Corinthians, it was appropriate for Paul to both warn and ask those he brought to the Lord to imitate him. The word "imitate" here means "to follow," similar to "exhort" in the previous verses. Paul was asking believers that he was shepherding to do what he does by following him.

In context, the believers were to imitate Paul in the way he served the Lord and ministered Christ to others. In general, when human fathers raise their children it is common for them to ask their children to follow in their footsteps — in their aspiration, diligence, philosophies, and positive characteristics. Yet, among believers, this kind of "fathering" to other believers is a foreign thought. Believers think only prominent ministers can have followers, but actually, every believer can and should have a few or at least one newer or younger believer as their follower, imitator, or disciple.

Consider how many prominent ministers have disappointed or led astray millions of followers because of moral failures or unhealthy teaching. What if there were tens of millions of ministers, rather than a culture of "celebrity" teachers and ministers? That way, failures among these ordinary ministers would only impact a couple of believers at a time. On the positive side, when every believer learns to be a nursing mother and exhorting father, the scriptural way of building the Lord's assembly will occur — His purpose fulfilled.

> And Jesus came and spoke to them, saying, "All authority has been given to Me in heaven and on earth. Go therefore and make disciples of all the nations, baptizing them in [into] the name of the Father and of the Son and of the Holy Spirit, teaching them to observe all things that I have commanded you; and lo, I am with you always, [even] to the end of the age." Amen.
>
> – Matthew 28:18–20

After the Lord Jesus resurrected and ascended, all authority was given to Him. He then commanded believers to go and disciple all the nations by immersing people into the Trinity and by teaching those who were immersed the entire counsel of God (Acts 20:27). The "sending" to make disciples happens only with the Lord's authority. This authority subdues Satan and all the demonic forces. When believers follow the Lord's command to "go," they must exercise the Lord's authority and not fear any of the attacks from the enemy. Making disciples spans the entire process of child-rearing: raising up believers by begetting through faith and baptism, growing them through nourishing teachings, eventually becoming functional disciples that will not waver in loving and serving the Lord to further His purpose.

When believers obey and "go" to do this service, the Lord promises He will surely be with them until the end of the age. This promise from the Lord was given in conjunction with commissioning the believers. The Lord's presence and the believers' experience of Him were more pronounced as they followed the Lord's command to make more disciples among the nations. In John 15:8, the Lord said disciples are those that bear fruit. Therefore, all believers, as disciples, are to bring sinners from regeneration all the way to bearing remaining fruit.

Some believers may have special gifts that enable them to excel in a particular service such as evangelism, teaching, giving to the poor, prayer or healing, but taking care of and making disciples one or two at a time throughout the Christian life is a basic call to every believer. One who is specially gifted and enjoys being a prayer warrior in a closet should still try and lead another person to the Lord, and cherish, nourish, and exhort that person to serve the Lord. This is similar to a human family. A parent may be a doctor, an entertainer, or a factory worker, but regardless of their prominence or any achievements in their career, they still have a responsibility to raise their family.

Believers tend to fall on one of two sides. On one side, are the gifted and stronger believers, who often want to do something great for the Lord; however, to take care of a couple of people over a long period of time seems too menial to them. They may think this job is beneath their calling and underutilizes their ability. On the other side, are the majority of believers who do not consider themselves qualified enough to take care of *any* people spiritually. Or, they consider that it is simply not their job. This is the cause of a major deficiency among God's people: the raising up of spiritual families from house to house.

The word for "go" in verse 19 means, "to go on one's way" (Vine's Expository Dictionary). This implies believers do not necessarily have to stop what they are doing and go on a mission to a foreign land. Instead, it emphasizes that as believers "go" from one location to another, living their life, they are to disciple others. Believers need to incorporate the Lord's commission of making disciples into their daily coming and going of life. Only some can actually go to a foreign land for mission work, but every believer has the opportunity to make disciples as they go about their daily life. There needs to be such an awareness that wasted time and opportunities can be seized for making disciples.

Never Force, Coerce or Pressure Others

It is important that ministers always respect others' free will and choices, and never force, coerce, or pressure others into doing anything.

> And the Spirit and the bride say, Come. And let him that hears say, Come. And let him that is athirst come; he that will, let him take [the] water of life freely.
> – Revelation 22:17, DBY

As believers practice making disciples — begetting, cherishing, nourishing and exhorting — there is danger of over zealousness. Boundaries may be crossed where the person receiving the help feels coerced, pressured, or forced to do something that they do not want to do. Free will has to be honored at all times.

God gave man a free will to choose at the very beginning when He made man; even at the very end of the Bible, in the last chapter of Revelation, free will is active and honored. Jesus calls people to "come" to drink the water of life, but their response depends on whether they desire to come or not when they hear the call. There is still the free will on the part of the person hearing the call whether to drink or not. Therefore, vigilance is needed for those who practice making disciples. They must always respect others' free will of choice. When care for people is out of true love, patience and forgiveness will be present, especially when those being shepherded disappoint the shepherd. Once a shepherd either tries to pressure people to follow the Lord or becomes upset with those that do not respond adequately to their discipling, it is no longer the Lord's service.

For example, a ministering believer may challenge a newer believer to study the Bible and pray regularly, or to share the gospel with friends. Yes, there should be exhortation — calling the believer to come alongside — but there should be sensitivity as well. The minister must guard against coercing others to do these things. Even more, no matter how much a minister may be a help to someone spiritually, it is dishonoring to the Lord Jesus as the Head of all the believers if they tell someone what to do. For example, they should not tell someone how to dress, what movies to watch, or what types of music they cannot listen to. The minister's calling is to feed and be a pattern to others and to trust the Spirit to work in the believers' conscience as to how they will live before the Lord.

Use Opportunities—Anytime and Anywhere—In Twos or Threes

> For where two or three are gathered together in My name, I am there in the midst of them."
> – Mathew 18:20

"In My name" in the Greek should be translated, "*into* My name." "In My name" to most people is understood as "one being a representative of the Lord," such as saying, "I am doing this in the name of the king." That means the king is not actually here, but the representative stands in for the king. A gathering "in" His name, then, would mean that the gathering is with a formal intention of representing the Lord's name.

However, "into" the Lord's name means that the gathering is in the sphere of or in the person of the Lord Jesus. That is why the Lord is in their midst — the gathering is *in Christ*. The gathering envelopes all that Jesus Christ *is* and *has accomplished*.

The "name of the Lord" is actually the very person of the Lord Himself. That is why there is no other name given to men whereby they must be saved (Acts 4:12), and why when men call on the name of the Lord, they are saved (Rom. 10:13). The name can save, because the name of Jesus is the very *person* of Jesus. His name is just Himself; otherwise, the name "Jesus" by itself, separated from the person, means nothing; it cannot save. The gathering into the Lord's name is with the direction, or the focus, of the gathering to be in the very person, presence, and Spirit of the Lord Jesus. This can and should happen anytime or anywhere when "two or three" believers are together; they should direct their conversation toward the person or work of the Lord Jesus. In doing so, the Lord will be in their midst, and they will be in the Spirit of the Lord with all of His riches.

Therefore, in caring for people — begetting (the gospel), cherishing, nourishing, and exhortation — ministers need to take every opportunity possible to bring others into the name of Jesus Christ.

The Lord Jesus was a perfect example. He took opportunities to minister at a wedding and also as He reclined to eat with people. As He journeyed from one point to another, He ministered at people's houses and taught along the way. Jesus spent much of His time ministering like this to individuals and small groups of people, compared to the few times in Scripture He preached to or taught large crowds. Jesus practiced what He commanded the believers to do: to make disciples as they went along their way.

Most Christians only consider going to church, or going to an organized event or meeting, to be a time for "fellowship" with other believers. Ministering or shepherding others also occurs in such venues, but such tradition makes shepherding and ministering to others limited and inefficient. If believers would consider ministry to occur "where two or three" are gathered into His name, all sorts of opportunities throughout the day and week would open up! They can be short periods of time, even for five-minutes. They can happen while commuting to work. They can occur over a coffee break, at a restaurant, or even while shopping with another person. Understanding this, every believer can find opportunities to minister Christ by meeting with another person or two, in the normal activities of life.

This verse cannot be emphasized enough. Practicing this verse will liberate believers to meet others anywhere, anytime, and for any length of time. They can even meet with just one other person. There is no need for set events, or a special place like a church. No agenda, schedule, or material is required. What freedom to be able to gather and have the Lord Jesus in one's midst, wherever they are! Practicing this brings freedom for every believer to serve and minister Christ. Without this understanding, believers may always think they need to be somewhere or do something special in order to do the work of their ministry.

Houses (Homes): The Preferred Place for Ministry

Jesus Himself regularly practiced visiting people in their homes, enjoying their presence. A person's own home is where they can truly be who they are. It expresses their personality and where they feel the most comfortable and most protected. It is their place of living, and the place where all family members gather.

It is significant that God's eternal purpose — the assembly — would be right inside believers' homes. Just as God Himself wants to live inside His people, His assembly is in His people's homes. God wants to be in the center of His children's life and family. Instead of going to a religious building such as a temple or a church to have a relationship with God, God comes to His people's homes to have a relationship with them. Since people's homes are so central to God's assembly (His eternal purpose), then it makes sense that homes were the very place where Jesus Christ ministered when He was on the earth.

Matthew's House

> After these things He went out and saw a tax collector named Levi, sitting at the tax office. And He said to him, "Follow Me." So he left all, rose up, and followed Him. Then Levi gave Him a great feast in his own house. And there were a great number of tax collectors and others who sat down with them. And their scribes and the Pharisees complained against His disciples, saying, "Why do You eat and drink with tax collectors and sinners?" Jesus answered and said to them, "Those who are well have no need of a physician, but those who are sick. I have not come to call the righteous, but sinners, to repentance."
>
> – Luke 5:27–32

Matthew (Levi) wrote the gospel of Matthew and was a tax collector. Matthew was working at his tax-collecting office when Jesus came to call him to be a disciple. The first place Jesus and the disciples went after Matthew was called was his house; they had a "party" with all of Matthew's fellow tax collectors and sinners. It would have been normal for Matthew to gather those in his same social circle to meet Jesus. At Matthew's home, the Lord was with those that were comfortable with each other, and enjoying food and drink together. After calling Matthew, the Lord didn't bring him to the temple or the synagogue to pray or to worship; rather, he went to his house to feast. The religious people were offended that Jesus was eating and drinking with tax collectors and sinners, but Jesus said that was exactly where He should be: as a physician hanging out with those that needed Him. Where did he find the "sick" that needed Him? Not in the temple, but in a home.

It is the same today. The "tax collectors and sinners" of today likely won't be going to church. They will be hanging out with friends and fellow "sinners" in each other's apartment or house. If a person is willing to invite a ministering believer to eat in his or her house, it shows that person is open to receive them as a friend.

It is clear Jesus specifically intended to minister in homes. Let's look at a couple more examples to see how Scripture affirms this.

Zacchaeus' House

Jesus visited and lodged at Zacchaeus' house, bringing salvation to his household.

> Now behold, there was a man named Zacchaeus who was a chief tax collector, and he was rich. And he sought to see who Jesus was, but could not because of the crowd, for he was of short stature. So he ran ahead and climbed up into a sycamore tree to see Him, for He was going to pass that way. And when Jesus came to the place, He looked up and saw him, and said to him, "Zacchaeus, make haste and come down, for today I must stay at your house." So he made haste and came down, and received Him joyfully. But when they saw it, they all complained, saying, "He has gone to be a guest with a man who is a sinner." Then Zacchaeus stood and said to the Lord, "Look, Lord, I give half of my goods to the poor; and if I have taken anything from anyone by false accusation, I restore fourfold." And Jesus said to him, "Today salvation has come to this house, because he also is a son of Abraham."
>
> – Luke 19:2–9

In this story, Jesus didn't even preach to Zacchaeus. He simply invited Himself to Zacchaeus' house. It is certain that Zacchaeus already knew what Jesus was about, and he was attracted to Jesus. As a result of Jesus' offer to go to Zacchaeus' house, Zacchaeus came to salvation.

The religious people, however, were upset that Jesus would go to a sinner's house. Religion cares for their worship places and people performing religious duties, but Jesus cared for people in their homes. It was not possible to perform a religious ritual in the midst of a bunch of sinners, but it was easy for Jesus to be Himself in peoples' homes – caring for people and enjoying eating and drinking with them. This is actually the best environment for salvation: in the sinner's home, rather than in a religious place. Zacchaeus received transforming salvation, such that he was willing to make restitution of his past wrongs, and to help those that were less fortunate.

One cannot be a good minister – a servant of the Lord – if one doesn't know how to visit peoples' home. Very few believers have the ability or the opportunity to preach to hundreds or thousands, but every believer has the ability to visit someone's home. Believers need to learn to invite themselves to a person's home, that Christ may be ministered so salvation can come to that household.

A Leper's House in Bethany

Another home Jesus visited was the leper's house in Bethany, where Jesus would also be anointed.

> After two days it was the Passover and *the Feast* of Unleavened Bread. And the chief priests and the scribes sought how they might take Him by trickery and put *Him* to death. But they said, "Not during the feast, lest there be an uproar of the people." And being in Bethany at the house of Simon the leper, as He sat at the table, a woman came having an alabaster flask of very costly oil of spikenard. Then she broke the flask and poured *it* on His head.

> Assuredly, I say to you, wherever this gospel is preached in the whole world, what this woman has done will also be told as a memorial to her.
>
> – Mark 14: 1–3, 9

What a contrast between religion and the Lord's way of relaxing and enjoying people in their home! In Mark 14:1–3, the religious leaders were planning to trick Jesus so they could kill Him while Jesus was enjoying fellowshipping with believers in a leper's house. In ancient biblical times, people with leprosy were to be shunned and avoided due to the fact that they could spread the disease. Yet, Jesus looked past the disease, and entered the leper's home where he was welcomed and comfortable. There is no home so sinful and worldly that Jesus will not visit. He enjoyed a meal there, and a woman came to anoint Him with a precious ointment. This was not in the temple or a religious meeting place, but in a home where Jesus was served and loved. Jesus Himself chose to take refuge there. Homes became the place that those who love Him could serve Him and have fellowship with Him.

The woman's act of pouring out costly oil on the Lord Jesus was most endearing to the Lord, because it reflected a responsive, sacrificial love. The preaching of the gospel speaks of the Lord's love for man, and this "pouring out" testifies of the believers' love for the Lord. Jesus poured out Himself for man, and man should respond by "pouring out" on Him. Thus, this story concerning the woman who poured out her expensive ointment on the Lord should be shared whenever the gospel is preached. This was the only instance of an action performed by a person that the Lord said should be a memorial…and it happened in a home. The woman didn't go out to do anything great in the sense of traveling the world to preach the gospel or feed the poor. She did something simple that touched the Lord's heart, right in a home. This didn't happen at the temple, at any preaching event, or at a "revival" meeting, but at a leper's home while having a meal.

Every believer can do something extraordinary in a home fellowship with Jesus. Visiting homes to bring salvation and nourishment also opens up the opportunity for any believer, both the believers doing the visiting and those being visited, to become remarkable lovers of the Lord Jesus.

Jesus Commissioned Believers and Sent Them to Peoples' Houses

Jesus sent the twelve disciples, then seventy others, and all subsequent workers to go out and spread the gospel in the exact same way.

> Then He called His twelve disciples together and gave them power and authority over all demons, and to cure diseases. He sent them to preach the kingdom of God and to heal the sick. And He said to them, . . . "Whatever house you enter, stay there, and from there depart."
>
> – Luke 9:1–3a, 4

> After these things the Lord appointed seventy others also, and sent them two by two before His face into every city and place where He Himself was about to go. Then He said to them, "The harvest truly [is] great, but the laborers [are] few;

therefore pray the Lord of the harvest to send out laborers into His harvest. Go your way; behold, I send you out as lambs among wolves. Carry neither money bag, knapsack, nor sandals; and greet no one along the road. But whatever house you enter, first say, 'Peace to this house.' And if a son of peace is there, your peace will rest on it; if not, it will return to you. And remain in the same house, eating and drinking such things as they give, for the laborer is worthy of his wages. Do not go from house to house. Whatever city you enter, and they receive you, eat such things as are set before you. And heal the sick there, and say to them, 'The kingdom of God has come near to you.'

– Luke 10:1–9

In Luke 9, the Lord first sent the twelve disciples into people's house. Then in the very next chapter, He increased the "sending" to seventy others. In fact, the Lord asked them to pray for more workers to be sent forth into the harvest. That means if the Lord has more workers (which would include all of the Lord's workers since then), He will send them in exactly the same way.

This is significant to consider. This is how the Lord wants believers to serve Him in the harvest. With all the power and authority He has given to the workers, one would think Jesus would have told them to hold a big meeting, or a conference, in order to preach the gospel and perform healings. No, they were commanded to go to people's houses — so insignificant, with a limited audience to witness their works of power, if they were to perform them. This is counter-intuitive to how people often think ministers should work! Typically, people think the bigger the audience the better; it is much more efficient this way. But that was not the way the Lord commanded the disciples. His way and direction, which is consistent with His eternal purpose of the assembly in the homes, is to go from house to house.

Note also that the Lord specifically directed them to "greet no one along the road." It seems that He didn't want them to become distracted by those along the road. Surely there are needy people along the road, but the Lord's desire was homes, households. People "along the road" can be defined as anyone who cannot be tracked or followed back to their homes. Since the Lord's goal here was households, He wanted His disciples to spend time in people's homes rather than with random people "along the road." Certainly there is nothing wrong with helping and preaching to people along the road, which Jesus and the apostles did. But in the Lord's instruction to His workers here, He specifically excluded those people so that they can spend time to find a "son of peace" and focus on households in homes.

Gaining the Entire Household

"Harvesting" takes place in peoples' homes. So, the Lord Jesus thrust workers out to houses, going house by house, looking for "sons of peace," or people of peace. He instructed workers to bring the peace of the Lord into a house; if the household accepted this peace, that meant there was a person of peace there. This peace included not just the words concerning the Lord Jesus as the gospel, but also the worker's care, concern, cherishing, and love.

When there is a person of influence in the house who welcomes the Lord's worker bringing such peace, a person of peace is present. When such a person is found, then the Lord instructs disciples to remain in that house. The worker is to stay and cultivate that house — to beget, cherish, nourish, and make disciples of those in the household. That household, and all of its friends and relatives connected with it, is the "field" for harvesting to bear remaining fruit. It is from such a house that an assembly is raised up.

This runs contrary to the Christian's usual way of doing ministry today. It is important to note that a house represents the entire city. One house receiving the Lord's peace means the entire city has favor with God. If no house receives the Lord's peace, then the entire city is condemned. How significant it is to work in the way that the Lord has directed — finding a house with a person of peace, and from that household, continuing to disciple and shepherd in order to gain all those connected to that house. As workers work from such a house, they will actually find the connections from that house will spread through the entire city. So from one house, more and more houses will be gained — people will come to salvation and grow to serve the Lord as remaining fruit.

Today, the method most Christian workers' use is to gain one person at a time through various venues: at church, open air, or TV for example. After individuals believe through the gospel, they are directed to leave their house to go to church to meet with other Christians and to hear more teachings and ministry of the Word. The person's household is basically neglected. It is not necessarily that today's methods are wrong; they are just completely different from the way the Lord outlined in this portion of Scripture, which is to work right inside the house until the entire household is gained and discipled.

One thing is certain: gathering people into churches builds up a worker's individual ministry. Building up the assembly has to be in homes. The Lord's way of directing believers to work is for building His heart's desire, which is the assembly, in house after house.

The Lord's way is actually available for every believer who wants to serve Him (which should be every believer) as a "worker." Every believer today, if they would follow what has been outlined in these chapters, will find a "son of peace" in their community — even within their social circles. If one cannot be found, that believer can join with another fellow worker who has found someone in the community that accepts the Lord's peace. Once such a person of peace is located, then over a period of time, through visitations to this person's house, the ministry of begetting, cherishing, nourishing, and exhortation can take place. With the faithfulness of a farmer, the "harvest" will spread to relatives and friends networked to that house.

If believers would heed the Lord's sending out in His way, they would find they indeed have authority over all the evil forces and have the ability to heal the sick. It is certain that believers going out to make disciples in the power and authority of the ascended Christ have nothing to fear. Those spiritually sick and psychologically struggling will be healed, and according to the Lord's will, physical healing will also transpire.

The First Gentile Assembly

After Jesus' death, resurrection and ascension, His apostles continued to spread the assembly from house to house, expanding to the Gentiles. The book of Acts tells how Peter went to Cornelius' house, where Cornelius gathered his relatives and friends.

> And they said, "Cornelius [the] centurion, a just man, one who fears God and has a good reputation among all the nation of the Jews, was divinely instructed by a holy angel to summon you to his house, and to hear words from you."
>
> And the following day they entered Caesarea. Now Cornelius was waiting for them, and had called together his relatives and close friends.
>
> . . . how God anointed Jesus of Nazareth with the Holy Spirit and with power, . . . whom they killed by hanging on a tree. Him God raised up on the third day, and showed Him openly.
>
> To Him all the prophets witness that, through His name, whoever believes in Him will receive remission of sins." While Peter was still speaking these words, the Holy Spirit fell upon all those who heard the word.
> – Acts 10:22, 24, 38–40, 43–44

The very first gospel preaching to Gentiles was divinely arranged to be in a house, in Cornelius' home. This meeting could have been arranged anywhere, but the divine arrangement sent an unmistakable message that God's move of initiating the building up of His assembly among the Gentiles starts in a home. Cornelius invited all his relatives and intimate friends. This was his extended "household." While his household was listening to the good news of Jesus Christ, the Spirit filled them, and they were saved by faith. What a wonderful sight! Everyone in Cornelius' household was filled with the Spirit. Cornelius was a "son of peace," and through him his entire household, relatives and friends, were saved... and the first Gentile assembly began. How significant! This is God's way of salvation: His salvation is for the entire household.

Isn't it a relief not to worry about which family member or friend is "chosen" by God for salvation? How sad it would be if the Spirit came to save a couple of relatives and friends but not others in the same household. Believers need to have the faith that God's salvation is for their entire household. Today, some may be quicker to believe and others slower, but it is important to believe God's heart of love is for the entire family. Although it is still up to each individual to choose the Lord, and it may not ultimately work out for every family, it is not God's choice to break up families; He treasures the family unit, and desires the entire family would be saved.

Paul's Gospel Preaching Gained Households

> Now a certain woman named Lydia heard *us*. She was a seller of purple from the city of Thyatira, who worshiped God. The Lord opened her heart to heed the things spoken by Paul. And when she and her household were baptized, she

> begged *us*, saying, "If you have judged me to be faithful to the Lord, come to my house and stay." So she persuaded us.
>
> – Acts 16:14–15

> Then he called for a light, ran in, and fell down trembling before Paul and Silas. And he brought them out and said, "Sirs, what must I do to be saved?" So they said, "Believe on the Lord Jesus Christ, and you will be saved, you and your household." Then they spoke the word of the Lord to him and to all who were in his house. And he took them the same hour of the night and washed their stripes. And immediately he and all his family were baptized.
>
> – Acts 16:29–33

The apostle Paul followed the Lord Jesus' way in Luke 10 by gaining households and abiding in the house of the person of peace. In fact, according to these verses, it seems that as soon as one believed, the entire household followed. In both of the stories above, Paul gained the whole household, not just one person at a time. Both Lydia and the jailer were persons of peace, and through Paul, their entire households were gained. Paul then took hospitality and stayed in their houses following the pattern given by the Lord in Luke 10. A person of peace, his or her house, and the whole household are inextricably linked — connected to each for salvation for God's purpose.

Man's need is for salvation, and God's need is for an assembly to be built up from house to house.

Paul Opened His Own Hired Dwelling for Shepherding

> Then he stayed two whole years in his own rented house. And he welcomed all who visited him, proclaiming the kingdom of God and teaching the things concerning the Lord Jesus Christ with full boldness and without hindrance.
>
> – Acts 28:30–31, HCSB

Paul's narrative in the book of Acts ends with two verses describing Paul fellowshipping in his house, declaring Jesus Christ. The greatest apostle purposely left this impression in the record of his acts. He was not preaching to thousands, teaching in synagogues, doing a healing ministry, or feeding the poor; rather, he was having home fellowship. He was teaching and preaching in his humble, rented house.

Remember that Paul was the same person who persecuted the assembly in Jerusalem by going from house to house. The memory of going into each house to drag away the believers was likely an unforgettable image in Paul's mind. Those fellowshipping in the houses may have been having a meal, singing, or praying. Each house Paul entered likely was doing something different at the time he arrived to arrest them. It is significant that this persecutor who went from house to house persecuting believers was now ending his story in Acts, himself in a house having fellowship.

What a contrast between the beginning and the end of Acts! In the beginning of Acts at the day of Pentecost, Peter preached to thousands at the temple and 5000 people were saved. Miracles became normal occurrences. At the very end of Acts, Paul is seen having fellowship in his house with a few people at a time. This may seem insignificant, but it is actually profound. Though this was the end of the Acts of the Apostles as recorded, in actuality, the acts of all the ministering believers as apostles (sent by the Lord) will never end until the Lord's return.

An apostle literally means "one sent forth" (Vine's Expository Dictionary), as in Matthew 28:19 when the Lord Jesus charged His disciples to "go therefore to make disciples." There may not be that many prominent apostles such as Paul or Peter, but every believer should be an apostle since each believer is sent by the Lord Jesus to go and bear remaining fruit (John 15:16). As a sent one, not every believer can preach like Peter to thousands and do miraculous work as in the beginning of Acts. However, every believer can be an apostle in a house, and can teach and experience fellowship as Paul did at the end of Acts. This conclusion opens the door for every believer to continue the writing of the book of the Acts of the Apostles by visiting homes and opening their own house to build the assembly. How wonderful would it be if each and every believer learned to share the good news of Jesus Christ? What if believers taught the truth in their own homes or in someone else's home?

This example of the greatest minister, apostle, and worker for the Lord Jesus was left for all believers as a pattern to follow. In homes, the gospel and teaching can continue boldly without hindrance. In many places around the world today, the gospel cannot be preached publically, and churches are either torn down or monitored. Yet people are being saved in their homes because the gospel is preached there. For example, the number of Christians increased dramatically in China after public Christian meetings were banned and believers started meeting from house to house in their own homes. It was a blessing in disguise; forcing believers to meet in homes brought boldness to believers, and advanced the spread of the gospel unhindered.

Therefore, all believers desiring to serve the Lord by being a minister of Christ to people around them have to learn both to open their own homes to teach and fellowship and to visit other homes for ministry. This is critical to any minister with a goal of building up God's assembly, which is from house to house. It is in homes that the gospel is preached for begetting, love is expressed for cherishing, Christ is unveiled for nourishing, and disciples are raised up through exhortation.

The author has no intention to disparage all the various ways and methods of preaching the gospel and teaching the truth. Philippians 1:18 states that believers should rejoice whenever and however the gospel is preached. The intention here is to bring to light what the Lord Jesus Himself commanded His disciples to do and how the early apostles followed that pattern. Believers today should follow as well.

Applying Love and Care Pragmatically

It is significant when a home is opened to receive believers for fellowship, whether it is for the first time or multiple times. Such a home needs to be cared for so that the host would not have undue burden for having a gathering for fellowship. Those going to such a home should be aware that if there is a meal, they should contribute food or money to help if possible. Before or after the meeting, there may be the need to prepare, clean up or put things back where they belong; thus, different ones should volunteer to help with the dishes, vacuuming, etc. The best practice is to leave the home as clean if not cleaner than when you first entered.

This is a real and practical cherishing, love and care for the host family. If this matter is not practiced, it can become too difficult for any homes to continue to be open for a fellowship gathering. Therefore, since the goal is to have home fellowship and even to have homes that would become a host of an assembly (a regular gathering place), then it is critical that the matter of food and cleanup be lovingly cared for. While performing these chores, fellowship can and should start or continue. As ones are preparing meals or washing dishes, they can sing, pray or share the Word together. How practical and enjoyable! This is the way to insure that more and more homes would be receptive to host and eventually become a regular place of assembly.

Practice: Visitation

Go out to visit neighbors, friends and family, even for a very short time. Be warm and hospitable, not trying to be spiritual. Have no religious forms or set ways. Hold a view of cherishing and nourishing. At the same time open your home and invite people over regularly, or on a semi-regular basis.

List a few names placed on your heart: _____

_____

Contact them to arrange a time for a visit.

Suggestions:

1. A meal or at least dessert together is preferred.

2. Depending on the situation, nothing spiritual needs to be brought up.

3. The easiest way to bring in Jesus Christ or the spiritual realm is ask if there is anything you can pray for them. This could open up a person's heart.

4. If there is an opening, reading a few verses together and having a short discussion will bring in spiritual nourishment. This can be done in 5–10 minutes.

18

BUILDING: ASSEMBLY IN ONENESS AND MUTUALITY

The Ultimate Goal of Workers

The ultimate goal of any worker is to build up the assembly from house to house — the body of Christ.

> And I also, I say unto you that thou are Peter, and on this rock I will build my assembly, and hades' gates shall not prevail against it.
>
> – Matthew 16:18, DBY

> Now, I rejoice in sufferings for you, and I fill up that which is behind of the tribulations of Christ in my flesh, for his body, which is the assembly; of which I became minister, according to the dispensation of God which [is] given me towards you to complete the word of God.
>
> – Colossians 1:24–25, DBY

Chapter 12 on the assembly *(ekklesia)* discussed how the assembly is God's eternal purpose. It is for the assembly that Jesus Christ came, died on the cross, and resurrected. His entire purpose for redemption and salvation was so that He could build up His assembly, His body. Therefore, any co-workers with the Lord, any ministers and servants of the Lord, should have the same goal: to build up the assembly, the body of Christ. It is critical for any minister of Christ to have this same vision of the assembly and to understand that is the goal of their ultimate labor — the building up of this eternal, yet practical, assembly from house to house. If that is not a minister's goal, their ministry is lacking at best and could be damaging to the body of Christ at worst.

Just as Jesus Christ suffered for the building up of His assembly, Paul declared that his rejoicing in suffering was for the body, the assembly. It was for the assembly that he became a minister. The Word is concise concerning the purpose Paul became a minister, and the purpose he suffered in his ministry: it was for the body of Christ, the assembly. Preaching the gospel to bring forth sons of God through the new birth, caring and nourishing new believers to help them grow, and exhorting believers to disciple them towards being mutually functioning members is all for the assembly. Each service provided by ministers to people around them is for the building up of the assembly. If their services are for any other reason, even their best effort will not advance God's goals.

Gathering Material for the Building

> Thus says the LORD of hosts: "Consider your ways! Go up to the mountains and bring wood and build the temple, that I may take pleasure in it and be glorified," says the LORD. [You] looked for much, but indeed [it came to] little; and when you brought it home, I blew it away. Why?" says the LORD of hosts. "Because of My house that [is in] ruins, while every one of you runs to his own house. Therefore the heavens above you withhold the dew, and the earth withholds its fruit. For I called for a drought on the land and the mountains, on the grain and the new wine and the oil, on whatever the ground brings forth, on men and livestock, and on all the labor of [your] hands."
>
> – Haggai 1:9–11

> ...but if I delay, in order that thou mayest know how one ought to conduct oneself in God's house, which is the assembly of the living God, the pillar and base of the truth.
>
> – 1 Timothy 3:15, DBY

God's house in the Old Testament is a type or prefigure of the assembly — the real house of God for eternity. Any believers, as God's people who are not building up His house, will not be satisfied with their Christian life. They will sense a lack of the blessings from the Lord and the lack of joy and supply of the Spirit. When a believer senses this lack, the Lord asks: "Consider your ways. Are you building up God's house, or are you just caring for your *own* house?"

This "caring for your own house" certainly can include the believer's physical house — which relates to their physical and psychological well-being on earth, but this actually includes the believer's ministry for the Lord as well. Is the worker's goal to build his or her own ministry — his own house (church) — or is it indeed for the Lord's house?

All believers (who should be workers of the Lord) need to consider their ways and rise up with renewed hearts to take action for the building up of God's house. All the people that are raised up through the labor of ministers are material for building God's house, or "wood." The minister's ultimate goal should not be to gather material for his own church or ministry, but for the Lord's house.

> ...as newborn babes, desire the pure milk of the word, that you may grow thereby, if indeed you have tasted that the Lord [is] gracious.
>
> ...you also, as living stones, are being built up a spiritual house, a holy priesthood, to offer up spiritual sacrifices acceptable to God through Jesus Christ.
>
> – 1 Peter 2:2–3, 5

In Matthew 16:18, the Lord called Simon "Peter," which means "a stone." Then when Peter wrote his letter, he told all the believers that they too were "living stones" for the building of God's spiritual house. Peter was not unique, but was a stone just like all other believers. All believers are stones for God's building. In the Old Testament, the physical temple was built with physical stones, but for the eternal house of God (which is spiritual), people are needed as living stones. Therefore, all the services by believers rendered to people surrounding them are to transform them from sinners through regeneration (newborn babes) to maturation — feeding them so that they will become living stones for the building of God's eternal assembly.

In the Old Testament only Israelites from one specific tribe were chosen to be priests. A priest was one who brought people to God — one who could offer sacrifices so that people could be brought into fellowship with God. In the New Testament, Peter stated that believers — living stones — are also a holy priesthood. This means every believer today is a member of the New Testament priesthood, qualified to serve God, to bring people to have fellowship with Him.

The Functioning of Every Member of the Body in Mutuality

There are about fifty-six incidences of the phrase "one another" in the New Testament in relation to members being in the body. This term means that believers should not only wait for someone to help them, to do something for them, but that each believer has the responsibility to help and do something for another. This is the mutual giving and receiving in the body. This is the body life, where each and every member functions in the body. This is the body building itself up as described in Ephesians 4:16.

Without every member of the body functioning, the body will be crippled or handicapped. No matter how little or how much, every believer needs to do their part to support and supply other members in the body. Below is just a sample in Scripture of the fifty-six uses of "one another," revealing activities needed in Christ's body.

1. Love one another

> "A new commandment I give to you, that you love one another; as I have loved you, that you also love one another.
>
> – John 13:34

2. Caring and serving

> …that there may be no division in the body, but that the members may have the same care for one another.
>
> – 1 Corinthians 12:25, ESV

> …through love serve one another.
>
> – Galatians 5:13, ESV

3. Speaking, singing and submitting

> And do not be drunk with wine, in which is dissipation; but be filled with the Spirit, speaking to one another in psalms and hymns and spiritual songs, singing

and making melody in your heart to the Lord, submitting to one another in the fear of God.

– Ephesians 5:18–19, 21

4. Considering, inciting, and exhorting

And let us consider one another in order to stir up love and good works, not forsaking the assembling of ourselves together, as [is] the manner of some, but exhorting one another.

– Hebrews 10:24–25

5. Teaching and admonishing

Let the word of Christ dwell in you richly in all wisdom, teaching and admonishing one another in psalms and hymns and spiritual songs, singing with grace in your hearts to the Lord.

– Colossians 3:16

6. Prophesying, listening and discerning

Let two or three prophets speak, and let the others judge [discern]. But if anything is revealed to another who sits by, let the first keep silent. For you can all prophesy one by one, that all may learn and all may be encouraged.

– 1 Corinthians 14:29–31

7. Bearing and forgiving

…bearing with one another, and forgiving one another, if anyone has a complaint against another; even as Christ forgave you, so you also must do.

– Colossians 3:13

Five Key Activities in an Assembly

Recall that the word *ekklesia* literally means, "a called out assembly." Therefore, building the assembly was to help facilitate the various activities among believers as they gathered in oneness.

And they devoted themselves to the apostles' teaching and the fellowship, to the breaking of bread and the prayers.

And day by day, attending the temple together and breaking bread in their homes [from house to house], they received their food with glad and generous hearts, praising God and having favor with all the people. And the Lord added to their number day by day those who were being saved.

– Acts 2:42, 46–47, ESV

And every day, in the temple and from house to house, they did not cease teaching and preaching that the Christ is Jesus.

– Acts 5:42, ESV

> But Saul ravaged the assembly, entering into the houses one after another, and dragging off both men and women delivered them up to prison.
>
> – Acts 8:3, DBY

As soon as people became believers in the Lord Jesus Christ, the assembly started — meeting in the believers' homes. In Jerusalem, the apostles taught openly in the temple, but the assembly took place from house to house in the believers' homes.

Since the assembly was in the homes then, it is imperative to understand five activities that were common in the assembly in the believers' houses. If these five activities are not present, then there is no assembly. All five activities may not happen in every gathering. However, if any one of these elements is missing, over time the assembly will weaken and suffer. The more of these activities that regularly take place, the more the assembly will grow and increase. These activities consist of the teaching of the apostles, the fellowship of the apostles, the breaking of bread, prayers, and the gospel.

In Acts 2:42, the apostles' teaching and fellowship is a pair. That pair is unique and the same in all home gatherings and for all assemblies, whereas the breaking of bread and prayers can be flexible depending on the homes. The timing of when to have a meal and how to break bread may very well be different from house to house. The subject of prayer and how to pray may also vary from house to house. It is unreasonable and illogical to assume what one eats and what one prays would be uniform in every home; however, the apostles' teaching and fellowship cannot be altered. They should be the unique focus of every assembly in every home, everywhere, throughout time. Let's look at each one in more detail.

Teaching of the Apostles

This portion is the very first preaching or teaching done by Jesus' apostles. It was completely on the topic of Jesus Christ — who He is and what He has accomplished. Peter used the Scriptures to expound on and describe Jesus Christ without deviating, setting an example for the teaching of Jesus Christ.

> Men of Israel, hear these words: Jesus of Nazareth, a Man attested by God to you by miracles, wonders, and signs which God did through Him in your midst, as you yourselves also know — Him, being delivered by the determined purpose and foreknowledge of God, you have taken by lawless hands, have crucified, and put to death; whom God raised up, having loosed the pains of death, because it was not possible that He should be held by it.
>
> Therefore let all the house of Israel know assuredly that God has made this Jesus, whom you crucified, both Lord and Christ."
>
> – Acts 2:22–24, 36

In the Greek, the word for "teaching" and "doctrine" is the same. Scripture sometimes uses teaching and other times, doctrine. Notice that the believers devoted themselves to the apostles' teaching (singular). It is a singular teaching or doctrine in which the believers are continuing steadfastly. This teaching is the unique truth of the New Testament, given to all the believers in John 17. All apostles only have one teaching or doctrine, and that teaching is Jesus Christ: His person and His work. It is critical that the assembly focus on this essential teaching of Jesus Christ. Without this doctrine, the assembly is missing the heart of the gathering. After the believers heard the teaching of Jesus Christ from the apostles, that became their topic of fellowship in the home gatherings. Acts Chapters 3 and 4 continue with more of the teaching of Jesus Christ. The teaching of Jesus Christ is so rich that it can include the entire Old Testament in addition to the New Testament, since Jesus Himself said that the Old Testament was all about Him (John 5:39; Luke 24:27). Because of this, the topic of Jesus Christ is unending and unsearchably rich.

Every minister of the Lord should only have one teaching, which is the teaching of Jesus Christ. To build up a gathering that is part of the assembly, believers — as ministers — need to keep the focus and topic on Jesus Christ. There is a differentiation between the doctrine of Jesus Christ and the many other items written about in the Bible. The Bible speaks of head coverings, baptism, giving to the poor, paying taxes, eldership, predestination, tongue speaking, the end times, and so on. But all these items by themselves can become a distraction from the focus: Jesus Christ. These topics may be related to healthy Christian living and practice, or they may be items that are mentioned in passing, but they are not the primary doctrine of Jesus Christ, the heart of the assembly.

Believers need to be vigilant knowing that just because something is in the Bible does not automatically mean that it is the "teaching." One can find many various doctrines in the Bible, but there is only one doctrine of the apostles. From the Bible, groups can quote verses and support a liberal political agenda, but from the same Bible other groups can advocate a conservative agenda. Only the doctrine of Jesus Christ can bring liberals and conservatives into the same mind concerning Him. Therefore, how well a person can minister depends on how skillful he or she is in bringing the focus to Jesus Christ and to facilitate the riches of Christ to be manifested in fellowship.

> For many deceivers have gone out into the world who do not confess Jesus Christ [as] coming in the flesh. This is a deceiver and an antichrist.
>
> Whoever transgresses and does not abide in the doctrine of Christ does not have God. He who abides in the doctrine of Christ has both the Father and the Son.
>
> — 2 John 1:7, 9
>
> And without controversy great is the mystery of godliness: God was manifested in the flesh, Justified in the Spirit, Seen by angels, Preached among the Gentiles, Believed on in the world, Received up in glory.
>
> — 1 Timothy 3:16

Believers only have one essential and critical doctrine, and that is the doctrine of Christ — that Jesus Christ is God in the flesh. This doctrine is not just related to the incarnation of Jesus (God born in flesh), but also His sinless living, His crucifixion, His resurrection, His ascension, His crowning as Lord and Christ, the outpouring of His Spirit, His indwelling of believers, His continuing work in the believers, the building up of His assembly, and bringing His body into glory. This is the doctrine of God manifested in the flesh.

As the apostles taught this doctrine in the Acts and throughout the epistles, it became the spiritual food that is the truth for believers to eat and enjoy in their assembly today. Any other topic can become a controversy and a source of contention, such as how to baptize, how to have communion, whether tongue speaking is allowed, or if abortion is right or wrong, for example. Believers, as ministers, need to bring any discussions and focus back to Jesus Christ. Without anyone feeling that they were ignored or corrected, a skilled and mature believer will be able to relate any topic back to Jesus Christ and help everyone in the assembly see Jesus only.

Fellowship of the Apostles

> That which was from the beginning, which we have heard, which we have seen with our eyes, which we have looked upon, and our hands have handled, concerning the Word of life — the life was manifested, and we have seen, and bear witness, and declare to you that eternal life which was with the Father and was manifested to us — that which we have seen and heard we declare to you, that you also may have fellowship with us; and truly our fellowship [is] with the Father and with His Son Jesus Christ.
>
> — 1 John 1:1–3

The fellowship of the apostles comes from the teaching of the apostles. The fellowship and the teaching of the apostles go together as a pair. The teaching brings fellowship, and fellowship is the very enjoyment of (sharing of) Jesus Christ, who is the content of the teaching. John declared Jesus Christ coming in the flesh, and through that the hearers were brought into fellowship. This fellowship was not just with the apostles, but also with the Father and His Son Jesus Christ. This is the one fellowship of the Spirit. In this fellowship believers find joy, peace, comfort, and strength — everything of the Spirit that is common and shared among believers. Fellowship is not one way. It is not just listening to someone talk; it is two ways — multiple ways — depending on how many believers are present. Every believer is a giver and a receiver in fellowship. Through this sharing, they experience the Father and the Son. How wonderful!

Fellowship means mutuality. It is not dictation or a one-way contribution, but a sharing from each member based on something that they all have in common, which is Jesus Christ. This fellowship has to be open and non-judgmental so that whoever is sharing does not feel rejected; this would cause not only the rejected person to shrink back and be withdrawn, but it would cause those observing the rejection to also withdraw. They could be next, they might think, if they share. Even if someone says something that is obviously wrong, great care needs to be taken whether to correct that person openly. It is much better to have a further discussion with that person privately.

> Finally, brothers, rejoice. Aim for restoration, comfort one another, agree with one another, live in peace; and the God of love and peace will be with you.

> The grace of the Lord Jesus Christ and the love of God and the fellowship of the Holy Spirit be with you all.
>
> – 2 Corinthians 13:11, 14

When the teaching of Jesus Christ — the truth — is the focus, then the fellowship of the Holy Spirit is the believers' experience. In the fellowship of the Holy Spirit, the grace of the Lord and the love of God are found, as well as restoration, comfort, harmony, and peace. When these items are present, that is the fellowship of Jesus Christ. If discussions among believers lead to the opposite — disharmony, suspicion, condemnation, arguments, and unhappiness, that then is not the fellowship of Jesus Christ. In this section (since the focus is on service), practical points will be shared to help facilitate fellowship.

Questions Are Good Openings to Unveil Christ

> He [Jesus] said to them, "How then does David in the Spirit call Him 'Lord,' saying: 'The LORD said to my Lord, "Sit at My right hand, Till I make Your enemies Your footstool"'?
>
> – Matthew 22:43–44

Jesus asked this question so people would consider that He is the Son of God. Genuine questions are the best opening for fellowship concerning the truth. Most people hear lectures at church with no room for questioning; the environment is generally not open to challenge what is being said. As a result, there is little fellowship and the more thoughtful people are left unsatisfied. In fellowship, however, it is important that people are encouraged to ask questions. It is through various questions that participants start to consider not only the truth, but also how the truth is applied in people's daily lives. Believers should not fear questions, but rather welcome them since it can lead to more fellowship.

When questions arise about teachings, practices and life choices, it is best that the most knowledgeable, mature, or talkative person not answer first. If they do, they may communicate a terminal answer or dominate the time; therefore, obstructing the fellowship. The less mature or knowledgeable people will automatically think they can no longer contribute since the "correct" answer has been given. So it is important for those more knowledgeable folks to remain quiet and allow those that are the least knowledgeable to speak first. In fact, the more knowledgeable believers should encourage someone to speak first by asking things like, "So John, how would you answer that question?" Remember, the definition of fellowship is "participation," and "contribution." Everyone needs to participate and contribute.

Contributions from the least knowledgeable may present a wrong answer according to the Scriptures, but that is okay because they are learning to participate. This is like a baby learning to speak, who will say things that are not intelligible; syllables may not be clearly enunciated. But it is through this learning process that eventually they talk. If babies had to remain silent until they could form a perfectly composed sentence, they would never speak!

Let the "unbelievers" or novices regarding the Bible speak. Many times their answer may be surprising. They may share exactly what the questioner or someone else in the room needs to hear. Their contribution can turn out to be more helpful than the more mature believer with all their scriptural references. The beautiful thing about fellowship is when all the contributions are added up in their aggregate, even with some wrong answers, the Spirit moves and brings light to both the questioner and the entire fellowship with love, joy, and peace. So by focusing on fellowship rather than the "correct" answer, the goal of fellowship is reached.

All believers when answering various questions should learn how to apply the truth of Jesus Christ as the answer. For example, let's say someone asks, "Can someone explain the matter of a wife having to submit to the husband? I think it is sexist." A question like that can quickly spiral downward if, for example, the discussion is centered on whether or not submitting to one's husband is true according to the authority of Scripture, or whether society has changed so that this Scripture is no longer valid. Those that are clear about the truth will bring up the fact that the portion in Ephesians is actually talking about Christ dying for His body, the assembly, with the assembly — man (male and female) — being the real wife. Bringing up Jesus Christ in context will steer the fellowship to appreciate Christ and the real eternal marriage in the universe.

Another example would be a question about baptism by immersion. The discussion could focus on whether believers should practice this or not, why immersion is more scriptural than sprinkling, or who is qualified to baptize or be baptized. All these points can be part of the conversation, but if the overall focus is not on the truth, then arguments and lingering questions may result. Eventually, the spotlight has to shift from the *practice* of baptism to the *reality* of baptism: believers are immersed into Christ. Jesus Christ is the entire universe for believers. They are in Him and will never be able to get out of Him. In Him they are a new creation, and it is of God that they are in Christ Jesus. The practice of baptism itself is only a symbol for the reality of believers in Christ. This fellowship would then exalt Jesus Christ based on the teaching of the apostles, the truth.

In some cases, some questions just cannot be answered or at least those participating in that group cannot answer. It is humbling to admit that either there is no answer, or one simply doesn't know *how* to answer. That is perfectly fine. After trying to answer a particular question, if a satisfactory answer is simply not available, it is good to just say, "Let's pray and give this to the Lord, and let Him give us the answer in due time." Those hard-to-answer questions can also be brought before the more mature believers afterward for further fellowship. In this way the network and circle of fellowship increases to include others, and their contribution may be exactly what is needed.

Be Open to Share Experiences and Difficulties

> O Corinthians! We have spoken openly to you, our heart is wide open.
> – 2 Corinthians 6:11

> ...that there should be no schism in the body, but [that] the members should have the same care for one another. And if one member suffers, all the members suffer with [it]; or if one member is honored, all the members rejoice with [it].
> – 1 Corinthians 12:25–26

In home assemblies there is real and genuine fellowship, which means believers have open hearts and can openly speak. If believers cannot speak openly what is in their heart, fellowship is hindered; everyone may be putting on a façade, putting on an act without really knowing each other.

Being part of a home assembly is different from going to church. One can go to church for years, listen to the sermons or messages, shake everyone's hand after service, and maybe even serve in the Sunday school program, but still not really know anyone. The reason? There is no openness to really know what is going on and what others are thinking or experiencing.

How can all the members rejoice or suffer with one another if open sharing of what each is going through, either in victory or in trials, is not present? So in fellowship, space has to be allowed for people to openly speak from their heart.

An open environment also makes the truth of Jesus Christ practical. Many times the doctrine of Jesus may seem theoretical, only affecting what may be in the future. A disconnect between doctrine and present experiences may exist. Many times believers simply don't know that the teaching of truth is very applicable to daily life, affecting practical challenges a person may be facing. When someone opens up about their difficulties, those who have been comforted and have overcome similar situations, can, through the Spirit, share their experiences. Others may bring up Scriptures to apply the teaching to the situation. This is the same care given to one another. In doing so believers will see that the truth is applicable and experiential, and grace, peace, and joy are supplied to all in the fellowship.

In an open, loving, and caring fellowship where judgment and fear do not exist, and the truth is its substance, the oneness of the body is expressed. There is no division, and mutual caring for one another is manifested. This is the apostles' doctrine and fellowship that the early believers started and continued steadfastly from house to house.

Breaking of Bread

Sharing meals with believers (the "breaking of bread") and the practice of the Lord's table are important in the assembly.

> So continuing daily with one accord in the temple, and breaking bread from house to house, they ate their food with gladness and simplicity of heart, praising God and having favor with all the people. And the Lord added to the church [assembly] daily those who were being saved.
>
> – Acts 2:46–47

> Now in giving these instructions I do not praise [you], since you come together not for the better but for the worse. For first of all, when you come together as a church [assembly], I hear that there are divisions among you, and in part I believe it. For there must also be factions among you, that those who are approved may be recognized among you. Therefore when you come together in one place, it is not to eat the Lord's Supper. For in eating, each one takes his own supper ahead of others; and one is hungry and another is drunk. What! Do you

not have houses to eat and drink in? Or do you despise the church [assembly] of God and shame those who have nothing? What shall I say to you? Shall I praise you in this? I do not praise you. For I received from the Lord that which I also delivered to you: that the Lord Jesus on the same night in which He was betrayed took bread; and when He had given thanks, He broke it and said, "Take, eat; this is My body which is broken for you; do this in remembrance of Me." In the same manner He also took the cup after supper, saying, "This cup is the new covenant in My blood. This do, as often as you drink it, in remembrance of Me. For as often as you eat this bread and drink this cup, you proclaim the Lord's death till He comes."

– 1 Corinthians 11:17–26

During the time of the apostles, the breaking of bread was typically accompanied with a meal. When the Lord Jesus first introduced the bread and the cup, for example, it was after a meal (Matt. 28:16). As previously pointed out, the breaking of bread can vary from house to house depending on what is practical for that home. Keeping this in mind, below are principles relating to this practice. This is not, however, a terminal interpretation of how to practice.

As a Meal among Believers – Satisfaction, Relaxation, and Enjoyment

A meal at the end of the day is the focal point of most households. It is the time to relax with family and friends. Eating and drinking together always brings satisfaction; being filled up with good food and drink is about the best experiences of human life. It is also a time of enjoyment, providing entertainment, especially back in the days when there was no television or video games. A meal with family and friends is what a party is about!

It is reasonable, then, that the verse that follows right after the phrase they "ate their food with gladness" says the believers were praising God, and finding favor with all their neighbors, family, and friends so that salvation could be brought to them. And many were added to the assembly daily.

Who wouldn't be attracted and want salvation when invited to a meal and witness believers eating and drinking together, full of peace, love, and joy? During a meal is when hearts are open, and there is time to really get to know one another. It may be like a "pot luck" or a "cocktail party" where a few people are gathered here and there conversing, some discussing meaningful topics of life, while others laugh and engage in lighter topics. Children and young people might play and chat happily. There is no hint of any religious rituals, but the name of Jesus is mentioned and lifted up; there, God is glorified.

A meal together will manifest either harmony as in Acts 2 or divisions as in 1 Corinthians 11. In Chapter 11, the rich believers brought their food and ate together, while the poorer believers didn't have enough to eat. Instead of sharing in harmony, there was division between those that had abundance and those that did not. Due to this division, Paul said it was not the Lord's Supper they were celebrating. The Lord's Supper (or the Lord's table) – the partaking of the bread and cup commonly known as "communion" – declares the body of Christ is one without any divisions. If there is division, it is no longer the Lord's Supper.

Therefore, mutual care for one another in the oneness of the body during a meal determines whether believers are truly practicing the Lord's Supper. If believers' practice the bread and cup for the Lord's Supper, and there is division, instead of partaking of blessings, they will be partaking of judgment.

This is a warning for believers. When gathering together for a meal as the assembly, cliques cannot exist. It is so easy for believers to congregate with people they are associated and not extend themselves to others with whom they are less familiar or do not know. It is also easy to gravitate towards others with similar ethnic backgrounds or towards those in the same age group or political leaning. However, believers need to proactively reach out to everyone in the assembly, and the best time and place to do so is during a meal.

As a Symbol to Remember the Lord Jesus

When it comes to the partaking of the bread and the cup, it is a symbol of the believers partaking of the Lord Jesus Himself. There are many ways to practice this, and Christians have argued and divided over this symbol for centuries. Opinions differ whether to use wine or grape juice, whether the bread has to be unleavened, whether female believers can break the bread and pass it, and many other points of potential arguments. The irony is (lost in all of these ritualistic concerns) the entire symbol of breaking bread is for remembering the Lord Jesus — His person and His work, producing His one corporate body.

Believers need to keep their attention on the various points of the truth shown by the symbol and not on the formality of the symbol itself.

The Bread is God Who Became Flesh to Be Eaten for Life

> Now as they were eating, Jesus took bread, and after blessing it broke it and gave it to the disciples, and said, "Take, eat; this is my body."
>
> — Matthew 26:26, ESV

Jesus as the "bread" is the bread from heaven (John 6:33, 51). When the bread as a symbol is presented, it is a clear reference that Jesus is God who became flesh that man may have eternal life through Him. God in the flesh (Jesus) came to give life to man, and if man would eat Him, then man would live by Jesus (John 6:57). Therefore, the symbol of eating the bread, which is the Lord's body, is a declaration that believers eat Jesus (God) who became flesh for man's life.

The Cup is the Death of Jesus for the Forgiveness of Sins

> And he took a cup, and when he had given thanks he gave it to them, saying, "Drink of it, all of you, for this is my blood of the covenant, which is poured out for many for the forgiveness of sins."
>
> — Matthew 26:27–28, ESV

The "cup" is the blood separated from the bread — the body — meaning death. It was through the shedding of the blood of Jesus, the sinless God–man that the sins of the world were taken away: God forgave man. Although God's original intent was that man would receive God's life, sin came into man and separated him from God; man was thus prevented from partaking of God. The death of Christ was needed for the forgiveness of sin so that man could come to God with boldness to receive Him.

The New Covenant: God Did Everything for Man

> And likewise the cup after they had eaten, saying, "This cup that is poured out for you is the new covenant in my blood."
>
> – Luke 22:20, ESV

The old covenant was conditional, based on whether man followed God's laws; if man could abide by God's laws, there would be blessing; if man broke God's laws, there would be death and God's people would be cursed. The new covenant, however, is based on faith that God did everything for man unconditionally. All man needs to do is to receive all that He has done by eating and drinking Him. This symbol declares that man's portion is to eat and drink of Jesus. Jesus, as the divine food in man, will automatically transform man into a new creation, in the image of Jesus Christ (see Chapter 14 on the new covenant).

The Mystical Corporate Body of Christ

> The cup of blessing which we bless, is it not the communion of the blood of Christ? The bread which we break, is it not the communion of the body of Christ? For we, [though] many, are one bread [and] one body; for we all partake of that one bread.
>
> – 1 Corinthians 10:16–17

Because the word "communion" is used in the popular King James Version translation of the Bible, communion is commonly associated with the symbol of the bread and cup. So when people say, "Our church is having communion this Sunday," it typically means the service will include the bread and cup in its liturgy.

However, the word for "communion" in the Greek, *koinónia,* is exactly the same word translated as "fellowship." Consider the phrases in 1 Corinthians 10:16–17 as "the fellowship (communion) of the blood of Christ" and the "fellowship (communion) of the body of Christ."

The bread is no longer just the body of Jesus; it is the corporate body of Christ. The physical body of Jesus, through His death and resurrection, has produced many "grains" (believers). These "grains," grounded and blended together, are baked into one bread — the body. It is out of the physical body of Jesus, buried and "broken" for believers, that His body has expanded and increased to include all of His believers as members of the one corporate body of Christ. They share in the same life, nature, and expression as Jesus, the original grain. Therefore, when believers partake of the bread, they are also declaring that there is only one body of Christ, and all believers are part of that one body. There is only one fellowship in this body. The fellowship of the body of Christ is one. That is why 1 Corinthians 11 indicated God's people could not possibly be partaking of the Lord's table because there was division during the believers' meals. As a result, judgment descended instead of blessing.

The Return of Christ

> "I tell you I will not drink again of this fruit of the vine until that day when I drink it new with you in my Father's kingdom." And when they had sung a hymn, they went out to the Mount of Olives.
>
> — Matthew 26:29-30, ESV

Finally, the symbol of the bread and cup reminds believers that Jesus Christ is coming again to bring forth the Father's kingdom. Believers are prompted to remember this every time they partake of the cup; the world today is *not* God's kingdom. It is still the kingdom of the evil one.

As believers eat and drink of Christ in the one fellowship of the body, they have a glorious hope — the hope of the Lord's second coming, the hope of a glorious and transfigured body, and the hope of a kingdom where love and righteousness reign. Because believers live and work in this world today, they are often caught up and distracted with all the things of the world: money, politics, sports, fashion, sins and unrighteousness. But the Lord's table recalibrates believers and turns them back to Jesus Christ and focuses them on His eventual and soon return. The world we are in today will end, and the Father's kingdom will be manifested in glory.

As a minor point, notice that singing hymns is clearly related to the practice of the Lord's table.

The key points revealed in examining the Lord's table match the teaching of the apostles exactly. The teaching (doctrine) of the apostles, which is the truth of the New Testament, is fully unveiled and enjoyed in the participation of the bread and cup.

Therefore, the practice of the Lord's table keeps the believers centered on the apostles' teaching and fellowship. The teaching and fellowship takes the practice of the Lord's table out of the realm of religious ritual, into the realm of praise and enjoyment, and into an appreciation of the reality of all that God is and is doing today.

The Prayer of the Assembly

In a previous chapter, the matter of unceasing prayer for personal life and fellowship with the Lord was covered. In this section, the focus will shift to the prayer of the assembly — a normal activity in a home assembly. As ministers desiring the building up of the assembly, believers should encourage prayer.

> So then Peter was kept in the prison; but a prayer was being made fervently by the church [assembly] to God concerning him.
>
> So, when he had considered [this], he came to the house of Mary, the mother of John whose surname was Mark, where many were gathered together praying.
>
> — Acts 12:5a, 12

When Peter was arrested and kept in prison, the assembly in Jerusalem offered prayer to God concerning him. Presumably, due to the prayer of the assembly, Peter was miraculously released from prison. After his release, he went to Mary's house, where many were gathered praying. This shows that the assembly was praying in the houses. One of the functions of the assembly in the homes is to pray. They prayed for whoever and whatever needed prayer at that time. Since Peter was put into prison, they prayed for him to be released. There was no human way for the believers to release or help him, but through prayer, the Lord answered and released Peter.

> And when they had prayed, the place where they were assembled together was shaken; and they were all filled with the Holy Spirit, and they spoke the word of God with boldness.
>
> – Acts 4:31

On one hand, prayer is to petition the Lord to do something that the believers cannot do. On the other hand, prayer does something to the believers. When believers pray, they are filled with the Holy Spirit. In this case, the apostles were threatened by the religious leaders to not preach Jesus any more. Hearing this, the saints prayed. While they were still praying, the place was shaken, the Spirit came and filled them so that they were energized with boldness, and with that boldness they went out to preach the good news of Jesus Christ. Those in the assembly were not praying for personal or material needs. They were motivated to pray because they wanted the Word to go out concerning Jesus Christ. They prayed when they were threatened to stop preaching. After they prayed, they were strengthened to speak even more.

> ...meanwhile praying also for us, that God would open to us a door for the word, to speak the mystery of Christ, for which I am also in chains.
>
> – Colossians 4:3

The primary burden of prayers of the assembly is for the Lord's purpose – that the rich Word of Christ would go out and that all the ministers (which should be every believer) would have an open door to speak the riches and the mystery of Christ. The mystery of Christ is His one body, the assembly (Eph. 3:4–6). Prayers are needed not just for the gospel concerning Jesus Christ to have an unhindered outlet, but also for the Lord's purpose concerning the oneness of the body of Christ.

This Word concerning the assembly may be needed even more than the gospel for salvation. Today there are millions of Christians, but there is a real deficiency relating to the oneness of the believers. Where is the oneness for which the Lord Jesus died? There are millions of Christians, but most are divided by various teachings and practices. Therefore, prayer is desperately needed for the unveiling of the oneness of the body, and for genuine assemblies where believers are one with all those in the same faith of Jesus enjoying the one fellowship of the body.

Prayer and Care in Mutuality

> Be anxious for nothing, but in everything by prayer and supplication, with thanksgiving, let your requests be made known to God.
>
> – Philippians 4:6

> Therefore I exhort first of all that supplications, prayers, intercessions, and giving of thanks be made for all men.
>
> — 1 Timothy 2:1

When believers fellowship and share meals together with open hearts, various needs will surface. Troubles relating to work, finances, family situations, and health will be made known. Burdens for various friends and relatives to know salvation will also be shared. All of these situations and people need to be lifted up to the Lord in prayer. Many situations today cause the saints anxiety. It seems that there is no way to be trouble free. So there are many opportunities and requests that believers can make known to God. Home assemblies are where these prayers can be offered after hearing people's various needs.

> If a brother or sister is naked and destitute of daily food, and one of you says to them, "Depart in peace, be warmed and filled," but you do not give them the things which are needed for the body, what does it profit? Thus also faith by itself, if it does not have works, is dead.
>
> — James 2:15–17
>
> My little children, let us not love in word or in tongue, but in deed and in truth.
>
> — 1 John 3:18

Along with prayers, consideration should be given as to whether a situation could use practical follow-up help. In many situations, practical help can be rendered to lighten the load of those burdened. As prayers are being offered to God, there should also be opportunities for those praying to help in some tangible way, if possible. Believers shouldn't just pray without doing anything practically to help, if they can. It can be simple things like visiting someone, offering a monetary gift, helping to "babysit," or maybe helping to clean a house. The point is that there should be an awareness to bear each other's burden, not just spiritually, but practically. If the need is not confidential, discussions can even take place in the group fellowshipping to consider how to render help as a group, or someone may volunteer to help.

Preaching of the Gospel

> And every day, in the temple and from house to house, they did not cease teaching and preaching that the Christ is Jesus.
>
> — Acts 5:42, ESV

The gospel preached and taught concerning Jesus Christ should take place from house to house. The same calling and burden that the apostles received to preach and to teach is the calling to which *all* believers need to respond, in their own homes. This may be the most enjoyable portion of the activities of the assembly: preaching and teaching the gospel and witnessing the regeneration of unbelievers when faith is received. When friends and relatives come to salvation in a home, it is at once exciting and becomes "normal." This excitement should occur on a regular basis. Otherwise, the home gatherings will become stale; people will settle into a routine. Believers should invite unbelievers (or new believers) to the gatherings to keep their questions and answers real, thus keeping the entire atmosphere of the gathering fresh with the Spirit — and believers will be full of anticipation to witness the work of the Spirit in bringing the lost to salvation.

Prophesying – The Most Profitable Gift for the Building Up

Every believer can prophesy; this is the most profitable gift for the building up of the assembly.

> Pursue love, and earnestly desire the spiritual gifts, especially that you may prophesy. For one who speaks in a tongue speaks not to men but to God; for no one understands him, but he utters mysteries in the Spirit. On the other hand, the one who prophesies speaks to people for their building up and encouragement and consolation. The one who speaks in a tongue builds up himself, but the one who prophesies builds up the church [assembly]. Now I want you all to speak in tongues, but even more to prophesy. The one who prophesies is greater than the one who speaks in tongues, unless someone interprets, so that the church [assembly] may be built up. Now, brothers, if I come to you speaking in tongues, how will I benefit you unless I bring you some revelation or knowledge or prophecy or teaching?
>
> So with yourselves, since you are eager for manifestations of the Spirit, strive to excel in building up the church [assembly].
>
> For if I pray in a tongue, my spirit prays but my mind is unfruitful. What am I to do? I will pray with my spirit, but I will pray with my mind also; I will sing praise with my spirit, but I will sing with my mind also. Otherwise, if you give thanks with your spirit, how can anyone in the position of an outsider say "Amen" to your thanksgiving when he does not know what you are saying? For you may be giving thanks well enough, but the other person is not being built up.
>
> Nevertheless, in church [assembly] I would rather speak five words with my mind in order to instruct others, than ten thousand words in a tongue.
>
> If, therefore, the whole church [assembly] comes together and all speak in tongues, and outsiders or unbelievers enter, will they not say that you are out of your minds? But if all prophesy, and an unbeliever or outsider [uninformed] enters, he is convicted by all, he is called to account by all, the secrets of his heart are disclosed, and so, falling on his face, he will worship God and declare that God is really among you. What then, brothers? When you come together, each one has a hymn, a lesson, a revelation, a tongue, or an interpretation. Let all things be done for building up.
>
> Let two or three prophets speak, and let the others weigh what is said. If a revelation is made to another sitting there, let the first be silent. For you can all prophesy one by one, so that all may learn and all be encouraged, and the spirits

> of prophets are subject to prophets. For God is not a God of confusion but of
> peace. As in all the churches [assemblies] of the saints.
> – 1 Corinthians 14:1–6, 12, 14–17, 19, 23–26, 29–33, ESV

In the previous section, the matter of the apostles' teaching and fellowship was pointed out as the content of the house gathering, as the assembly. This chapter is a detailed description of *how* that was practiced in the homes. 1 Corinthians 14 is the only portion in the New Testament that describes the building up of the assembly by the functioning of each member gathered in a home. It is significant that the assembly, God's eternal purpose, will be practically built up from house to house where each believer can function to minister directly for the building up of the assembly.

The use of the words "build up" and "assembly" together occur in only five verses in the English Standard Version of the New Testament. The first and the most important was when Jesus Himself said that He would build up His assembly (Matt. 16:18). That was His purpose as the anointed one, the Christ. Then, Paul stated in Acts 9:31 that the assembly throughout all Judea was being built up; it was multiplying. Each of the remaining three verses that use the words "build up" and "assembly" is found in 1 Corinthians 14. In fact, the word for "assembly" or "building up" is used in this chapter significantly more than any other chapter in the entire New Testament. This shows Paul's purpose in writing 1 Corinthians 14 was to show how believers could practically build up the assembly that the Lord Jesus was (and is) building. Therefore, any believer who desires to serve the Lord needs to understand the pattern laid out in 1 Corinthians 14 in order to have a clear direction in their ministry to build up the assembly.

Every House Gathering in Oneness Represents the Whole Assembly

Though this gathering in Corinth happened in a home (it was in Gaius' house according to Romans 16:23), it was considered to be the "whole assembly" coming together. If the whole assembly were in Jerusalem (or let's say in Los Angeles) today, it would include tens or hundreds of thousands of people, since every believer is part of the assembly. If that were the case, it would be impossible for each person to practice taking turns to speak, and it would not be practical to gather so many believers all at once in each locality. Therefore, the only way to understand this verse in 1 Corinthians 14:23 is that every home gathering of believers, as the one body of Christ, represents the whole. Even though there may only be twelve believers gathered in a home in a city of 100,000 believers, those twelve believers represent the whole.

When Jesus said that He was in the midst of any two or three people that were gathered into His name, it was the *whole* Jesus — not a part of Him. In 1 Corinthians 12:27, referring to the assembly in Corinth, Paul said, "Now you are the body of Christ." The body of Christ should include every believer throughout time and space, but Paul referred to the believers in Corinth at that particular time as the body of Christ. Shouldn't he have said, "Now you are a part of the body of Christ"?

Just as when two or three who gathered back in the first century had the entire Jesus with them, and as the assembly in Corinth was the entire body of Christ with all the functions, so too any home assembly today is also the whole. This is significant. Even though an assembly may be a small group of believers, it does not lack the gifts of the body. If all the members in the home assembly participate and exercise the gift and function given to them by the Spirit, then there is no lack. Everyone will be supplied, filled with joy and love, and there will be spiritual growth and increase. This is the practical building up of the assembly in the homes, house by house. The "whole assembly" is present and represented by any home gathering in the Lord's name as the one body of Christ. By this, there is a realization of the utmost importance of home gatherings as the assembly.

The Building Up of Individual Believers in a Particular House is the Building Up of the Assembly

The building up of the assembly is not building up a particular group of Christians as if that group has an identity that is separate from other believers. All believers are individually part of the assembly, the body of Christ (1 Cor. 12:27); therefore, to build up an assembly, the emphasis is practically on the building up of each individual believer. If believers are built up, then the assembly is built up. Many Christians identify or associate believers based on the ministry that they follow or the church they attend. Often, how Christians interact with each other or relate to each other depends on whether that person is within the same group or not. If people are in the same church or follow the same ministry, they may treat each other a certain way — such as more caring and friendly. But, if one is an outsider to that group, they are treated another way, and if one departs from that group, then they are treated even worse. This happens when believers do not understand there is one body. Believers need to treat each other the same, because each are individual members in that one body (1 Cor. 12:25). Therefore, in a home assembly, the goal is to build up each one in that house, no matter what church some may attend or what ministry some may prefer or follow.

When an individual progresses and has genuine experiences in the following areas, "building up" occurs:

1. When the person becomes one with other diverse believers and appreciates each member (1 Cor. 12:12–14)

2. When there is no division with other believers, and the person cares for everyone the same (1 Cor. 12:25)

3. When the person functions more and more according to the gift given to each one (1 Cor. 12:4–11)

4. When they pursue the love as defined by 1 Corinthians 13 (1 Cor. 14:1)

5. When they are encouraged and comforted (1 Cor. 14:3)

6. When the person receives more knowledge and revelation concerning the person and work of Jesus Christ: the mysteries of Christ and His assembly (1 Cor. 14:6)

7. When the person is motivated to go forth and bear fruit as they witness unbelievers receiving faith unto salvation (1 Cor. 14:23–25)

If the above is the experience of an individual attending and participating in a home gathering, the assembly is being built up, God's eternal purpose is progressing, and those serving toward this end are doing their job.

Prophesying Brings Light and Understanding to the Hidden Mysteries of Christ and His Body

Prophecy is any utterance that brings light and understanding to the hidden mysteries of Christ and His body, the assembly. In 1 Corinthians 14:2, believers are told to desire the ability to prophesy — it is prophesying that builds up (v. 3, 4). In the assembly, all the believers can prophesy one by one (v. 24, 31). According to this chapter on building up the assembly, prophesying is the best and highest gift; therefore, it is critical to understand exactly what "prophesying" is.

Most people automatically assume that prophecy means predicting the future, but that is not the primary meaning. According to Vine's Expository Dictionary, "prophesy," "prophecy," and "prophet" are from the same Greek word meaning, "To speak forth the counsel of God, His message." The etymology of that Greek word includes enlightening and explaining by bringing a hidden thought into light for understanding. Some Christians practice prophesying by bringing to light something hidden in another person's heart or by speaking forth what God has intended for that person in the future. This certainly can be the Spirit's special gift and there should not be a despising of any prophecy. Yet, this form of prophecy may or may not be true and may or may not come to pass; therefore, the prophecy that this section is focused on is the prophesying that every believer can pursue and practice, and it is true for building up every single time.

What is hidden in God that needs to be brought to light, to be explained, for people to understand? Ephesians 3:9 reveals Paul was charged to bring to light the economy of the mystery that was hidden in God (see Chapter 11 on God's economy). Continuing with this thought of the hidden mystery, Paul in Colossians 1:26–27 said that the hidden mystery is, "Christ in you the hope of glory." Colossians 2:2 states that Christ is the mystery of God. Jesus Christ manifested all that is hidden in God; therefore, unveiling Jesus Christ is unveiling God's mystery. In Ephesians 3:4–6 Paul said that the one body of believers is the mystery of Christ.

Today, Jesus Christ is also hidden, but the one body of believers manifests and unveils the riches and attributes of Christ. This called out assembly is the mystery of Christ. When both are combined, Ephesians 5:32 says this "Christ and the assembly" is a *great* mystery. Therefore, any speaking that unveils, teaches, brings to light, and causes people to understand and appreciate the many aspects of Christ and His one body of believers, is prophesying.

Prophesying as described in this chapter can come in many forms, as long as it brings light and understanding concerning the mysteries of Christ and the one body. For example, Paul said in 1 Corinthians 14:24, "If all prophesy…" Then verse 26 described Paul expanding on what these "all" should be doing. He wrote, "Each one has a hymn, a lesson, a revelation, each has a tongue with interpretation, let all these things be done for building up." Paul listed various speech-related activities as prophesying, and any of these items, when they unveil the mysteries for building up, are the goal of prophesying. Prayer, singing, and even "five words" can be a prophecy as long as they uplift and bring to understanding and appreciation some aspect of Jesus Christ and His body (v. 14–19).

No wonder all believers, men and women, can desire to be prophets; everyone can function in this way. How wonderful that the building up of the body of Christ is not limited to a few gifted believers or the need to wait for a miraculous manifestation, but each one of the believers in the home assembly can participate directly in the building up of one another. Thus, this "gift" of prophecy really depends on a wider and deeper knowledge and enjoyment of the mysteries of Christ and the one body, so that speaking, singing, and praying will be full of light and inspiration.

Preparation Needed before Assembling

Normally when Christians go to church, they do not have to prepare to contribute anything other than some money for the tithing plate in their "Sunday best." They go to listen and watch those who have done the preparations carry out their professional services. Therefore, there is a hard shift in the concept that assembling according to the New Testament is very different and will require preparation, if the goal is to build up the assembly. Since an assembly's activities depend on member's contributions, if no one prays, sings, or says anything concerning Jesus, it will be a very dead and boring gathering – or the gathering will end up focused on other things.

Therefore, a proper assembly requires every member to prepare something to bring and share. Again, this is why 1 Corinthians 14:26 speaks of each one having a hymn, a lesson, a revelation, etc. "Has" means that it is something that they already possess and bring to the assembly. During the week, believers should consider what song they can bring to share. This is not just to call a song for everyone to sing together. What if this person is so inspired and touched by the Lord that he or she sings a solo to everyone? Or maybe a husband and wife that enjoyed a song together sing a duet? Christians are so programmed to professional-sounding singers in church that they will not dare sing out a solo for shame it will sound out of tune. But what will feed both God and man is a song that unveils something of Christ sung with the person's experiential knowledge and the inspiration of the Holy Spirit. Then, after, the entire assembly can sing together.

Or what if there is consideration on what testimony to give to glorify an aspect of the person or work of Christ? If every believer commits to being a minister of the Lord, each will prepare something to bring and contribute. They will not come before the Lord in His congregation "empty handed." They will not come to be spectators, but ready and willing to share. This sharing is based on each one's capacity; whether little or much, eventually everyone will be filled, and there will be no lack. The point is that such preparation and sharing will fully enrich the assembly. Christ is unveiled one by one through various prayers, songs, and speaking.

Two or Three Prophets to Take the Lead

In every assembly, there should be two or three believers that have a fresh burden to speak for the Lord to unveil the mysteries of Christ and His body. It should be something that they have prepared from their enjoyment of fellowshipping with the Lord in the Word during the week. When they present their message or revelation and minister the Spirit, an unveiling of mysteries will occur and an enlivening to everyone listening and discerning. When their speaking enlightens someone, and something of the riches of Christ and His body is revealed, that person will want to speak forth what inspired them by the Spirit. Then the prophet who is speaking should stop, and let the newly unveiled person speak. This becomes a kind of chain reaction, speaking to speaking, that can be intermingled with singing and prayers.

In fact, this kind of speaking generates more prophesying due to the increasing number of participants being inspired by the unveiling of mysteries that were hidden from them previously. Each one will have something to say with eagerness under the inspiration of the Spirit. This kind of excitement and enlightening will cause everyone to speak, sing, or pray at the same time, which would, of course, become confusing. So Paul says that they can all prophesy one by one. They should have control over their own spirit, so as to wait their turn to minister and not interrupt others too quickly. Let peace prevail among the believers in the assembly.

The initial two or three prophets who started the chain reaction are not to dominate the assembly. Their burden and goal is to unveil the mysteries until the others listening and discerning are inspired to jump in and interrupt them. Actually, interruption means that the prophet did their job well in sparking others to speak the things that were unveiled to them, inspiring them.

Since everyone can speak and teach in the assembly, everyone also needs to listen and discern or weigh whether the speaking is healthy to take in as from the Lord, or to be challenged and rejected if unhealthy. This type of listening to one another in conjunction with the inward teaching and witnessing of the anointing Spirit is needed for active participation in the assembly. Typically, once a believer joins a particular church, they become passive listeners in the sense that they no longer use their discernment to consider whether what the pastor or preacher teaches is healthy or not. There is almost a mechanical acceptance of whatever is spoken. And if one does not agree, the only recourse is to find another church with a different preacher. But in the assembly, with active listening, one can question what is being spoken or interject with a different point of view.

The above description is completely different from how church is practiced. Since church today is really the ministry of one person or of one school of thought, one of the clergy of a church speaks the entire sermon or message, and no one interrupts the speaker. The speaker will not become silent if someone in the audience is inspired by the Spirit to say something for the Lord. There is a time and place for giving an uninterrupted message, or for teaching a lesson, but it is not in the assembly. Church is really more like a school with some performances to inspire the audience. Proper uninterrupted sermons and messages to expound the Word and teach the truth certainly have their place, but not in the assembly that has been described, located in homes from house to house.

The early apostles did this kind of teaching and preaching messages in the public area of the temple. For example, Paul rented a school to teach regularly for two years in Ephesus, but that school was not the assembly. The assembly in that city was located in Aquila and Priscilla's house. Similarly, in Jerusalem, much of the teaching and preaching was done at the temple, but the assembly took place in the homes, from house to house. The apostles' goal of preaching and teaching publicly or in a dedicated place was so that the believers could be equipped with the teaching of Jesus Christ and function for the building up of the assembly in the homes.

There is a clear distinction between Christian workers and their teaching and preaching in their church, and the believers' assembly from house to house where everyone is prophesying for the building up of the body of Christ.

A normal assembly should include "outsiders and unbelievers" so that they can see God and come to salvation through witnessing the functioning of the body in oneness. It is not normal to have the same believers in a home gathering week after week and month after month. Unbelievers should be invited regularly, and those novices concerning the things of Christ should be asked to "come and see" and enjoy the meals and fellowship in the home. The Lord, who loves all men and desires all men to be saved and come to the full knowledge of the truth, wants the unbelieving and uninformed to be included in the gathering of an assembly. It is here that unbelievers can witness the love and oneness of believers, the living testimony from each, and the unveiling of Christ and His body in an understandable message in singing, praying and speaking. This situation fulfills the Lord's Prayer in John 17, and causes unbelieving and uninformed men and women to see the practical manifestation of God. Witnessing this will lead them to believe and worship God, who is real and expressed in the assembly of believers. Therefore, it is profitable and normal to regularly include unbelievers whenever believers assemble in the homes. It is actually spiritually unhealthy (and the gatherings become stale) if a home assembly does not have young and new believers regularly. This is how the Lord was able to add to the assembly day by day those that were being saved.

The Culminating Work of a Minister of Christ

> ...to be a minister of Christ Jesus to the Gentiles. I serve the gospel of God like a priest, so that the Gentiles may become an acceptable offering, sanctified by the Holy Spirit.
>
> – Romans 15:16, NET

The offerings in the Old Testament were supposed to be God's food, and certainly man ate them. They were the offerings that satisfied God, and physically satisfied man as well. God ordained that the offerings could only be made at the temple in Jerusalem. In typology that is the place of God's dwelling in the oneness of all His people.

What is God really satisfied with? What is God truly hungry for? What food will satisfy Him? It is not dead animals, but people (Gentiles). It is not fallen people of the old creation, but living people that are full of the eternal divine life and whose entire lives are being sanctified by the Holy Spirit.

Paul, as a priest of the gospel, ministered Jesus Christ to people in order that he could offer them as living offerings to satisfy God. The unbelievers were hungry for God, so Paul served (ministered) Christ to them as food. The babes in Christ were hungry for more of Christ as food, so Paul ministered more of Christ to them that they would grow and be sanctified by the Holy Spirit. Paul brought those he ministered to as an offering to God as food for God's satisfaction.

All believers are hungry for this offering; therefore, the very offering for God is also food for all people at the feast to enjoy.

This means that all the services relating to preaching the gospel to beget a new birth in Christ, the cherishing and nourishing for growth in younger believers, and the work of discipling to establish believers is ultimately for an offering to satisfy God and fellow believers in the body. Just as the feasts in the Old Testament demanded offerings to God, in the New Testament, the place of offering to God is in the assembly from house to house. That is the real temple where God's people are one. Whomever a minister is serving should be brought to the assembly as an offering to God.

In other words, if a ministering believer is sharing Jesus Christ to an unbelieving friend or relative, the unbeliever should be brought to the assembly. If someone just came to the Lord and is being nourished to grow, that newer believer needs to be brought to the assembly. If believers are visiting a home to be established in fellowship according to the pattern in Luke 10, those believers also need to be at the assembly. God would be satisfied by those offerings, and all the other believers would be encouraged and rejoice.

This is why Paul said in 1 Corinthians 14 that in the assembly there were unbelievers as well as the uninformed or "outsiders." They were brought to the assembly as an offering to God. It is these offerings that make the feasting for both God and man rich for the building up of the assembly. How unpredictably enjoyable is the fellowship when all the believers serving the Lord bring with them those that they are serving, all together as one assembly, to magnify Christ and glorify God.

The culminating work of the believers' service, ministry, and labor, in whichever stage it is as outlined in these last four chapters, is ultimately all for God and His purpose in the building up of the assembly, the one body of Christ.

Practice: Prepare to Prophesy

Remember that your goal in prophesying is to inspire others to see and appreciate something concerning Christ so that they will be motivated to speak and participate in the fellowship. In fact, if those listening are so inspired that they interrupt you, then you are a good prophet. Therefore, you are not preparing to give a long message. Typically, material for about three minutes is enough to inspire, and anything more than five minutes can be too much, since it may appear that you are dominating the time. There are three things that you can consider as a preparation:

1. A scriptural portion – Consider verses that recently inspired you in your reading, and write some notes on how these verses unveil something of Jesus Christ concerning His person or work. Ponder on the verses with the points while considering prayerfully those that might be at the gathering. As you do this, the Spirit may give you a special word that you can speak to the assembly.

2. A song or hymn – During the week you could be singing and praying over some hymns and songs. You may even compose your own lyrics with some familiar tunes. These songs that you are enjoying before the Lord and have inspired you should be brought to the assembly. Then in the assembly you can sing the hymn or a portion of it. Before or after your singing, you can speak a word concerning the song. This is very different from just singing a hymn in a program or calling a hymn for everyone to sing; rather, this is bringing a song as your portion to share.

3. A testimony – Do you have a testimony of your experience this week that would give glory to God and highlight the Lord Jesus in your experiences? If you do, then testimonies are always inspiring, real, and applicable for the assembly to enjoy.

Typically, you will not be able to do all three of the above within 3–5 minutes so just one or two of the above items will be adequate. But if you have all three ready, then the Spirit, during the gathering, will move you according to His will what and when to share without dominating the meeting and taking up all the time. It is better to share multiple times than one long period of time. How rich will be the assembly even if just some of the believers will have such preparations – and all those assembling will be inspired and speak their inspiration concerning Jesus Christ!

CONCLUSION

The Heavenly Vision

> Where [there is] no vision, the people perish…
>
> – Proverbs 29:18 KJV
>
> But rise and stand on your feet; for I have appeared to you for this purpose, to make you a minister and a witness…to open their eyes, [in order] to turn [them] from darkness to light, and [from] the power of Satan to God, that they may receive forgiveness of sins and an inheritance among those who are sanctified by faith in Me.
>
> Therefore, King Agrippa, I was not disobedient to the heavenly vision.
>
> – Acts 26:16, 18–19

Have you seen ONE? Have you seen this heavenly vision from the Lord after considering all the verses highlighted in this book? Proverbs says that God's people need a vision so that they will not perish. Other translations say that without a vision, people will have no restraint. God's people need a controlling vision. Without a controlling vision, there is no guidance. This will cause a person to flounder; there will be nothing to restrain them from living a destructive or at least an unproductive spiritual life.

Paul, on the other hand, could declare that he was not disobedient to the heavenly vision that the Lord showed him. God appeared to Paul to make him a minister and a witness, that he would turn people from darkness to light, from the power of Satan to God, and bring forgiveness of sins. What a calling and what a vision! God is giving this same vision to all His people and calling them to rise up and stand on their feet. Have you seen this heavenly vision? Will you rise up? Will you be a minister and a witness with the life and power of God to bring people around you into the righteousness, peace and joy of the Holy Spirit? Will you be a person bringing people into ONE?

The Vision of the One Body

I have no doubt that after reading this book — if all the verses highlighted and the thoughts behind them are understood — you will be motivated to commit yourself to living and serving toward God's purpose. Are you seeing this vision of God's eternal purpose of the oneness among believers as the building up of the Lord's body, the assembly? Seeing this vision will fundamentally change your view toward other believers, toward the world around you, and toward your own earthly purposes. Seeing and living according to God's purpose and keeping this as a priority, will make clear your own personal pursuits and goals, whether earthly or spiritual. You will have peace, joy, and life direction as you align yourself to God's eternal purpose as clearly unveiled in the Scriptures.

The oneness as unveiled in John 17 is the building up of the Lord's body. Receiving God's eternal life is for this. Knowing and understanding the truth is for this. And receiving the Lord's glory is for this. If you see this, then you will also see how many things among Christians are being used by Satan to distract believers from this oneness. Keeping and obeying this vision will cause you to stay true and put away all distracting things, no matter how scriptural they may be. You will live and take action according to the heavenly vision of the building up of His assembly.

The heavenly vision will cause you to enjoy and steadily grow in the divine eternal life through eating, drinking, breathing, exercising, and sleeping. You will love the truth, which is the knowledge of Jesus Christ. This love will cause you to study the Bible with a hunger to expand your knowledge of the truth, and to have your mind renewed by it, so that you will be on a solid foundation for the building of the assembly. Finally, you will find joy and purpose in serving and ministering Jesus Christ to people for salvation and building. There is glory in being nothing but a servant in God's purpose. In this glory, self-pride is absent; you will be a peace-maker in the body of Christ — a humble, yet peaceful and joyful servant. Your function is truly as a member of Christ to fulfill the mission of accomplishing God's eternal purpose.

Take Action

> ...but the people who know their God shall stand firm and take action.
> — Daniel 11:32 ESV

What is highlighted in this book is not just a vision. There are many practical actions that need to be taken in order to fulfill the heavenly vision of ONE. For growth of life, eating, drinking, breathing, exercising, and sleeping must occur; action is needed. For the practice of the assembly, action is needed to expand the one fellowship with other believers. And certainly for a life in the Lord's glory, action is needed to be a minister — in sharing the gospel, in cherishing, in discipling, and in the building up of an assembly in the homes, house by house.

If you know God and His purpose, and you are ready to take action, one of the best ways for consistency is to connect with or find companions that have the same heavenly vision and take action together. To do this, it is recommended that you gather a few people together as a study/action group and go over the verses with the associated points in this book chapter by chapter. Set up a regular time (once a week preferably) to consider and fellowship over the verses. It is not a matter of whether you agree with all the points; the exercise to fellowship and pray over what is presented through the Scriptures in these chapters will cause a fresh move of the Lord in your group.

I can assure you with testimonies that if you do this even with just one or two other people, you will be instrumental in the building up of an assembly according to the Scriptures that is living, functioning, fruitful, and full of the joy of the Lord.

Remember, this study/action group can include those attending institutional churches, those already meeting in homes, or even those unassociated with any groups. What you will build up is an independent assembly that exists in oneness with all believers, with no human hierarchy, and where everyone can function just as they are as a member of Christ.

The study/action group itself should be considered as a class to learn and to help keep each other accountable. It is what you will do outside of this class that is the building up of the assembly. If you will practice according to what is highlighted chapter by chapter, within 4–8 months you will be able to testify to a transformation in your living — a witness to the Lord using you for the building up of his body, the assembly. Something fresh and dynamic of the Holy Spirit will transpire as you take action in accordance to the heavenly vision.

Let's have the same dream: Reset to ONE; Revival Next!

May the Lord's Prayer in John 17 continue to be fulfilled through you. May the Lord Jesus bless you and be with you. Grace and peace to you. Amen.

SHARE THE VISION AND DREAM OF ONE

It is our hope that the matter of ONEness among people and specifically among the followers of Jesus Christ becomes a major topic of conversation. This discussion would not just be on a theoretical level or relegated only to a future reality. Neither can it be a political mediation among Christian organizations. Becoming, functioning, and manifesting ONE among believers has to start with each individual at a "grass root" level. The ONEness of the Trinity among believers cannot happen organizationally, rather organically.

Therefore, if you have come to the same dream of "Reset to ONE; Revival Next!" then it is up to you to spread the word and bring others into this conversation and vision. In other words, ONEness cannot be dictated from the top down. ONEness has to be viral, spreading from one to another at a personal level.

This book, ONE, is not intended to be a concluding word, nor a terminal definition of the practice of oneness among Christians. Rather, our hope is that it will be a catalyst for expanding fellowship that would allow the Spirit to move freely among God's people for new and fresh discoveries, insights, and experiences.

Here are a few suggested ways to make use of this book in order to spread the conversation of ONE, God's eternal purpose:

1. Quote from this book and reference it through your social media postings. Use it to start and expand on the topics of ONE, life, truth and glory.

2. Refer people to our website where the entire book is freely available to be read online: www.ONEbody.life.

3. Buy the book at bulk pricing to give away in order to spread the message of ONE.

4. Sell the book through your channel by either purchasing the book at wholesale or be an Amazon Associate direct purchasing ONE in amazon.com.

For more information contact us at:
www.ONEbody.life

BIBLIOGRAPHY

Austin-Sparks, T. The Centrality and Supremacy of the Lord Jesus Christ. Online Library of T. Austin-Sparks.

Brother Lawrence. Practice the Presence of God. London: Epworth Press

Coneybeare and Howson. Life and Epistles of St Paul. Grand Rapid, MI: WM. B. Eerdmans Publishing Co.

Jacobson, Wayne. Finding Church. Newbury Park, CA: Trailview Media

Lee, Witness. The All-Inclusive Christ. Anaheim, CA: Living Stream Ministry

Lee, Witness. The Economy of God. Anaheim, CA; Anaheim, CA: Living Stream Ministry

Lee, Witness. Exercise and Practice of the God Ordained Way: Anaheim, CA: Living Stream Ministry

Mackintosh, C.H. Genesis to Deuteronomy. Neptune, NJ: Loizeaux Brothers

Mackintosh, C.H. The Mackintosh Treasury. Neptune, NJ: Loizeaux Brothers

Murray, Andrew. The Two Covenants. New Jersey: Spire Books

Murray, Andrew. Abide in Christ. New Kensington, PA: Whitaker House

Murray, Andrew. The Spirit of Christ. Minneapolis, MN: Bethany House Publisher

Nee, Watchman. Normal Christian Life. PA: CLC

Nee, Watchman. Normal Christian Church Life. Colorado Springs, CO: ISP

New Testament Recovery Version (with footnotes). Anaheim, CA: Living Stream Ministry

Rodriguez, Milt. The Priesthood of All Believers. Box Elder, SD: The Rebuilders

Scroggie, W. Graham. The Unfolding Drama of Redemption. Grand Rapid, MI: Zondervan Publishing House

Vine, W. E. Vine's Expository Dictionary of New Testament Words. Public domain: www.blueletter.org

Viola, Frank. Reimagining Church. Colorado Springs, CO: David C. Cook

Zens, Jon. 58 to 0. Lincoln, NE: Ekklesia Press

Bible Versions Used

Unless otherwise noted, all scriptural verses are taken from New King James Version (NKJV). Copyright © 1982 by Thomas Nelson. Used by permission. All rights reserved.

[DBY] Some of the scriptural verses taken from Darby Version have been revised to conform to modern English. Public domain version.

[ESV] English Standard Version copyright © 2001, 2007 by Crossway Bibles, a publishing ministry of Good News Publishers. Used by permission. All rights reserved.

[RSV] from the Revised Standard Version of the Bible, copyright © 1946, 1952, and 1971 the Division of Christian Education of the National Council of the Churches of Christ in the United States of America. Used by permission. All rights reserved.

[NET] THE NET BIBLE®, NEW ENGLISH TRANSLATION COPYRIGHT © 1996 BY BIBLICAL STUDIES PRESS, L.L.C. NET Bible® IS A REGISTERED TRADEMARK THE NET BIBLE® LOGO, SERVICE MARK COPYRIGHT © 1997 BY BIBLICAL STUDIES PRESS, L.L.C. ALL RIGHTS RESERVED

[NIV] THE HOLY BIBLE, NEW INTERNATIONAL VERSION®, NIV® Copyright © 1973, 1978, 1984, 2011 by Biblica, Inc.® Used by permission. All rights reserved worldwide.

[ASV] Thomas Nelson & Sons first published the American Standard Version in 1901. This translation of the Bible is in the public domain.

[WBT] The Webster Bible was translated by Noah Webster in 1833 in order to bring the language of the Bible up to date. This version of the Bible is in the public domain.

[HNV] The Hebrew Names Version is based off the World English Bible, an update of the American Standard Version of 1901. This version of the Bible is in the public domain.

[KJV] The King James Version. Outside of the United Kingdom, the KJV is in the public domain. Within the United Kingdom, the rights to the KJV are vested in the Crown. This Bible is printed and published by Cambridge University Press, the Queen's royal printer, under royal letters patent. The text commonly available now is actually that of the 1769 revision, not that of 1611.

[HCSB] Scripture quotations marked HCSB are taken from the Holman Christian Standard Bible®, Copyright © 1999, 2000, 2002, 2003, 2009 by Holman Bible Publishers. Used by permission. Holman Christian Standard Bible®, Holman CSB®, and HCSB® are federally registered trademarks of Holman Bible Publishers.

[WEB] The World English Bible is a 1997 revision of the American Standard Version of the Holy Bible, first published in 1901. It is in the Public Domain.

Made in the USA
Lexington, KY
15 November 2017